# HUMANISTIC
# EXISTENTIALISM

# Humanistic Existentialism

*The Literature of Possibility*

*Hazel E. Barnes*

UNIVERSITY OF NEBRASKA PRESS · LINCOLN

*This book was originally published as*
The Literature of Possibility:
Studies in Humanistic Existentialism.

Manufactured in the United States of America

TO DORIS
WHO HELPED MAKE IT POSSIBLE

# ACKNOWLEDGEMENTS

To the following I am greatly indebted, and I wish to express my sincere thanks and appreciation:

To the University of Colorado, which granted me a faculty fellowship for the spring semester, 1958, that I might have time free to spend in making this study.

To the University of Colorado Council on Research and Creative Work, which supplied funds to aid in the preparation of the manuscript.

To the Ford Foundation, which has provided a grant to make possible the publication of this book.

To the friends who have read the manuscript and whose criticisms have improved it.

To the many other scholars in the field. While I have made specific references to these writers in all instances where I have knowingly made use of their work, I must acknowledge a heavy debt of gratitude to those who have provided me with the background of general knowledge without which this book could not have been written.

# CONTENTS

# Intentions

*FREEDOM IS POSSIBILITY*
—Nicola Abbagnano

# INTENTIONS

FOR ALMOST A CENTURY NOW, prevailing psychologies and the literature written under their influence have agreed that men cherish the illusion of freedom while being in fact determined by heredity, by environment, and by early childhood experiences. Humanistic existentialism challenges this doctrine and claims that exactly the reverse is true: every man is free, but most men, fearing the consequences and the responsibilities of freedom, refuse to acknowledge its presence in themselves and would deny it to others. So radical a shift in point of view can be effected only when accompanied by a reorientation of all human attitudes. It requires a specific psychology to support it; it demands a reappraisal of the human situation. The literature which shows that men are free presents to the world a new philosophy of man.

The term "humanistic existentialism" may be applied most appropriately, in my opinion, to the work of three French writers: Jean-Paul Sartre, Simone de Beauvoir, and Albert Camus. I am well aware that the decision to isolate these particular authors and to treat them as a group may appear somewhat arbitrary. They are not the only ones to work with the themes commonly associated with existentialism. Nor is the desire to ask and to answer once again the question, "What is Man?" limited to existentialists. Perhaps we could put it another way and say that the existentialist mood *is* the temper of our times. But to paraphrase Kierkegaard's remark about Christianity—where everyone is existentialist, no one is existentialist. It is one thing to describe man's anguish and

3

despair; it is quite another to provide an adequate philosophical and psychological analysis of these feelings and to suggest a solution which does not merely dismiss the protest as adolescent and mistaken. Camus, Sartre, and de Beauvoir have all written philosophical treatises setting forth their ideas on man's ethical dilemma, his metaphysical and psychological possibilities. For literature, however, the important thing is that from the pages of their imaginative writing emerge fictional men and women whose acts are consistent with a psychology based on freedom and who, taken all together, provide a comprehensive picture of contemporary man's attempts to live significantly in a world in which he can find no God nor any over-all, more than human meaning. As a total view, it is the synthesis which is unique, not the sum of the details.

An opposite sort of objection might be raised, perhaps even by the three authors themselves. Camus' and Sartre's political dispute is famous; Camus has declared in so many words that he is not an existentialist.[1] Can there be any justification for grouping together those who have emphasized their differences? Certainly we must recognize that each is an independent writer. De Beauvoir is more than Sartre's interpreter. The characters of Camus' fiction are explicable in the light of his own essays without reference to *Being and Nothingness*. There is no common creed to which each writer is pledged. Admittedly there are areas of sharp disagreement; yet I am convinced that these are less weighty than the marked similarities. It is significant that on more than one occasion the three have used one another's books to illustrate points in their own writing. Most often, it seems to me, the unique development of each one's thought supplements rather than contradicts the work of the other two. We might, of course, avoid the controversial term "existentialist," particularly since Sartre himself has indicated a preference for "phenomenologist." But with apologies to my subjects, I prefer to call them humanistic existentialists. Rightly or wrongly, the public is accustomed to think of them as existentialists. I hope by adding the word "humanistic" to suggest that what they offer us is a concept of man which is related to, but not identical with, that of other existential philosophies.[2]

In my discussion of what may be named descriptively "the literature of possibility," I am particularly concerned with the manner in which the creative writing reflects the philosophy and psychology which it presupposes and of which it is the exemplification. This is not a propaganda literature either in intention or in fact. At the same time it is a literature which *means* something, and its fictional beings move in a world where values and motives are not the same as those found in the naturalistic and psychoanalytic novels and dramas of the last hundred years. If we are fully to comprehend and evaluate it, even our aesthetic criteria may need to be modified. Moreover, this new interpretation of man and his behavior challenges more than our aesthetics. It makes a demand upon us, compelling us to decide whether or not this is indeed a true picture of the human situation, whether people actually act as they are here described. If we judge that the analysis is valid, then we must consider the implications of the existentialist ethic which follows as a corollary.

Part One of this book discusses the literary theory of Sartre and Camus. (De Beauvoir has never explicitly formulated an aesthetics but appears to share Sartre's perspective.) After examining their ideas on the nature and proper function of literature, I hope to show that the fiction of these authors is concerned primarily with the revelation of man's metaphysical and psychological possibilities and with the actual choices which he confronts in the world today. In Part Two we shall examine the literature from this point of view; that is, we shall observe the ways whereby men and women either seek in bad faith to avoid the responsibilities which go with being human, or find the courage to recognize and "engage" their freedom. Having studied these case histories, so to speak, we shall turn to the psychological theory behind them. In finding out just what are its formal principles, we shall want to know three things: Does the theory convincingly demonstrate the real existence of that freedom which is the mainspring of all existentialist heroes and heroines? Does this psychology stand alone as a purely theoretical speculation, or does it find support in contemporary empirical psychology? Finally, when this set of principles is used for the purpose of analyzing historical or living subjects, does the result bear any resemblance to the fictional creations of the authors of these biographies? In pursuing these themes, it seems best to me to present each new idea in terms of the writer who has been chiefly concerned with it. Thus, for example, we first meet the concept of bad faith within the framework of Sartre's exposition, then go on to see it portrayed in a short story of his, later in the imaginative writing of Camus and de Beauvoir. On the other hand, our discussion of how one may live meaningfully in a meaningless universe finds a natural starting point in Camus' *Myth of Sisyphus*. It is important to remember throughout that the literature of humanistic existentialism does not exist in a vacuum. For this reason I have chosen on several occasions to show how a particular point of view is set forth in the works of other authors closely related to the three whom I have selected. In the concluding section, "Possibilities," I shall try to define more precisely the place of the literature of possibility in the contemporary literary scene and to evaluate what we have found in examining it.

# PART ONE

# Myth, Society,
# and Case History

# MYTH, SOCIETY, AND CASE HISTORY

ABOUT THE MIDDLE of this century novelists and playwrights stopped making men and women to order for the psychologists and began to re-create Man. The movement began in France. Such at least is the view of Jean-Paul Sartre, who maintains that there is a sharp cleavage between the literature produced before World War Two and the works of the last two decades. Albert Camus concurs, though without stressing the abruptness of the change. "The subject matter of art," he says, "has been extended from psychology to the human condition." [1] Both authors believe that contemporary literature is concerned primarily with metaphysical problems. Yet in their preoccupation with man as a whole and with his philosophical view of himself, they have not forgotten the social dimension. Their claim is this: The significant writer today presents in his imaginative works characters wholly engaged in a specific social situation and confronted with the necessity of making a definite choice, but the conflict is always such that the solution is somehow a commitment as to the nature and possibilities of man. In the first number of *Les Temps Modernes* Sartre wrote, "We are with those who want to change both man's social condition and the conception which he has of himself."

Since Sartre has been the most specific in defining the new trend in literature, we may best approach the subject by following along the lines of his analysis. The first detailed formulation of his position appeared in this country in *Theatre Arts* in 1946, in an article called "Forgers of Myths." Although concerned here exclusively with the drama, Sartre laid down a distinction which he later extended to the whole field of fiction. The pre-war drama, he said, was a "theatre of characters," whereas the new French playwrights have been giving us a "theatre of situations." This is to say that the older authors' purpose was to create personages of depth whose total personalities were so thoroughly revealed to us that their every act appeared inevitable in the light of what their creator showed us of their background and gradual character formation. Thus the drama was successful if at the end of it the audience felt that they "knew" the characters as living beings. Its degree of success was roughly proportionate to the complexity and interest of the persons portrayed.

> The theatre, as conceived of in the period between the two world wars, and as it is perhaps still thought of in the United States today, is a theatre of characters. The analysis of characters and their confrontation was the theatre's chief concern. The so-called "situations" existed only for the purpose of throwing the characters into clearer relief. The best plays in this period were psychological studies of a coward, a liar, an ambitious man or a frustrated one. Occasionally a playwright made an effort to outline the workings of a passion—usually love—or to analyze an inferiority complex (p. 324).[2]

One's immediate reaction is to object that Sartre is ignoring the quite extensive output of American writers of the twenties and thirties who focused specifically on the social dimension. What of *Tobacco Road* or *Anna Christie?* Or if we leave the theatre proper (as Sartre does in his later literary criticism), what of the naturalistic novels—*Studs Lonigan,* for example, or *The Grapes of Wrath?* Sartre does not mention any of these works, but he makes his position clear in criticizing what he calls the "realistic theatre." His objection here is the same as that which he offers elsewhere to the nineteenth-century naturalistic novelists of France.[3] The author's focus of attention, he claims, is always the psychological make-up of the protagonists. In the realistic drama we watch what happens when fully constituted natures are buffeted by external social forces.

> "Realism" has always offered plays made up of stories of defeat, laissez-faire and drifting; it has always preferred to show how external forces batter a man to pieces, destroy him bit by bit, and ultimately make of him a weathervane turning with every change of wind (p. 329).

Camus' evaluation of the realistic American novel of the thirties is different from Sartre's in that Camus feels that its characters have no inner life whatsoever. All are reduced to certain elemental reactions, are presented through merely a series of external responses to events so that persons are almost indistinguishable from one another.[4] I think that Camus' judgement here is rather less fair than Sartre's. The important point, however, is that both men criticize the realistic writer for having too little respect for his characters' ability to act as free individuals.

There are two reasons why Sartre believes that the literature of characters is neither appropriate nor adequate for the existentialist writer. In the first place, he holds that it stems from a false view of man. A person does not possess a ready-made character, formed by hereditary and environmental pressures and developing in accordance with strict psychological laws. Man is not determined by passions which sweep over him like external forces. His emotions, like every one of his attitudes, are the result of the way he has decided to relate himself to the world around him. He is free at any time to make a new choice of himself, to choose a fresh way of living out his existence and to remake his so-called "nature." Hence we may expect to find in the new theatre not the inevitable action but the free decision. We will be interested, not in seeing how the present has been determined by the past, but in perceiving how the act before us is outlining the pattern of an imminent future.

Sartre's second reason is a historical one. In its concern with individual behavior, the older writing was what we might also call a "literature of average situations." It tended to shy away from the heroic. It implied a comfortable acceptance of the human condition as a natural, infinite milieu within which the individual worked out his everyday problems. But war and the Occupation changed all that. A man confronted with probable death or actual torture could not avoid taking full stock of his capabilities as a human being. The situations in which he found himself were such that his choice committed him only to one of two extremes—cowardice or heroism. Moreover, one had a real and present sense of history. One knew that by one's actions one was helping to write the record of the French nation under stress. Even more than that, one was affirming what it meant to be human. It was no longer "natural" to be a man. Rather it was a question asked and an answer given.

For the French writer, the result of these experiences is the literature of extreme situations or, to use another of Sartre's terms, "the literature of great circumstance." What precisely is this literature and what does

Sartre think that it ought to be? One obvious conclusion might be that it would stress the freedom and the responsibility of its heroes, whatever their situation; and this is true. A corollary assumption might be that the plots of the new literature would concentrate on those situations where the heroic choice is possible and clearly evident. Such is the case in part, especially in some, though not all, of the works of Sartre himself. But it is not always so. Camus' *The Plague (La Peste),* for example, is the account of a city struck by bubonic plague, and the plague itself is a thinly disguised symbol for the Occupation in particular, and in general for any widespread disaster. In *The Fall (La Chute),* on the other hand, Camus' hero never confronts any social or political crisis. The conflict is wholly an internal one. Yet this novel fits almost perfectly the Sartrean requirement in that it is essentially the story of a man's attempt to meet head-on the question of what it means to be human. Moreover, the hero, while individualized as to nationality, profession, and so forth, meets with no crisis which depends upon his particular background or which influences his basic character structure. Rather the problem is presented as that of every person, and its solution—or lack of one—might be any man's answer. The sense of urgency in the book comes not from a particular conflict in which grave issues are at stake, but from the fact that the hero cannot accept *any* situation as normal so long as the human condition itself seems to him unacceptable.

The obviously heroic setting, therefore, is not essential, nor is any particular type of character. If we want to understand more precisely the nature of the literature of humanistic existentialism, we will seek it rather in three things, none of which is absolutely clear at first glance and all of which, taken together, are paradoxical but not, I think, actually self-contradictory.

First of all, Sartre says, this literature will seek to present from a new point of view basic human situations and will not be much concerned about laws of human nature. "What is universal . . . is not nature but the situations in which man finds himself; that is, not the sum total of his psychological traits but the limits which enclose him on all sides." [5]

Sartre's second requirement is formulated in relation to the theatre, but I hope to show that with but slight modification it can apply equally well to other literary forms. We must realize, he says, that the theatre is or should be in essence a collective, religious phenomenon. As such it will reject realism and will work with myths. [6] Camus adds a qualification with which Sartre would be in hearty agreement: The creative writer who has rejected the possibility of any more than human destiny for man will not cease to delight in myths. But they will be myths "with no depth other than that of human suffering and, like it, inexhaustible." They will not be like "the divine fable which amuses and blinds," but rather myths which contain the difficult wisdom of earth and a passion which knows that it has no tomorrow.[7]

Finally, the literature of hexis must be abandoned in favor of a literature of praxis. By "literature of hexis" Sartre refers to writing which seeks merely a synthetic, explanatory view of life; by "literature of praxis" he means a literature which inspires action.* His view here is closely bound up with his belief in the social mission of the author. The function of literature, he claims, is to lead society to reflect upon itself. "Through literature the collectivity turns to reflection and mediation; it acquires an unhappy consciousness, an unstable image of itself which it forever seeks to modify and to improve." [8] Thus the purpose of those writers whom Sartre approves is to change the world. Yet the new literature, while concerned with concrete issues of the writer's own environment, is not mere propaganda. It never forgets man himself. It remains a "total" literature in that it is always conscious of the human against which all specific conflicts are posited and resolved. In a sense it acts as the mediator between the human condition of all men and the specific situation in which each man is writing his own history. As Sartre puts it, literature is preoccupied with the relation between what man *is* and what he is choosing to make himself within the historical perspective. Man cannot choose his age, but he must choose himself within it. Literature today raises the question of what specific ends man should choose for himself. What means for achieving these ends does the existing social structure allow? And in a society based on violence what should be the relation between means and end?

> Works which are inspired by such concerns cannot aim primarily at pleasing; they irritate and disturb, they offer themselves as tasks to be performed; they invite us to quests without conclusion; they lead us to share in experiences in which the outcome remains uncertain.[9]

The responsible writer is oriented toward the future, but the future which he wants to help determine is the future of this generation, not a dim area on the near side of eternity. "We write for our own time." [10]

---

* *Hexis* and *praxis* are both Greek words. *Hexis* refers to a permanent state or condition; *praxis* means action.

Camus is not really in disagreement with Sartre on this point. "Authentic creation is a gift to the future," he says.[11] And Camus believes that today the stakes are high. "When the passion of the age puts the whole world at stake, then artistic creation wants to be in full control of destiny." [12] In his acceptance speech when he received the Nobel Prize, Camus stated that the artist must accept the two trusts of his calling, "the service of truth and the service of freedom." For since the writer's purpose is to unite men, he must oppose falsehood and slavery.[13] All of this is quite in harmony with Sartre's view that literature should aim at the liberation of man. Yet Camus is much more reserved in his assertion that the writer must make a political commitment. In the first place, he stresses that the artist should not be expected to engage himself *as an artist*. It is *as a man* that he will feel it necessary to speak out on specific social issues.[14] Furthermore, Camus is completely opposed to the thesis novel or play. Such a work is so pervaded with an *idea* that it kills *thought*. Great novelists are "philosophical," the very opposite of thesis writers.[15]

Camus believes that an artist must neither sever himself from the world nor let himself be engulfed by it.

> He runs the risk, if he stays in his ivory tower, of cutting himself off from reality, or, if he gallops forever around the political arena, of drying up. The ticklish paths of true art lie somewhere between the two.[16]

An amusing short story by Camus, "Jonah" (*"Jonas"*)[17] makes the same point. A good-natured, self-confident painter wins spectacular success with his first efforts. Critics praise him, society lionizes him, young would-be artists come to him for advice. The demands of the public plus the domestic needs of his growing family absorb most of his time and literally shove him into a corner of his own house. Lacking both adequate time and space, Jonah paints little and badly. The critics turn cold. In desperation Jonah builds a little loft under the high ceiling of the living room. There in isolation he works feverishly until finally he dies from exhaustion and malnutrition. A friend looks at Jonah's recent work. There is only one canvas, perfectly blank save for one word in letters so small and illegible that no one can be sure whether they spell *solitaire* or *solidaire*. In excess, solitude and solidarity are both disastrous to the artist. Camus would agree—though with some reservation—to Sartre's statement of literary purpose.

Here then is the new literature. It denies any interest in the usual sort of psychological characterization. It is concerned with the fundamental situations within which human freedom asserts itself. It works with myth. It has an acute sense of social responsibility. One will find no difficulty in pointing out seeming contradictions in this set of principles. To mention only the more obvious: How can a forger of myths in a nonrealistic drama deal with concrete problems of the contemporary world? Is it possible that the duty of a writer is both to serve a society and to change it? If this be his social function, then in the name of what society is he so directed? Finally, how can any literature which concerns itself with human problems afford to neglect the psychological?

I should like to consider the question of psychology first, both because it seems to me the most fundamental and because I think that Sartre's statement in this connection is misleading. Aside from the fact that it is hard to conceive of any work of fiction or biography which would not in some way depend on the author's knowledge of the principles of human behavior, there are several reasons why the literature of existentialism would seem to lean even more heavily on psychology than most other writing. There is a particular paradox in the case of Sartre who has presented his existential psychoanalysis as the culmination, so to speak, of his entire philosophy as developed in *Being and Nothingness (L'Être et le Néant)*. Since the time of Kierkegaard, existentialists have used fictional characters to convey their philosophical views. Presumably their reason for doing so was the belief that the total living individual is both the subject and the object of philosophy and that the principles of a philosophy of existence can be expressed only in a concrete setting. Hence the conflicts, the problems, and the possible solutions of philosophical questions have been embodied in the situations and reactions of imaginary persons. But what is this need for a human setting if it is not a recognition of the psychological dimension? One wonders how Sartre or anyone else can produce a literature which presents real problems (social or metaphysical) in a real world without providing real people to meet them. If the existentialist writer should disregard all particular psychology and individual characterization, would we not be left with an indefensible discrepancy between philosophical theory and literary practice? How could either the literature or the strictly philosophical writing of existentialism throw any light upon the other? And most vital of all, can a literature without psychological characterization be of any value whatsoever in describing twentieth-century man?

Obviously it cannot. Apparently Sartre himself felt the need of softening his earlier statement. For later in the same article in *Theatre Arts* he writes, "We do not reject psychology, that would be absurd: we integrate life" (p. 329). Yet Sartre, I believe, has not quite realized the full significance of his remark. When he speaks of integrating life, he is emphasizing the necessity of not studying a passion—a love affair, for example—as though it were isolated from all other phases of existence. Any emotion is played against and is colored by a background which includes not only other emotions and personality traits but a complex system of values: concepts of rights, economic and political views, basic hostility or friendliness toward other individuals, etc. Sartre does not mean merely that everyone *ought* to be concerned with all aspects of the life around him but that in everything he does, whether he is actively involved with larger issues or not, he *is* affirming his position as regards the whole. Now this is all very well and good, but there is more back of the statement than a simple plea to broaden the scope of a novel or play. Actually, the plots of Sartre and other existentialists and near-existentialists tend to be compressed rather than extended, to focus on a single conflict rather than to give the whole story of a life in which a man confronts as many as possible of the problems of existence. In the passage just mentioned, Sartre is objecting that psychology is too abstract and that the study of any individual is meaningful only when pursued in the full social context. But he is not merely replacing psychology by sociology. He is attacking the very definition of psychology, and he is arguing in line with his own peculiar view of the unitary nature of consciousness. Furthermore, this is not an isolated instance. It is my firm conviction that Sartre never plays down psychology either in his strictly philosophical works or in his imaginative writing. What he does do is portray fictional characters who behave entirely consistently with the precepts of his own precise psychology.

The details of Sartre's existential psychology emerge as one studies the particular situations presented in his fiction and the reactions of the characters engaged in them. There are, however, three basic assumptions so fundamental that they condition the literary theory itself. All three are essential for Sartre but by no means accepted by most other psychological schools. First, there is the belief that man functions as a total unit, that any act or reaction, important or insignificant, can be fully explained only as the expression of a basic choice of existence, a choice so fundamental as to underlie and determine the quality of any particular complex or passion or even any intellectual attitude. Second, such psychic unity is possible only on the supposition that the being of man is wholly conscious. Sartre goes all the way here, rejecting entirely the Freudian structure of id, super ego, and conscious ego. Finally, we must assume that when a man chooses his way of life, the choice is a free decision; it means also that man is at any time free to change his existence and to choose himself anew—though in practice this happens only rarely.

Several consequences for literature of this psychological position appear immediately. Obviously a writer agreeing with the tenets of existential psychoanalysis will not employ the methods of earlier psychoanalytically inclined authors who tried to show us the unconscious determination of a hero knowing less about himself than the reader knew. Nor will heredity and environment be of interest as conditioning factors; instead they will be simply the matter by means of which the hero reveals himself and expresses his basic choice. Moreover, we may expect that just as the exciting work of Freud stimulated writers to produce novels illustrating the Oedipus complex, to utilize dreams, *lapsus linguae,* etc. in their character portrayal, so the existentialist writer will want to show us characters who are in the process of discovering or remaking the basic choice of themselves, of first confronting their existential freedom. The crisis in the new "literature of crisis" is precisely this choice of a way of existence, a choice of Being, which every man is constantly making but which is more clearly made and more often remade at times of "great circumstance." Thus we see that far from being divorced from psychology, Sartre's characters behave consistently with their creator's psychological analysis. More than this, they frequently and designedly serve as specific illustrations of the various principles of Sartrean psychology.

At this point one might well raise the question as to just what the existentialist character has become. If he is to demonstrate abstractly the possible human choices and their consequences, then he is little more than a philosophical personification. Sartre's statement that the new theatre will deal in myth suggests that such may be the case. On the other hand, if he is to serve as documentation, so to speak, for Sartre's existential psychology, then we would seem to have a new type of fictional case history. For still a third possibility, we must recall Sartre's statement that the writer is to present to society a picture of itself and a program for change. Are his characters then to serve as mouthpieces for their author's social theories?

It is quite evident that Sartre uses his actors and his plots to express his own views with regard to philosophy, psychology, and politics. Does this make his work bad art? The history of literature from Aeschylus to Dante to Tolstoi to Shaw forbids us to maintain that no creative writer can successfully use fiction as a vehicle for his own strong convictions. So far as Sartre or any other writer is concerned, the test appears to lie in whether or not the ideas concerned are sufficiently penetrating to be a true picture of man and the universe even if only a partial one. A specific problem arises, however, in connection with Sartre's approach since the constituent elements of his theory might seem to be inconsistent with one another. Can an author write at once myth, case history, and contemporary social comment?

Just how Sartre has combined these three intentions we can see clearly even by a superficial examination of three widely different examples of his work—*The Flies (Les Mouches),* a full-length drama; *No Exit (Huit-Clos),* a one-act play; and *Saint Genet, Martyr-Comedian (Saint Genet, comédien et martyr),* a biographical study. In each of these Sartre is passing judgement on society (though less specifically in *No Exit* than in the other two), and he is illustrating basic principles of his psychology. In each he makes use of myth but not in the same way in all three instances. I have in fact chosen these particular examples because they provide illustrations of three different approaches to myth, three distinct concepts of what myth is and what may be its value to the writer.

*The Flies* is the only one of these examples which actually retells an ancient myth. In the story of the house of Atreus, Sartre has chosen not only a familiar tale but one which had already been overlaid with a wealth of interpretation, beginning with three Greek tragedians. I am sure that his choice of a myth which comes to us, so to speak, already furnished with an explanation is no accident. The myth itself was raw material, but the Athenian interpretations were a direct challenge.

Whatever may have been the origin of the Greek myths, they certainly provide in their amazing diversity a prototype for most, if not all, conceivable emotional conflicts and human situations. It is not surprising that the Greek writers of tragedy seldom felt the need to invent a plot or to turn to historical sources. Instead they employed their imaginations either in searching for the kind of characters who would have been involved in the situations described in the myth, or in demonstrating some universal meaning which the myth could be shown to contain. We find both approaches in the Greek treatment of the unhappy Agamemnon and the events following upon his murder by Clytemnestra and Aegisthus.

Sophocles and Euripides are interested in the creation of the appropriate characters. Of the two, Sophocles in his *Electra* comes closer to giving us a Sartrean type of characterization. The play focuses upon the person of Electra, who has chosen to identify her life so completely with her hatred of her mother and her mother's lover that she is little more than the embodiment of the will for vengeance. In existentialist terms, one would say that she has chosen herself as revenge and that Sophocles is interested in showing us the effect of this choice upon her life before and during the act in which she finds her fulfillment. To this end all else is subordinate. Orestes is dwarfed in comparison, serving almost as her instrument. Chrysothemis, Electra's sister, is brought in only that her weak character may serve to illuminate Electra's strength still more clearly. Even Clytemnestra serves largely as a foil, as the visible object upon which Electra's anger and resentment are vented. In Euripides' *Electra,* on the other hand, Electra is more three-dimensional. We know a great deal about her. We are aware of the passionate hatred for her mother, which seems to go beyond what is elicited simply by Clytemnestra's crime, and of Electra's proud condescension toward her peasant husband to whom she is married—thanks to his respectful courtesy—in name only. We know of her dislike of poverty, her wish that she could wear pretty clothes to parties, her tendency to self-pity. Euripides is more interested in the woman Electra than in the basic situation, and in this case he is farther from Sartre in his approach than is Sophocles. Both playwrights, however, have produced here (though certainly not in all of their work) what Sartre would call the theatre of characters.

Aeschylus, on the contrary, in his trilogy the *Oresteia* takes the other approach to myth, seeking in it universal truth. His characters are not wholly lacking in individuality, particularly not Clytemnestra nor Agamemnon, but all are subordinate to the basic problem posited by their situation. At the end of the first play, *Agamemnon,* the King, who to some extent deserved his death, has been slain by Clytemnestra and Aegisthus for motives stemming from personal passions of hate and desire. At the end of the second play, the *Choephorae,* Clytemnestra, even more guilty than Agamemnon, has been killed by her son, Orestes, who acted reluctantly and at the command of the god Apollo. The concluding play, the *Eumenides,* must somehow resolve the problem in such a way as to show whether the first two actions, externally alike, are in reality the same or different. By the end of the trilogy we have almost forgotten Orestes the person. The real issue, simply symbolized by Orestes, lies in the struggle between the old concept of justice, represented by the Furies, and the new law, represented by Apollo. When the *Oresteia* is over, Aeschylus has set forth several very comprehensive ideas: that there is a divine power of justice in the very structure of things; that justice is a spiritual concept, concerned with motive as well as with objective act; that the State is the guardian of justice; that the fearful Erinyes, or angry spirits of vengeance, have voluntarily become the Venerable Goddesses or kindly ones; that the new patriarchal religion of the Olympians has superseded that of the old earth-deities of a pre-Greek matriarchy but has been forced to make certain concessions in return. It should be clear, I think, that in Aeschylus' treatment of the myth we have an earlier form of Sartre's "theatre of situations." Sartre himself has recognized the resemblance between the ideals of contemporary French drama and those of Greek tragedy. In the same passage in which he asserted his disinterest in the usual kind of psychology, he says, "In this we return to the concept of tragedy as the Greeks saw it. For them, as Hegel has shown, passion was never a simple storm of sentiment but fundamentally always the assertion of a right."

Yet as I have tried to show, in their handling of the Orestes story Sophocles and Euripides both concentrated on the character portrayal of their heroine, thus not conforming in this particular instance to the requirements of a "theatre of situations." And those philosophical ideas which Aeschylus presents are decidedly not those of existentialism. Hence we are thrown back once more upon the question as to why Sartre chose to retell an ancient myth already so thoroughly worked over. We may arrive at an answer most easily by considering what possibilities the myth as handled by the Greeks offered to him. Disregarding any idea of simply rewriting the story with no important change, there were two things which Sartre could do in *The Flies*.

First, he might have accepted the Greek interpretation and attempted to show the universality of the theme and its pertinence to our own day by modernizing the situations and the characters. This is Eugene O'Neill's approach in *Mourning Becomes Electra*. The Trojan War has given place to the American Civil War. The palace of the royal house of Agamemnon has become the wealthiest mansion in a small New England town. A few townsmen have replaced the chorus. With full awareness of Freudian psychoanalysis, O'Neill has developed the principals in such a way that Orestes' faintly suggested Oedipus complex is full-blown in Orin and finds its counterpart in a more than suggested Electra complex in his sister. Lavinia (Electra) had loved before she came to hate Captain Adam Brant (Aegisthus). The affectionate dependency of the brother and sister has about it a decided aura of incest. At the end it is Lavinia, not Orin, who is to live out her life pursued by her own psychological furies. Yet Christine (Clytemnestra) and Ezra (Agamemnon) are rather filled in than transformed. In fact, with very slight exceptions the story remains the same and motivations almost the same as in the *Oresteia;* they are simply adjusted to fit a period of more psychological sophistication. This is not to accuse O'Neill of a lack of originality but to point out that essentially what he has done has been to develop still further, along the lines already laid down by Euripides, a study of complex personalities interesting only in and for themselves. *Mourning Becomes Electra* is as clear an example of the "theatre of characters" at its best as one could hope to find.

What Sartre has achieved, however, is an altogether different thing. So far as the characters of *The Flies* are concerned, they are, if anything, still less individualized and less obviously "human" than those in Aeschylus' trilogy. The situation and the characters' choice of themselves within the limits of the situation are all that matters. It is significant that the Furies, who were leading protagonists in Aeschylus' drama, who disappeared entirely in Sophocles' play, and who were wholly internalized as mere psychological reactions in the work of Euripides and O'Neill, are now portrayed as actual living spirits of vengeance, as the Flies.[18] This is but one of several indications that Sartre, like Aeschylus, is interested primarily in the basic problem and in the ways in which human beings may hope to solve it—more than he is in creating specific individual personalities to come alive for us and engage our sympathies.

Sartre differs from O'Neill in another way. O'Neill has realistically reproduced the ancient situation in an environment which is relatively familiar to us and with characters who seem contemporary, as though to point out that the Greek view of the problem and its resolutions are today as pertinent as ever. Sartre has done quite the opposite. He has kept the Greek setting and the Greek protagonists, but he has changed the ending and hence the whole meaning of the myth. Whereas the Greek Orestes acts in accordance with the god's command and is ultimately justified by a heaven-directed court, Sartre's hero defies Zeus and affirms that he alone is responsible for his act and is the only one who can judge it. There is no longer any question of an Oedipus complex. The problem faced by both Orestes and Electra is whether they will or won't be willing to accept the fearful solitude of human freedom. In other words, whereas O'Neill seems to be saying, "See, human nature has not changed!" Sartre is launching a violent attack on Aeschylus and saying essentially, "For man as we know him in the twentieth century this basic human situation no longer holds the same significance. For us Aeschylus neither posed the question correctly nor gave the right answer. Therefore, let us rewrite the story and see what it has to tell us today." Ironically, Sartre, although specifically challenging Aeschylus' solution, is adopting Aeschylus' dramatic method—to interpret the myth in such a way as to force it to reveal a philosophical truth bigger than the concerns of any of the individual characters in the drama.

In a period when values are relatively stable, authors tend to use the classical myths merely allusively, enriching the poetic quality of their work with layers of older connotations. In an age more obviously transitional, there is likely to be more of new interpretations.[19] The myth itself seldom, if ever, presents any clear solution, but the Greek dramatists, in their attempt to find solutions, outlined for posterity the Greek view of man and human nature. In *The Flies* Sartre has directly challenged this answer and offers a new theory of what it means to be human. Later we shall examine this portrait in detail; for the present we may look at it in broad outline so as to see how *The Flies,* like most of Sartre's literary works, is at once myth, case history, and social comment.

As myth, *The Flies* is not only a retelling of a story dealing with the Greek gods and heroes. Like any myth it takes up the question of man's place in the universe. In opposition to Aeschylus, who claimed that there is a divine Justice concerned about the affairs of men, Sartre's Orestes declares, "What do I care about Zeus? Justice is men's business, and I need no god to instruct me in it." [20] Sartre's hero leads a humanistic revolt against the whole concept of deity and says that man must make himself fully responsible for his destiny.

At the same time, although Orestes is in one sense any human being courageous enough to accept the full responsibility of being human, and while he cares enough about his fellow men to suffer for them voluntarily, still Sartre is concerned to show us the inner feelings of a man thus discovering himself. In this way Orestes becomes a kind of individual illustration of a general psychological principle, functioning for Sartre much as the report of a case history serves a psychoanalyst in establishing a new theory. Three positions of Sartre's are particularly delineated: the inevitable sense of futility in the man who tries to avoid in any way engaging or committing his freedom (Orestes in Act One); the anguish with which a man first realizes that his freedom is absolute and inescapable but paid for by estrangement from the world of nature (Orestes in Act Two); the concept of "bad faith" by which man tries to escape being responsible for himself (the townspeople throughout and Electra especially in Act Three).

Finally, this humanistic doctrine of man's freedom is developed in such a way that the political reference is inescapable even if one does not know that the play was intended to be in part, at least, an attack on the German Occupation. Zeus, the god, talks with Aegisthus, the king, as one tyrant to another. They both harbor the same dread secret, says Zeus, the knowledge that men are free. When Aegisthus learns that Orestes has made this tremendous discovery, he says, "He knows that he is free. Then it's not enough to put him in chains. To have a free man in a city is like keeping one mangy sheep in a flock. He is going to infect my kingdom and undo all my work" (p. 79).

Summarizing then, we see that *The Flies* as myth deals with the relation of man and god; as psychological study, it is concerned with principles as general and fundamental as the Oedipus complex and as specifically related to Sartre as the complex is to Freud; as social comment, it is a plea to the French people to have the courage to work for national freedom against their oppressors. In a broader sense, it is also a manifesto for freedom against social or economic oppression, hence appropriate among the works of a Leftist writer such as Sartre has consistently been.

Although there are many occasions on which Sartre points up a philosophical conclusion by means of a brief explanation of a familiar myth, *The Flies* is his only full-scale treatment of one. Among his French contemporaries there are several particularly interesting examples of similar studies. Two of these are works by Camus: *The Myth of Sisyphus* and *Caligula*.

*The Myth of Sisyphus* provides an original interpretation of the tale of one of Greece's most spectacular and unfortunate criminals. During his life Sisyphus defied the gods and even for a time cheated death itself. In Hades he was sentenced to push a huge rock up a mountain, a rock which inevitably rolled down again just before Sisyphus got it to the top. Camus' analysis is not fiction but a philosophical essay which, as Sartre has pointed out, serves as a sort of commentary for Camus' novel, *The Outsider (L' Étranger).*[21] For Camus, Sisyphus is a symbol of absurdity, a concept common (with variation) to both Camus and Sartre. "The absurd" refers to the discrepancy between man's aspirations and his possibilities, and to the lack of any ultimate, external justification of man and his projects.

Sisyphus is the absurd hero. He becomes so as much through his passions as through his torment. His scorn of the gods, his hatred of death, and his passion for life got for him that unspeakable punishment in which all one's being is spent in accomplishing nothing. This is the price which must be paid for the passions of this earth (p. 164).

Still, for Camus, Sisyphus represents also the grandeur of man. As Sisyphus decides each time to try again to roll the rock up the hill, he gives of his own free will a meaning to what he is doing.

This universe, henceforth with no master, appears to him neither sterile nor futile. Each particle in this stone, every mineral splinter in that night-enfolded mountain is a world in itself. The very struggle toward the summit is enough to fill a man's heart. We must picture Sisyphus as happy (p. 168).*

A parallel analysis in drama is *Caligula*. Caligula, of course, is a historical rather than a mythological figure, but Camus' picture of him in no way pretends to be a historical study. Caligula, too, is represented as having discovered the essential absurdity of life. Sartre finds Camus' re-creation of the Roman emperor a perfect example of the new type of characterization in which the person is interesting, not as a complex individual, but as a personification of a possible human attitude.

If one of us happens to present character on the boards it is only for the purpose of getting rid of it at once. For instance, Caligula, at the outset of Albert Camus' play of that name, has a character. One is led to believe he is gentle and well-behaved, and no doubt he actually is both. But that gentleness and that modesty suddenly melt away in the fact of the prince's horrifying discovery of the world's absurdity. From then on he will choose to be the man to persuade other men of that absurdity, and the play becomes only the story of how he carries out his purpose.[22]

An example from another playwright, Jean Anouilh, is especially interesting since it was his *Antigone* and its reception by New York

---

* Socrates' friend Critias wrote a tragedy on the subject of Sisyphus. A fragment from it, probably spoken by Sisyphus, though this is not certain, sets forth the idea that since laws were not sufficient to keep men from sinning, someone invented the belief that there are gods who know everything and who have the forces of the thunder, etc., at their disposal to use in punishing men.

critics which led Sartre to formulate the aim and methods of the "theatre of situations" in his article "Forgers of Myths." The play illustrates the new theory of drama in two ways. First, Antigone represents a human will, an affirmation of right. Sartre writes of her,

> Thus, Anouilh's Antigone may have seemed abstract because she was not portrayed as a young Greek princess, formed by certain influences and some ghastly memories, but rather as a free woman without any features at all until she chooses them for herself in the moment when she asserts her freedom to die despite the triumphant tyrant (p. 325).

Here we find that preoccupation with a person's basic choice of himself which is at the very heart of existential psychology. In the second place, the play was, like *The Flies,* a commentary on the political situation under the German Occupation. To a certain extent even the original *Antigone* of Sophocles had political implications. When Antigone's betrothed, Haemon, challenged his father's right to condemn Antigone to death for acting contrary to his law, Sophocles set forth Haemon's arguments in such a way that Creon stands for dictatorship and Antigone and Haemon for the right of the individual and democracy. Sophocles, however, allowed Antigone no possibility of compromise. She was caught between duty toward heaven, represented by her individual conscience, and duty toward the State. No perfect solution being possible, Antigone had to pay a penalty—in a sense even a deserved penalty—and her choice lay between heroic death and shame for herself and her dead.* In Anouilh's tragedy, on the other hand, Creon has become quite benign, and Antigone dies largely because of her own self-willed martyrdom. Apparently it was clear to almost everyone in France that Anouilh was not interested primarily in the individual psychology of anyone in the play but that Antigone's position symbolized that of France under the conqueror. Debates were carried on in the newspaper arguing as to just what was the real message of the play, but the argument was conducted almost always on the political level. At present it seems quite clear that the author was responding to the very early attempts of the Germans to win over the French by a policy of conciliation and that Antigone represents what seemed to Anouilh the

---

* In *Antigone,* unlike *Electra,* Sophocles obviously produced a "drama of situations."

right choice—a refusal to cooperate in any way, this being the only path to freedom.

In his *Antigone,* Anouilh is certainly writing an example of the "theatre of situations." Anouilh is even less an "existentialist" in the strict sense of the term than Camus, and he is in no way committed to the principles of existential psychoanalysis. The existence of the tragedy is one of many examples which indicate that Sartre's criticism is applicable to more than those works which are deliberately designed to illustrate strict existentialist doctrine. On the other hand, this approach is not typical of all of the work of Anouilh. When he is not concerned with the symbolic presentation of his country's political situation, he can produce plays as purely illustrative of the "theatre of characters" as any of the pre-war writers. *The Lark,* for example, is a psychological study of Joan of Arc. In contrast with Camus' *Caligula,* it seeks to explain and re-create the full character of Joan, even using bits of the actual trial records to establish the accuracy of the interpretation.

So far we have considered only the use of *established* myths by Sartre and his contemporaries. The truth is, however, that the existentialist writer is far less likely to retell an old myth than to invent a new one. Sartre's *No Exit (Huit-Clos)* is an example of a myth which he himself has invented. The play is laid in hell and deals with the reactions of three people who have just arrived there, who gradually learn what exactly is the nature of hell, who try and fail to escape their punishment. Another example from Sartre's work is *The Chips Are Down (Les jeux sont faits),* a scenario in which the dead move invisibly among the living. The hero and heroine are informed after their death that they had been "meant for each other" but that an administrative error had prevented their meeting. They are given permission to return to life for twenty-four hours with the understanding that if they succeed in loving each other fully and with perfect confidence, they may remain for a long life together. (They fail!) A third example, this time from the work of Simone de Beauvoir, is the novel *All Men Are Mortal (Tous les hommes sont mortels).* Here the hero is given a drink which makes him immortal. The story concerns his gradual realization that life without mortality is meaningless, that between an immortal and a mortal no significant relation can be established.

I call these and comparable other examples myths. One could, I suppose, classify them as fantasies or even as science fiction. But there is an important difference. The emphasis in these works is not on the imaginary setting or the "gimmick" involved, nor is the train of consequences in any significant fashion derived from the fantastic situation. Rather the plot is ancillary to the metaphysical question. Its purpose is to serve as a framework within which human possibilities may be developed and a man's choice of himself made evident. It would not, I think, be a far-fetched comparison if we were to say that the invented myth of the existentialists is a not too remote descendant of the Platonic myth. As with Plato, the imagination is used to portray man in what is, from one point of view, a purely fictional situation but at the same time a revelation of man's actual philosophical or human condition.

Looking a little more closely at this use of myth in *No Exit*, we find that Sartre has retained the popular concept of hell as an actual place to which one goes and is punished. At first, however, no tortures are evident. All is polite and comfortable. Three people are locked in a room together, and we learn that the only punishment to be administered is whatever they will do to each other. Sartre uses this device partly to express some of his ideas on the meaning of death. In addition he depicts in the interrelations of his trio his own views as to the fundamental character of human relations in actual life.

So far as Sartre's philosophical position on death is concerned, we see in *No Exit* only the bare outline of his concept: that death is the moment at which each man ceases to be responsible for his being, the point after which other people will determine the significance of his life, will decide what he has been. In the play there is a brief period in which each of the characters can watch this process beginning; he watches the events on earth which immediately follow his death and sees what others have made of him.

But Sartre's chief interest here is less metaphysical than it is, in his own specific sense, psychological. Thus we have once more a study of bad faith as each character seeks excuses for his former failings. We have again an affirmation of Sartre's belief that each man is wholly responsible for his acts.

> *Garcin:* I died too soon. They didn't leave me time to achieve
> *my* deeds.
> *Inez:* One always dies too soon—or too late. And yet your
> life is there, completed. The line is drawn, you have
> to add up the figures. You are your life and only your
> life.[23]

Finally *No Exit,* more emphatically than any other of Sartre's literary works, illustrates his statement that the basis of any human relationship is a conflict of subjectivities, each man trying ceaselessly to assert his own subjective supremacy by making of the other an object. In *No Exit* the struggle is triangular. Turn by turn, each of the three persons is on the point of setting up some kind of satisfactory relation when all is destroyed by the awareness of the subjective observation of the third. "Hell is—other people," concludes Garcin. As the three face an eternity of this futile struggle, Sartre obviously is not merely indicating the eternal damnation of his trio; he is pointing out that hell is not in the next world but in this one.* In *No Exit* there is little reference to contemporary political issues. Garcin was a pacifist, and his cowardice lay in being unwilling to face the consequences of his position. The judgement passed upon him is consistent with Sartre's prejudice against any doctrine of passivism, but the point is not essential to the play. The social comment here lies rather in the analysis of what seems to Sartre the intrinsic nature of the social as such.[20]

In the group of works deriving from this type of "literary myth," there is one play by Camus which is a little different from the other examples chosen. This is *State of Siege (L'État de siège)*, which is actually less a myth than an allegory. In it Camus attempts to do more overtly what he had already done indirectly and more skillfully in *The Plague;* that is, he describes and comments on the German Occupation—or any totalitarian regime—by representing it symbolically as a plague epidemic. In *State of Siege* the political reference is more obvious, but the characters have lost all reality as people. Instead of a real pestilence there is a character named "The Plague," who personifies both the disease and arbitrary dictatorship. The persons who work with or against him are hardly anything but personified political attitudes. The play was produced in Paris in 1948 but was not a success. I suspect that there were two reasons for its failure. One is that allegory is less easy to handle than myth. The other is that Camus has so completely suppressed the psychological (the case-history aspect) that we are left with little more than the thesis play which he himself has so strongly condemned.

It is not too surprising that in fiction based on traditional or newly invented myth the problem and its solution supersede any interest in the individual characters as such. On the other hand, one would not expect to find this same combination of myth, case history, and social theory in a biographical study. Sartre has done two major works in biography. In the first, *Baudelaire,* his method is exactly what one would

---

* We shall see later that neither Sartre nor one sympathetic with him is forced to leave things quite at this negative point.

expect of any psychologist; that is, he attempts to re-create and explain the person of Baudelaire by applying the principles of his own existential psychoanalysis. If the results are startling, it is because of the unusual character of the tenets of the psychology rather than because of any novelty in literary method. On the other hand, in *Saint Genet, Martyr-Comedian* Sartre appears to be as much interested in the general psychological and social consequences of his analysis as he is in establishing the personality of Genet. His treatment of the subject offers a third method of approaching and using myth.

Jean Genet, professional thief and homosexual, was given a pardon and relieved of the necessity of serving out the rest of his prison sentence by the President of the French Republic at the instigation of Sartre and Jean Cocteau. Sartre and others in French literary circles evidently believed in Genet's talents as poet and novelist as well as in the sincerity of his resolutions to make of himself a new person. As Sartre writes the biography, Genet is for him literally a case history; that is, he provides material for Sartre's study; he is not merely the subject of the study. Sartre analyzes in minute detail the events in Genet's life and his reactions to them; the result is not only an explanation of Genet according to the principles of Sartrean psychology, but an exposition of the theory and methods of existential psychoanalysis. Furthermore, although Sartre attempts to give an exhaustive description of the inner and external life of Genet, the individual, he makes it quite clear that he regards Genet as a symbol of the victims of society, embodying all the suffering which human beings endure as the result of oppression and social justice. In fact, Sartre's plea that society is ultimately responsible for Genet is so strong that it poses at least a threat to Sartre's doctrine that every human being is absolutely free. Finally, and perhaps most surprising of all, Sartre states that the life of Genet can be understood and explained only in terms of myth. This is not merely to say that Genet, like all men, lives by myths, meaning that we are all guided by ideals and inexact images of physical and social realities. Sartre's title *Saint Genet* has a more specialized significance than that. In a very specific sense he says that Genet lives, so to speak, *outside* the daily episodes of his life. What happened was that Genet reacted to a few decisive incidents of his childhood in such a way that everything which he later did or suffered held significance for him only as a repetition of the earlier experiences. Sartre compares Genet's attitude toward his own life with that of the ancient Egyptian toward his national history, and says, "He condescends to pay attention to the circumstances of his life only to the extent to which they appear to repeat the original drama of the lost paradise." [24] Referring to the moment at which Genet, when still a young child, was suddenly made to feel that he was a thief—not just that he had stolen but that he *was*, once and forever, a thief and an outcast—Sartre writes,

> In the same way that Jesus does not cease to die, Genet does not cease to be metamorphosed into vermin: the same archetypal event is reproduced in the same ritualistic and symbolic form by means of the same ceremonies of transfiguration; for Genet, as for the faithful of a religious community, sacred time is cyclic; it is the time of the Eternal Return. . . . Genet has no profane *history;* he has only a sacred history; or if you prefer, like those societies called "archaic" he continually transforms history into mythological categories (p. 12).

Proceeding upon this assumption, Sartre sets about to seek the true significance of the facts of Genet's life by analyzing the myths by which he lived. In a sense these "myths" are only Genet's successive choices of himself. What is different here is that in each case Genet's choice was essentially an acceptance of a judgement passed upon him from the outside, the source being variously conceived by him in the course of his life as coming from his immediate associates, from society in general, or from God. The judgement was so specifically connected with a definite episode that it was easy for him to think of it as being repeated in a succession of similar patterns. The very process of seeing one's life as lived in this manner is in itself a choice of oneself as myth rather than as freely self-creating history.

In all of the examples discussed, though the specific view as to the nature of myth and its value for literature has varied considerably, there is one thing which we may say about all these works. This is that Sartre and the other writers mentioned have in all instances been unanimous in seeking a new concept of the human, a new definition of man. Whereas the authors of the "literature of characters" sought for variations on the basic themes, thus seeking complexity of character or novelty produced by unexpected turns of events within the basic plots, Sartre and his associates turn to a re-evaluation of human attitudes in the face of the most typical and the most fundamental situations. Since the essence of myth is always to point to the universal, the basically human, it is not strange that the new writing should either return to older myths or deal with contemporary events as if they were myths. We must remember, however, that for Sartre it is the human limits and situations which remain the same, not the collection of human traits which it has been customary to think of as human nature. Therefore, in the treatment of myth the existentialist seeks to portray a new human reaction to basic situations; he does not try to point up "the universally human" in characters reacting to a new form of the situation.

One might ask whether the new definition of man is any more likely to be final than that of the Greeks. Sartre would be the first to claim both that the definition is not final and that no definition ever would be. For the essence of man is to have no fixed essence but to be constantly in the process of freely making his own nature. It is therefore important for the contemporary writer to realize that the picture of man which he is drawing is of necessity only the portrait of man as he is right now in the mid-twentieth century, and this is one reason why Sartre stresses the writer's responsibility to make a commitment with regard to the social context. On the other hand, Sartre would not deny that there are certain metaphysical and material limits which remain fixed for man, and here, I suppose, he would be forced to acknowledge a certain absoluteness in his point of view. I refer here partly to what Sartre calls man's "facticity," his existence as a combination of specific body and consciousness, his finiteness not only in that he is mortal but in that his choices are limited by his material situation and by the laws of logic. Man cannot, for example, simultaneously have two things which are mutually and absolutely exclusive; he cannot undo by his wish what has actually been accomplished, though of course he can change its significance for him or modify its effect by another act, etc. In short, there are limits for man which collectively Sartre calls "the human condition," and it is within these limits that all human choices must be made. Furthermore, the statement that human beings are free and that human nature is not fixed—this is in itself an absolute position. Moreover, it demands a psychology to justify it, and here we find the real reason for Sartre's tendency to create fictional characters or to use biographical subjects who perform for existential psychoanalysis the same function provided by the actual case histories in the writing of the various branches of Freudian and post-Freudian psychoanalysis.

To understand either the principles of Sartre's psychology or its application to individuals, we must, of course, examine the literature itself. On the other hand, before we can even begin to understand the literature, we must know something about Sartre's basic metaphysical position regarding man's relation to the rest of the universe; for Sartre's whole theory concerning the freedom of man and the nonexistence of any determining human nature is derived directly from his peculiar view of human consciousness.

It is here that we meet Sartre's famous distinction between Being-in-itself and Being-for-itself. Being-in-itself *(L'Être-en-soi)* is all of nonconscious reality. Being-for-itself *(L'Être-pour-soi),* which is the being of man, is not actually a separate kind of being. For consciousness is not a thing, but a Nothingness. Man is the being who has at his heart a nothingness, a power to "nihilate" Being. This means in simple terms that man by the power of consciousness is able to withdraw, to stand off—as it were—from Being and reflect upon the rest of Being and upon himself, thus introducing meaning into a universe which without consciousness would be utterly undifferentiated and without significance. Consciousness is always consciousness *of* something; without the "something" it would be, in fact it *is,* nothingness. Moreover, the very fact that consciousness *is not* Being, even though it depends upon Being, means that it is identical with freedom. The discussion of how man discovers and lives his freedom is essentially the theme of this book.

There is a further development of Sartre's thought which is almost as fundamental as his position on Being and Nothingness. This is his idea concerning the relation of consciousness to the ego. For Descartes, of course, consciousness and the ego were identical. So are they, probably, in the mind of the average person. Sartre, however, makes a distinction between consciousness and the ego. In his view, although a man's consciousness is differentiated from other consciousnesses by means of that of which it is conscious, it is nevertheless not determined by the daily experiences and memories which gradually form what we think of as the "personality." The basic core of a man is a free consciousness for which present and past psychic experiences are objects to be determined and evaluated in the same way as objects of the outside world. It is here that we find the possibility for a new choice of oneself, which we discussed earlier. Our awareness that we *are* this undetermined and unpredictable consciousness comes to us at those anguished moments of crisis when we realize that *nothing* prevents our suddenly behaving in a fashion which nothing in our previous lives could have foretold. Such moments may be "big" moments, acts of heroism, religious conversion, a change in a fundamental outlook on life. Or they may be trivial moments, such as those when one recognizes within oneself an impulse to scream out in a silent auditorium or to blurt out unwelcome opinions at inappropriate moments, or to throw oneself over a cliff for just no "reason" at all.

The consequences of this view for Sartre's literature are tremendous. It not only explains his refusal to depict characters determined by heredity and environment; it explains as well those sudden shifts in orientation which we see so often in his heroes and heroines. It is the reason also why they experience so acutely an anguished sense of responsibility together with the realization that both internal and external guarantees are lacking for any values. We can see too why there is so much concern with the problem of the self, why any attempt to find a definite self which one can know, understand, and use as a guide for future conduct is doomed to frustration. For if consciousness is undetermined and free, then there is, in reality, no present self; there is a past self which has been and a future self which one must make, but that is all. Even the future self, of course, never exists save as the outlined project of a present consciousness.

There is another consequence of this theory of Sartre's which is of importance in connection with his statement that the existentialist writers must integrate psychology and life. The concept of a free consciousness working through, but not determined by, the personalized psyche involves two corollaries: first, consciousness is a totality, which means that every act and decision is to be interpreted in the light of consciousness' basic choice of itself; second, since consciousness exists only as consciousness *of* something, this means that when consciousness chooses itself, the choice must be presented to it in concrete terms. Thus, although admittedly much of my discussion has been presented in abstract terms, Sartre as an existentialist philosopher never forgets that an individual exists as a whole, not piecemeal, and that when he chooses, his choice is between two objects or two issues. For this reason, Sartre's heroes are presented to us as living in a real world with concrete choices, and the real world which Sartre provides for them is either directly or indirectly the real world of the twentieth century.

Inevitably, this view of the proper goal of literature will have an effect even upon the more superficial characteristics of a writer's work. One of the interesting consequences of Sartre's position is reflected in his ideas as to the novelist's narrative technique. In an essay in which he criticizes François Mauriac, Sartre complains that Mauriac, like many novelists, does not allow his characters to work out their own destinies. It has always, of course, been a law of fiction that the author must not seem to manipulate his characters, and it is commonplace to hear novel-ists complain that a character has got out of hand and changed the course of the story. Sartre, however, is referring a little more specifically to the technique of the novelist. He dislikes having the author put into the novel an analysis of the fictional character's thought or action when the analysis is neither that of the character himself nor an openly acknowledged reflection on the part of the author. This is the basis of Sartre's criticism of Mauriac's treatment of his heroine, Thérèse Des-queyroux, in *La Fin de la nuit.*

> M. Mauriac . . . passes from Thérèse-subject to Thérèse-object within the same sentence: "She heard the clock strike nine. She must kill a little time yet, for it was too early to take the tablet which would guarantee her a few hours of sleep—*not that this was one of the habits of this careful but desperate woman,* but this evening she could not deny herself this help." Who here is judging Thérèse to be a "careful but desperate woman"? It cannot be she herself. No, it is M. Mauriac, it is myself. We have the Desqueyroux dossier in our hands, and we pronounce judgement upon her.[25]

The omniscient novelist, says Sartre, "takes God's standpoint on his characters" and sees the whole universe within the novel, inside and out. But, "the time has come to say that the novelist is not God!" Sartre has two objections to the idea that there is outside the fictional situa-tion some absolute truth by which the characters may be judged. First, it presupposes that there is a purely contemplative narrator looking on at the action, and this is not true. The novelist-creator is not uninvolved and impersonal. In the second place, Sartre objects that the absolute—because it is nontemporal—destroys the novel, which is always in some form at least a narration of temporal events. If the absolute once takes away the train of duration, there remains only "a dull truth, *sub specie aeternitatis.*" Mauriac is correct in claiming that we may conceive of the novel as "an action related from various points of view," but the points of view must be open and acknowledged. If the author does not speak in his own name, he must reveal the fictional characters entirely through their own actions and their reflections upon themselves and others.

> Fictional beings have their own laws, of which the most strict is this  the novelist can be their witness or their accomplice but never both at once. Inside or outside. Because he does not

abide by these laws, M. Mauriac kills off his character's consciousness (p. 48).

Sartre himself is quite consistent in observing the principle which he lays down in this discussion of Mauriac. So, I believe, is Simone de Beauvoir. The most interesting example, however, is Camus' *The Plague,* though I have no reason to assume that Camus was consciously following Sartre's directions. Until the last ten pages of this more-than-three-hundred-page book, the story is told by a narrator who apparently takes no part in the action, who refers to "our fellow citizens," etc., but who for all practical purposes might be the author himself. One might easily assume that Camus was merely pretending to have witnessed the events—so as to give more verisimilitude to the account. The main characters in the novel are all described in the third person, seemingly from the same point of view, except that references are made to a diary of Tarrou's which the narrator has read, and that Dr. Rieux seems rather more than anyone else to be in the center of things. Suddenly when the book is almost ended we read, "It is time for the doctor, Bernard Rieux, to confess that he is the author." [26] Rieux goes on to explain his motives in writing the preceding record, his attempts to be objective, his own observations as to the lessons to be learned from the terrible experience. Then as we look back, we realize that we have had precisely what Rieux says; i.e., the account which Rieux would have written if he had tried to give an impersonal report. Inevitably the whole has been stamped with his personality; one realizes that in the passages where the "omniscient author" seemed to be working, these were all analyses of the kind Rieux would have made. The only places where emotional reactions were described a little too fully were those depicting Rieux' own reactions. *The Plague,* if we were to assume Rieux actually the author, might well serve to illustrate the fact that the impersonal narrator is impossible. While it is almost certain that Rieux' personality is sympathetic with that of Camus himself, yet the type of intrusive analysis to which Sartre objects is wholly absent.

A second technical consequence of Sartre's literary theory is found in his concept of style. Feeling as he does that the function of the writer is to reveal to man his own possibilities, Sartre is naturally as far removed as possible from any position which would emphasize style at the expense of content. His own writing, while frequently difficult because of the thought involved, is never intentionally obscure. For him language is always an instrument; it is a means of revealing man to himself. Sartre compares style to glass.

> One is not a writer for having chosen to say certain things but for having chosen to say them in a certain way. The style, of course, makes the value of the prose. But it must pass unnoticed. Since words are transparent and since we look through and beyond them, it would be absurd to slip in among them panes of frosted glass. Here beauty is only a gentle, imperceptible force.[27]

Poets, to whom Sartre rather unenthusiastically grants status as a special case, "are men who refuse to *utilize* language" and treat words as strange things in themselves, as the painter does with color. But the prose writer must communicate.

> The function of a writer is to call a spade a spade. If words are sick, it is for us to cure them. . . . There is nothing more disastrous than the literary practice called, I believe, poetic prose, which consists in using words for the sake of the dim overtones which they set up and which are made up of vague meanings in contradiction with the word's clear signification.[28]

Consistent with this position, Sartre steadfastly rejects extensive use of "allusive" imagery or that based on unconscious association. This is not to say that he spells out his meaning nor that the interpretation of his literary works is apparent at first reading or exhausted by any number of readings. But there is never a barrier created by the language itself.

Camus, like Sartre, says that great style is invisible.[29] In general, however, his approach to the subject is entirely different from Sartre's. This is partly because he has presented his aesthetic theory in such close connection with his doctrine of the absurd and of revolt that, for the most part, it becomes an appendage to his unique philosophical position. In part, however, Camus differs from Sartre because he gives emphasis to an idea which Sartre tends to neglect (at least in theory)—that the goal of literature is not only to instruct but also to delight. Sounding a little like John Dewey, Camus says that the express purpose of the novel is to give style to life's constant "becoming."[30] "The novel makes destiny to measure."[31] * In a sense, the novelist satisfies what Camus

---

* It is interesting that Camus generally uses the novel for illustration, whereas Sartre turns more often to drama.

believes is the fundamental meaning of revolt—that man both can and does refuse to be what he is.* In the novel—but not in life—there is a universe "where action finds its form, where final words are pronounced, where people give themselves wholly to each other, where all life takes on the appearance of a destiny." [32] The novelist does not provide mere wish-fulfillment but a legitimate intensification of the possible significance of life. To add style to reality is to *correct* reality. Another way of expressing the same idea is to say that beauty like true revolt "contests the real while bestowing unity upon it." [33] But just as the conscientious political leader must be careful neither to sacrifice living individuals to an abstract ideal nor to refuse all idealism in the interest of an existing order, so the creative writer encounters his Scylla and Charybdis. If he rejects the world completely, his work becomes wholly formalistic and empty; but if he allows himself to be entirely engulfed by the world, the result is an extreme realism which is little more than the stale enumeration of details.[34]

As we turn now to examine the literature of humanistic existentialism, we can see why it is also a literature of possibility. Because it presents to us a new picture of man, and because this picture·is one which includes the view that man is free to determine future portraits of himself, the existentialist is concerned above all else with pointing out to us what are the possibilities of man. In order for us to see these possibilities, we must know something about man's metaphysical situation (hence the use of myth), about his psychological capabilities (hence the case history), and about the actual problems which he confronts (hence the social comment).

---

* Not, of course, in the way of a self-evasion but in refusing to confine his aspirations and efforts to those appropriate to a being defined by finitude and mortality.

PART TWO

---

Self-encounter

# I. THE DEFINITION

---

THE APPLE WHICH SENT the Greeks off to Troy was made of gold. The apple which tempted Eve and the one which crashed the theory of gravitation into the head of Isaac Newton were presumably sound natural products. But the existential apple suggested in an image given us by Jean-Paul Sartre is imperfect. "Nothingness lies coiled in the heart of Being—like a worm." It is right that the figure should suggest something rotting. For according to the existentialists, man discovers his Being in anguish and nausea, he more often than not lives out his life in bad faith, and he determines the quality of his existence by the attitude which he assumes toward his inevitable death.

Twentieth-century literature is interested no less than Genesis in the question of original sin and man's reason for being. In spite of Darwin it persists in regarding the human race as qualitatively different from the rest of Creation, and it is obsessed with the necessity of arriving at a new definition of man.

In Sartre's formulation, Nothingness is always present. Man is, in fact, the being through whom Nothingness comes into the world. He is the being who is what he is not, and who is not what he is. He is freedom, and freedom is a lack of Being. Yet there is an existentialist imperative as well. For if man is to live a life appropriate to the truth of his existence, then he must make himself a lack of Being in order that Being may be *there*.[1] He must set himself apart from the totality of Being in order to assign significance to the particular Being which he confronts and to the relation which he establishes with it.

Sartre bases his definition of man on the premise that consciousness is a process of continual negation, a nihilation—to use Sartre's term. Man differs from the rest of the universe only in the one explosive fact that his consciousness is able to effect a psychic distance between itself and its object, which may be all or any part of the rest of Being. In a sense, this negative view of consciousness actually gives more importance to the human individual than any previous philosophy. For while the whole weight of Being is thrown over onto the side of the In-itself, this is an undifferentiated plenitude, only a brute being-there. Even the "there" suggests a situating consciousness. Strictly speaking, all one can say of nonconscious Being is that it is. The For-itself, consciousness, is but a Nothingness (or a power to create a Nothingness); its existence, like that of a shadow, is wholly dependent. Yet only through its nihilating recoil can there be differentiation, change, meaning, significance; and from a human point of view, which is the only point of view we can take, these things are what really matter. Even idealism, religious or otherwise, gives importance to a controlling deity or to a universal Mind or at least to transcendent Ideas; but for Sartre, it is only the particular consciousness which brings into the world anything more than what we might call an unmeaning itness.*

Thus man attains to a certain philosophical dignity after all, even though he *is* chiefly a "hole in Being." The psychological implications are something else again. It is one thing for man to be actually a creature so separated from the rest of reality that he is free to give to Being whatever meanings he chooses. It is quite another for him to realize his status and to live in such a way that he never pretends to himself that his particular way of being is guaranteed—like that of a stone or a tree. I hope to show that it is possible to have a positive ethics and a significant existence consistent with the existentialist position, but I think that Sartre is right in pointing out that the immediate consequences of man's discovery of himself as a free nihilating being are almost inevitably shattering—or, at the very least, extremely depressing.

To say that man must make himself a lack of Being in order that Being may be there is to say that man must recognize—not in a single flash of inspiration but continually—that he alone determines the values by which he lives, that he is not endowed with a ready-made self or nature but rather must be constantly making himself. He *is* nothing; he

---

* I apologize for adding this term to the already appalling collection of coined words in existentialist writing; but when one is trying to describe a reality which by definition precludes description, it is hard to be either precise or elegant.

is always about-to-be whatever he chooses. Interestingly enough, Martin Heidegger, who gave so much to Sartre, has recently altered completely this ethical imperative so as to give preponderance to Being. Man must let Being be, he says, thereby meaning that man must somehow let nature or objects reveal themselves as they really and essentially are. This statement implies both that man is somehow fulfilled or healed of his alienation from Being and that there is a priority of essence over existence. But for Sartre, man is a creature in whom existence always precedes essence. Man makes himself a lack of Being; that is, he recognizes that he as a consciousness is *not* Being, hence can, so to speak, let Being stand before him for judgement.

The view that man is somehow characterized by a lack, by a fundamental rift or ambiguity within him, by a species of estrangement from nature and even from himself is not peculiar to existentialism. It is not limited to the twentieth century either, but I believe it is a mistake to claim that there is nothing new in the contemporary statement of it.

Colin Wilson in *The Outsider* has attempted to show that the "existentialist hero" is a familiar type in twentieth-century fiction. I do not believe that his analysis of the "hero" is an adequate one, and it is difficult to see how an existentialist, or anyone else for that matter, could accept the mixture of physical culture and elementary mysticism which Wilson calls religion. Furthermore, he almost entirely misunderstands Sartre. In one passage he claims that Sartre maintains that man is never free; yet Wilson describes the Sartrean hero as discovering within himself an absolute freedom.[2] But Wilson is right in pointing out that recent fictional characters are marked by a "self-division," a feeling of unreality, a sense of isolation from other people, and a loss of belief in even the possibility of any certain values.

That man is separate from the rest of nature is the central theme of Vercors' *You Shall Know Them (Les Animaux dénaturés)*.[3] This novel, a clear example of the literature of situations, is concerned directly and almost exclusively with arriving at a definition of the human. It is a story of a scientific expedition in New Guinea which discovers a tribe of Tropis. These creatures appear to be the long-sought Missing Link and resist any final classification either as men or as apes. Immediately there arises a multitude of difficult questions. When one of the native tribes kills and eats some of the Tropis, are they to be condemned for cannibalism? Can the defenders of the equality of men any longer defend their position before the advocates of white supremacy? Is it the duty of the Church to make the Tropis Christians when religious instruction appears to be impossible? And is baptism an obligation or a sacrilege? Matters are brought to a head when the Takura Development Company conveniently assumes that the Tropis may be considered beasts of burden and proceeds to train them for manual labor in the factories—unlawful exploitation if the Tropis are men, but justifiable (at least by human standards) if they are animals. The scientists who have discovered the Tropis and who are fond of them feel that the question of classification must be settled. Biologically there is a definite answer. The Tropis unquestionably belong to the same species as humans, for a species is defined as including those beings, and only those, which can mate with each other. Douglas Templemore and one of the female Tropis have by artificial insemination produced a male offspring. If Vercors had wished, he could have resolved the problem by merely having the Court accept the biological definition; we should be left with a neat piece of science fiction and only that. But the author has given us a philosophical novel by raising the question as to whether man may be defined simply by a biological classification. In order to force the Court to determine the status of the Tropis, Templemore deliberately kills the· baby. If the offspring is human, then of course the State must hold Templemore guilty of murder. Gradually the Court and all of England realize that no decision can be made since there never has been any adequate definition of man. And Parliament is asked to determine what it means to be human.

There are several points of interest in Vercors' resolution. First, the jury agrees with the Counsel for the Defense that "humanity" is not so much the possession of certain biological potentialities as a particular use of these. It is not something strictly determined by biology but a quality defined by men themselves.

> No one is a human being by a right of .nature. . . . Mankind resembles a very exclusive club. What we call human is defined by us alone. The rules within the club are valid for us alone. Hence the need for a legal basis to be established, as much for the admission of new members as for setting up rules and regulations applicable to all (p. 240).

Here of course is the possibility for Templemore's acquittal. Since the status of the Tropis had not yet been decided, he cannot retroactively be said to have murdered a human child.

Such a conclusion throws everything into relativity, including the act of murder itself. Earlier, before the trial, Douglas' wife, Frances, was filled with horror as she realized that even her own feelings toward him would be affected by the ultimate decision as to whether her husband had committed murder or merely killed an animal. To Douglas, on the other hand, the thought of the importance which men attach to formal designations is filled with exciting possibilities.

It shows that at bottom murder doesn't exist. Not by itself, I mean. Since it doesn't depend on what I have done but on what men—and you, and I, too, perhaps, after all—eventually decide I've done. Men, Frances, men alone. The human species. And we feel such a profound solidarity with the human species that what it thinks, we can't help thinking with it. We are not free to think differently: what they decide, that's what I am, that's what you are, that's what we all are together. And we shall decide it ourselves, for ourselves alone, without bothering about the universe. That's perhaps what strikes me as beautiful (pp. 219-220).

But what is this quality which the human club demands and which all its members share? Vercors says that it is the spirit of religion, but it is a religion less characterized by a reliance on the supernatural than by a self-conscious wrenching away from nature.

Now, in order to question there must be two of you—the one who questions, and the one who is questioned. Intimately bound up with nature, the animal cannot question it. That seems to be the point we are seeking. The animal is *one* with nature, while man and nature make *two*. To pass from passive unconsciousness to questioning consciousness, there had to be that schism, that divorce, there had to be that wrenching away from nature. Is not that precisely the borderline? Animal before the wrench, man after it? Denatured animals, that's what we are (pp. 224-225).*

A man is a being who questions. As Sartre has put it, man is a being such that his very Being consists in putting his Being into question. Such questioning is indicated, Vercors argues, by ritual, by tabu, by "ju-jus." In the novel we are informed that whereas all the Tropis preferred raw flesh and could not be induced to eat cooked-meat, those who resisted the explorers' influence continued to observe a seemingly pointless ritual in

---

* There is an obvious similarity between this view and that of Erich Fromm in *Man for Himself*. I am reserving discussion of Fromm for Part Three.

which they lightly smoked their meat before eating it. The native tribe which secretly used Tropis for cannibalistic religious ceremonies would capture only the meat-smoking ones and scorned the others. Clearly, in the eyes of the natives, some Tropis qualified as human and others did not.

Vercors' attitude toward man as defined in *You Shall Know Them* is essentially that of Pascal, who declared that man as a "thinking reed" is greater than the storm which breaks him, for man can reflect on the situation while the storm cannot. The separation from nature is not so much an estrangement as the achievement of a new point of vantage from which man can look down on nature. Frances says,

> Humanity is not a state we suffer. It's a dignity we must strive to win. A dignity full of pain and sorrow. Won, no doubt at the price of tears. . . . But now I know, I know that all this isn't "a tale told by an idiot, signifying nothing" (p. 244).

Vercors' conclusion is easier, more optimistic, and, in the final analysis, less original than that of most of the existentialists. Vercors as a Communist (albeit one with existentialist tendencies) stresses the grandeur of the destiny of the human race as a collectivity rather than the psychological consequences for the individual. Moreover, his definition of man is arrived at abstractly through intellectual discussion. It bears no more relation to the actual experience of what it means to be human than the description of an illness bears to the real aches and pains. Although there will always be a discrepancy between words and the thing described, still, in their imaginative writing, Sartre, de Beauvoir, and Camus have tried to emphasize the *quality* of an experience as much as its intellectual signification. Especially apropos of man's relation to nature they have sought to portray the insecurity and ambiguity of his situation.

One of the best short statements of the negative response to man's unique position can be found in a nonexistentialist work, in Eugene O'Neill's *Long Day's Journey into Night*.[4] The dramatic katharsis in this play is achieved as each of the characters attains for the first time to some measure of self-understanding. For three of the members of the Tyrone family the recognition involves a comprehension, by each one, of his individual character and earlier motivations. But for Edmund the insight is not so much an illumination of his own personality as a revelation of what it means to be a human being.

It was a great mistake, my being born a man, I would have been much more successful as a seagull or a fish. As it is, I will always be a stranger who never feels at home, who does not really want and is not really wanted, who can never belong, who must always be a little in love with death (pp. 153-154).

Edmund here touches on several of the fundamental themes of existentialism. There is first the nostalgia for a return to nature, a forbidden longing more basic in the eyes of the existentialist than the Freudian yearning for the lost security of the womb. Just as the return to the foetal state symbolizes rest, security, an absolute belonging to an all-embracing mother-home, and freedom from the burden of being a separate individual, so the return to the womb of nature represents a oneness with the environment in which man is no longer responsible for himself, where he has the certainty of instinctual living and the security of belonging so completely that the question of being wanted or of being necessary cannot even arise. This is the same idea which Sartre expresses by saying that man as a for-itself longs for the security of the in-itself. The desire is irrational, for what man actually wants is to be conscious of having the sureness of nonconscious Being. Man cannot go back to the heart of nature any more than the individual can return to the womb. His life as himself is paid for with estrangement, isolation, uncertainty. Edmund is not at home in the universe, and he sees that he is not necessary to the universe. Since his existence is thus not "justified," he can never wholly give himself to wanting anything in this universe. Nor is there any absolute relation which can be established between him and other persons since they, like him, have no fixed being or place. Finally he is half in love with death as being the one certainty of his life; he cannot, however, fully desire death, for a consciousness can never really experience the idea of its own unconsciousness.

If one were to attempt a concrete picture of man as the existentialists—and other of our contemporaries—see him, I think the result would be a combination of some of the forms of Dali—a strange figure, partly organic, partly mechanized, with a hole in the middle, with bony excrescences jutting out into the distance, all of this set in a background of melting or disintegrating time. If the portrait seems absurd, we must remember that the absurdity of man is an existentialist concept.

# II. BAD FAITH AND

# THE SERIOUS WORLD

---

## 1. THE MEANING OF BAD FAITH

W HETHER OR NOT we feel that the existentialists are unduly pessimistic in their view of the human situation, I think we must begin by giving full weight to the negative side. In the first place, any proffered solution or any more positive picture of man must at least take into consideration these feelings of insecurity and isolation. Secondly, if we are to understand their literature, we must know why. existentialist writers believe that man generally feels unable to face the truth about himself and seeks various modes of escape.

Essentially the position is this: that man cannot bear the realization that all the values he lives by, his purposes, his projects are sustained by his own free choice; he finds it too great a strain to accept sole responsibility for his life. Therefore he takes refuge in the belief that somehow the external world is so structured that it guarantees the worth of its objects, it provides specific tasks which have to be done, it demands of each person a definite way of living which is the *right* one. Whether God, Nature, or a transcendent Society is responsible, the order of things is absolute. It is a *serious world*.

Sartre contrasts this "spirit of seriousness" *(l'esprit de sérieux)* with the lighter attitude of one playing a game. No matter how serious the stakes, the player knows that the rules have been *invented*. If they are to apply to him, it is because he has consented to regard them as binding. There is always the possibility of initiating a change in the regulations or of playing an entirely different game. To use another analogy, man is like an artist—in this case one forced to paint *something*. If the artist is to produce the picture he has in mind, he will have to observe certain principles of composition, of form, of color. But he is free at any moment to change his artistic purpose and so adopt an entirely different set of criteria.[1]

According to Sartre, man, if he honestly reflects, cannot help realizing that his situation is like that of the player or the artist. Herein consists the absurdity of existence. Life has the same value as a game has—that is, whatever value the players choose to give to it. One has to play the game, but one is never given a book of rules.

Here we should note one important fact. I have been speaking almost exclusively of nontheistic existentialism. If we were to consider the religious branch, then of course the metaphysical description would be different as well as the ultimate solution. Surprisingly, the concept of man's absurdity and the presentation of man's psychological predicament are remarkably similar. In the eyes of Kierkegaard, man's position is absurd in that he is a finite rational creature who seeks salvation in the infinite. For God to be united with the finite (as in Christ) is for reason the greatest absurdity of all. Yet only this absurdity is commensurate with man's need. Moreover, there is never any guarantee for man. that the leap in faith is anything more than a jump into unreason. Even if God should send a special messenger as he sent his angel to Abraham, still each man—like Abraham—must decide whether the angel is real or a hallucination.[2] As man he can never be *sure*. Franz Kafka stands midway between Kierkegaard and Sartre. Even though Kierkegaard insists that there is no rational or objective proof of God's existence or nature, his faith in the specific Christian revelation is unshakable and ultimately determines all of his judgements. Kafka seems certain that there is a goal which ought to determine man's actions, and there is great emphasis in Kafka's work on guilt feelings and judgement. But he appears to be equally sure that there is no way for man to know what is demanded of him or what exactly *is* his relation to the utterly transcendent Judge. For humanistic existentialism, of course, man's absurdity and insecurity stem from the fact that there is no ultimate standard of reference, that *sub specie aeternitatis* all actions are equal. As regards these two positions, a person's own temperament, I believe, must decide for him whether it is easier to believe in an incomprehensible God one does not know how to reach or in a world with no God at all.

According to Kierkegaard, men sometimes reject completely the appeal of the Infinite; more often they delude themselves by thinking they can reach the Christian God by merely accepting a second-hand experience via the institutions of Christianity. Kafka apparently feels that most of us simply give up the search and live a half-life in which we become like automata or insects, functioning as social units but not as individuals. Sartre says that man escapes into the Serious World by *bad faith*.

Bad faith *(mauvaise foi),** although it is roughly a synonym for self-deception, is not simple in its philosophical formulation, and it is much more complex as a chosen mode of living. Considering first Sartre's analysis in *Being and Nothingness*,[3] we find that bad faith always involves a shift between two meanings of the verb "is," a failure to be accurate in designating whether the state of Being referred to is that of Being-in-itself or Being-for-itself. Existentialism has been accused of being "an exercise in the art of misusing the verb 'to be.'"[4] Sartre also seems to base humanity's troubles on ignorance of verbal paradigms. One might ask—not wholly facetiously—whether a mere grammatical confusion can be so consequential or whether we could improve the situation by providing syntactical clarification and coining a few new terms. But aside from the fact that man chooses the grammar to express his thought rather than a thought to fit his grammar, the ambiguity here is existential. Grammar has accurately reflected existence. For man *was* and *is* in the two modes of Being. He *was* in the manner of Being-in-itself. His past action *was* an event or object in the world. If, for instance, a man has stolen or has behaved like a coward, then he *was* a thief or a coward just as the table *was* a table or the tree *was* a tree. Yet in the present and for the future, man is wholly in the mode of Being-for-itself. We cannot say that he *is* a thief or a coward as the table *is* a table, for it depends on him to choose whether to be a thief or not. Thus man with his finite body has, especially in the past, the Being-in-itself of things in the world; but at the same time he *is not*—in any final sense—that

---

* Walter Kaufmann, in including in his existentialist anthology a section of my translation of Sartre's chapter on bad faith, made a point of changing my translation of *mauvaise foi* to "self-deception." This procedure seems to me entirely unjustified. The French means "bad faith" and nothing else. *Mauvaise foi* is a technical term and should not be translated by some sort of explanatory equivalent. Cf. Walter Kaufmann, *Existentialism from Dostoevsky to Sartre* (New York: Meridian Books, 1957), p. 222.

which he chooses to make himself. This vacillating structure of Being makes it easy for the man in bad faith to deceive himself by a metaphysical play on words.

Manifold as are the outward expressions of a life in bad faith, the psychological structure is reducible to a description involving three types of conduct: (1) the simultaneous use of both meanings of the word "is," not as they apply existentially but as they are advantageous to the purposes of the person using them; (2) a pursuit of sincerity which is actually insincere; (3) an unauthentic attitude toward "faith."

Sartre introduces his analysis of the first structure—the dishonest exploitation of the two meanings of "being"—by an amusing example. A woman is having dinner for the first time with a man whose amorous intentions are obvious though not as yet put in so many words. The man is trying to make the first approach; his words are suggestive but so calculated that taken at face value they may appear to be merely respectful or admiring. The woman decides so to take them. Since she is not sure of her own feelings, since she wishes neither to commit herself for the future nor to remove all possibility of any involvement, she elects to give everything the quality of being-in-itself; that is, she pretends that words are absolute with only their dictionary meaning, that the respectful attitude of the man *is* what it is with a fixed meaning as the table *is* a table. When she accepts her companion's compliments, perhaps his hints of future meetings, she has no sense either of being deceitful or of making promises, for she assumes that any future is but a continuation of the absolute present, that any words of hers are but literal answers to his statements literally taken. Yet the woman is wholly in bad faith; for what gives the moment its charm is the very undercurrent of danger, the suggestion of future change which she denies. Although she pretends to herself that she and her escort are merely two people having a friendly conversation, although she is not ready to acknowledge that theirs is a man-and-woman relation, yet she would resent the fact if the man's feelings toward her failed to recognize her femininity. What she wants is to prolong this uncertain hour in which she may *feel* her freedom without committing it.

The man is unwilling to leave things as they are. He tries to force a decision by taking the woman's hand. Now she alters her tactics. Where before she was all for emphasizing the "facticity" of their situation, for acting as if they and their words existed only in the present, like things, now she suddenly becomes entirely a free consciousness so fully liberated from the present that what she does with her body loses significance.

> The young woman leaves her hand there, but she *does not no-tice* that she is leaving it. She does not notice because it happens that she is at this moment all intellect. She draws her companion up to the most lofty regions of sentimental speculation; she speaks of Life, of her life, she shows herself in her essential aspect—a personality, a consciousness. And during this time the divorce of the body from the soul is accomplished; the hand rests inert between the warm hands of her companion —neither consenting nor resisting—a thing (pp. 55-56).*

The duplicity here is made possible by the fact that the human being "is at once a facticity and a transcendence." As a finite creature, occupying a definite place in space and history, man's being *is* a fact as things are facts. But in the freedom of a consciousness which transcends time and space, which allots to them their very significance, man never *is*—finally—what at any moment he may make himself. There is always a film of nothingness between him and the role he chooses to play.

So far, bad faith is fairly easy to detect, and one might well wonder how anyone even slightly introspective could be so self-deceived. But the statement that a person never fully is that which he is making himself be leads us into a more subtle structure of bad faith—the pursuit of sincerity. Sincerity may be easily defined as the determination to be for oneself and for others whatever one really is. At first thought, sincerity appears to be the evident antithesis of bad faith, which we found earlier to consist in not letting oneself be pinned down to any one position. That this view is incorrect is shown by Sartre in a remarkably subtle analysis of an imaginary conference between a homosexual and a friend who is trying to help him.

The homosexual in Sartre's example is not a homosexual in good faith; that is, he has not deliberately chosen a life in which he acknowledges to himself that his sexual needs are best satisfied by other men. Rather he is a man who declares that he "is not really a paederast" even though he admits to having indulged on occasion in homosexual relations.

---

* Apparently Sartre and de Beauvoir must have discussed this example. In de Beauvoir's novel, *L'Invitée,* which appeared in the same year as *L'Être et le Néant,* she gives a brief sketch of a woman behaving in exactly this way.[5] What strikes me as odd is that neither Sartre nor de Beauvoir points out that there is some bad faith on the man's side as well. His choice of ambiguous words is explicitly designed to allow him to retreat rapidly to the plane of polite friendship in case he has misjudged the situation.

His case is always "different," peculiar; there enters into it something of a game, of chance, of bad luck; the mistakes are all in the past; they are explained by a certain conception of the beautiful which women cannot satisfy; we should see in them the results of a restless search rather than the manifestations of a deeply rooted tendency, etc., etc. Here is assuredly a man in bad faith who borders on the comic since, acknowledging all the facts which are imputed to him, he refuses to draw from them the conclusion which they impose (p. 63).

At this point the homosexual's position is not different from that of the young woman in the first illustration. He chooses to think of himself *only* in terms of his freedom. He is quite right in thinking that he is not a homosexual absolutely in the way that a thing is a thing. Or to put it another way, he is right in holding that you cannot define a man's essence merely by pointing to his established patterns of conduct. But he is wrong when he tries to maintain this same freedom with respect to his acts in the past. In so far as a paederast is defined as a person who commits certain acts, and in so far as he has committed those acts, he has been a paederast. To say that he is, in an absolute sense, not-a-paederast is as incorrect as to say that he is absolutely a paederast. What he is trying to do is to use simultaneously and dishonestly the two meanings of "to be"; he says that since as a for-itself he cannot *be* a paederast (or anything else), therefore he is (in the sense of being-in-itself) not-a-paederast.

The homosexual's conduct is a common enough type of rationalizing resorted to by many people who do not like to see applied to themselves a term which carries opprobrium when they apply it to others. A new element enters in when we examine the attitude of the homosexual's well-meaning friend. He is impatient with the homosexual's duplicity and urges him to be "sincere." If the homosexual will just admit that he *is* a paederast, urges the friend, then he will show himself trustworthy and perhaps the friend can offer understanding and help. This argument, Sartre claims, is just as much in bad faith as the excuses of the homosexual. The friend wants the homosexual to admit to being a paederast absolutely as a thing is a thing. His motive is a double one: first, the homosexual's self-classification would remove the disturbing element of a freedom which makes his friend a bit uncertain as to how to proceed; second, it would enable the friend by "pardoning" to offer him as a gift the freedom to make a new choice and no longer be a paederast.

I am not sure that in the particular example chosen, Sartre's interpretation is necessarily correct. There seems to be no reason why the friend should be incapable of trying to help the homosexual by pointing out to him that his being a paederast in the past and his being one in the present and future are two different things. Yet in the broader sense I believe that Sartre is right in pointing out that sincerity may easily become an avenue leading into bad faith. With regard to the past, sincerity is possible and necessary; if a person is to be in good faith, then he must admit that he has been what he was, he must acknowledge his own acts. With regard to the present, I should go further than Sartre; it seems to me that sincerity is in good faith in so far as one describes his projects as they actually seem to him to be rather than as he merely desires another to see them. But if a person makes of himself the project of *being* what he is, this is not sincerity but bad faith. For the individual does not have a fixed nature; to assume that he must continue to be what he is becomes the equivalent of saying that some gift of heredity or previous experience is determining his being, is cutting off his future. It is no better than if the homosexual should say that since he *is* a paederast, he might as well just give up any attempt at change and be a paederast. From this point of view "sincerity" becomes a lie and an excuse.

The third structure of bad faith is an unauthentic attitude toward faith itself. Bad faith—like good faith—is aware that "a belief is only a belief." One cannot believe without being to some extent aware that a belief is an idea based on incomplete evidence, and the result is that the act of believing tends to undermine itself. "Every belief is belief that falls short; one never wholly believes what one believes" (p. 69). Good faith cannot escape this tendency to self-destruction, but it "finds refuge in Being." Sartre has not said just what he means by this. Presumably a man in good faith will assume responsibility for his actions even though he has no assurance that he is right, and he will carefully distinguish between what he believes (even if he *only* believes) to be true and what he (only) believes to be false. He will seek to approach as near as possible to the certain Being of things. The conduct of the man in bad faith is easily recognized. Since all belief is only belief, he makes no distinctions. "If every belief in good faith is an impossible belief, then there is a place for every impossible belief" (p. 69). If all faith is insecurely anchored, then he will give as firm allegiance to any idea which satisfies his irrational impulses as he will to one supported by at least a probable degree of reason. From assuming that nothing is sure, he passes to the attitude that everything is equally sure; from there to the conviction that a particular belief is absolutely sure.

For the existentialist, bad faith is almost original sin. One is not, to be sure, born in it. But bad faith is so prevalent in the world that one can hardly escape its contagion. Moreover, the philosophical vision required if one is to avoid bad faith is such as could hardly be attained by one living in a state of complete innocence. The existentialist hero comes face to face with the truth about himself when he recognizes within him the structures of bad faith—in much the same way that the Christian convert is saved from sin at the moment when he acknowledges that his soul must be cleansed of it.

It is time for us now to examine the patterns of bad faith which are delineated in the lives of the characters of existentialist fiction. Some of this conduct is easily recognized as self-deceptive. For example, we will hardly be surprised to see that anti-Semitism and unthinking conformism are examples of bad faith. It soon becomes obvious, however, that bad faith may be found "coiled like a worm" at the heart of most human relations, in political attitudes, in religion, even in the uncritical acceptance of psychoanalysis.

## 2. A STUDY OF BAD FAITH

The various ways in which one can *live* bad faith deserve separate analysis. First, however, I think it may be profitable to examine carefully one of Sartre's early works, *The Childhood of a Boss (L'Enfance d'un chef)*, a novella which introduces in quick succession a number of themes developed more extensively in Sartre's later books. It is the case history of a young man "destined" to succeed his father, a wealthy industrialist. There is no missing the fact that while Sartre has attempted to create a three-dimensional individual, Lucien also typifies for him a member of the employer class. The social comment is unmistakable. At the same time, Sartre's procedure and the details which he has selected—especially those showing us the very early influences on his hero —parallel so closely the case histories of psychologists as to suggest deliberate satire. The whole is a study of bad faith as manifested not in one but in many interrelated attitudes. Since it is Sartre's contention that the individual is a unit and functions as a whole, it follows that a person who has chosen bad faith is hardly likely to manifest it in a single pattern but will more probably reveal it in everything he does. Let us look then at the life of Lucien Fleurier.

When we first meet him, Lucien is being fitted for an angel costume! (The irony here is so broad as to be almost unworthy its author.) A visitor pretends to take him for a girl, and Lucien "was afraid that people would decide all of a sudden that he was no longer a little boy" and that then his sex would actually change. The passage is prophetic both in foreshadowing the later theme of homosexuality and in indicating that Lucien will ultimately be content to be what other people make of him. Freud, of course, would relate the episode to a castration complex. For Sartre it becomes an illustration of how our ideas of ourselves are formed in part, at least, by perceiving what others think of us. The self-for-others is something which we cannot quite grasp but which we must live with, and our realization that it exists inevitably influences our own attitude toward the elusive self.

The next episode is rather more Freudian than Sartrean. Lucien, who sleeps in the same room as his parents, dimly realizes that they have had intercourse. He is disturbed, imagines that thieves have come to steal his parents from their bed and have put two strangers in their place. Or perhaps his parents by day are not the same as those by night. He decides now that when he grows up he will *not* marry his mother. He becomes aware of his mother's body but with disgust, not with desire. When she laughs, he thinks that the back of her throat is dirty, and he would like to spit inside it. (Later in *Being and Nothingness* Sartre describes the obscene as arising from the awareness of human flesh as flesh when one is not in the state of desiring that flesh.)

Lucien pretends to himself that he is an orphan. Suddenly he confronts the truly existential question: Is he playing at being an orphan or at being Lucien? He cannot answer the question, nor can he escape the feeling that he is merely playing. He is troubled and wishes he might be like his father's friend, M. Bouffardier, "who was so heavy and so serious." At this point Lucien has actually glimpsed the truth of the human situation, though he seeks already to avoid recognizing it. Further realization comes to him a little later when he is alone in the garden. He has been inwardly disturbed by a question as to whether he loved his mother, although he had answered firmly that he did. Now he cries aloud,

"I love my Mama! I love my Mama"; there was a big blue fly buzzing around him: it was a dung fly [*une mouche à caca*];

Lucien was afraid of it—and an odor of something forbidden, powerful, putrid, and tranquil filled his nostrils. He repeated, "I love my Mama," but his voice seemed strange to him; he felt a terrible fear and fled at once back into the living room. From this day on Lucien understood that he did not love his Mama (p. 160).[1]

This episode with the unpleasant symbol of the dung fly both illustrates Sartre's ability to handle symbolism of the conventional sort and touches on something new. The suggestion of excrement reminds Lucien of childhood experiences, of being made to sit on the potty, of certain of his mother's prohibitions. Dwelling on the forbidden, he is impelled to press on into other prohibited areas. Suddenly he realizes that he does not love his mother as he is expected to do. In part this is simply Sartre's statement that human relationships do not necessarily elicit the emotional response which they "are supposed" to produce—hardly a new idea, but one which is frequent in existentialist literature: for example, in Camus' *The Stranger,* where Mersault is condemned to death not so much for having murdered a man as for not having behaved with the customary sentimentality at his mother's funeral.

In a more fundamental sense Lucien's self-discovery is an extension of his perception that he cannot be sure of *being* Lucien. He has expected to find the emotion of love recognizable within himself, like an opaque cloud which has come to fill and engulf him. But when he looks, there is nothing there. Emotions are not things-in-themselves; they are not even drives or forces which irresistibly overwhelm one. One makes an emotion moment by moment as one chooses oneself.[2] Sartre claims that with emotions, as with almost everything else, man longs for an unattainable absolute. He has in his mind an idea of a pure emotion which is itself and nothing else, which is all-absorbing and possessed of a certain density. Take suffering, for example. If a man suffers, he adopts an attitude toward the world which somehow devalues everything save that which he has lost or failed to attain. Even his bodily postures and expressions are designed to express the new outlook. In a sense one works at suffering, as is illustrated by the wonderful question of the cuckold in *The Baker's Wife:* "How can I bake bread when I am busy being deceived?" [3] We have a tendency to judge the suffering of others by its outward expression, or, as Sartre points out, we feel that we can see real suffering in an artistic portrayal. If, for example, we see a statue of a person suffering, that, we think, is suffering absolute. By comparison, our own feeling, which is never possessed of this opaque density, which is never an all-embracing suffering pure of any contamination with other feelings—this next to the imagined "form of suffering" seems somehow lacking. And "we suffer from not suffering enough." In addition to skirting perilously close to a Platonic Idea, Sartre is presenting here further application of one of his most fundamental principles. Man's freedom is asserted even in the face of his own feelings. He can never truthfully say that an emotion sweeps over him and compels him to certain acts; rather he chooses the manner and degree in which he will live emotionally.

But to get back to Lucien—-he reacts to the discovery that he does not love his mother by resolving to spend his life in a convincing pretense that he does love her. This is not from a feeling of pity for her or guilt with regard to his own feelings. It is simply the belief that if he did otherwise he would be a "bad little boy." In short, the revelation has been cut off half way. Lucien has acknowledged to himself the truth of his own feelings toward his mother but has not gone far enough to question the conventional judgements of the world around him.

At about this time Lucien becomes aware of Being-in-itself. He is bewildered by the unresponsive self-sufficiency of the chestnut tree which is impassive before Lucien's insults, whereas words of his spoken to his mother or nurse evoke an immediate, more or less predictable response. He is troubled, both by the obvious limitations to his subjective power and because the fullness of being of things underscores his uncertainty as to his own elusive being. He is constantly troubled by a feeling of unreality, and he tries to comfort himself by pretending that there is another Lucien who has a Being as absolute as that of the chestnut tree and who loves his papa and mama as he ought. At this point Lucien has widened rather than tried to close up the gap between the "I" and the "Me."

Sartre touches but lightly on the subject of religion in this story. Lucien as a child thinks of God only as a kind of projection of all external regards. God knows all of Lucien's secret and evil thoughts and acts, and for this reason Lucien hates him. More important to Lucien's development are the Sunday walks with his father. Then they meet the workers, his father's employees, who greet them so respectfully that Lucien is filled with a delicious sense of self-importance. He learns that his destiny is to be their employer, and he sets to work at once trying to learn the names of the workers whom he meets; for M.

Fleurier says that remembering the names of the men is the way to make them love him.

Now it is time for Lucien to go to school, and the half-somnolent experiences of childhood are replaced by the more self-analytic intro-spections of adolescence. Lucien's first realization of what his school-mates think of him is an almost exact literary equivalent of the analysis of our first relation with others—the Being-for-others—which is found in *Being and Nothingness*. In the school lavatory one day Lucien notices on the wall the words "Barataud is a bug." Remembering the small-statured Barataud, he smiles and resolves to call him a bug to his face the next day. But suddenly Lucien's eye shifts and he reads, "Lucien Fleurié is a beanpole." He is shocked and horrified. Imme-diately his imagination builds up the details of the conversation in which he has been unknowingly and helplessly the object of his school-mates' judgement. From then on he can hardly bear his object-state. He continually feels that everyone is looking at the back of his neck. When he is alone, he pretends that someone is looking at him through a keyhole. In revenge he himself begins actually looking through key-holes at others.

In one of the best-known passages of *Being and Nothingness* Sartre develops the thesis that my original encounter with the Other occurs at the moment when I am first aware that he is looking at me. The Look or the Stare *(le regard)* reveals to me that there are other subjec-tivities in the world; it forces me to realize my possibility of being an object, whereas I had thought of myself as wholly subject. At the same time I discover that my being or not being an object depends not on me but on the Other. I am at his mercy, and my only recourse is to enter with him into perilous conflict in which I try with my own Look to make him so completely an object that he cannot look at me in return.

In *Being and Nothingness* the analysis is more intellectual than emo-tional, though Sartre does point out that the first revelation of the Other is often effected in shame. Most typically, I am sitting alone and ap-parently unperceived. I begin to talk to myself or smile or make an awkward gesture. Suddenly I look up and see someone looking at me. My shame is not so much due to what I have been doing. It is not in-trinsically shameful to have spoken aloud or to have smiled. My em-barrassment is due rather to the sudden shift from a state in which I felt myself to be wholly a subject, a center of reference around which the world is organized—from this to a wholly different situation in which I am but an object in a world organized by the Other. Sartre has made brilliant use of the keyhole example too. If I am looking at people through a keyhole and am unexpectedly caught doing so, it is no bourgeois sense of unbecoming conduct which makes me blush with shame. It is because the reversal of situation has been too dramatically complete. As observer I was actively conscious of myself as subject, gloating in the fact that my human objects did not know I was there, when all at once I find that I have been not separate from them but rather with them in unconscious ignominy. To my mind the example in *The Childhood of a Boss* is even better than Sartre's later analysis. In everyday experience, I believe that it is possible for a look to be an exchange as well as a judgement or a calculation. But everyone knows the shock of first realizing that he is no more exempt from the easy judgement and ridicule of his acquaintances than they are to his.

Lucien's subsequent reactions illustrate another aspect of the experience. Even when he knows that his friends call him a beanpole, he cannot quite convince himself either that he really is or is not one. He cannot feel just what was meant by the word when his friends pronounced it even though he can easily perceive intellectually the height and leanness which provoked the epithet. The self-for-others—that is, the self which we appear to be to the Other—is something which only the Other really knows.

All of these experiences have so intensified Lucien's uncertainty as to who he is that he begins to despair as to whether he *really* exists at all. (He even considers writing a treatise on Nothingness!)* He has been playing with the idea of shooting himself to prove that he exists, when he meets a new student named Berliac. Berliac is a poet. Sartre uses him in part for some rather gentle satire against the surrealists, who in their abuse of language have always appeared to Sartre destructive as well as ridiculous. More important, however, is the fact that Berliac introduces Lucien to psychoanalysis. Any reader, Freudian or not, may find amusement in Sartre's satiric description of how the two adolescents discover in themselves the symptoms of the Oedipus complex and other nervous disorders, how with grim delight they predict their probable mental breakdown. But within all this are indications of the more serious criticism which Sartre was later to make not only of

---

* On the basis of this and a few other superficial similarities some critics have attempted a sort of psychoanalysis of Sartre himself—as though he actually were Lucien. This seems to me particularly foolish since Sartre's novella is designed to show the development of a man who is the antithesis of Sartre in almost every respect.

the easy misapplication of Freudian psychology but against the basic theory of psychoanalysis. Actually, Freudian psychology offers Lucien his first real escape into bad faith. Hitherto he has been disturbed and anxious because of not being able to pin down and classify his *self*, for he senses already the terrifying responsibility of an existence penetrated by Nothingness and lacking opaque Being. Now he is suddenly relieved of his anxiety, for psychoanalysis enables him to take seriously the role he had been playing as a game. He used to pretend that there was another Lucien who was what he was and who knew what he was. Now he discovers that "the real Lucien was deeply buried in the unconscious; one could only think about him without ever seeing him as in the case of an absent friend" (pp. 84-85). It is this Lucien, living deep within like a volcano, who controls the destiny of Lucien's outward semblance. Lucien is afraid of this inner self, but at least the fear is relieved of responsibility. For everyone has to follow his innate disposition. There is no escape. Lucien, although he cultivates a pathetic sadness before his blighted life, is actually happy for the first time. At last he knows that he exists and he knows who he is. He is a young man with an Oedipus complex. He *is* the unconscious Lucien. He can no longer be disturbed by a sense of not understanding or of never coinciding with his Self; for while by definition the Self is beyond the reach of consciousness, still it is there and one can await its decisions.

Unfortunately the ultimate results of surrealism and psychoanalysis are for Lucien a rather unsavoury homosexual episode which he has not even really wanted. There is an element of bad faith in the whole affair. Lucien goes on a trip with another surrealist, Bergère, who has introduced him to the work of Rimbaud and the Marquis de Sade, and who has endeavored to teach Lucien that not only women but anything— living or not—can serve as an object of sexual desire. Lucien keeps telling himself that everything about the journey is aboveboard but actually is not surprised to learn what Bergère really wants of him. Sartre with an excess of realism represents Lucien at the critical moment as suffering from an attack of nerves, bringing on nausea and diarrhoea. In any other author one would take this illness as indication of the boy's inner conflict. By analogy with Sartre's theory of the emotions, I suspect we should see Lucien's trouble as psychosomatic in a different sense. Sartre would almost certainly say that Lucien becomes ill as a method of trying to escape the impending crisis. In any case he finally gives up and comes to bed. Significantly, the moment at which he gives in to Bergère is the one at which he suddenly remembers a time in his childhood when someone had called him a little doll. He sees himself as Bergere's little doll and submits. Here is one more example of Lucien's allowing himself to become whatever someone outside will make of him.

Lucien is ashamed of the episode afterwards. He convinces himself that Bergère had taken advantage of his inexperience, that he himself really did not know what he was doing, that he had felt no great pleasure, hence he cannot be "really a paederast." Now that he has been guilty of conduct which is so shocking to him, Lucien can no longer feel the same reassurance with respect to psychoanalysis. What had been a means of escape becomes a burden, for he fears that he may be driven into actions still worse. Typically enough, his release comes not from within himself but from a chance comment made by his former philosophy professor. Lucien asks him what he thinks of psychoanalysis, and the man replies that it is a passing fad, that the best of Freud was already in Plato, and that the rest is nonsense. This is enough for Lucien. The burden slips from his shoulders. For a short time he comes close to a proper recognition of his being as freedom. He realizes that he does not have to remain what he has been, that his self does not at any moment come to him fully constituted by previous experiences. But the discovery brings anguish as well. The old question "Who am I?" comes up once again, and Lucien almost faces the fact that he *is* the Nothingness from which his freedom derives. This he cannot bear. Again he looks outward for reassurance, and he finds it in the person of a new friend Lemordant, "a man of convictions," who is planted so firmly in the Serious World, who possesses such full certitude and absolute being, that he seems to be "an adult by birth." Lucien looks at him with envy. "That's how I should be—a rock" (p. 218).

Lucien learns that Lemordant and his group of friends are members of a fascist, anti-Semitic organization. He is impressed, not because he is intellectually in agreement with their aims, but because their convictions are so strong, their sense of purpose so firm, their being so "guaranteed." For awhile he hesitates.

> Lucien still had fits of depression: he had the impression of being nothing but a little gelatinous transparency which was trembling there on a chair in a café, and the burning agitation of the Young Royalists seemed to him absurd. But at other moments he felt himself to be hard and heavy as a stone, and he was almost happy (pp. 229-230).

Two things finally persuade Lucien to join the movement. First he feels that in the eyes of others he would gain in importance by such a commitment. It is not that all his associates would approve the act. In fact his parents beg him not to join. But he senses in them a new respect. The very fact that they fear his decision indicates that the possibility makes him a person to be reckoned with. Chiefly, though, it is the definiteness of purpose which attracts him. His companions do not feel the need to justify their acts by reason. To them, Jews by definition are self-evident enemies. Lucien delights his companions by pointing out how he can recognize strangers as Jews by certain evident signs. Now he reflects retrospectively that his former friend Berliac, whose grandmother had been a Jew, had shown "typical" signs of Jewish stinginess. Lucien had never been aware of this tendency before; his "recollection" illustrates Sartre's claim that while acts in the past are absolute, their significance is something which we are constantly remaking. Lucien, without ever rationally examining what he is doing, becomes so intoxicated with the new emotions of hate and the admiration which his attitude wins from his friends that he soon surpasses them in the energy of his emotions. When they make an unprovoked attack upon a Jew whom they meet in a lonely street, it is Lucien who delivers the apparently fatal punch. He decides at last to become a member of the Young Royalists.

The immediate result of his decision is that his girl Maud is impressed and finally becomes his mistress. This episode, though but briefly developed, is both another example of bad faith and an illustration of Sartre's usual gloomy view of human relationships. Maud is a girl who has some leanings toward the Left politically, but she "has a generous spirit" and finds "that there is good in all parties." Her earlier resistance had been merely conventional; her final giving in is not actually the result of either love or extreme desire: rather it is an acknowledgement of the power of that same heaviness of Being which Lucien has been seeking and believes that he has now attained. When their first lovemaking is over, she convinces herself that she had not really wanted what happened, that she had momentarily been carried away by something stronger than herself; yet her actions all through the evening had been designed to make the outcome inevitable. On his side the sexual triumph is short-lived and basically disappointing. What he had wanted was to possess the subjectivity of Maud. It was her particular appearance, "her dignified bearing, her reputation as a serious girl, her disdain of the masculine sex, everything which made of her a person who was a stranger, truly *an Other,* hard and definitive, always out of reach with her own little thoughts" (p. 235). But what he possessed was not her Otherness. As an Other she could not be possessed. For a moment they were one flesh, but it was a meaningless flesh, divorced from the minds which remained separate. Maud became a mere object and no longer really Maud. Lucien concludes that Maud is not a person to be respected and begins to think with some interest of his friend's sister Pierette, toward whom he maintains the somewhat exaggerated respect which some men conventionally entertain with regard to womanhood rather than toward particular women.

The climax of the story comes at Pierette's birthday party. Her brother Guigard introduces Lucien to a friend of theirs who is a Jew. The boy extends his hand. During the last few weeks Lucien has gradually made of himself a person to be defined by a single phrase, "the man who hates Jews." Now he cannot bring himself to act inconsistently with this image. He says nothing in response to the introduction. Instead of shaking hands he plunges his hands in his pockets and walks away. Hearing Guigard say of him that he is mad, Lucien is crushed. If his being as "one who hates Jews" is not recognized, he feels that he "will never be *anybody.*" Even his dislike of Jews seems to melt away beneath his regard, and he can no longer feel his hatred as the almost tangible support which it had been to him.

The next morning all is changed. Guigard apologizes. " 'My parents say that you were right, that you could not do otherwise since you have such a conviction' " (p. 239).

*Being* settles down on Lucien once again. He is at last a "man of convictions." He feels that he is no longer the insect-like self which he had been. He is "as neat and clean as a chronometer." Going alone into a café he takes new stock of himself and his life. How mistaken had been his previous attempts at self-discovery! One did not find the truth by looking inwards. "The true Lucien was to be sought in the eyes of others, in the timid obedience of Pierette and Guigard"—and in the respectful regard of the workers. He goes further, remembering his father and how he has been training Lucien to carry on the family traditions. Lucien sees now that just as the Jew *is* an object of contempt, so he himself *is* a man with *rights.* And rights are absolute, just as circles and triangles are absolute, though their existence is equally intangible. Generations of workers could never exhaust his right to give orders. "His rights were beyond existence like mathematical objects and religious dogmas," hence beyond attack or question. And Lucien himself is "an enormous mass of responsibilities and rights." He had been wrong in thinking that existence was something haphazard or derived. Even before he was born, his place in the sun was prepared for him. He meditates on the great life of responsibility which awaits him. He will need a wife, someone like Pierette, if he is to fulfil his role effectively. She will, of course, be a virgin who will recognize Lucien's sole right to possess her. She will be *his* woman and they will have many children. He wonders how long he will have to wait for his father to die so that he can take over the business. Lucien arises in the full sense of his destiny. Some outward token of the change is needed, he thinks. He will grow a moustache.

The portrait of Lucien is a study of a man in bad faith. One thing in particular must be noted. Although even in his childhood Lucien had been presented with a future essentially the same as the destiny which he finally embraces, Sartre makes it quite clear that the final choice, as well as all those preceding, is freely made. Lucien is no H. M. Pulham, Esquire, struggling in vain for a freedom which he glimpses but which he cannot attain because of family and social pressure. On the contrary, every decisive action is the result of Lucien's own desire to escape from a freedom which terrifies him. His bad faith—like all bad faith—consists in his refusing to accept a true view of himself as a combination of being and nothingness and in evading the responsibility of free decisions, whether with respect to the past or the future. It would be impossible at the end of the story to extricate Lucien's anti-Semitism from his political attitudes, and this is not due simply to a "natural" link between racial prejudice and fascism. It is because Lucien has chosen himself as a man who will live as though he is an in-itself (albeit a highly privileged one) in a Serious World. The innate rights of the Gentile and of the industrialist and of the male are all manifestations of a single attitude. So were Lucien's earlier responses to religion (though but lightly touched on in this story) and to psychoanalysis—all of them attempts either to flee from himself or to pin himself down as though he were classifiable once and for all—like a thing. Yet while the existentialist cannot consistently represent environment as a determining force, he does not ignore it. Man is in-the-world. If his own free choice gives form to his way of life, still the situation in which he finds himself provides the matter or content. If Lucien had been brought up in the home of poverty-stricken fundamentalists, his bad faith might have manifested itself in Communism or in religion.

Now that we have examined a fictional presentation of a life in the Serious World, it may be well to consider individually the various types of conduct in bad faith, looking both at other examples of fiction and at pertinent philosophical analysis by Sartre and other humanistic existentialists.

We may group the patterns of bad faith under four headings. We shall see how it manifests itself in prejudice, in political attitudes, in religion, in human relations.

### 3. MANIFESTATIONS OF BAD FAITH

*Bad Faith in Prejudice*

It has always seemed strange to me that in discussions as to whether or not there is any positive philosophy of value in existentialism, both critics and defenders have almost universally ignored the constructive work of Sartre and de Beauvoir with regard to the oppression of minorities and the psychology of racial prejudice. *Les Temps Modernes,* of which Sartre has been editor since 1945, has had a high proportion of articles, some of them by American writers, decrying segregation and oppression of Negroes in the United States. Sartre and de Beauvoir along with Camus and Malraux have actively championed the cause of oppressed peoples in Africa and Asia. But it is not merely that the sympathies and political platforms of existentialism have been against racial, religious, or national prejudice. Sartre and de Beauvoir in particular have attempted to provide both a psychological explanation for the views of the prejudiced and a philosophical justification for their own belief in the basic equality and rights of all people.

Sartre's fullest discussion of the nature of prejudice, *Anti-Semite and Jew,*[1] is of particular interest in that it provides a full commentary, as it were, on Lucien's conduct, an explanation which is completely consistent with the philosophical theory of *Being and Nothingness.* Sartre is not original in holding that the explanation of anti-Semitism must be sought not in the Jews but in the minds of the prejudiced. Yet he goes rather far in this direction when he says that if the Jew did not exist, the anti-Semite would have to invent him. In another passage he makes an even stronger statement—that the anti-Semite has *created* the Jew. The two views—that the anti-Semite *needs* the Jew, and that he hates the Jew because of this need and not because of any real or imaginary Jewish characteristics—stem from the fact that (according to Sartre) anti-Semitism is not an *opinion.* It is not simply an intellectual idea, not even a mistaken one. Anti-Semitism (or any similar prejudice) is a global attitude, a passion and a way of life. Sartre claims that no doctrine expressly designed for the oppression or extermination of a group of people can be dismissed as mere opinion. We must note, of course, that he is talking about the persecution of people as *people;* one might easily be convinced on intellectual grounds that it was necessary to destroy the program and impede the actions of a group; e.g., those of the Ku Klux Klan or of the Nazis—or even of the Zionists or supporters of the United Nations. Sartre argues that when we speak of someone holding an opinion, we mean that he holds an ideal which seems to him to be reasonable. If he is given information which shows that the opinion is based on insufficient evidence, then he will change his mind. For no reasonable man will knowingly cherish an idea which he knows to be false. Prejudice, however, is not an opinion based on lack of information. Proof of this is our realization that it cannot be stamped out by the presentation of new facts. Evidence of the falsity of the beliefs about which racial and religious bigotry are centered is readily procured and easy to understand. But prejudice is not opinion; it is emotion, a choice of oneself as a particular "passion."

That prejudice is not just an opinion formed on insufficient evidence is shown by two other facts. First, says Sartre, the order of events in prejudice is precisely the opposite of that involved in arriving at an opinion. Any supposedly rational idea is formed on the basis of experience, but prejudice is not caused by experience; it determines the experience. The hatred and dislike come first, and then one seeks for reasons to explain them. It is as though a person should say, "There must be something about tomatoes because I can't bear them." Sartre uses two familiar examples. A woman says that a Jewish furrier has robbed her of her furs; so she hates Jews. Now why, asks Sartre, if she must generalize from this one incident, does she hates Jews rather than furriers? Or someone complains that there are too many Jewish doctors. But no one complains that there are too many doctors from Brittany. If all Bretons were doctors, people would only say, "Brittany provides doctors for the whole of France" (p. 7). The complete lack of concern for any reasonable basis for such beliefs is evidenced by the ease with which the same person can entertain two flatly contradictory ideas. He will cheerfully say in the morning that all Jews are sympathetic with Communism, and in the evening he will claim that all Jews are capitalists controlling the nation's economy. Or he will say almost in the same sentence that Negroes are so shiftless and lazy that they need to be managed by superior whites and that they are so pushing and ambitious that they must be kept in their place by force.

None of this analysis is really new. It is the familiar logic of all prejudice, and even the prejudiced know it. But Sartre provides a philosophical framework. In the first place, he denies that a man can incorporate prejudice—in this case, anti-Semitism—into the rest of his attitude as if it were a separate atom among others. "It is an attitude totally and freely self-chosen, a global attitude, which is adopted not only in regard to Jews but in regard to men in general, to history and society; it is a passion and at the same time a concept of the world" (p. 8). We have seen how Lucien's anti-Semitism was inextricably interwoven with his political views, his attitude toward women, and his decision to *be* the self he saw in the eyes of others. Sartre makes the same point as a kind of joke in his play *Nekrassov*. A swindler and fugitive from justice, Georges de Valéra has been caught in the apartment of a reactionary journalist, Sibilot. Knowing of Sibilot only that he is in general conventional and that he writes for a right-wing newspaper, Valéra baits him by showing his ability to guess that Sibilot never has any doubts about what is right, that he does not "listen to subversive doctrines which would make the criminal a product of society," that he would not take into consideration any extenuating circumstances of Georges' past. Finally he says, "You have an answer for everything. Nothing threatens your convictions. Ah, sir, with that bronze forehead, those enamel eyes and that stone heart, you simply must be an anti-Semite" (p. 79). Georges goes on to wring from Sibilot the confession that he hates Arabs as well as Jews. He ends by concluding that the two of them (Georges and Sibilot) are alike, that their convictions are all based on an exaggerated respect for private property. Sibilot as a private citizen owns it; Valéra as a confidence man lives off the owners.

But granted that the anti-Semite is a man who has chosen an emotional way of life rather than a rational one, the question remains as to why he has done so. The answer is that he is afraid. He has a "nostalgia for impermeability"; he wants to be, as Lucien longed to be, "hard as a rock." The anti-Semite is seeking some absolute justification for his existence. It is inevitable that he will reject reason; for a man who lives by reason knows that his beliefs are never more than probable and that new facts may appear to make him change his mental adjustment to the world. But the anti-Semite is afraid to change. He is afraid of himself, or more accurately he is afraid to face the fact that he does not have a self in any final sense but that he is a limitless freedom which is constantly making a self. This endless pursuit of a self with which he can never quite coincide is too much for him. Moreover, he is afraid of the truth, not of any particular truth, but of the very nature of truth, "an indefinite approximation." Prejudice, an obvious form of bad faith, is a rejection of the human condition, which demands that we look to an open future with no guarantee that the step we are taking is the right one. Prejudice is a refusal to live by reason because reason does not give absolute certainty, because reason as it answers one question opens up the need for further investigation, because reason is a guide and a challenge, not a sedative.

The anti-Semite has chosen to exist as a passion. He is all emotion. As such, Sartre points out, his way of life is *magical*. It is Sartre's view that any emotional reaction is in a sense magical. Emotions enter in when one is faced with a situation in which one cannot attain one's object by observing what reason calls "objective" means. Since one cannot alter the world, one through emotion alters oneself in relation to the world. For example, a person fleeing an angry bear cannot annihilate the bear but can for the moment annihilate himself by letting his fear cause him to faint. Or a speaker who sees himself cornered by an opponent may begin calling names, thus transforming—in his own eyes—the situation from one which calls for rational arguments to one which allows mere intensity of feeling expression. Or a girl wanting and yet afraid to confess the whole truth about herself to priest or psychiatrist may find a solution by sobbing so vehemently that she appears unable to continue.[3] Similarly the anti-Semite. Since the human condition, if faced squarely, does not provide absoluteness and security or an automaton self, the anti-Semite reconstructs the world in his own mind. He convinces himself that there is, after all, something higher than reason. He follows the pattern which we discussed in the analysis of bad faith. That is, he passes from the attitude that any belief is only probable to the attitude that he may then—on nonrational grounds—be convinced of any improbable belief.

According to Sartre, the life of every one of us is a pursuit of self. From one point of view it is a futile quest, for a person never finally *is* anything and hence—quite literally—can never find himself. Yet in another sense the "pursuit of self" is but a synonym for a dynamic life, for freedom. When one recognizes that he spends his life in pursuing the self, this is the equivalent of realizing that life is a process of freely making oneself, of gradual but never completed self-realization. The anti-Semite tries to escape from himself; it is the pursuit itself which he seeks to flee; and his evasion consists in pretending that his self is already captured or indeed has been there from birth with all the weight and massivity of a stone statue. Yet deep within him the anti-Semite lacks a real self-respect. He has never learned to know the evanescent self which he really is, and he does not trust himself to engage in the free making of a self capable of change. Thus he seeks an easy way of winning a feeling of importance and security. With no confidence in his ability to win distinction in open competition, or in the fear of losing what he already possesses in this unstable world, he longs for a distinction which cannot be lost by any stroke of fate and which he himself does not have to struggle to achieve or maintain. Therefore he looks for something which is his by accident of birth. He trains himself in the belief that being other than a Jew or a Negro, or a member of whatever minority group is at hand, is in itself a priceless virtue, a secure possession of superiority. Thus no matter what heights of distinction the man of another race or religion may attain, it makes no difference to the anti-Semite's self-esteem. The other is still only a member of an inferior class and so may be safely despised. The prejudiced man belittles the other's achievements to his own glory. He exists simultaneously on two levels of thought (if we can call it such) with two discrete sets of values. Self-respect in himself becomes arrogant pride in the other. Sober economy becomes avarice. All admirable qualities are marvelously and magically transformed by the mere fact of the other's possessing them.

The anti-Semite escapes from himself (or tries to) in another way. Although Lucien used his hatred of Jews partly to convince himself that he was a man of convictions, someone weighty and definite, yet the episode at the party showed that what he craved was distinction among those who had already accepted him. What he valued fully as much as the sense of absolute hate which seemed to possess him was the sense of being accepted by the group of Young Royalists. Since anti-Semitism is based, according to Sartre at least, partly on the sense of having an automatic and unquestioned ticket for admission to social approval, the anti-Semite not only need not be alone; he *cannot* be. We observed that immediately after the party when Lucien thought that his friends had disapproved of him, he could not feel any reality in his hatred of Jews. His hatred, which he had thought of as something which possessed him, suddenly became merely one attitude among many, a point of view which he could choose to recognize or not to recognize and which at the moment seemed to vanish from him. In the mystic brotherhood of the mob, the anti-Semite can deny his human isolation.

He can glory in his very mediocrity, for the crowd receives most readily him who is distinguished by neither marked inferiority nor outstanding excellence. Thus in its most basic sense the anti-Semite becomes but one example of the type of person most prevalent in recent decades, the man who represses all impulses to be an individual or a leader and submits to the pressure of the cult of conformity. One might perhaps object at this point that avowed anti-Semites have not, except in certain totalitarian countries, been given social approval. This is true, but we must remember that those who are opposed or indifferent to anti-Semitism are not organized. One never strives to conform to mankind as a whole but rather to that part of society in which one finds oneself. Just as any conformist will choose his own clique within the larger group, so the anti-Semite will search for the association which satisfies his passion for a life centered on unreason.

One further point made by Sartre is that the anti-Semite is openly or secretly a sadist. He may resent superior Jews, but he attacks only those who are weak and defenseless. Anti-Semitism, particularly when raised to the level of a political movement, satisfies the hostile and destructive impulses of the man who hates the world and others because he cannot face them on the basis of an honest acknowledgement of who he is. In the eyes of the anti-Semite, good and evil are absolute. A political program of anti-Semitism allows its adherents to do Evil in the name of Good. I feel that there is a certain parallel here with the attitudes of Mickey Spillane's detective, Mike Hammer, who persuades himself that he must be evil in order that he may accomplish the good which others cannot achieve, who has no hesitation in annihilating those persons who his passion convinces him are opponents to an absolute political order.

In brief, the anti-Semite of Sartre's analysis is in bad faith because he refuses to face either reality or himself. He is, as Sartre says, a pathetic figure and might even win our sympathy if the consequences of his refusal were not so tragic.

> We can now understand him. He is a man who is afraid. Not of the Jews, of course, but of himself, of his conscience, his freedom, of his instincts, of his responsibilities, of solitude, of change, of society and the world; of everything except the Jews. He is a coward who does not want to admit his coward-ice to himself; a murderer who represses and censures his pen-chant for murder without being able to restrain it and who nevertheless does not dare to kill except in effigy or in the

anonymity of a mob; a malcontent who dares not revolt for fear of the consequences of his rebellion. By adhering to anti-Semitism, he is not only adopting an opinion, he is choosing himself as a person. He is choosing the permanence and the impenetrability of rock, the total irresponsibility of the warrior who obeys his leader—and he has no leader. He chooses to acquire nothing, to deserve nothing but that everything be given him as his birthright—and he is not noble. He chooses finally, that good be ready-made, not in question, out of reach; he dare not look at it for fear of being forced to contest it and seek another form of it. The Jew is only a pretext: elsewhere it will be the Negro, the yellow race. The Jew's existence simply allows the anti-Semite to nip his anxieties in the bud by persuading himself that his place has always been cut out in the world, that it was waiting for him and that by virtue of tradition he has the right to occupy it. [Compare Lucien's attitude toward a career in his father's factory.] Anti-Semitism, in a word, is a fear of man's fate. The anti-Semite is the man who wants to be pitiless stone, furious torrent, devastating lightning; in short, everything but a man (pp. 26-27).

Sartre's position that the anti-Semite has created the Jew—as well as his statement that the man who is an anti-Semite in one country will be anti-Negro or anti-Oriental or anti-Arab in another—inevitably results in an analysis of the psychology of prejudice rather than a study of a social phenomenon. To some extent this is as it should be; for without the individual fears and evasions—without bad faith—I do not believe that anti-Semitism and comparable prejudices could exist. Yet I, at least, get an uneasy feeling from the book, a suspicion that Sartre by insisting that the anti-Semite has created the Jew is theoretically annihilating Jewry just as much as the anti-Semite. This is, of course, emphatically not his intention. Furthermore, he is right in pointing out that Jews are not distinguished from other people by language, by customs, by a geographically determined nationality, nor even by religion, since there is infinite variety in the kind of religious beliefs held by Jews. Yet the fact remains that the Jews do share a national history, and this, I believe, should be taken into account even if Sartre is right in pointing out that in part the preservation of this national history has been forced upon the Jews by anti-Jewish feeling. In the last part of his book Sartre discusses the authentic and unauthentic conduct which the Jew may adopt in the face of anti-Semitism.[4] He may seek to deny the reality of any such trait as "Jewishness," or he may choose an authentic way of living *as a Jew*. But in each case the Jew is facing the portrait of himself which the anti-Semites have created; he is not considered by Sartre either as the source of the picture or as a man confronting a national heritage.

Before leaving this subject we should consider Sartre's fictional treatment of anti-Negro prejudice in *The Respectful Prostitute*. It would be impossible, I think, for an American to have written this play. The episode from which the plot evolves is improbable. Lizzie, some white men, and four Negroes have all been riding together in a train in a Southern state. Since apparently the train was a coach and not a Pullman, the presence of both white and black is unlikely. Moreover, though I should be the last to deny the existence of white provocation of Negroes in the deep South, still the unmotivated decision of the whites to throw the four Negroes out of the window of the moving train strikes me as oversensational. (The same may be said for the denouement, in which the crowd—without any explanation on Sartre's part—cheerfully and apparently without much concern lynches the wrong man.) In any case, the disturbance on the train results in the shooting of a Negro by a white. When Lizzie, a prostitute from the North, arrives at the town in which she hopes to establish herself, she soon discovers that Fred, her first customer, is a cousin of the man who did the shooting. Fred and his father, a Senator, try to get Lizzie to substantiate a story which they have spread about to the effect that one of the other Negroes had tried to rape her. Meanwhile the Negro in question appeals to her to state what actually occurred. Lizzie at first persists in telling the truth but finally reluctantly signs the paper presented by the Senator. Her surrender is partly due to threats that she will be jailed for prostitution if she does not sign. Even more persuasive are the mellifluous words of the Senator, who makes her believe that she will win the respect and personal appreciation of the influential relatives of the white man who did the shooting. When Lizzie receives only money and no sign of social recognition, she realizes that she has merely been bought, and she is filled with revulsion toward herself as well as toward Fred and the Senator. Thoroughly beaten and having lost any belief in herself as a person with a will of her own, she ultimately resigns herself to being supported as Fred's mistress—after the wrong Negro is hanged and the one accused has escaped.

Interwoven with all this sensationalism are those ideas of Sartre on prejudice which we encountered in connection with the anti-Semite. Fred and the Senator have all of Lucien's convictions of natural, sacred rights. The Senator argues that whether the Negro has been guilty of rape or not, still since someone must be sacrificed, the "better" man must be saved. The better man is obviously he whose ancestors have built up that part of the country. Fred in particular, in addition to depicting the Freudian concept of the close bond between lust and murder, is an example of the absolute man, "impermeable as a rock." He lives in a world where good and evil are definite, almost tangible entities. To him the Negro and Lizzie are both "devils," incarnations of sin. Hence he wants to destroy the one and possess the other. Convinced that his relations with Lizzie are sinful, he finds the fascination of known evil too much for him. He feels that he must have her even though he is filled with guilt after being with her. His possession of her has more than the allure of the forbidden. By feeling that he owns her, by denying to her any freedom as a person, he destroys this Evil at the same time that he enjoys it.

One new theme in this play is the unstable sense of solidarity existing between Lizzie and the Negro. Both victims of the social order, they understand each other. But there can be no real appreciation, for there is in neither of them enough self-respect to enable him to respect the other. Both are so cowed by their oppressors that even in the moment of revolt they realize they cannot pull the trigger of the gun which would save them. What ultimately happens to the Negro we do not know. But Lizzie in her final submission to Fred has come as close as any woman can to becoming nothing but a thing.

## Bad Faith in Political Attitudes

Although existentialism is rightly thought of as a philosophy of individualism, it is only the religious branch which has presented the possibility of deliverance in wholly personal terms. The humanistic writers have without exception linked self-realization with some kind of social commitment. There is, however, considerable disagreement as to the nature of the social—especially between Sartre and Camus. For this reason the problem of what constitutes an authentic political position as contrasted with one in bad faith is best considered in connection with man's acceptance of freedom and his voluntary engagement in the world.

There are, however, a few attitudes which would be said to be in bad faith by any one of the authors whom we are considering.*

First of all, existentialist writers agree in rejecting any society in which some men are sacrificed either for a privileged minority or for a mystic State. They disagree with regard to the extent to which they are willing to compromise in order to achieve a classless society, but they are alike in condemning either fascism, unrestrained capitalism, or a communism which sets a mythical Whole above existing individuals. They oppose the view of a Serious World in which one is born with a particular place prepared for him and in which social values are pre-established and not to be questioned. They are against the principle of sacrificing persons to abstractions. The State is nothing but the individuals who compose it. They will not destroy a whole present generation for the sake of a future one. To think of *man* as existing independently of men is in itself an attitude in bad faith.

As one would expect, humanistic existentialism is unalterably opposed to the exploitation of less developed peoples. As Simone de Beauvoir has put it, any attempted justification of a "superior" ruling class (whether benevolent or otherwise) is synonymous with a false view of the nature of the "human." Such a view denies that freedom which is man's dynamic essence. It pretends that a man is predetermined to be one thing rather than another, whereas each man is free to try to make of himself what he will. De Beauvoir is particularly scornful with regard to the arguments often advanced by white colonials to the effect that the natives are patently unable to look after themselves, that they would be better off under more highly civilized protectors, and that perhaps they even prefer a position of dependency. To this she replies that the conditions which seem to indicate inferiority are frequently the result of the oppressors' own efforts; moreover, any theory that the natives feel "by nature" more comfortable as dependents is instantly exploded if one merely looks at a child. The child has no inborn sense of where it belongs in the social scale and will develop one attitude or another depending on the world within which it makes its choices.[1]

Since French existentialism developed during and immediately after World War Two, one subject with which it was concerned was collabora-

---

* Martin Heidegger, who found it expedient to support the Nazis under Hitler, has often been used to support the charge that existentialism can just as well lead to fascism as to a political theory based on freedom. But it is questionable whether Heidegger ought to be called either "humanistic" or "existentialist." In any case he has written nothing in the way of imaginative literature and does not come within the sphere of this discussion.

tionism. Very often existentialist writers have tried to show that collaboration was the natural consequence for someone who for one reason or another had been living a life characterized by bad faith. But neither Sartre nor anyone else has attempted to give for it a universal, comparatively simple explanation of the kind which Sartre provided in his study of anti-Semitism. In an article entitled "What Is a Collaborator?" [2] Sartre pointed out that French collaborationists were of no single class or type. The only thing which they had in common was the fact that all had lacked any real sense of being integrated in the society in which they had formerly been living. Potential collaborationists, Sartre claimed, have always existed, even in peacetime with no known enemy. War makes them known to themselves as well as to others. In this sense the problem of collaborationism is identical with that of criminality and suicide. Society is partly responsible; but the causes are manifold and the final resolve to collaborate is an individual one, not the result of a class attitude or a group decision.

Sartre has presented a skillful and convincing portrayal of a collaborator in Daniel in his novel sequence, *The Roads to Freedom,* where collaboration completes the picture of Daniel in much the same way that anti-Semitism put the finishing touches on the character of Lucien. Daniel is, however, so lacking in any real interest in politics that it seems better to me to consider his complex struggle under the subject of religion; for while he is not essentially religious any more than he is political, the nature of his problem is more clearly evident in the religious context. Less complex examples of collaborators may be found in the works of Camus and de Beauvoir, who seem to share Sartre's view that collaborationism is merely an unusually spectacular manifestation of more familiar types of social and personal disintegration.

Camus has depicted two collaborationists in his work—Cottard in *The Plague* and Nada in *State of Siege.* Both remain types and symbols more than individuals. For Cottard, the plague comes as a reprieve. Knowing that he was about to be arrested for a crime, he had tried unsuccessfully to commit suicide just before the epidemic broke out. Owing to the emergency he escaped notice for a while, became a black marketeer, and worried about the day when the town would recover. Once things are back to normal, he faces arrest again. This time he goes mad and fires upon the crowd gathered beneath his window. Cottard is an unpleasant character. At the same time Camus' presentation is two-edged. While the implication is clear that collaborationists are likely to be those who have been enemies of society under normal conditions,

Camus' criticism of a social order which would produce a Cottard and drive him to suicide or madness is sufficiently apparent so that one's disgust with the man is tinged with pity.

Nada in *State of Siege* is quite clearly an allegorical figure representing intellectual cynicism or nihilism. When The Plague, Camus' personified symbol for Fascism, learns that Nada believes in nothing, he says that he can well use such a man. Nada collaborates, apparently without a qualm. Then when The Plague has been driven out and the usual order of things restored, Nada drowns himself. But he is driven to death neither by conscience nor by fear of punishment. He dies "because one cannot live if one knows that man is nothing and that the face of God is frightful." [3] Nada has denied God through the play, and there is nothing to indicate that he has experienced any religious conversion. "The frightful face of God" seems to stand for the hostile Universe in which man feels himself a stranger. Nada cannot believe in God; he will not believe in man. There is nothing else.

In de Beauvoir's *The Blood of Others (Le Sang des autres)*,[4] collaboration is one of many political attitudes examined in a novel in which self-discovery and political commitments are inextricably interwoven. The basic theme of the book is the problem of our responsibility for others. The question is posed directly to Jean Blomart, a leader in the Resistance, as he spends the night beside the bed of his mistress, Hélène, who has been fatally wounded on a mission which Blomart had directed. As he awaits Hélène's death, Blomart knows that at dawn he must decide whether or not to send a close friend out on another equally dangerous assignment. As he inwardly debates the question, the author reviews for us the events of the last few years during which Blomart and his friends had tried to work out their own sense of purpose in life against the political background of appeasement, war, and the Occupation.

Of the half-dozen principals, only two, the Communist Perrier and the pacifist Gauthier, follow unwavering lines of conduct leading them to what de Beauvoir in 1945 apparently thought were inevitable actions. Perrier from the start favored active intervention against the Nazis and moved most easily and naturally into the work of the Resistance. (De Beauvoir makes no mention of any troubled conscience during the early days when Russia seemed to be working with Germany.) Evidently Perrier's attitude is taken as that which is politically correct. Yet there is a hint that de Beauvoir does not regard him as a wholly sympathetic character. Hélène, who was engaged to him before she met Blomart, had always found Perrier rather uninteresting as a person. He was apparently little more than the embodiment of the political ideals which he cherished. Moreover, he seems to be a worker who has recognized his place in the worker's party, rather than a man who has made a free and passionate choice. Although de Beauvoir's patriotism has prevented her from representing Perrier as a man actually in bad faith, there is a sense in which he does not really exist as a man.

Gauthier, on the other hand, is quite obviously an example of one in bad faith. At first his pacifism manifests itself as a great love of mankind which will not allow the sacrifice of any individual. Gradually, as Nazi aims and methods become more evident, Gauthier shifts uneasily to the view that some people may have to be sacrificed because "there is nothing worse than war." Finally, under the Occupation he prepares to continue publishing his newspaper with German approval. He uses the excuse of pacifism for what is actually a policy of collaboration but which he refuses to recognize as such. His conduct is exactly like that of Sartre's homosexual, who admitted all the actions of the paederast but refused the title which logically followed. Clearly Gauthier is in bad faith. What de Beauvoir does not quite make clear is whether he is in bad faith as a man or as a pacifist. She implies that it is pacifism which is in bad faith. But pacifists are not necessarily collaborationists; moreover, de Beauvoir as an existentialist should not explain motivations and actions by means of pure abstractions.

The reason for de Beauvoir's too-easy equating of pacifism and collaborationism is probably the simple fact that in France many pacifists did collaborate. Of course this is no excuse either for her failure to make the explanation more convincing in the case of Gauthier or for leaving us with the impression that *all* pacifists behaved in this way. Sartre in his article "What Is a Collaborator?" makes specific mention of the pacifists. Their bad faith, he says, lay in an illegitimate evaluation of the Occupation. They were against war; for France the war was ended. They persuaded themselves that they had achieved their end, merely changed their means. Hence the incongruous alliance between the pacifists and the most military of nations. One is reminded, says Sartre, "of Gribouille throwing himself into the river in order to escape the rain." [5]

In the life of Hélène during the years before she finally joined the Resistance movement, two other patterns of bad faith are represented. Throughout the period of appeasement and the early months of the war, she sought to lose herself in Jean Blomart. Unable by herself to find any meaning in life, she attempts to justify her existence by her love for him. In doing so she becomes as "unauthentic," as much an *object* as Lizzie in *The Respectful Prostitute,* and she is not much happier. Since for her, life is wholly centered in Blomart, she cannot view the political situation except as it is a threat to their relationship. She feels quite simply that if Blomart goes to the front, he will be killing her. She is furious at his talk of responsibility toward others since this is, in her eyes, only lack of concern for her. Finally she succeeds in making arrangements to get Blomart transferred to a safe job away from the army. He is so revolted by this betrayal that he refuses to see her again, and Hélène is left in despair.

Until now Hélène's refusal to assume any kind of responsibility for what was happening in Europe had been the result of too personal an outlook. Yet in reality her conduct, which seemed pure selfishness, was the result not of too great a love for herself but of a lack of self-confidence resulting from the fear of confronting herself. Like Lucien she could not bear the lack of a fully constituted self and sought to find one in the eyes of another. Once she has lost Blomart, Hélène adopts another pattern of bad faith, quite the reverse of her former attitude, though based on the same self-evasion. Instead of looking at events only as related to her own personal situation, Hélène now tries to depersonalize herself. She cultivates a deliberate numbness and lethargy, persuades herself that she does not really exist. To a limited extent she is facing the truth. The person she had tried to see herself as being no longer exists, in fact had never existed. But instead of accepting the responsibility of choosing herself as an individual, she tries to convince herself that she is simply a puppet, a moment in History. When the Germans entered France, "she looked on at the march of History, which was not *her* history, which did not belong to anyone" (p. 270). Since History appears to her both impersonal and inevitable, Hélène sees no point in resisting.* She continues at her old job in a clothing firm, now under the management of the Germans. She drifts into a friendly relation with a German employer and even considers going to work for him in Berlin. While she is not altogether oblivious to the suffering of her

---

* Sartre discusses this point in the article on collaborationism from which I have already quoted. He adds that sometimes this attitude toward the march of History assumes the form of a tough "realism." "The man who is always talking about 'the hard lesson of facts' looks only at those facts which are to his advantage. In his haste to get rid of what embarrasses him, he is perpetually in bad faith. For example, Déat, fifteen days after the Germans entered Russia, was not afraid to write, 'The Russian Colossus has now collapsed' " (p. 16).

former friends, she keeps herself from actively feeling anything by stressing the necessities of History, by assuming the existence of an impersonal Destiny before which all are inert objects. Although Hélène's apathy is a little more pathological, her frame of mind is that of any citizen who refuses to accept responsibility for what is done by his government. It is also that of the man who will not support any wide-sweeping change, even one aimed at an end he approves, because "you can't change human nature" and the way things are is the way they will be.

Inevitably Hélène's free self demands to be heard. She cannot go on forever pretending not to exist, and she realizes at last that she must choose what part she will play, that even by refusing to choose, she is choosing. History does not decide things for her. The first sign of awareness had occurred during her attempt to return to Paris after a blind flight into the country at the time of the Germans' arrival. While waiting in line for gas, she was suddenly aware of a child staring at her in seeming reproach. This is, of course, the typical Sartrean confrontation with the Other; also, as we have seen, de Beauvoir has used the child elsewhere as an illustration of the falsity of belief in any absolute social order. As Hélène looks, she remembers suddenly a conversation with Blomart in which she had said that she did not *feel* the reality of others' existence, hence had no sense of responsibility for them. Now she seems to hear and for the first time to sense the significance of his words: "Others exist; you have to be blind not to see them" (pp. 274-275). Helene gives her place in line to the woman with the child. The second self-realization comes when she is in a night club with the German. This is again a self-revelation through the eyes of others. The German offers to buy her a box of chocolates of the kind which she had seen in her parents' candy shop. A customer had bought several, saying to Hélène's mother, "I sell them again for four hundred francs to the Fritzes" (p. 290). When she heard the remark, Hélène had seen the "Fritzes" as separate from herself, as the nation's conquerors, who could not be resisted but of whom she was not one. Now she perceives herself as one of them and as they are looked at by the French, and she decides not to go to Berlin. The final awakening comes when Helene's childhood friend, a Jewess, is about to be deported to Germany. Hélène saves her temporarily and ultimately goes to Blomart for help. The realization that the fate of the Jews, which she had known only abstractly, was about to be made real in the girl who had shared so much of Hélène's own life—this renders impossible any pretense that people are merely moments in History. It is an emotional response which forces her to a new rational decision. She decides to work with Blomart, who is now leading a group of workers for the Underground. Two things happen: for the first time she finds happiness in her love for Blomart, since she can now love him as an individual with a life of his own and not just as an emotional justification for her own existence; also she now finds that life has a significance—one finds meaning in life when one is committed to something for which one is willing to accept death.

Hélène's bad faith had consisted in trying to avoid any awareness of others' need of her. In Jean Blomart there is no self-deception in the usual sense but rather, at the beginning, a false view of the human situation. He is a true existentialist hero in that he is absolutely honest with himself and has always recognized both his responsibility for his own life and the necessity of respecting the freedom of others. For him the problem is that he does not know how to act in accordance with the values which he has chosen and at the same time not imperil the lives of others. The novel is the presentation of Sartre's thesis that the only limit to freedom is the freedom of other men. Here is the existentialist paradox: Everyone is free and everyone is totally responsible.*

Blomart's first sense of involvement with other people came when at the age of eight he learned of the death of a servant's baby. Stricken with horror and guilt he experienced "the sin of being another being." He perceived that despite any feeling or expression of sympathy on his part, the servant was alone in her sorrow; moreover, in the face of gratuitous and irremediable evil, his own life and that of his family continued as though the horror did not exist. At about the same time he became aware of poverty, and again he was shocked at the indifference with which rich and poor alike seem to regard it. When he reaches adolescence, Jean's sympathy with the workers leads him to break with his father and to join the Communist Party. He is self-confident for a while, though mildly disturbed by the knowledge that his background will never allow him to be really one with those who are workers by necessity rather than by conviction. Then a tragedy completely alters his point of view. Blomart persuades his friend Jacques to accompany him to a Communist demonstration, and Jacques is killed. Blomart feels that he is a murderer. He breaks with the Party and devotes himself to advocating nonviolence and trade unionism. Although he still works for what he considers the good of men in general, he refuses to perform any

---

* On the dedication page of the novel de Beauvoir quotes Dostoyevsky, "Each man is responsible to everyone for everything."

action which will jeopardize or radically change the life of any one individual. Gradually he realizes the untenability of his position. When Hélène falls in love with him, even though he is attracted to her, he tries not to get involved, both because he realizes that she is trying to make him psychologically responsible for her existence, and because he knows that he cannot honestly love in the way that she does. He cannot make her the absolute justification for his life that he is for hers. Eventually, however, he realizes that by his very existence, he *is* determining her life, and he reluctantly makes her his mistress, pretends that he loves her as she desires, and even plans to marry her. Meanwhile his political attitude has been changing. After Jacques' death he had resolved not to take any political action. "To take part in politics was to reduce the rest of men to their classifiable external functions, to treat them like blind masses, so that I might reserve to myself alone the privilege of existing as a living thought" (p. 163). During the period of appeasement, Blomart was unhappy and less firmly convinced that non-intervention was the solution. He began to see that refraining from action was making the nation as responsible for injustice and death as action would have done. Still he refuses any personal advocation of decisive action. When war breaks out, he insists on fighting in the front, manages to return after a temporary absence due to Hélène's machinations, is wounded, and for this reason is still in Paris during the Occupation. Still harassed by philosophical doubts, he nevertheless is among those who organize the Resistance. But he is in anguish at the thought of the innocent hostages who are killed as the result of Underground activities and is never quite sure that he is justified in determining that some individuals shall die when they themselves have not freely chosen to do so. The question, on the philosophical level, can no longer be evaded as he sits by the dying Hélène and faces the decision as to whether to send his friend out to risk his life. Blomart seeks a way out; he himself will go instead or at least will accompany his friend. But he is prevented by other members of the group, who insist that he is too valuable as a leader to risk death merely to satisfy his own conscience. Finally at dawn after spending the night reliving the experiences of the last ten years, he sees things in what is to him (and to de Beauvoir) their true light. His earlier attitude had been in bad faith in the sense that he cherished the illusion that it is possible for a human being either to be guiltless or to avoid making decisions which will alter the lives of others. He had been aware of the pain of human isolation, aware of his own freedom, but he had not adequately grasped the meaning of freedom in a world in which there are many other subject-beings.

The existentialist concept of freedom in the human sphere is closely related to the idea of man's freedom in relation to the physical world. Since by definition man is a finite being, a freedom without limitations would not only not be human, it would be a meaningless concept. For freedom involves choice. If one lived in a world where one could be simultaneously in more than one place, where one could do and be mutually exclusive things, then there would be no choice, no distinction between wish and achievement, between dream and reality. Freedom is the capacity to choose one's action, to bestow what value one likes upon one thing rather than another. The physical world offers a certain resistance to activity, but it is the human being who determines the significance, the very idea of limitation. Is a mountain, for example, a reason to alter one's course or the opportunity to climb to a better view? One has to choose within existing circumstances because a man is a creature who exists. If freedom is to exist, it must exist "in situation." Hélène suggests this at the end of her life when she tells Blomart that she chose him and the Resistance freely and that he must not feel guilty. "I have done what I wanted. You were just a stone. Stones are necessary to make roads, otherwise how could one choose a way for oneself?" (pp. 325-326). Blomart reflects, "I believe you, I must believe you. No harm has come to you through me. Under your feet I was only an innocent stone. Innocent as the stone, as that piece of steel that pierced your lung."

This is not an evasion but the acceptance of an existential tension: The individual must make his decisions alone, with no certainty of being right, with no possibility of knowing the total effects of his acts or of passing an absolute judgement upon them. Within whatever situation he finds himself he must choose among the limitations offered him. There is no escape from choice and no complete escape from the burden of lone individuality. Yet at the same time one knows that by each choice he is affecting the arrangement of the world within which others will make their choices. Thus on each side there is total freedom and total responsibility. Hélène alone chose what she on her side would make of her relation to Jean; but he on his side could not avoid the fact that his existence was bound to alter her life one way or another, that at the very least it forced upon her a choice. Thus no man is guiltless, for everyone has taken upon himself to mould the world within which others will choose their lives; and this is a violation of their freedom.

Yet at the same time within the situation offered, each one chooses freely and responsibly. Each man is isolated from all others, and each man affects all others.

> Those who will be shot tomorrow have not chosen; I am the rock that crushes them; I shall not escape the curse; forever I shall remain alien to them, forever I shall be to them the blind force of fate, forever separated from them (p. 328).

Blomart concludes by realizing that at last he has the courage to live with his anguish and guilt, that he will work for a cause (universal freedom) which inevitably he will betray in the process of striving for it.

Throughout her work de Beauvoir has stressed the painful tension inevitable for the man who does not want to destroy the present generation for an ideal future and who is equally unwilling to refrain from all action while waiting for an impossible perfect solution. For her, Saint Just's claim, "No one governs justly," is inescapable, but it must never be made an excuse for accepting injustice easily. We are equally wrong if we give up the struggle for innocence or if we seek to evade that guilt which is inseparable from the human condition.

## Bad Faith in Religion

The most obvious form of bad faith in religion is of course hypocrisy; that is, hypocrisy is bad faith if it involves a degree of self-deception, otherwise it is merely a lie. Hypocrisy by definition implies that there is a definite and recognizable set of attitudes which one pretends to embrace but actually does not. As such it has been for centuries one of the sins most frequently portrayed in literature. Dante, looking at the inner life, represented the hypocrites as walking through hell beneath the weight of gilded cloaks lined with lead. Molière in *Tartuffe* and Samuel Butler in *The Way of All Flesh* reversed the picture: Tartuffe and Pontifex wear a cloak of humility to cover up the flames of greed and sadism. Hypocrisy has not received great attention in the writings of either religious or atheistic existentialists. The reason, I think, is not simply the abundance of previous treatment but the fact that the existentialists take no absolute code of behavior for granted and are more interested in seeing how established patterns may in themselves be structures of evasion and self-deception. For Kierkegaard bad faith in a Christian consists in letting himself believe that he can be saved vicariously through the Church, or that a half-hearted commitment is enough, or that God can be made to conform to the demands of human reason.

Writers like T. S. Eliot, Reinhold Niebuhr, and Paul Tillich have continued to stress the need for a total passionate commitment and have delineated patterns of bad faith in their analyses of the more subtle forms of spiritual pride. Since Sartre, de Beauvoir, and Camus have all rejected Christianity, they naturally do not attempt to say what does or does not constitute a valid position with regard to Christian doctrine. Yet religious themes abound in their writing. Sartre and Camus, in particular, have been interested in investigating religious attitudes which are manifestations of bad faith.

The two works of Sartre most directly concerned with religion are *The Flies* and *Lucifer and the Lord*. In both plays the religious struggle of the hero is inextricably bound up with his attempt to achieve a new self-understanding and a proper concept of responsibility toward others. The final decision is religious, ethical, and political.

In *The Flies* Orestes, like his Greek prototype, kills Clytemnestra and Aegisthus, punishing them for their murder of Agamemnon. Here almost all resemblance between Aeschylus and Sartre ceases. Orestes does not come back with the explicit purpose of avenging his father; in fact he decides to kill the King and Queen more because of what they are doing to the people of Argos than because of their original crime. Moreover, his real antagonists are not Aegisthus and Clytemnestra but Zeus and his own Tutor. The Tutor is of major importance symbolically. He is in the play to remind us that the existentialist alternative to the acceptance of conventional religion is not an easy, irresponsible humanism. The Tutor, who longs for "that gentle land of Attica where my reason was always right," has brought Orestes to Argos reluctantly, and he tries his best first to persuade Orestes to leave without becoming involved with the Argives and then to remain in sanctuary when his crimes have been discovered. The Tutor has trained Orestes to appreciate the cultural treasures of the past, to contemplate life with a reasonable interest but without commitment. He represents both the existentialists' distrust of pure rationalism and Sartre's dislike of the uncommitted intellectual. Zeus has certainly nothing in common with the Olympian god unless it is his sophisticated behavior. Part of the time he seems to represent Jehovah, but he is too much lacking in moral fervor to fit either the Jewish or the Christian God precisely. So far as the plot is concerned, it is perhaps most accurate to say that he represents not God himself but the traditional concept of God in Christianity. This interpretation seems more appropriate to Sartre's contention that God does not exist and to Orestes' assertion of independence. Ironically, Zeus comes alive as a dramatic creation even more than some of Sartre's "human" characters and presents a quite believable mixture of urbane good will, cynicism, and self-interest.

In contrast to Orestes, who portrays in a rather abstract and purified form the "existentialist hero," the play contains two detailed studies in bad faith—the people of Argos and Electra. The bad faith of the populace is identified with the central theme of Christianity—the doctrine of original sin and atonement. For Adam and Eve we have Aegisthus and Clytemnestra; instead of Satan and the apple we have the murder of Agamemnon. It is the Argives' conviction that their King's and Queen's sin is their own, that they themselves must spend their days groveling in guilt and remorse in order to atone for the original crime. Argos is like a dead city, or rather it is like a town inhabited only by insects. Both the Tutor and Zeus refer to one of the old women as being like a black beetle among a host of vermin. The image, I suspect, may have been derived from Kafka's *Metamorphosis,* where the hero actually turns into the cockroach which his soul has metamorphically become. Or perhaps Sartre and Kafka have both borrowed the idea of "beetle men" developed by Dostoyevsky in *The Brothers Karamazov.*

The dual association with death and insects is strengthened by two other things: the ceremony for Dead Men's Day, around which the action is centered, and the presence of the Flies. The Flies are the everyday symbol of the guilt and remorse of the inhabitants; when the avenging Furies appear in the last act, they too are represented as giant flies. Sartre, I believe, has taken both ideas from Greek religion. In ancient Greece the Anthesteria was a three-day festival built upon rites of purification. While it was being celebrated, the dead were invited to come back among the living, just as in the scene described by Sartre. The spirits of the dead were represented in art as little winged creatures called Keres. The word "Keres" (which in parallel forms in Latin and German comes to mean "germs") applied to more than the souls of the dead. It referred as well to invisible insect-like spirits who, something like modern bacillae, were believed to cause disease, putrefaction, and death. The Anthesteria involved both the invitation to the dead ancestors and purifying ceremonies to get rid of the harmful Keres, who were thought to fill the air so full that one could not help breathing them in. Thus the Greek festival, like that in Sartre's play, indicated a fear of the dead and a belief in the need for purification. I think it is not coincidence that Sartre has combined the Christian concept of atonement for spiritual guilt with the primitive Greek idea that one must magically get rid of evil spirits. Both in his eyes are clear evidence of man's failure to assert his potential human dignity.

In his presentation of the guilt-ridden Argives suffering under the plague of the Flies, Sartre seems to me to have pointed out at least three objections to the doctrine of Atonement. First, in so far as the idea of original sin refers to a specific event, it is false. The newborn child cannot be said to have been responsible for the death of Agamemnon. Second, the inculcation of feelings of guilt is psychologically degrading and unhealthy. Finally, the doctrine of original sin as actually lived constitutes conduct in bad faith. The people are all willing to acknowledge their guilt abstractly. They dwell upon their wickedness, even derive a masochistic pleasure from it. They train their children in a piety rooted in terror. But they will not recognize their responsibility for any specific guilt. The old woman will not admit that she had secretly satisfied a lust for bloodshed and reveled in the gory details of Agamemnon's slaughter. Clytemnestra like the rest of the city delights in public confession. She enjoys the process of reliving her crime and she likes to be the center of attention. (This is, of course, an obvious thrust at the "testimony meetings" of certain religious sects.) But Clytemnestra will not allow criticism of her remorse. As Electra says to Orestes, "People are going to beg you to condemn them. But be careful to judge them only on the faults they admit. The rest of their sins are nobody's business, and they would be quite annoyed with you for pointing them out" (p. 36).

Acknowledgement of guilt for all things becomes a device in bad faith by which one may avoid being held guilty for any one thing. In addition the doctrine of original sin may become an excuse for brooding over one's past or abstract guilt instead of striving to avoid actual guilt in the future. The belief that one is guilty no matter what one does may easily pass into the attitude that then one may as well do whatever one pleases. It is the frame of mind reflected in a limerick about a convert to the Neo-Orthodox movement.

> At Ipswich when Niebuhr had quit it,
> A young man said, "Ah, now I've hit it!
>   Since nothing is right,
>   I'll go out tonight,
> Find the best sin and commit it!" [1]

Although admirers of Niebuhr may maintain that the rhyme exaggerates, the fact remains that those who hold to the doctrine of original sin have frequently opposed progressive efforts on the ground that a corrupt human nature would prevent their ever succeeding. What we have here is the equivalent in religious terms of the movement in bad faith with respect to intellectual belief. We saw earlier that the man in bad faith will pass from the attitude that all belief is only probable to the position that he may embrace any improbable belief. Here the man who believes that he is irreparably guilty will believe that he may as well take on any specific guilt.

The existentialists, as we have seen already in connection with *The Blood of Others,* and as we will see in several other examples, have their own concept of original sin. And there is in some cases, at least, a question as to whether their attitude with regard to it is any less an impediment than the Christian. But in *The Flies* Sartre represents Orestes as taking a firm stand to the effect that man is fully responsible and as such not only is without excuse but must be without remorse. Man must accept the responsibility for all his past actions, but they can never constitute an excuse for not acting in the way that seems best with respect to the future. The fact that man cannot live without being guilty of crimes does not allow him to treat all acts as being equal. A man is in bad faith, Sartre is saying, if he allows preoccupation with his own spiritual guilt to prevent his recognizing his responsibility to prevent the existence of particular evils which might be avoided. Sartre suggests also that for some people the surrender to guilt feelings is a device to escape from the real problem of discovering a way to live life significantly. When Orestes wants to free the Argives from their burden of guilt, Zeus says, "And what would you give them in exchange? Good digestions, the gloomy repose of provincial life, and the boredom—ah, the inescapable boredom of happiness" (p. 21). Zeus feels that even the guilt and anxiety of a false religion are easier for man than a confrontation with the truth about humanity's contingent, unnecessary existence. But to Orestes the pain of lost illusion is but a stage on the way to a life of *human* significance.

> *Zeus:* Poor people! You are going to make them a gift of loneliness and shame. You're going to snatch from their eyes the veils with which I had enfolded them. And suddenly you will show to them their existence, their obscene, tasteless existence, which has been given to them for nothing.

*Orestes:* Why should I deny to them the despair which is in me—since this is their lot?

*Zeus:* What will they do with it?

*Orestes:* What they will. They are free, and human life begins on the far side of despair (p. 102).

Electra's bad faith is totally different from that of the general population. Her problem is not intrinsically one of guilt, nor is her conflict primarily religious. She is rather a person who is nourished by a dream in which someone else will accomplish for her that which she both desires and fears. So long as the dream is there to sustain her, she is capable of acts of courage and defiance. But she cannot face reality. When she finally recognizes Orestes and his purpose, she is filled with fear both for him and for herself. She gains enough support from him to join in the plot against Aegisthus and Clytemnestra, but later she cannot face the realization of what she has done, nor can she assert that her act was good in the face of public disapproval. She allows herself to be persuaded by Zeus that she had not really fully desired the murders, and she joins the rest of Argos in works of atonement. On the religious level she perhaps stands for the person who can do without religion until he encounters trouble, the "foxhole convert." In the first act when Electra is under the illusion that a deliverer will come to free her and the city, then she can throw garbage at the statue of Zeus and dance shamelessly before the mourning populace. But when she has committed irrevocable acts, when she has no guarantee for the future and no assurance that what she has done is right, then she returns for refuge to the god she had defied.

There are in the play a number of other attacks on Christian doctrine. Although these are not specifically examples of patterns of bad faith, they indicate what Sartre believes to be false attitudes and should be included in our discussion of his view of religion. In this connection the characterization of Aegisthus is significant. Although he is a murderer and a tyrant, and although his death is necessary if the people are to be freed, he is more like Orestes than any of the other characters. This is because he alone of the Argives is without illusion. He has chosen to let himself be made the tool of Zeus. He knows that his power depends on his being able to keep the people blind with fear and guilt. Sartre is using Aegisthus to attack the traditional alliance of Church and State to protect the interest of a minority against the people, especially as manifested under the doctrine of the divine right of kings. There is one further point. In Act Two after the ceremony for the dead, Clytemnestra approaches Aegisthus, and he repulses her, asking her if she is not ashamed to come to him under the very eyes of Agamemnon. Clytemnestra realizes with surprise that Aegisthus, like one of the people, means that Agamemnon has actually come forth from the cave at the ceremony. She replies, "But the dead are underground and will not trouble us for many a year. Have you forgotten that you yourself invented that fable for the people?" (p. 71). There is an echo here of the idea known at least as early as the author of the Greek play *Sisyphus*— that rulers had invented the idea of the gods to keep their subjects obedient and had ended by believing in their own invention as did everyone else.

Sartre's second objection to religious doctrine relates to the idea of the justice of God, though he gives less emphasis to this point than others of the existentialists have done. In Act One Orestes hears the story of Agamemnon's murder and says, "So now the assassin reigns. He has known fifteen years of happiness. And I believed the gods were just!" (p. 16). Later Zeus comes to warn Aegisthus that Orestes is coming. Aegisthus asks Zeus why he should try to prevent this crime when he had permitted the earlier one. Zeus replies that it is not that he loves Orestes more, in fact he loves nobody. As for crimes, "The first crime was mine; I committed it by making man mortal" (p. 75). Here Sartre touches lightly on a theme much more extensively developed by Camus —that it is impossible to maintain a belief in a just, all-powerful God if one takes seriously the sufferings of finite man. As James put it in one of his more sombre moods, mortal life is doomed to failure simply because it is mortal. With death at the end of it, what human project can be said to have succeeded?

Two other traditional arguments for the existence of God are touched on briefly. One is that based on miracles. Sartre does not in this play try to disprove the reality of miracles, though obviously he would hold them to be impossible in view of the rest of his philosophy. In *The Flies* we have two genuine miracles: The first occurs just after Electra has come in a dress of dazzling white to dance in among the black-clad mourners. She has almost persuaded the Argives to renounce their guilt- and fear-ridden way of life when Zeus intervenes by causing a great rock to roll down from the cavern into the midst of the people. The miracle brings the populace back into line, though it does not intimidate Electra. At first thought this might seem to be evidence of Zeus' power, but

Sartre has so constructed the scene that the miracle appears childish and incongruous. After the passionate logic of Electra's speech, the fact that a mere boulder could undo all that she had said seems not to witness to the glory of God but rather to the tragic indignity of man. The second miracle comes just a little later when Orestes hesitates between his conviction that he ought to kill the King and Queen and the realization that Zeus has apparently forbidden the act. He asks Zeus for a further sign, and Zeus obliges by making light flash about the rock. But Orestes does not obey. The scene is in striking contrast to the Abraham story so often used by Kierkegaard. Abraham, confronted with the choice between loyalty to his own "human conscience" and obedience to an "inhuman" command from God, chose obedience. Orestes chooses disobedience, thereby asserting his sense of right in the face of God himself. Existentialism has often been attacked as a philosophy which degrades man, and it is true that existentialist writers have often been unkind to man's pretensions. Yet it would be difficult to find any philosophy which goes further in asserting man's responsibilities or his dignity if he is willing to face his situation honestly.

One other religious attitude is examined in a passage where Zeus and Aegisthus discuss their relation to their subjects. Aegisthus realizes that he can see himself now only as the figure whom his subjects see; the political role has absorbed the person. In reply Zeus hints that he himself will go on living before men's eyes only so long as they forget to look into themselves, the implication being, of course, that Zeus has been but a projected ideal or fear which human consciousness may replace or abandon. What follows suggests the origin and nature of this ideal. Aegisthus and he himself, Zeus says, have a passion for order. Sartre's reference here, I believe, is to men's tendency to accept even a doctrine hostile to themselves, provided it seems to explain things, to contain the universe and human life and all events in a logical system. This is one of the comparatively few places where Sartre expresses the existentialist claim that the irrational cannot be ignored and that any so-called rational method of ironing out all contradictions and evidence of chaos is to be distrusted.

The climax of the religious conflict in *The Flies* is effected in a scene where the Biblical parallel is patent. As God spoke to Job out of the whirlwind, so Zeus appears to Orestes. He is no longer the affable, sophisticated companion but speaks with the true voice of God. He opens to Orestes a vision of the universe, and he reveals himself as the Creator. Zeus' speech, like that of God to Job, begins with a rehearsal of the wonders of Creation. Like proponents of the Cosmological Argument, Zeus points to the wonderful regularity in nature, the limits of the spheres, the determination of organic and inorganic species, the miracle of growth, all functioning by divine law. He goes further than God in his word to Job and explains the nature of Good and Evil. The argument advanced here is a somewhat pantheistic version of that given by the early Christian Fathers: God is all good; evil is but the negation of Good and is due to a lack in man.

> For the world is good; I created it according to my will and I am The Good. But you, you have brought evil into the world. Things with their stony voices accuse you. The Good is everywhere. . . . Your very body betrays you, for it fits my specifications. . . . And this Evil of which you are so proud, which you think you have created—what is it but a reflection of being, a by-path, a deceptive image whose very existence is sustained by the Good? . . . Return to Nature, Nature's unnatural son (pp. 98-99).

Undaunted, Orestes replies, "You are King of the Gods, Zeus, King of the stones and of the stars, King of the waves of the sea. But you are not King of men" (p. 99).

The Apocalypse ends. Zeus returns in his usual form and reminds Orestes that he owes his very existence to Zeus. Now in addition to the Cosmological Argument, based on the wonders of Nature, and the Augustinian argument that Evil is but the lack of Good, we have another Augustinian doctrine, that freedom is found only in obedience to the will of God. Zeus asks, "Who, then, created you?" Orestes replies, "You, but you should not have made me free." And Zeus answers, "I gave you freedom so that you might serve me."

Confronted with this philosophical array, Orestes (or anyone who has read *Being and Nothingness*) has three ready answers. To the statement that Evil is only relative and a lack of Good, Sartre replies that Evil is absolute. To deny that the gratuitous death of a child or a plague or slavery or political oppression is an evil is to blaspheme against humanity. Even if certain evils are necessary in order to attain a greater good, they are not thereby prevented from being evil. Orestes' answer to this particular doctrine is less in words than in action. By choosing to draw the Furies upon himself instead of letting Zeus make him King of Argos, he asserts that the presence of the Flies *is* evil and frees the people from it. At the same time he refuses to recognize the essential justice of things. His attitude is that of John Stuart Mill, who said that if one could prove to him the existence of an all-powerful God but one who was not good according to human standards, Mill would recognize his existence but refuse to call him good. "And if he sends me to hell, then to hell I will go."

In answer to Zeus' statement that man had been given freedom in order that he might serve God, Orestes replies that freedom has turned against its giver. "I *am* my freedom. No sooner had you created me than I ceased to belong to you." This is—in simplified form, to be sure —the argument about the relation between Creator and creature which Sartre painstakingly worked out in *Being and Nothingness*. Either the created being is still a part of the mind of the Creator, in which case he is not an independent being and cannot be considered or judged as such, or he is separated from the Creator, fully independent and totally free. To assert this freedom against the Creator is, in the eyes of the Christian, blasphemy. (And this is how Orestes' affirmation appeared to Electra.) But if for a personal God, we substitute some impersonal Force, the case alters and Sartre's position is no longer shocking. It is, in fact, practically the same as that of Schopenhauer, who argued that the consciousness which the Will had created for its own self-preservation is now capable of turning back against the Will and refusing to perpetuate its meaningless existence. Or—to turn to the more positive aspect —the view is not unlike that of more optimistic biologists who suggest that the mind of man, which has evolved as merely one more device for survival (like the turtle's shell or the weasel's changing color) can now in part direct its own future evolution and determine the circumstances under which it wills to survive.

Finally, Orestes refuses to be overawed by his vision of the firmament and the wonders of nature. Marvelous as it may be, Nature does not impel him to accept the idea that in itself it constitutes the Good or that man can find himself by seeing his place in Nature. Essentially, Orestes has discovered what the Judge decided in Vercors' *You Shall Know Them*. What distinguishes man from the rest of life is that he is *not* at home in Nature. Vercors explains man's detachment in terms of his ability to question nature and himself. Sartre expresses it as man's recognition of freedom. In a terrifying moment Orestes simultaneously realized that he was free and that he was exiled from Nature.

Suddenly freedom swooped down upon me and chilled me through and through. Nature leapt back, I was ageless, and I found myself all alone in the midst of your benign little world, like someone who has lost his shadow. And there was nothing left in the sky, no Good, no Evil, nobody to give me orders (p. 101).

Orestes knows fully all that his rebellion involves. It means that he accepts for himself no standard, law, excuse, or remedy which comes from either God or Nature. He must decide alone and find his right way, must determine his own goal.

At this point we can see the full significance of the conclusion of the play. There is one more Biblical parellel. Aegisthus and Clytemnestra had brought original sin into the world. Zeus sought to justify the demands made by God and the inevitability of guilt and repentance for man. There is still lacking a divine sacrifice and the offer of Grace. The end of the play provides the Passion as Orestes leaves Argos and voluntarily takes upon himself the punishment by the Furies. The symbolism is obvious, but there remains the question as to just how this act fits into the existentialist scheme of things.

First of all, we must recognize that existentialism of any variety denies that any person can live another man's life for him or free him from his own guilt. To an extent I believe that Sartre's desire to complete the Christian symbolism of the play has led him into a certain inconsistency. Actually, if the Argives thought that Orestes' sacrifice freed them from further responsibility, they would once more be leading lives in bad faith. Electra has clearly shown that she is incapable of anything else. What then is the existentialist significance of Orestes' act? There are, I believe, two points. First, Orestes is doing what he had earlier told Zeus that he would do. By taking away the Furies, he is forcing the people to look at life squarely instead of being preoccupied with abstract guilt and remorse. He is making it possible for them to see the truth about their freedom; what they will do with it is for them to decide. In this sense Orestes is performing a human act equivalent to the divine one. Christ died that men might know Truth through Him. Orestes will live in suffering so that the people may know the truth of their freedom. A second, not inconsistent interpretation might see in Orestes all of mankind assuming the Cross which is the burden of human life. As Man, Orestes is willing to take on the responsibilities and agonies of a life which is wholly human, a life which has no transcendent assurance, one which inevitably involves guilt for which there can be no forgiveness because there is nobody to give forgiveness. Man, in short, will no longer shift responsibility for his life to a god but will decide for himself what can make his life significant.

Before leaving *The Flies,* I want to point out once again that the play is not exclusively religious or metaphysical, not only myth. On the political level, obviously Orestes represents any movement for freedom against an oppressive regime. If one wants to make the parallel with the Nazi Occupation more precise, we could say that Zeus represents the Germans, Aegisthus the Vichy Government. The people of Argos are the humiliated and despondent French, Orestes the Resistance movement, Electra the patriotic Frenchman who hated the Germans but did not have the courage to face the killing of hostages, etc. which resulted from the work of the Underground. In this case the "passion for order" perhaps represents the deadly German efficiency, the Creation vision a reference to the earlier stupendous achievements of the Germans in Europe, etc. But while the play allows for such equations, I think that Sartre is interested in making a basic appeal to freedom rather than in presenting a detailed allegory. Similarly, *The Flies* can be interpreted as the study of human psychology. The populace represent the vast majority of human beings who never leave the Serious World and the realm of bad faith. Electra is one who tries to achieve an existentialist katharsis but does not quite have the courage to accept the basic loneliness and insecurity which comes with the loss of illusions. Orestes, of course, is the existentialist hero who has never been really engulfed in the Serious World but who had at first deceived himself into thinking that an uncommitted freedom could satisfy him, who had to learn that since the world includes others, one cannot remain detached from them. Electra meets despair and retreats into the Serious World. Orestes passes through the Slough of Despond into a new value-world of his own creation.

*Lucifer and the Lord (Le Diable et le bon Dieu)* was written at least ten years after *The Flies.* It belongs with a group of plays *(Dirty Hands, In the Mesh, Nekrassov)* in which Sartre is seeking a valid political commitment for the intellectual. The problem is how to recognize and maintain a mean between an idealism leading to no action and a political expediency which in sacrificing means for end would undermine its own cause. *Lucifer and the Lord* is as definite in its political reference as *The Flies.* In addition, as Sartre has said, "The play throughout deals with man's relations to God, or, if you prefer, with man's relations to the Absolute."

The action takes place in and near Worms. The background is clearly that of the Reformation and the Peasant Revolt, and there is some obvious satire directed against both the Catholic Church and the early Lutherans. Sartre, however, does not press the political allegory and concentrates on the spiritual struggles of a central character, Goetz. At the beginning of the play Goetz has betrayed both the Church and the people and is interested in nothing but his own worldly power. Then as the result of a bet, he decides that instead of opposing God and serving Evil, he will show that he can work with God and do nothing but Good. He fails, not as the result of weakness of will but because of the ignorance of the others and because he can never foresee the consequences of his acts. Finally he discovers that God does not exist, and at last he feels free to work realistically for the good of mankind. One might say that he has made three successive existential choices of himself; first as the Devil, then as God, finally as a man.

Certain ideas which we have met in *The Flies* are repeated. Sartre offers an almost Kierkegaardian criticism of easy, vicarious religious experience. This he effects by incorporating into the play Luther's old opponent, the priest Tetzel, who comes selling indulgences. Sartre satirizes also the excessive Puritanism and masochistic self-abasement often associated with the Church. Somewhat more serious is the effort (already encountered in *The Flies*) to show that spiritual preoccupation is often an excuse for self-aggrandizement at the expense of others. Thus Goetz' saintliness results in the death of his former mistress, who in despair became a prostitute when he cast her off. The serfs whom he had freed are prevented by Goetz (in the name of love of mankind) from helping their neighbors in their struggle for freedom. In another passage Sartre points out that when God is silent, his followers make him say whatever they please. One theme is a little further developed than it had been in *The Flies;* this is Sartre's objection to belief in the existence of a perfectly just God. In Scene VI the villagers have been told that Goetz' mistress has died, and they want to pray and ask forgiveness for "this poor dead woman who has seen hell and who is in danger of being damned." Hilda, who becomes Goetz' companion at the end, addresses God defiantly.

> Ask your forgiveness! What need is there for you to forgive us? It is you who should beg our forgiveness. I do not know what you have planned for me and I scarcely know this woman. But if you condemn her, I do not want your heaven. Do you think

that a thousand years of Paradise would make me forget the terror in her eyes? I have only scorn for your stupid Elect who have the heart to rejoice when there are the damned in hell and the poor on earth. As for me, I am on the side of men, and I shall never forsake them. You can cause me to die without a priest and summon me without warning to your Tribunal. But you will see then which one of us will judge the other.[2]

Hilda's statement is stronger than Orestes' and more specifically an attack on Christian doctrine. It is reminiscent of James' question, asking who of us would enjoy an eternity of Paradise if he knew the world's happiness was paid for by an eternity of torture for one damned soul.

There is one wholly new theme in the play, an explanation of conduct before God which is derived from Sartre's view of human relationships, a view which is almost the equivalent, one might say, of Freud's theory that God is a gigantic father-image. We have seen that according to Sartre a person first realizes the existence of other subjects in the world when he finds himself the object of another's Look. The process of "staring the Other down" becomes in the fullest sense the origin of most of human relations. Between any two people there is, of course, a potential alternation in the subject-object relation. But even in those cases where one of the pair is able to establish himself as virtual Master, the couple is forever threatened by the appearance of a Third, who as subject will transform both the others into objects. Such a shift among the trio in hell, each one of whom in turn upsets the bond between the other two, is the theme of *No Exit*. But there is a further step. One may postulate (either in love or fear) the existence of an unseen subject who is always present and who by definition cannot be made an object. This subject is God. There are three types of conduct possible before this God: First, one may accept one's object-state in shame and fear. This was the attitude adopted by the people of Argos. It is a self-evasion, for to accept oneself as an object is to avoid the responsibility for choosing what kind of self one will become. At best it involves learning from the outside what one is to be. A second possibility is to accept the concept of the absolute Subject and then revolt against him. This type of rebellion is not of the same nature as Hilda's declaration. Hilda rejected traditional religious attitudes in the name of what seemed to her a higher good. But there is a way of accepting the absolute Subject as the Good and still rebelling against Him. In *Being and Nothingness* Sartre says,

Black masses, desecration of the Host, demonic associations, etc. are so many attempts to confer the character of object on the absolute Subject. In desiring Evil for Evil's sake I attempt to contemplate the divine transcendence—for which Good is the peculiar possibility—as a purely given transcendence and one which I transcend toward Evil. Then I "make God suffer," I "irritate him," etc. (p. 290).

Sartre goes on to explain that of course such attempts are logically self-contradictory. Either God is an absolute Subject, and hence none of my attempts to make him my object can possibly succeed, or else I am able to make him an object, in which case there has been no absolute Subject against whom to launch my rebellion. It is the inner contradiction which renders this conduct so peculiarly appropriate to bad faith.

During the first act of *Lucifer and the Lord* Goetz has deliberately set himself against God and has chosen Evil. Having been born a bastard, he feels that he has always been an outcast from the world (God's world). By trying to lay claim to a place in this world, he must act contrary to the claims of Society and the Church. Thus from his first action he feels that he is damned and that God can do nothing more to him. "Monsters and saints are both raised up by God." Goetz feels that by doing evil he is making himself responsible for what he is instead of simply accepting his condemnation from God. Yet every action is calculated in terms of how it appears to God. By committing crimes, Goetz forces God to appear responsible for allowing injustice. He boasts that he is without equal. "I am the man who makes the Almighty uncomfortable. Through me God finds himself repulsive." When the priest Heinrich taunts him by saying that far from being unique, Goetz is like everyone else, that it is impossible for man to do anything but evil, Goetz proposes a bet—he will do nothing but good for a year. When Heinrich hesitates about accepting, Goetz throws the dice to decide whether to do good or evil, calling upon God to send a sign. The dice signify that he is to do Good, though Goetz' mistress sees that Goetz has cheated in order to be sure that Good will be indicated! By a neat turn it is Heinrich who for the rest of the play makes himself an object by seeking God in bad faith as a way of self-evasion. Heinrich is tortured by the memory of having betrayed a city in order to save himself and a few other priests. Although he leads a wretched existence in which he thinks he is condemned by God and that an actual devil walks around with him, still he finds it preferable to be judged by an

Infinite Being rather than by his fellowmen. His reasons are two: first, he feels that his punishment can wipe out the effect of his crime, and second, he cherishes a secret hope that by acknowledging to God that he is guilty, he can persuade God to pronounce him finally not guilty. While neither of these attitudes is precisely un-Christian, they are in bad faith according to the existentialists. Repentance does not wipe out guilt; one must accept the responsibility for what one has done and strive to do and be different in the future. Neither God nor anyone else can wipe out the past—or determine what one is to be for the future.

In Sartre's eyes Goetz the saint is fully as reprehensible as Goetz the incarnation of Evil. Wherein lies the bad faith? In the political context Sartre's intention is fairly clear. One cannot "force ·men to be free," nor can one set up a perfect state by merely assuming that all men are perfect. On the personal level, if we return to the subject-object relation again, we see that Goetz is still positing an absolute Subject before whom he is an object. Hatred has been replaced by love, but Goetz awaits guarantees from the outside and assumes that his course of conduct is pre-established. Ultimately, of course, he realizes that God has never been more than the projection of his own attitude.

Goetz' conduct poses a peculiar philosophical problem. To posit God as an absolute Subject whom one defies by doing Evil is obviously wrong. It is, in the first place, self-contradictory; moreover, it springs from self-hatred (a feeling that one is rejected by the source of good, hence is inevitably evil), and it can lead only to a deeper sense of alienation and to more and more destruction. But what about positing an absolute Subject, who is good, and whose approval and love one strives to win? In this case it seems that one's conduct would be as good as one knew how to make it. For the God one believes to be all Good would be pleased by actions one believed to be good. Even granted that such a Being is but a projection of human thought, do we not have here that drawing power of the Ideal celebrated alike by Plato, Dante, Santayana, and even John Dewey? And can such an attitude be properly said to be in bad faith?

While Sartre has not proposed the problem in just these terms, I believe that Goetz' behavior in the play can provide us with an answer. Although Goetz finally realizes that he himself has invented God, the fact remains that so long as he considered himself an object before a Subject, he had not fully exercised his right of free choice. Once he is convinced that he can never finally *be* anything in the eyes of God, that God is "absence and the loneliness of man," then he feels free for the first time to take those steps which seem to him best for mankind in existing situations. Until then, whether he was choosing Evil or Good, his hands had been tied by allegiance to the conventional ideas of the nature of that Good which God represented. The concept of the absolute Subject logically demands eternity and changelessness. As the Subject to whom man is object, God tends to become one of the furnishings of the Serious World, usually one of the most antique. The Ideal ceases to be a drawing power toward the Good and becomes simply a fetter binding one to the status quo. If man is to progress toward the Good, he must recognize that part of the process involves a constant redefining of the goal. If man is merely an object, he is incapable of any free determination. The truth is that Goetz the saint is in bad faith whether God exists or not, for he assumes that what others have said about God has once and for all delimited not only God's nature but Goetz' own.

*Lucifer and the Lord,* in spite of its historical setting, is almost pure myth. Sartre makes no attempt to individualize his characters as living people. They are embodiments of various points of view, illustrations of possible ways in which man may choose himself. The social reference is clear enough. Obviously Goetz' final choice is to embrace a realistic program for social reform, rejecting laissez faire or reaction on the one hand and Utopian idealism on the other. What is lacking in the play is any concern with individual psychological structures. To find a case history of bad faith in which the religious element is important, we may turn to Sartre's study of Daniel in the trilogy *The Roads to Freedom (Les Chemins de la liberté).*[3] Precisely because he is presented to us as a case history, Daniel's turn to religion is understandable only in the light of his total outlook—just as we saw with respect to Lucien's anti-Semitism. The central figure of the three novels is not Daniel, but Mathieu, a teacher of philosophy who seems to represent Sartre himself (at least the earlier Sartre) more closely than any other single character in Sartre's work. As an intellectual who has discovered his freedom but who does not know what to do with it, Mathieu is almost a twentieth-century Hamlet. He is contrasted on the one side with Brunet, the committed Communist, and on the other with Daniel, who seeks in bad faith to escape his freedom. Daniel is a homosexual; *therefore* he is filled with guilt and self-hate and feels the need to punish himself. The "therefore" is of course a connection in Daniel's own mind. Mathieu asks him why he does not accept his inclinations, hold up his head and choose to *be* homosexual. But Daniel replies that one cannot be an invert without the feeling of guilt. Whether or not this be true, in general, we cannot simply accept the conclusion in the case of Daniel. The question is why —since Daniel feels guilty—he continues to be a homosexual. Sartre provides absolutely no explanation of the sort one would expect from a Freudian. We are given no information whatsoever about Daniel's parents, his childhood experiences, his first knowledge of sex, or anything else which is usually thought to be pertinent. Nor is there any hint that the reason is physiological. Daniel is more than ordinarily handsome, and he is physically strong. He says explicitly that he is able to have sexual relations with women—though he hates them. This silence on Sartre's part in what is otherwise a very careful study must be deliberate. It means that the explanation must be sought not in any external forces of heredity or environment but on the philisophical level. It means that we must find in Daniel's own attitude the answer as to why he chooses himself as a homosexual. Why? At the risk of seeming to introduce circularity, I suggest that it is because he *wants* to feel guilty and to have something for which to punish himself.

If Sartre were discussing Daniel in *Being and Nothingness,* he would have an ontological formula ready at hand. In order to escape from the Self which he *is* (in the mode of not-being) Daniel tries to make himself into a Self which he is not (in the mode of being). In simpler terms —Daniel cannot bear the thought that his consciousness is a nothingness, his essence the freedom to make himself what he will. He is willing to be anything so long as he can *be* it absolutely—"as an oak tree is an oak tree." Daniel feels that such being (a being-in-itself) may be attained only by an emotion of self-love or self-hate so great that it wipes out any feeling of separation between the "I" and the "Me." The way of love is closed to him, although he is wistfully attracted to narcissistic types. But he cannot aim at experiencing self-coincidence through self-love because he knows that his project is in bad faith. (We must remember that while bad faith is nonreflective, it is not unconscious.) Knowing very well that he can never really *be* anything in a final sense, he is forced to embark upon a policy of self-deception. The knowledge that he is trying to deceive himself makes it all the easier for him to choose the way of self-hate. By becoming a homosexual, he is aware of social disapproval (and there is in Daniel a certain regard for the values of the Serious World); moreover, by convincing himself that he really does not want to be a homosexual, he can continue to hate himself after each lapse.

Whether or not I am correct in thus explaining the reason for Daniel's guilty homosexuality, his self-hatred and his desire to attain self-coincidence through self-punishment are clearly established. Daniel attempts to experience himself as a hateful object in three different ways. First, he does things which he himself believes to be contemptible in order that he may be filled with self-loathing. In this he fails, for the self-contempt he should feel is too tangible, too much dependent on his own efforts. At best he remains a neutral "I" contemplating a hateful "Me," but there is a distance between the two. Then he tries inflicting physical or psychic hurt upon himself. He cuts off a pimple so as to scar his face, he wears a heavy jacket on a hot day when he would prefer a light one. But in serious efforts he fails again. Remarking cynically that if he hasn't the courage to kill himself all at once, he can do it bit by bit, he tries to force himself to drown his cats (the only beings for whom he has any real tenderness); but at the last moment he is unable to do so. He attempts to castrate himself, but he cannot force his hand to move the razor. At length he finds that he can come closest to achieving his purpose by making himself an object of hatred to others. Toward the end of the first novel, *The Age of Reason,* he has formed a project which at last seems to promise success.

Most of the book has been directly or indirectly involved with the consequences of the discovery by Mathieu's mistress, Marcelle, that she is pregnant. Mathieu, who feels that settling down in a bourgeois marriage would destroy him, assumes that of course Marcelle will have an abortion. He tries in vain to borrow the necessary money and finally in desperation steals it from a friend (though he intends to pay it back eventually). Meanwhile Daniel has been secretly seeing Marcelle. He does not love her, rather despises her in fact, but he enjoys playing the role of "archangel" so that he may under a pretense of friendship manipulate her life and undermine Mathieu. Learning of her pregnancy from Mathieu, who comes to him to ask for a loan, Daniel refuses him the money and then persuades Marcelle that he did so because he thought she might prefer to have the child. Secretly she does want it and is persuaded by Daniel to let him tell Mathieu that she does. Mathieu, not knowing that Daniel is going to tell her of their conversation, ignores all reference to it. At the moment when she thinks he is going to propose marriage, he hands her the money for the abortion. Marcelle is hurt and enraged and breaks off with him completely. Now Daniel carries through on his plan to punish himself and make himself hated both at once. He proposes to Marcelle and tells Mathieu almost in a single breath that he is going to marry her, that he intends to make it a marriage in the full sense of the word, and that he is a homosexual who has no use for women. Mathieu is filled with despair at the thought of his responsibility in bringing about what promises to be an unhappy life for Marcelle. For a brief moment Daniel thinks that he has finally succeeded. Mathieu knows his secret and hates him. Daniel can almost feel that he exists absolutely as an object of another's hate. But the elation does not last. Mathieu is too understanding to hate Daniel completely and too much of a philosopher to think that Daniel *is* the evil thing he has made himself. Instead, he immediately appeals to Daniel's free choice of himself and asks why he cannot accept himself as a homosexual without guilt. Daniel can only refuse. Rather surprisingly he says that this would mean accepting himself as a swine, and this he will not do. Besides, "I have accepted myself only too thoroughly. I know myself inside out." Just as Mathieu's knowledge has not made him *be* a paederast as a tree is a tree, so Daniel finds too that marriage is not the ultimate in punishment. Although he has mostly contempt for Marcelle, he finds to his disgust that he is less bored with her than without her.

So far Daniel has tried to achieve an absolute Being by making himself wholly an object either to his own self-contemplation or before the Look of another human being. Now he carries the idea to its logical conclusion, pursuing the same pattern that we saw followed by Goetz in Act One of *Lucifer and the Lord*. Sitting in the garden soon after his marriage to Marcelle, Daniel has a kind of mystic experience. It is not a conversion, for there is no exchange of evil for good nor any radical alteration in his way of life. Rather Daniel feels suddenly the presence of an absolute subject and experiences an intense joy, surpassing all pleasures of the flesh, at the thought that he is at last the object of an absolute Look. He writes in a long letter to Mathieu,

> God sees me, Mathieu; I feel it and I know it! . . . "I am seen, therefore I am." I need no longer bear the responsibility of my turbid and disintegrating self; he who sees me causes me to be; I am as he sees me. . . . At last I am transmuted into myself. Hated, despised, sustained, a presence supports me to continue thus forever. I am infinite and infinitely guilty. But I *am*, Mathieu, I am. Before God and before men, I *am*. *Ecce homo.*[4]

Daniel prepares to enter the Catholic Church, and he shows that he is still the same Daniel by rejoicing that the priest who prepares him for the Church is a man whom he cannot like or respect.

We have seen already the contradiction involved in the positing of absolute Subject. In the case of Daniel, Sartre does not show us how the disintegration occurs. This lack is, I think, a fault from a literary point of view. The reason is probably that Sartre was impatient to show the reactions of his group of characters under the Occupation and wanted to use Daniel as an illustration of how bad faith leads naturally to collaboration. In the article "What Is a Collaborator?" Sartre claimed that homosexuals furnished numerous recruits for the Nazis. He explained the fact by pointing out that during the Occupation "ravished" France somehow assumed a feminine role. Journalists habitually used sexual metaphors in referring to her relations with Germany. Collaborationism produced its own "climate of femininity."

> The collaborator speaks in the name of force, but he is not force; he is the ruse, the guile which gets its strength from force; he is even charm and seduction since he seeks to bring into play the attraction which, according to him, French culture exercises over the Germans. It seems to me almost certain that there is in collaborationism a curious atmosphere of masochism and homosexuality (p. 17).

Obviously Daniel as a masochistic homosexual perfectly illustrates Sartre's thesis.

When we meet him again, the earlier mystic experience is forgotten and he has found a new type of deliverance. When the Germans entered Paris, Daniel felt that it was a triumph against all the forces of respectability which had judged him. Since the Parisians, in whose eyes he had felt his culpability, had fled the city, Daniel seemed to himself to be in some way vindicated. Although he still manifests a basic hostility toward mankind (a reflection of his own self-hate), he finds release in a new sense of solidarity with the Germans, the Apostles of Hatred. For the first time he shows a genuine if perverted joy in living. Although he sets about systematically seducing a young French deserter and planning a course of collaboration for them both, he is for the moment without a sense of guilt and he seems to be filled with genuine tenderness for the boy. But in the very midst of his excited preparations for winning over Philippe (Daniel plans to make use of Rimbaud and the systematic disordering of the senses, Bergere's procedure with Lucien), he suddenly feels that someone is looking at him. This time the Look is not the reassuring eye of God. Rather his sense of having someone observe him sets up in Daniel once again the weary treadmill of the pursuit of absolute Being and need for self-punishment which he had known before. Even in the new morality which the Occupation had seemed to present him, Daniel is afraid to accept freedom and the responsibility for his acts. " 'This time,' he thought, 'it'll be the end of me,' and in his mouth he could taste the bitterness of the agonies still to come."

Daniel's ultimate failure to achieve even a perverted adjustment within himself is clear evidence that the cause of his anxiety was not merely a sense of guilt before society. The brevity of his happiness within the Church bears witness to the inadequacy of his effort to make himself object to absolute Subject, or rather to the inconsistency inherent in such a position. But there is still more to be said. Along with Daniel's struggle to become so much an object that he could escape his freedom and simply *be,* in the manner of a thing, there runs a counter melody, as it were. Much as he may want to make Mathieu—or God— responsible for his being, there is something in him which resists reduction to an object-state. When a friendly bartender greets him and is about to pour out the usual double whisky, Daniel curtly refuses the drink and gives a different order. He does not wish to be classified even to the extent of being "the man who always takes a double whisky." In the final scene with Mathieu, Daniel refuses to be one with those men who simply accept their homosexuality as inevitable. Earlier he had declared, "It must be very entertaining to do the exact opposite of what one wants to do. One feels oneself becoming someone else." This seems at first thought simply another kind of self-evasion. Yet actually Daniel's self-punishing acts had been in one sense an assertion of self-mastery and freedom, an affirmation to the effect that no natural inclination could determine him. It is in this sense that Mathieu views Daniel's decision to marry Marcelle.

> "He is free," he thought. And the horror with which Daniel inspired him was suddenly combined with envy. . . . "He has *acted;* and now he can't go back: it must seem strange to him to feel behind him an unknown act which he has already almost ceased to understand and which will turn his life upside down. All I do, I do *for nothing*." [5]

In contrast to Daniel's misuse of freedom Mathieu finds in himself only "A sort of embodied refusal, a negation." Daniel's act is not what we should call free in the fullest sense because it is too closely related to his desire to avoid at all costs a life which is wholly in good faith. But it is at least a species of revolt against the idea that he must follow his most immediate inclinations.

This combination in Daniel of the desire to become wholly an object (a being-in-itself) and the will to assert his freedom (as being-for-itself) is not a chance inconsistency in Sartre's portrayal. Daniel is not really any more willing to become the unconscious in-itself than he is to recognize himself as the translucent, totally free for-itself. What he wants is to be the conscious cause of his own absolute being, to have the full permanence of an unconscious object and yet to be consciously responsible for this kind of being. He wants to be a Self-Cause. As Sartre expresses it in *Being and Nothingness,* Daniel wants to be God. Sartre believes that Daniel's destructive desire is nothing more than the basic attitude of every man but exaggerated until it has become an obsession. God as *causa sui* is simply the projected irrational wish of man to have both the surety of the things in nature and the free choice of man. Man wants to escape the responsibility of being-for-itself and still remain superior to being-in-itself. He wants to be an in-itself-for-itself. According to Sartre, man cherishes this wish whether he actually maintains a belief in an individualized God or not. Its corollary is, of course, a universe in which values and rights are absolute and clearly defined—the Serious World. As Sartre expresses it, the existentialist passion is precisely the opposite of the Christian. Man every day kills himself in order that God may live. But Man dies in vain. There is no God, and "Man is a useless passion."

In spite of Sartre's startling reversal of terms in thus defining the human situation, the curious fact is that sin in his humanistic terms is essentially the same as that in Kierkegaardian or Neo-Orthodox Christianity. Ultimate sin is the aspiration to be God. But whereas Kierkegaard believes that man's final abdication precedes the gift of Grace, Sartre urges that man must renounce his claim, not because it is blasphemous to God but because it destroys all possibility of man's building a significant life based on an honest recognition of his own being. In renouncing the desire to be God, Kierkegaard acknowledges his guilt as man, Sartre his freedom and responsibility.

Sartre finds that all religious attitudes are in bad faith because they are all based on self-evasion or wishful thinking. His rejection of religion is ontological; that is, religion is not consistent with the condition of man as Sartre sees it. To some extent his objections are in part psychological as well since religious beliefs are, he holds, largely projections of man's wishes and fears. Although it is possible in Sartre's literary works to find veiled references to Christianity, he seems to be concerned with the general aspects of man's relation to God rather than with any specific religion. Even Daniel, while he writes to Mathieu that he is going to enter the Church is never shown to us as an accepted convert. Nor is there a single word referring to specific Church doctrine or to anything other than Daniel's preoccupation with the Eye of God. One might as well be dealing with the primitive belief in the Evil Eye and the practice of wearing a blue bead as a protection against it.

In contrast, Albert Camus in his fiction has presented three clerical representatives of Christianity—the Curé at the end of *The Stranger (L'Étranger)*, the Missionary in a short story called "The Renegade or A Confused Mind" *(Le Renégat ou un esprit confus)*, and Father Paneloux in *The Plague*. Camus is as vehement in his rejection of religion as Sartre but on a less abstract basis. It is the injustice of things which lies at the basis of his refusal. To some extent he would go along with the Marquis de Sade: If one is to postulate God's existence, then human sin is but the answer to divine sin.[6]

Of the three clerics presented, the Curé in *The Stranger* comes closest to being a mere type. His character is scarcely developed, and he appears to serve chiefly as a means of awakening Mersault to an awareness of what he himself believes. The Curé's abstract immortality seems an insult to Mersault both because it is founded on mere wishful thinking and because it denies the earthly happiness which Mersault is about to lose and of which he now for the first time realizes the value. The Curé may be said to be in bad faith because he devalues existence at the same time that he holds out the promise of its being extended. Although the mood is much different, Mersault is like Orestes in that the suggestion of heavenly refuge results in his passionate affirmation of himself as man.

The Missionary in "The Renegade" is much more carefully portrayed. His bad faith resembles the Sartrean variety, though the specific pattern is a little different from any we have met in Sartre. The story employs a technique midway between stream of consciousness and the dramatic monologue. The Missionary is seated alone on a little rocky elevation in the desert. There beneath the blazing sun he awaits with poised rifle the arrival of his replacement, whom he is intending to kill. His tongue has been torn out by his recalcitrant parishioners, but to his half-crazed mind it seems that another tongue is constantly talking, telling the story of his past, commenting on his present watch. Although to the reader the tale is completely horrifying, the Missionary himself has no self-pity and does not look upon his history as a mere story of suffering. Rather it is the account of his transformation from Disciple of Love to Apostle of Hate. As a boy in a gloomy Protestant country in the North, he had heard from a Catholic priest the words, "Catholicism is the sun." Taking the words both literally and figuratively, the boy entered training as a priest, went to Algeria, and requested an assignment among savage natives, salt miners in one of the most isolated parts of the Sahara. Since no Christian worker had ever been able to live among these people, his superiors refused. The Missionary then took off his robes, stole the requisite money from the station's cash box, and went off on his own. The inhabitants of the City of Salt immediately seized him, beat and tortured him, and imprisoned him in the dark dwelling of their fetish-god, whose servant he was forced to become. At first he rejoiced to suffer these humiliations for the God of love, but gradually his attitude changed. He began to pray to the fetish-god, then really to worship him and to kiss—with sincerity—the hands of his captors. One day he overheard French soldiers outside his prison; he learned that a military garrison was to be set up outside the town and that another priest was to come, a chaplain to look after the children. This news plunged the Missionary in despair. He managed to escape and to steal a rifle. Now he watches for the priest's arrival and kills him. Suddenly the first person narrative breaks in the middle of a sentence. And we are told "A handful of salt fills the mouth of the garrulous slave." His masters have followed him and killed him, probably having deliberately allowed him to shoot the new priest first.[7]

The transformation in the Missionary is carefully anticipated by Camus in such a way that we do not have one of those sudden new choices of being which occur so often in Sartre but rather a consistent characterization of such a kind that the Missionary at the end is still the same man, not really changed but reacting appropriately to his altered circumstances. At all times he is a man who worships power. He wants to dominate others but always against a background of authority which guarantees his actions. Thus he seeks an Absolute as much as Daniel does. But he is also a symbol of the person who uses religion as a way of self-aggrandizement. His defiance of Church authorities in Algeria and his escape from the natives do not constitute an exception. In each case, there is a limited defiance in the name of a higher authority—the perfect blend, in fact, of that desire for self-assertion and need for self-abasement which constitutes the peculiar quality of the Missionary's character.

Looking at the Missionary's history, we can see how from the beginning he manifested the martyr's arrogant humility. He turned to the Catholic Church although he lived in a Protestant community, thus bulwarking himself with stricter authority and satisfying his wish to win distinction by doing what is difficult. His dreams of missionary work were pure thirst for power. He was determined to go where nobody else had dared or been able to go, and he would succeed because "they didn't have faith and I had it." He expected insults but dreamed that by his way of submitting to these insults he would subdue those who reviled him. He would be like "a powerful sun."

> Powerful. Yes, that was the word which I continually rolled over my tongue. I dreamed of absolute power which brings the world to its knees, which forces the adversary to surrender, which at last converts him. And the more the adversary is blind, cruel, sure of himself, and entrenched in his own conviction, the more his capitulation proclaims the royalty of the one who has brought about his defeat (p. 50).

The Missionary longs to "rule by the word alone" over an army of the wicked. The use of the word as a symbol anticipates, of course, the Missionary's defeat on the day when his tongue is torn out.

In view of his worship of power, the apostasy of the Missionary is inevitable. It is notable that when he is arrested by his captors, there is a brief moment when one feels that the outcome might have been otherwise. There is a period during which they merely look at him and he at them (an exemplification actually of the Sartrean Look). It is the Missionary who breaks. He looks away and weeps, and it is then that they contemptuously punish him. From the moment that he has seen that humility will not win over the enemy, the Missionary not only is forced to be a slave but thinks of himself as a slave. Almost from the start he feels that his God of love has been proved the weaker and he is ready to shift allegiance to the deity of hate. It is still power that he worships, and he even regains a mocking semblance of his old career; for he willingly becomes the careful, jealous servant of the fetish-god. The Missionary is possessed by the new god in a way that he had never been by the God of love. This is because he realizes that only Evil can reign absolutely. In a regime based on Good there is inevitably compromise; the very act of being a beneficent ruler is in itself partly evil, for it is a violation of the subjects' freedom. "There are no good masters." The rule of power and evil is without limits. The Missionary achieves a kind of happiness in his dark prison and regrets his lost tongue chiefly because he wishes that he might use it to further the reign of Evil through falsehoods.

When he hears of the coming of the new priest, the Missionary feels that he must destroy him for two reasons. One is the desire to allow no hindrance to the complete supremacy of Evil. In addition he resents the ease with which the Curé will be able to enter the village safely and pursue his work. This is, of course, jealousy of the most petty sort, but the Missionary feels no need to justify himself. In the religion of hate there is room for petty spite as well as crime.

Yet when he has shot the new arrival, the Missionary is tortured by doubt. Having taken the decisive step, he needs the assurance of his new god that he has done rightly. But Evil can give no comfort and no pardon. In parody of the Christian passion he cries out, "O Fetish, why have you forsaken me?" He dies in anguish, remembering too late his sense of fraternity with men. With his last words he implores the fetish to change with him, to become good and join with the Missionary in rebuilding "the city of mercy."

"The Renegade" as a study of bad faith is not out of harmony with those works of Sartre's which we have been examining. Quite different is Camus' treatment of the Jesuit Father Paneloux in *The Plague*. Father Paneloux is a man of strong intellectual convictions who has attained considerable distinction for his research on St. Augustine and the history of the Church in Africa. During the first month of the plague the Church authorities organize a week of prayer and ask Father Paneloux to preach the Sunday sermon. What he says is dramatic and uncompromising. Beginning with the words, "My brothers, disaster has struck you and, my brothers, you have deserved it," he goes on to say that the plague is both a punishment for sin and a discipline to lead them to God. Let the people accept the rebuke and heed the warning. Then let them be comforted. If they will but offer to Heaven a prayer of love, God will see to all the rest (p. 111).

Individuals in the audience vary in their reaction to these words. The Judge finds it "absolutely irrefutable." Others take a Kafka-like view that they seem to be sentenced for an unknown crime to an indeterminate imprisonment. During the interval between this sermon and one which the Jesuit gives late in the course of the plague many things happen to change both the priest and his parishioners. There is a general turning from religion to superstition. Church attendance falls off, but the sale of healing medals and all kinds of old and newly invented prophesies skyrockets. People seem not much interested in learning why the plague has come or what their fate in the next world will be; on the other hand they are feverishly anxious to find something tangible which they can do to insure their survival now or at least give them knowledge of how long the plague will last. As for Father Paneloux, he gives up his historical research and joins the corps of Sanitation Workers. That his work is influencing his spiritual views is shown when he remarks to the doctor that he is writing an essay on the subject, "Ought a Priest to Consult a Physician?" One day he joins the doctor in witnessing the long death-struggle of a child. At the end Paneloux observes that such a death moves one to revolt because it is beyond human understanding. He adds, "But perhaps we ought to love what we cannot understand." Dr. Rieux replies, "No, Father. I have a different view of love. And I shall refuse until I die to love this creation in which children are tortured" (p. 240). Soon afterwards Father Paneloux invites Dr. Rieux to come to hear another of his sermons.

The second sermon does not take back all that was in the first. But it is a different man who preaches it. Father Paneloux now says "we" instead of "you." There is tenderness and searching instead of passionate conviction. He is still convinced, he says, that in this world all things are designed ultimately for the good of Christ's people. But this is not an easy truth to accept. When faced with the death of a child, he is not sure that it is enough to say that heavenly delights will be compensation to the child for his suffering here. Who can say that an eternity of joy can compensate for one instant of human grief? Paneloux goes on to say that at certain times God lays extreme commands upon his people. One must contemplate the problem honestly. The suffering of one child is a horrifying fact. But one must accept all or deny all. "The suffering of children is our bitter bread, but without this bread our soul would perish from its spiritual hunger" (p. 248). Whatever is shown to be God's will, this we ourselves must will. There is no middle way. We must wholly love God or hate him. Father Paneloux concludes by showing that the Church's ministers of God must go all the way in sharing the afflictions which God has sent. After hearing this Kierkegaardian Either-Or, Dr. Rieux reported the sermon to his friend Tarrou, who tried in his own life to prove that one could live the life of a saint without God. Tarrou said that Father Paneloux was right, and he referred to a priest he had known who had lost his faith during the war as the result of seeing a young man with both eyes blinded. " 'Paneloux is right. When an innocent man loses both his eyes, a Christian must either lose his faith or consent to lose his own eyes' " (pp. 251-252).

In the days following, Paneloux showed that he had not lost faith. He went quietly about his work and then one day fell ill. He refused to let a doctor be called until he was too weak to protest. Although he died of what seemed to be the plague, the symptoms were not right. His name was entered in the registry as "a doubtful case." The implication obviously is that he had willed to die to demonstrate his complete acceptance of God's will.

Camus has called *The Plague* the most un-Christian of his books. His reason must surely be because of the events themselves. It is certainly not because of the bad faith of any Christian character. Father Paneloux dies to prove his good faith. The book seems to show that the totally committed Christian is closer to the humanistic existentialist than either is to the Easter Sunday Christian. In religion the extremes seem to be closer to each other than to the mean.

## Bad Faith in Human Relations

In *The Childhood of a Boss* we have seen already the outline of what will constitute bad faith in human relations. Lucien uses people in two ways, neither of them justifiable. In general he employs others to provide him with an image of himself so that he may escape the responsibility of deciding on his own what he will be and what he will choose to make of his life. This aspect of his relation to others is essentially a denial of his own freedom, an attempt to see himself as an object instead of as a free subjectivity. But the consequence of this most fundamental position is that the image of himself which Lucien accepts is such that he must use *certain* other people as though they were only objects for his subjectivity. He thinks of them as things by which he may attain the realization of his own absolute Being. Thus in hate he uses the Jews to make himself a person to be reckoned with in the eyes of his friends. He is a man of conviction, "the one who hates Jews." In indifference he uses his father's employees to support his economic position, to endow him with "rights." In love (or what seems to him to be love) he plans to possess the woman who as his wife will make him the center of her existence and so justify Lucien's.

It is not doing violence to existentialism to say that it still retains Kant's categorical imperative as the basic ideal of human relationships—treat the Other always as an end and never as a means only. But the existentialist seems to be more acutely aware than Kant that most situations demand that someone be treated as a means or else there would be no ends for anyone. Moreover, they have enriched Kant's formulation by the addition of their own interpretation of Hegel's Master-Slave relation between consciousnesses.

For our study of bad faith in human relations we are fortunate in having both Sartre's formal analysis in *Being and Nothingness* and de Beauvoir's *She Came to Stay (L'Invitée),* a novel which follows so closely the pattern outlined by Sartre that it serves almost as a textbook illustration. In dealing with Sartre's discussion we must keep one fact in mind: In reading his analysis it seems that he is putting the whole realm of human relations in bad faith, but this is not actually true. At the beginning of his treatment of "concrete relations with others" he states that all relations with other people are based on conflict. He concludes by saying that there is no escape from a circle in which one is tossed back and forth between two unsatisfactory positions. Yet at the very end we are brought up short by a footnote saying, "These considerations do not exclude the possibility of an ethics of deliverance and salvation. But this can be achieved only after a radical conversion which we cannot discuss here" (p. 412). We have encountered a similar situation already in our study of Sartre's religious views. The whole of *Being and Nothingness* is designed to show that man's basic tendency and most of his projects are guided by the false ideal of realizing a missing God, that man is a useless passion. But this does not prevent Sartre from presenting to us characters like Orestes and Goetz who go on to live by a purely human ethics. And Sartre says at the end of *Being and Nothingness* that he will in the future investigate the possibility of an ethics not based on the search for an in-itself-for-itself. If then we take the whole of Sartre's analysis (in *Being and Nothingness*) of human relations to be in itself a study of bad faith, this is undoubtedly what Sartre intends us to do. But it does not mean that Sartre believes that human relations must always be as he has portrayed them.

We may recall first the basic structure upon which Sartre's discussion is based. I may encounter the Other first as another "center of reference." Whatever may be the geographical or mathematical organization of space, my private world is one in which objects and distances are always experienced in relation to me. If I am sitting on a park bench, the path represents so many paces between me and the fountain, the statue at the far side of the lawn marks the point at which objects merge into a background for my field of clear vision, a certain tree is the apex of a triangle for which I and an ice-cream wagon form the other two angles, etc. But if a stranger whom I had been including as part of the general background suddenly stirs on his bench and looks at me, then

I am aware that objects are not fixed within my own organization of the world. There is another center of reference, and to the extent that I feel myself a part of the Other's subjective organization of the landscape, my world suffers from a sort of "internal hemorrhage"; it "bleeds in the direction of the stranger." This sudden transformation from absolute subject to complete object is more strikingly exemplified in the keyhole episode where the watcher becomes unexpectedly and shamefully the watched.

What is revealed in these experiences is the in-itself aspect of the for-itself. This is no contradiction. The for-itself can never be other than for-itself in its own eyes. But because of our bodies and because our presence to others must be made manifest through objects in the world (through the space we occupy or the gestures we make or the sound vibrations we send through the air or the words we write), we are external to the mind of the Other and so—for him and in a very special sense—a part of the In-itself. This in-itself side of ourselves is what Sartre calls the self-for-others. We discussed the concept in connection with Lucien, especially in the passage where he realized that to others he was a "beanpole" and tried in vain to see himself as one. Naturally we can never fully grasp this self-for-others, for it exists only in the mind of an Other. We can, however, through the power of the imagination understand something of what he sees, and we can strive to influence his concept either by looking into ourselves and trying to make ourselves appear to be one kind of object rather than another or else by making the Other so conscious of his object-state that his self-for-me takes precedence over my self-for-him.

Limiting ourselves to *Being and Nothingness,* we find that in my relations with others I either seek in some way to destroy them because they threaten me, or I seek to escape from myself and my problems by making others take over responsibility for my existence. Throughout the infinite varieties and combinations of emotional relationships which are possible between me and the Other, I embrace either or (alternately) both of two procedures: I try to modify my own subjectivity by making myself an object before the Other, or I try to guarantee my subjectivity as the only one by making him wholly an object before me. Since each attitude bears within it the seeds of its own failure and collapses into the other, we are involved in a frustrating circle, and it does not really matter where we begin. Hence we may as well start as Sartre does with love. Our journey into hate will thus seem more in keeping with the general pessimism of Sartre's discussion.

The first attitude—that in which I exploit my possibilities as an object—may be lived as love or as masochism. In love one wants illogically to absorb the Other while still preserving within him his "otherness," to possess his freedom as freedom, to delimit his free determination. Although this may sound like an assertion of the lover as Subject, this is not really the case. For the subjectivity of the beloved must be preserved at all cost, and this means that the lover's attempt will be to force the beloved to choose him as an all-absorbing object. Sartre points out that the lover's method (though not his goal) is the same as that of the seducer. He seeks to make himself so fascinating an object that the beloved is trapped by the intensity of his own contemplation. He is seduced into choosing, and yet he remains the one who has chosen. In spite of Sartre's insistence to the contrary, I cannot help feeling that there is a kind of compromise here in the subject-object relation, at least an armistice or armed truce as opposed to actual conflict. As Sartre himself says, a reciprocated love gives to the lover a release from the fear of being made simply an instrument for the Other or a means to an end. And the beloved in turn is not forced to accept him as a fascinating object. But to return to Sartre's analysis, love is essentially the desire to be loved. When I love, I desire that the beloved will make me the limit, the horizon, so to speak, of his life. This is in a sense an assault both on his freedom and on mine. For while I want him to do so of his own free will, still I am trying to force upon him a system of values such that my own value is secure. This, says Sartre, is the reason for the many passages in novels in which a woman will test a man to see if he would steal or kill for her; she wants him to prove that no morality is binding if it does not place the lover at the center of things. The lover wants to be the necessary intermediary between the beloved and the world so that objects will appear cloaked with the feeling which love has inspired. At the same time the lover wants to have his own existence justified, and this means that the beloved must be free. Yet the lover dares not think of the beloved's choice as being like any other choice, easily made and easily revoked. The result is that familiar mixture of fatalism and freedom by which those in love claim both to be "made for each other" and to be freely re-creating their love with each new repetition of the words, "I love you."

In being loved the lover feels that his existence is no longer *de trop,* that in being essential to the beloved he is essential absolutely. Now to D. H. Lawrence and to Aristophanes in Plato's *Symposium* this kind of mutual fulfillment is both possible and desirable. But Sartre finds that it is doomed to failure on three counts. First, the formula itself involves an infinite regress; if I want the Other to love me, this means that I want the Other to want me to love him, etc. It seems doubtful that the philosophical implications here actually disturb many lovers very deeply. On the other hand, Sartre is right in saying that it is impossible actually to make another responsible for one's own subjective being. And to the degree to which the ideal is approximated by one of the pair, the relation is destructive to the personality of the other. It is this type of self-evasion through emotional dependency which de Beauvoir was attacking in her portrait of Hélène. Absorption of one partner by another impairs both; for the dependent one lives in bad faith, choosing never to develop the free possibilities which are his (it is usually *hers*), and the dominating partner can no longer derive from the other anything more than what has been put there by himself. That each one could be equally responsible for the other's being seems to Sartre a self-contradiction and an impossibility. Probably it is. A relation in which each partner is actually enabled to find self-fulfillment would seem of necessity to be founded on the recognition that each one must work out his self-realization on the lines which he freely chooses. This is not to make another the source of one's existence but quite the opposite, and it is not a structure of bad faith. Whether it precludes the necessity of the Other is another question. We shall return to this.

Sartre's second reason for the failure of love is that the beloved may suddenly make of the lover an object of the wrong sort. The lover wants to have his being secured, but he wants it to remain free. If he suddenly finds that the beloved is after all using him as a means to an end, he has lost. Actually the lover's goal is essentially the same as the elusive being-in-itself-for-itself which we meet elsewhere in Sartre's philosophy. He wants to be free and yet to make the Other provide a meaning for that freedom.

Finally, Sartre claims that even if the lover and the beloved succeed in approximating a relation of mutual justification, the balance is always shattered before the Look of a Third who transforms both into objects and so destroys all chance for either to be justifying subject for the Other. This, says Sartre, is why lovers like to be alone! This third failure is the theme of *No Exit*. In less abstract form it has been the *leitmotif* of a host of other works of fiction depicting the impossibility of a life lived only for love. Most illustrative is Dante's treatment of Paolo and Francesca in *The Inferno*. Or there come immediately to mind the lovers in Faulkner's *The Wild Palms,* in Tolstoi's *Anna Karenina,* in Rolland's *Jean Christophe.*

It is easy to see how love thus defined bears within it the seeds of masochism. If instead of using my being-as-object in order to fascinate the Other's freedom, I myself become fascinated by my object-state and no longer demand that the Other make me the limit of his freedom, then my attitude is wholly masochistic. Masochism is "a species of vertigo, vertigo not before a precipice of rock and earth but before the abyss of the Other's subjectivity" (p. 378). In order to be assured that he is wholly determined in his being and nothing but object, the masochist must be treated by the other as a thing. Hence he demands pain and suffering, for these are things which one would never—in good faith—choose save perhaps as a means to a satisfying end. But the end set up by the masochist is a spurious one. At best he gets a relative pleasure stemming from relief at not being forced to confront his total situation honestly. Masochism too fails. One *is* not an object and can never quite avoid having at least an unreflective realization of the fact. Moreover, if a person *lets* another humiliate and torture him, his subjectivity is—in the very permission—asserting itself and cannot be denied. If one can continue in the masochistic attitude, it is because at last one grows to love even the inherent failure. Like any "will to fail," masochism demands that a person deceive himself into thinking that he wants the opposite of what he strives to get. Hence masochism can never provide more than compensatory satisfaction, and it is forever in bad faith.

Masochism and love are linked in that both depend on maintaining the Other as a free subject. The second attitude toward others consists in trying to deny or to destroy the Other as subject and make him wholly object. Sartre considers indifference, desire, sadism, and hate as manifestations of this approach.

In indifference we simply pretend that people have *only* that quality of being-in-itself with which we come in touch directly. Despite all evidence to the contrary, we act as if they were not other centers of reference, as if they had no life except that which they exhibit when serving as the material, so to speak, out of which we fashion our own experience. To some extent a certain amount of indifference, of identifying people with their functions is inevitable. One cannot in more than a superficial sense establish a personal relation with every tradesman who serves one, with every boy who delivers a telegram, with each person who walks on the same sidewalk. But indifference as a fundamental life-attitude involves exaggerating the confusion of person and function to the point where almost every Other is simply part of one's own life-furnishings. Sometimes this indifference is disguised and may pass for a highly scientific theory of human relationships, but it is a technique for dealing with people as if they were mechanisms. In this connection Sartre refers to seventeenth- and eighteenth-century French writings on ambition and ways of achieving success. He might well have mentioned Carnegie's *How to Win Friends and Influence People* and the flood of comparable works which succeeded it. Indifference toward others is not only a dishonest attitude; it is also, Sartre says, a dangerous one. It is dangerous because it means that I am defenseless before the Other's Look, which cannot be annihilated simply by my pretending it is not there. At any moment he may suddenly catch me unaware and force me to realize my object-state before his subjectivity. Moreover, my implicit realization that I am pretending causes me to be anxious. I am thrown back even more forcibly upon myself to justify my own being. Finally my refusal to see the Other as he really is blunts my ability to make practical use of him. One thing Sartre does not say which it seems that he might have added: My refusal to see the Other as a subject means that I must surely fail to realize many of my own potentialities. The horizons of my life are infinitely shrunken. Indifference, of course, is not an attitude which can wholly succeed even within its own limited terms. One can never really escape the Other's Look. But as Sartre says in an almost poetic passage,

> This state of *blindness* can be maintained for a long time, as long as my fundamental bad faith desires; it can be extended— with relapses—over several years, over a whole life; there are men who die without—save for brief and terrifying flashes of illumination—ever having suspected what the *Other* is (p. 381).

Indifference is the pretense that the Other is only an object. There are other attitudes which recognize the Other's subjectivity but aim at capturing or destroying it. The most basic of these is sexual desire. Sartre takes the rather surprising position that sexuality is explained as an ontological structure of human beings rather than as a psycho-physiological one. Reminding us of the existence of desire in persons whose sex organs cannot provide fulfillment (children, eunuchs, the very old), Sartre claims that sexuality is a fundamental characteristic of a person in a world where there are others and that it does not depend upon sex organs. On the contrary, it is desire which reveals to the human being that he is sexed. This may be true if we go on the premise that a person has sex to be revealed, though I cannot see how the for-itself could feel sexual desire if there were no special physiological structure to serve as a medium. In desire, Sartre says, consciousness deliberately lets itself be troubled. It deliberately makes itself body. The desiring consciousness tries by making itself flesh to incarnate the consciousness of the Other.* It is still the Other's freedom which he wants to capture, but "Since I can grasp the Other only in his objective facticity, the problem is to ensnare his freedom within this facticity. He must be 'caught' in it as the cream is caught up by a person skimming milk" (p. 394). The true fulfillment of desire is not coitus but the caress, by which desire is expressed as language is by thought and "the full pressing together of the flesh of two people against each other" (p. 396). At this point there is a certain reciprocity of consciousnesses, for each one by willing its own incarnation has elicited the incarnation of the other. But once again the harmony is fleeting, and the relation established by desire collapses. If coitus is achieved, desire's fulfillment is also its limit and its death. It has failed in its object, for what it possesses is only a body, not the other's subjective consciousness. Moreover, pleasure is likely to introduce a reflective consciousness which soon becomes preoccupied with only its own consciousness. Then the other becomes too much or too little an object. If one forgets the other and becomes absorbed in the pleasure of *being* caressed, then desire leads to that embracing of the object-state which we encountered in masochism. If, on the other hand, one wants to remain sole subject and concentrates exclusively on *taking* his pleasure, which means making the other wholly an object, then desire leads into sadism. "Sadism and masochism are the two reefs on which desire may founder" (p. 404).

The aim of sadism is to use the Other as an object but as a particular type of object, one which is an incarnation of a captured freedom. It differs from desire in that desire seeks to enchant the Other's freedom by a mutual incarnation. In sadism the mutuality is lost even as an ideal. The sadist wishes to remain wholly a subjective consciousness while forcing his victim to reduce himself to pure flesh-object. His wish is to incarnate the Other through violence. He wants to possess the Other's flesh but at the same time retain the illusion of not being flesh himself. To accomplish his aim the sadist will employ physical and psychic pain, and he will introduce the category of the obscene. The function of pain

---

* "Incarnate" is used with its literal meaning of "putting into flesh."

is obvious. It signifies that the victim has been forced by another consciousness to experience what he himself would not have chosen; pain seems to annihilate the victim's freedom. The question of the obscene is a little different. Blasphemy or ridicule of what the victim holds sacred is part of the sadist's desire to inflict pain. But for the meaning of the obscene, Sartre provides a particular and interesting interpretation. We can best understand the obscene by contrasting it with its opposite, "grace." When the Other performs a graceful act, he appears to me as a harmonious blend of finely perfected body and governing consciousness. The body, like a precision instrument, is perfectly adapted to the task it performs and suggests a neat inevitability. But the psychic element is there too, the psychic which "for others is the unpredictable object." In the graceful act the flesh is, as it were, clothed by the act it is performing. The graceful person makes his body seem more than body in the very act by which he displays his body to us. The obscene enters in when the body is revealed to us as wholly a thing of flesh, stripped of the acts which give it meaning. The obscene is our apprehension of inert, unsignifying flesh when we are not in a state of desire for that flesh. Sartre explains in amusing fashion that it is not mere nakedness which is obscene but a particular situation.

> The sight of a naked body from behind is not obscene. But certain involuntary waddlings of the rump are obscene. This is because then it is only the legs which are acting for the walker, and the rump is like an isolated cushion which is carried by the legs and the balancing of which is a pure obedience to the laws of weight. It cannot be justified by the situation; on the contrary, it is entirely destructive of any situation since it has the passivity of a thing and since it is made to rest like a thing upon the legs. Suddenly it is revealed as an unjustifiable facticity; it is *de trop* like every contingent (p. 401).

The sadist by inflicting pain and by forcing the victim to assume obscene positions shows that the victim's body is to the sadist a thing or instrument like any other object. But his victory is not assured until the victim himself acknowledges that he is nothing but obscene flesh. The sadist's moment of triumph comes at the point at which the victim denies what he has felt to be most essentially himself and begs for mercy for the tortured flesh. And at this same moment the sadist realizes his failure. For he has not actually captured a freedom. What he has there groveling before him is nothing more than a body. It is not an end in itself nor does it point to any further end. Furthermore, the Look of the victim is something which the sadist cannot kill. It torments him with the realization that he has not only failed to catch the Other's freedom *qua* freedom but that he himself is not protected from being made an object before the Look of the victim who judges him. This is why the sadistic officials in Sartre's play *The Victors (Morts sans sepulture)* feel that they have to kill the captured Underground workers even though the officials believe (mistakenly) that they have got all the requisite information from them by torture. The torturers' knowledge of what they have been in the eyes of the victims is something which they feel that they must wipe out at all cost.

The failure of sadism can lead to only one other attitude—hate. In despair at the impossibility of any satisfying relation with the Other, I may long to get rid of him completely. Hate is the wish for the Other's death. It may arise at any moment when I feel that I have been made irremediably subject to the Other's freedom. What I hate is the Other's very existence. Hence hate is a total passion, quite different from contempt or disapproval, which are directed more toward specific actions or character traits. Sartre goes on to say that hate of a particular Other is in reality hate of all others. If I cannot tolerate the sense of being an object before one Other, this is because I cannot stand the thought of any factual limit to my freedom. Symbolically I will the death of all others when I wish it for one. It is easy to see that hate too is inevitably frustrated. Even if we regard the death wish as one which would be satisfied by symbolic fulfillment, still I cannot annihilate all Others or even one Other. If I were actually to kill the one I hate, I could not thereby kill his Look. For the memory of the Look which has been there will haunt me all my days and alienate my freedom from me. I can never see myself except as having been the object of a particular judgement passed upon me.

As I pointed out earlier, Sartre has surreptitiously weighted the scales in this discussion of circularity by choosing a procedure in which he begins with love and ends with hate. But even if he had progressed from hate to love, we would not be much better off. The circle of human relations is as unstable as the ball on which the Greco-Roman goddess Fortune used to stand. By the very process of assuming a position upon it, one turns it.

This emotional labyrinth is all faithfully illustrated for us in Simone de Beauvoir's novel, *She Came to Stay*. Although this book and *Being* *and Nothingness* were published in the same year (1943), the similarity between them is too striking to be coincidence. As with all of de Beauvoir's early fiction, the reader of *She Came to Stay* feels that the inspiration of the book was simply de Beauvoir's decision to show how Sartre's abstract principles could be made to work out in "real life." * This is not to say that the novel has no merit in its own right. De Beauvoir is skillful in portraying emotional moods, and she has considerable ability in delineating character, especially in whatever fictional personality she has chosen to represent herself. But she is not yet the novelist of *The Mandarins.* The basic problem is handled more like a *quod erat demonstrandum* than a life situation, and the analysis of human relationships and personalities is more philosophical than psychological. Perhaps de Beauvior and her fictional counterpart are accustomed to think in this way about themselves and their reactions, but most people are not so metaphysically articulate.

On the frontispiece de Beauvoir gives us the theme of the novel—the same quotation from Hegel which Sartre had used as the basis of his discussion of Being-for-Others: "Each consciousness pursues the death of the other." As in *No Exit* we have a triangle consisting of a man and two women. They are Pierre, writer, director, actor, and—quite evidently —an early version of Jean-Paul Sartre; Françoise, who is clearly Simone de Beauvoir and hardly to be distinguished from Anne in *The Mandarins,* and Xavière. Who is the original of Xavière, I do not know. But there must have been an original, for Ivich in *The Age of Reason,* which appeared two years later, is obviously Sartre's portrayal of the same girl. Both Ivich and Xavière have long golden hair which they generally allow to fall over the face (apparently de Beauvoir liked the hair style and Sartre did not); both girls are selfish, egocentric, gratuitously disagreeable. Both—without being actually homesexual—like to appraise other women's sexual attractions. Both are mad about dancing and have an odd habit of ordering and drinking cocktails which they do not like. It is possible that the model for Xavière and Ivich was the Olga Kosakievicz to whom both books are dedicated. I am inclined to hope not.

Besides Pierre, Françoise, and Xavière, there are two other important characters in *She Came to Stay.* Of these one is Elizabeth, Pierre's sister,

---

* I do not at all preclude the possibility that de Beauvoir has contributed to the formation of Sartre's philosophy. I suspect that his debt to her is considerable. All I mean in the present instance is that the novel serves as documentation for the theory, regardless of who had which idea first.

who, chiefly from jealousy at the happy self-absorption of the other three, urges a young actor, Gerbert, to try his luck with Xavière. Gerbert's success not only destroys the self-containment of the original trio but sets up another triangle impinging upon the first. He and Françoise had always felt a certain attraction toward one another. When they finally go on a hiking trip together, their relation does not seem to bother Pierre but is disastrous in the eyes of Xavière.

Xavière is unquestionably the apex of the first triangle. But it is not a triangle of the usual sort. Pierre and Francoise have for almost ten years maintained a relation which we are obviously meant to take as a reciprocal love in good faith. They are not married and they do not maintain a common household. But they sleep together, work together, and believe with all the fervor of pre-existentialist romances that they are united by a firm bond for the rest of their lives. Each means that the other shall be entirely free. Pierre occasionally makes use of his freedom for a light affair with other women. Françoise cannot bring herself to behave in similar fashion but feels in no way threatened by such conduct on the part of Pierre. It seems quite clear that de Beauvoir intends this relationship to serve as a model of love in good faith against which is played the conflict of love in bad faith initiated when Xavière, a little girl from the provinces, comes on a visit to Paris.

Relations at the beginning are on the plane of indifference. Francoise enjoys showing Paris to the provincial, feels vaguely sorry that Xavière must return to her dreary existence at home. When Pierre proposes that Françoise might suggest to Xavière that she come to live in Paris, that they might support her until she could shift for herself, Françoise is mildly disturbed at the prospect of complicating her life, but agrees. Then as she persuades Xavière to come, Françoise herself becomes enthusiastic. But she has not actually ceased to be indifferent, for what she envisions is a picture of herself moulding Xavière's life into the image of what she thinks it ought to be. She does not see Xavière as a self-determining subject or as an Other who might in any way affect Françoise's life. She is but the material for one of Françoise's projects.

Xavière accepts the invitation. There is a bit of friction from the beginning, for Françoise finds that Xavière is not content merely to share Françoise's leisure time. That there is an actual problem becomes evident when the two women spend an evening with Pierre. Pierre takes Xavière's immature pronouncements seriously. What had seemed to Françoise selfish irritability takes on for Pierre a fascinating quality of pure emotional intensity. Horrified, she seems to see Xavière changing shape, ceasing to be a harmless sulky child and advancing in heavy menace.

> Françoise tried with all her strength to push back this precious and encumbering Xavière who had just been revealed; it was almost hostility which she felt within her. But there was nothing to do, no way of going back. Xavière existed (p. 69).

Xavière's emergence as a subject threatens Françoise in two ways. In the first place she forces Françoise to become aware in a new way of her self-for-others and to see her whole life in a different and dubious light. Françoise had developed through her relation with Pierre and her work a quiet contentment. She assumed that one pursued happiness; she had developed a routine to guarantee its future. She lived by a code based on complete honesty toward herself and others. While she was not unaware of a certain complacency in her outlook, nevertheless she tried to make her way of living a base of support for such changes as might come rather than an ironclad "adjustment." It seemed that one could do no more. Xavière challenged all this. By scorning Françoise's work program as a regimented "living by bells," by declaring that she hated intellectual discipline and purity, by expressing contempt for the desire to find happiness in life, she thrust upon Françoise a view of her life as being nothing but a dull subservience to the demands of the Serious World, and of herself as a combination of awkward prudery and pedantry. Although Françoise had always known, as an existentialist heroine should, that values are chosen and created, nevertheless the violent confrontation with those of Xavière seemed to undermine her own, to alter and transform them. She might refuse to accept Xavière's, but she could not close her eyes to their existence.

The second threat is to Françoise's relation to Pierre. In part this is simply the Sartrean disintegration of a dual relation under the Look of a Third. Before Xavière's lofty disdain of human bonds, their mutual dependency begins to appear ridiculous. More seriously, Françoise is forcibly reminded that she and Pierre had not really been one. Although they had scrupulously respected each other's freedom, still Françoise, at least, had come to believe that they not only shared all experiences with each other but that either one could penetrate to the unspoken thought of the other. Now the difference in their evaluation of Xavière makes her see Pierre as an opaque being with whom she can no longer feel an absolute unity. A little later there inevitably arises the question as to whether either one can achieve any significant relation with Xavière without excluding the other.

Rather cold-bloodedly the two of them discuss the situation, or rather the possibility of there being a situation. Pierre inquires first whether Françoise, having discovered Xavière, would not prefer to remain the most important person in her life. Later he puts the question on another basis. Would Françoise feel that a personal bond between him and Xavière was any threat to their own relation? In each instance Françoise declines to stand in the way, though not without some misgiving. Once all have abandoned the pretense of indifference, once Xavière's being-as-subject has been recognized, the problem arises as to whether all three parties can remain subjects or whether inevitably one or more must be reduced to objects. The action develops through three stages.

During the first part where there is conflict without even a temporary resolution, the novel comes closest to following the conventional treatment of the triangle. Françoise's relation with Xavière is not primary, though she feels an occasional pang of disappointment at the thought that Pierre is becoming more important to Xavière than she had been. But the real question is whether Xavière is threatening Françoise's position in Pierre's life. From the beginning it is clear that any relation between Pierre and Xavière will not be the light sexual affair which he has had with other women. Although he explains his interest by saying that he cannot resist the idea of making a conquest and that it is always the beginning of an affair which fascinates him, yet it is plain to him as well as to Françoise that Xavière is not to be conquered without demanding a commitment in return. De Beauvoir is careful to tell us that Françoise is not at any time jealous of Xavière. But it is a little difficult to classify her reactions if they are not jealousy. She observes the difference between Pierre's gravely polite attention to what she says and his eager look toward Xavière. She feels that they have come to take each other for granted, that their love is growing stale. When she tries to discuss the matter with him, he is a little impatient. He feels that their love is beyond question and needs no constant reaffirmation. Nevertheless he offers to give up all thought of Xavière if this will reassure Françoise. But faced with this possibility she refuses. She does not want a love based on the refusal to accept the truth of Xavière's existence. She insists on their continuing in the same way and faces the inevitable risk, not with resignation, but with "an impersonal curiosity so violent that it had all the warmth of joy." Her fears are soon realized. Pierre begins to show signs of accepting Xavière's values. He seems to encourage her in irresponsible evasions of duty. Françoise feels that her attempts to make them think of a future for Xavière result only in spoiling their pleasure and making herself hateful in her own eyes. On a lonely midnight walk she realizes that she had allowed herself to become somewhat lost in Pierre. She could use only "our" with respect to the future. Pierre quite obviously could still say "my." She feels utterly abandoned, isolated even from herself. At this point, quite understandably (since the other two had prevented her from either working or sleeping), she comes down with pneumonia.

Françoise's stay in the hospital somehow solves the problem of her relation to Pierre. His devotion and his passionate anxiety convince her finally that her relation to him is secure. Stage One is ended. But the conflict resumes. And now it is openly a struggle for Xavière. The lines are laid down before Françoise is even ready to leave the hospital. During her illness the other two had apparently concentrated wholly on serving her. But at noon on almost the first day of her convalescence, they come in together to tell her that they had decided that they were in love with each other. Françoise is disturbed. "She was not jealous of him, but that silky little golden girl whom she had adopted early one acid morning—Françoise was not giving *her* up without a struggle" (p. 209). Pierre had inadvertently given her an opening. Xavière had consented the night before to telling Françoise that she and Pierre had decided they loved each other, but she turns sullen when he actually begins to discuss their relation and leaves in a fit of temper. Later with Pierre's consent Françoise tries to pacify Xavière by proposing a three-way relationship.

> "A closely knit couple is already beautiful, but how much richer still are three people who love one another with all their strength."
>
> She hesitated a bit. Now the moment had come to commit herself also and to accept the risk.
>
> "For after all there is, isn't there, a kind of love between you and me?"

Xavière admits to the bond between them, and Françoise continues:

> "You see, if there is also a love between Labrousse and you, that makes a beautiful, perfectly balanced trio. It is not the usual way of living, but I don't believe that it is too difficult for us" (pp. 218-219).

For a time the triangle appears to be equilateral and set firmly on its base. Although to outsiders the mutual absorption of the three seems slightly ridiculous, they seem to themselves to have captured an elusive and precarious happiness. The bonds uniting them are not overtly sexual, though a hidden sexuality is certainly present. De Beauvoir's restraint is not, I think, primarily due to a fear of offending good taste. The real reason is her resolve to document Sartre's statement that, whereas all human relations are implicitly sexual, they do not have sexual intercourse as their specific goal. De Beauvoir gives full weight to both parts of this theory. There is much made of the caress (an occasional chaste kiss or a handclasp), but there is an express denial that Pierre wants to seduce Xavière or that Françoise wants a full homosexual relation. But as both agree that it seems a kind of profanation to think of Xavière as a sexual object, neither can bear the idea of her sleeping with anyone else. Their reasons are somewhat different. Pierre declares that he is not a sensualist. (As a matter of fact, he displays little real passion at any time.) His desire to establish a relation between himself and Xavière is in the beginning based almost wholly on vanity, which has taken the form of the need to dominate. He is interested in Xavière because she offers resistance; he is jealous of anyone else who might attract her because this threatens his own supremacy. Later he becomes the pure embodiment of the Sartrean project of love (love in bad faith, of course). In loving Xavière he wants to *be loved* by her. He wants her to choose him as the center of her existence. Recognizing the intensity of her will to be the subject in any relationship, it will be the supreme conquest if she voluntarily chooses him as the limit of her freedom. This is not the same as reducing her wholly to an object, for in that case she would be no more than the women of his other affairs. (This is another reason for his not wanting the relation to become simply a sexual one.) Pierre must somehow keep Xavière wholly free and yet be assured each day that she is freely entrusting herself to him. It is a relation in bad faith, for in the name of guaranteeing her freedom he is actually trying to ensnare it.

Françoise's position is a little different. In a sense her project is also one of love, for she wants to be important in Xavière's life and she tries to guide and direct Xavière's existence. She acts in tenderness and in good will, but she is nevertheless trying to give shape to Xavière's life. In one sense she is more violently offending Xavière's freedom than is Pierre. During the consultation with Pierre at the hospital, she had taunted Pierre by saying that in his need for assuring himself of Xavière's dependency he would continue to ask for more and end up by sleeping with her. The thought is repugnant to Françoise but not because of sexual jealousy of either one of them. The picture of Xavière which she has cherished is of the little girl from the provinces; Françoise would like to arrest her at that level. She feels that if Xavière should awaken sexually in Pierre's arms she would be like all the other women Pierre had known and no longer Xavière. Yet while this reaction belongs to Françoise-subject, she begins to assume more and more of an object role toward Xavière. Sartre follows Freud in holding that all love is to a certain extent a blend of masochism and sadism—or more accurately it bears within it the seeds of both and almost inevitably collapses into one or the other. Whereas Pierre, whose subjectivity is never really in question, uses Xavière as a test of his own power and hence skirts the edges of sadism, Françoise has more at stake. Already even in her relation with Pierre she came dangerously close to accepting a dependent kind of being. She saw the world through his eyes, waited for him to give the final stamp to any mood or opinion. Even Xavière did not assume real importance until Françoise began to see her as she appeared to Pierre. Françoise had never quite accepted the status of object. In a crisis she could still judge Pierre, though it shocked her to find herself doing so. She never really became masochistic.

True masochism is represented by Pierre's sister. Elizabeth had for years let her life be made almost unbearable by an unsatisfying relation with a married man. For a time she deceived herself into thinking that Claude would break with his wife. Then she realizes that he never will and tries to break away. She is unable to give him up, partly because she cannot resist his physical attraction but mostly because even her unhappy relation to him gives her a kind of justification for her existence which she is unable to find anywhere else. She is pathetic—as well as in bad faith—in that she is neither able to accept an irregular, subordinate position for what it is worth nor to reject it. Like all masochists she prefers to be tormented rather than to face things squarely and enter into a way of life which would necessitate a change in her choice of herself. Rather surprisingly, Françoise and Pierre seem to feel that she is incapable of such adjustment and deliberately try to keep her in bad faith.

Elizabeth's example is influential in preventing Françoise from ever giving in to the temptation to lose herself in Pierre. She is never in real danger of falling into masochism. With respect to Xavière, however, the risk is greater. This is partly because Xavière, unlike Pierre, is not willing to maintain a relation in good faith with Françoise. It is also because the whole relation with Xavière had from the beginning been in bad faith on all sides. While not as domineering as Pierre, Françoise had from her first recognition of Xavière sensed that they were involved in a conflict. The relation was never one of mutual enrichment and growth. As she becomes more closely involved with Xavière, she allows herself to become more and more dependent on her. Her mood for the day is determined by Xavière; the slightest word from her is sufficient to exalt Françoise in happiness or plunge her in misery. More important, Françoise feels herself alienated from her own life. All that she had treasured is made to seem contemptible beneath Xavière's scornful look. Even her own body seems an awkward excrescence which finds no place in Being except when Xavière "makes her dance well" or compliments her on her appearance. Hers is a project of love in which she is almost snared in the object-state with which she has hoped to fascinate Xavière's freedom; it is love on the masochistic side. She is saved from complete reduction only by the habit of reflective thought, which never quite deserts her, and by the fact that the shifting relation among the three of them prevents any subject-object relation from being final.

So far we have seen, in terms consistent with Sartre's analysis, exemplifications of indifference, of two projects of love, and of masochism. In Xavière we see a portrayal, in very delicate terms, of sadism. There was obviously no place in this novel for the torturer-sadist whom Sartre described. Such a description de Beauvoir provided later in her study of the Marquis de Sade.[1] But Xavière is no less a sadist because as her instruments of torture she uses cutting words and a look of helpless appeal. She is the pure form of sadist in that she wants to keep her own subjectivity supreme at all cost. She demands the enslavement of all those with whom she comes in contact, and she makes no commitment in return. For her even generosity is a form of enslavement.* She gives imperiously, not as an expression of tenderness but to assert her own supremacy. She enters into the triangular arrangement with Pierre and Françoise because she sees herself as its apex, which she is for a time. But all the while she is trying to break down the relation between the other two. It is significant that her efforts are directed more toward Pierre. This is in part due to sexual vanity; much as Françoise may try to deny it, Xavière is a passionate woman in spite of her sheltered vir-

---

* In *Being and Nothingness* (pp. 594-595) Sartre discusses generosity as a combination of destruction and enslavement.

ginity. In addition, Xavière realizes that Francoise is more dependent upon her than Pierre is, and she senses that in the relation of the other two, it is Pierre who is more free. Thus by winning him away from Francoise she can prove her power over them both. As with most, if not all, sadists, Xavière sometimes turns toward herself the hostility which she generally manifests toward the world. Her demands upon herself are excessive, and she punishes herself if she does not meet them. Thus, for example, after sentimentally letting herself wear a faded rose given her on the night before, she not only suddenly resolves to destroy the rose but takes a cigarette and with deep, voluptuous pleasure burns a deep hole in her hand.* Mostly, though, she worships her own subjectivity and transfers allegiance back and forth between Françoise and Pierre, playing one against the other in an endeavor to use both of them for her own ends.

De Beauvoir's analysis of the emotional fluctuations of her trio is brilliant. It is done largely from Francoise's point of view. On the whole, the occasional moments of happiness she finds alone with Pierre or with Xavière are not enough to make up for the friction when all three are together—even during the weeks when she still has hope that the trio may achieve a satisfactory *modus vivendi*. She suffers alternately for Pierre and for Xavière as they hurt each other in their struggle for dominance, and she is miserable when a temporary reciprocity between them seems to shut her out. When Pierre suggests that they might all go on a holiday together, a vacation she had expected to spend with Pierre alone, Françoise can hardly bear the thought and resolves to make the trio a duo at all costs.

As I mentioned earlier, it is Elizabeth who (although actually a fourth person) functions here as a Third to upset completely the uneasy equilibrium which they had established. At her suggestion, Gerbert invites Xavière out for an evening. Xavière has been attracted to him all along. In fact her interest in Gerbert, her admiration for his good looks and boyish charm, is almost the only thing about her which makes her seem like a normal girl instead of a self-worshiping monster. One feels that if at the start she had met Gerbert and not the other couple, she might

---

* In a night club scene described in *The Age of Reason* (pp. 254-259), Ivich, with less clear motivation though apparently from a mixture of self-hate and revolt against things in general, cuts her hand with a knife. Mathieu, not to be outdone, plunges the knife into his hand and pins it to the table. The waiter, who "had seen many such incidents," calmly sends them to the cloakroom attendant for first aid. Ivich and Mathieu rub their bloody palms together as a kind of "mingling of the blood."

have developed some of the more graceful outgoing qualities of youth instead of merely its narcissism. As the situation develops, however, Xavière is too proud to let Gerbert see that she is interested in him. When she finally consents to go out with him, it is chiefly because she is offended that Pierre and Françoise had earlier had an appointment with Gerbert at which she was not included.

The evening which the two spend together is like a breath of spring to Xavière and Gerbert—and to the reader—but the consequences are disastrous for all concerned. Pierre is furiously jealous. When the trio meets the next evening, he so torments Xavière with insinuations about the evening that she thinks Gerbert has talked about her. The thought of having been made an object by him is so repugnant to her that she turns from him with hatred, renewing her allegiance to the trio. But Pierre goes too far. He forces Xavière to admit that her unpleasant behavior has been motivated by jealousy of Françoise and resentment that she cannot destroy the relation between the two of them. For the moment Xavière does nothing. It is Françoise who snaps. Ever since Xavière's arrival Françoise has felt menaced by her. Now the threat seems suddenly to take on a metaphysical character. Just as mystics in religious ecstasy experience in intensified form the reality of the God in whom they have always believed, so Françoise *feels* for the first time the perilous quality of her subjectivity before the existence of another consciousness. What she experiences now is no more like her intellectual comprehension of the existence of separate consciousness than St. Theresa's trance resembles the recitation of the Creed.

> Across Xavière's mad possessive pleasure, across her hate and jealousy, the shocking scandal burst forth as monstrous, as definitive as death. Face to face with Françoise and yet apart from her there existed something which stood as a condemnation without appeal: free, absolute, irreducible, an alien consciousness was rising up. It was like death, a total negation, an eternal absence, and yet in staggering contradiction, this abyss of nothingness could render itself present to itself, could make itself exist for itself in absolute fullness; the whole Universe was swallowed up in it, and Françoise forever dispossessed of the world, was herself dissolved in this void whose infinite circumference no word, no image could encompass (p. 301).

In this passage de Beauvoir has compressed the essence of Hegel's conflict of consciousness and of Sartre's idea that the emergence of another consciousness effects an internal hemorrhage of my world. The keyhole example soon follows.

Incensed by Pierre's accusations, Xavière not only goes out with Gerbert again but becomes his mistress. The haughty Pierre, whom Françoise on more than one occasion had gently accused of thinking that he was God the Father, this unchallenged subject, not only paces the floor above Xavière's room but is reduced to looking through the keyhole. He is not discovered there like the man in Sartre's example, but he becomes momentarily an object of shame as he confesses to Françoise what he has done and feels her half-compassionate, half-scornful appraisal. The next morning they find a note from Xavière under Françoise's door.

> I am so disgusted with myself. I ought to have thrown myself out of the window, but I will not have the courage. Do not forgive me. You yourself must kill me tomorrow morning if I have been too cowardly (p. 321).

On her door is tacked up another note with the words, "No forgiveness." Xavière's reaction is not simply that of a girl frightened or disillusioned by her first sexual experience. Once again she hates herself for having given in response to a demand, for having for the moment lost her subject-being. It is not enough to punish herself afterward. She also turns against Gerbert and throws him out. Her insistence that she must not be forgiven is in itself a defense of her being-as-subject, for forgiveness as much as judgement throws the weight of Being over upon the one who makes the decision. Later in the same day Xavière withdraws even more completely by disclaiming all responsibility for the note, pleading intoxication and pretending that nothing of significance has taken place.

Xavière's night with Gerbert brings to an end the second stage of the story. She continues to see Gerbert occasionally, but he no longer has any real interest in her. Pierre, after first breaking with her completely, consents to a sort of truce and secretly hopes to make her give up Gerbert. The two of them fall into a sort of complicity which Francoise feels excludes her. This time she neither tries to win back Xavière nor takes steps to insure that her own relation with Pierre will not suffer. Utterly disgusted with Xavière's egoistic duplicity and Pierre's blindness toward Xavière and lack of consideration for herself, Françoise at last refuses to be an object before either of them. Toward Pierre she feels almost indifference.

> Facing Xavière she felt with a kind of joy the upsurge within her of something black and bitter which she did not yet recognize, something which was almost a deliverance: powerful, free, bursting forth in full bloom—it was hate (p. 369).

Rejecting all hope of reciprocity with Xavière, unable to make her an object and unwilling to give up her own subjectivity, Françoise finds recourse in the one attitude untried. For the moment she does not pursue the emotion to its logical outcome; since she is leaving Paris for a vacation, she can pretend that Xavière does not exist. She is not forced to recognize hate for what it really is, the will to annihilate the Other.

In the last and decisive phase of the novel events move swiftly. Françoise and Gerbert have set off alone on a hiking trip. Although the arrangement was intended to be a platonic one, she eventually becomes his mistress and they live a summertime idyl based partly on sexual attraction and partly on tender friendship. De Beauvoir's intention is apparently merely to show that Françoise is finally able to live for herself again, that there are other interests in life besides Xavière and Pierre. Though the thought is perhaps unjust, I cannot myself refrain from thinking that there is a bit of sadism in Françoise's action. Although she does not recognize in the love affair any connection with those left behind in Paris, the fact remains that by sleeping with Gerbert she is both hurting Xavière (who had never wholly relinquished her claim to him) and rather forcefully asserting her subjective independence of Pierre.

Upon returning to Paris, Françoise learns that Pierre has given up all but politely casual relations with Xavière. Rather inconsistently he explains his decision by accusing Xavière of bad faith. Xavière had suddenly lost all importance to him, he says, precisely when she became all repentance and tenderness.

> If she had thrown herself unreservedly into my arms, I would have been really moved; perhaps too if she had remained on the defensive, I would have been challenged by her resistance. But when I saw how greedy she was to get me back and how anxious she was to sacrifice nothing for me, I felt only a faintly disgusted pity (pp. 386-387).

Françoise allows herself to gloat just a bit over her victory. In her eyes it is the old-fashioned virtues which have won out over obstinacy, egoistic caprice, and deceit. Defeated, Xavière is no longer a threat. Françoise "once again existed alone, without an obstacle, at the heart of her destiny."

I am inclined to think that it would have been better from a strictly literary point of view if the novel had stopped at this point. But de Beauvoir has not examined quite all of the philosophical implications of being-for-others. There still remains the exploration of hate. Now we are thrust into the midst of World War Two. Pierre and Gerbert both go off to the army. Françoise continues to see Xavière. Suddenly the conflict is on again between the two of them more violently than ever. First, Françoise discovers that Xavière has been telling Gerbert a false version of the story of her relation to Pierre and that she is trying to build up even yet a picture in which she and Françoise play respectively a sort of Mary and Martha role with regard to him. This is bad enough, for Françoise's knowledge of how things really have been cannot prevent her from being aware of a possible different interpretation. But the decisive engagement takes place when Xavière breaks open Françoise's desk and reads letters she has had from Pierre and Gerbert. Françoise, confronting her, now sees the story of recent events as they appear to Xavière: she sees herself jealous of Pierre's love for Xavière and getting revenge by taking Gerbert from her. It does not seem to Françoise that this is exactly how things were and she feels that somehow innocent love has been tortured into sordid betrayal; but she is horrified at the picture of herself which she sees in Xavière's eyes. She begs for forgiveness, for the chance to make it up somehow to Xavière. Xavière refuses. Now it seems to Françoise that she and Xavière cannot both go on living.

> *There* was Xavière, existing only for herself, entirely self-devoted, reducing to nothingness everything which she excluded. She inclosed the whole world in her own triumphant solitude, she expanded without limit—infinite, unique. Everything which she was she drew out of herself. One could get no hold upon her. She was absolute separation (p. 418).

"It is she or I," thinks Françoise. And arranging things to look like suicide, she turns on the gas to kill Xavière while she sleeps. Françoise has "chosen herself."

Strictly speaking, de Beauvoir has not gone quite to the bitter limit of Sartre's analysis. As we have seen, hatred of one Other is hatred directed toward all Others. There is no reason to think that Françoise will never encounter another Xavière. Moreover, she can never erase the memory of Xavière's Look. She will never be able to think of herself and Gerbert without taking Xavière's view of things into account. But of all this de Beauvoir tells us nothing.

I think we should not be afraid to say that this is a shocking book. There are, of course, allowances which must be made. In all fairness we must grant that the denouement is a metaphysical murder rather than a real one. There is no sign in the rest of her work that de Beauvoir actually believes it justifiable to kill anyone blocking the way to one's self-realization. In essence Françoise's decision to kill Xavière is but the dramatic conclusion of a philosophical proposition: If one insists on choosing bad faith as the mode of living one's human relationships, then only one's own death or that of the Other will end the conflict. To the extent to which the emotional involvements of the characters in *She Came to Stay* are intended as an illustration of bad faith, the novel is an exposé of the way in which many people use love and friendship as a cloak for their exploitation of others. It attacks the notion that through love one is justified either in living another's life for him or in letting one's own life be determined wholly by another. In these respects, and in its denunciation of egotism, selfishness, and deceit, the book is as moral as a sermon by Billy Graham.

But difficulties arise when we try to find the other side of the picture. Is there anywhere in the novel a standard for human relations in good faith? Abstractly this is easy to find. Pierre defines it when he points out how his relation with Françoise is different from any they have been able to establish with Xavière. "Between us there is reciprocity. . . . The moment that you recognize me as a consciousness you know that I recognize you as a consciousness too" (p. 312). The trouble is that this recognition on Pierre's part seems to be restricted to Françoise, and even in her case it is sometimes a little myopic. Pierre acknowledges a need for frequent light affairs with women, "conquests" which are not even in answer to sexual needs but rather the result of his compulsion to dominate. He and Françoise profess a strict code of honesty, but it does not prevent them from lying to Gerbert when they want to have Xavière to themselves. Moreover, their demands upon Xavière are no more justified than hers upon them. To ask that this impulsive, highly emotional girl, who loathes nothing so much as introspection, should conform to their continual demands for reflective self-analysis and consistency is doing violence to her right at the start. Of course we may say that Pierre's and Françoise's defections are the result of their having forsaken their usual life in good faith and that it is Xavière's peculiar character which has seduced them into the way of bad faith. They have "backslid," as it were, and return to the fold when the evil of sin is made manifest. But Françoise's choice of herself through murder is not an act in good faith. By existentialist standards she should have had the courage to accept the consequences of her own acts and to live with her own view of things no matter how Xavière tried to picture them. Perhaps we are to assume that de Beauvoir recognized this, that she meant to represent Françoise as so utterly destroyed by having entered into the wrong kind of relation with Xavière that redemption is impossible. In that case the novel is an unrelieved tragedy, and Françoise's choice of herself is as much a defeat for her as death is for Xavière. But then what becomes of the existentialist theory of the unity of the personality? Sartre maintained that a man could not be an anti-Semite and in other respects a good citizen. Hatred of any one Other, as we have seen, is hatred of all Others. Françoise herself recognized the universal nature of her first perception of Xavière as an alien consciousness confronting her. Is it possible for Pierre and Françoise to be in good faith with respect to each other and in bad faith toward most of the rest of their world? It seems to me that there are only two possibilities: Either all of the novel's characters are in bad faith and no one has been able to maintain a true reciprocity—or else de Beauvoir's picture of human relations in good faith is such that there is little reason for anyone to choose good faith rather than its opposite.

In *She Came to Stay,* as we have seen, de Beauvoir has been content chiefly to give flesh and blood to Sartre's analysis of Being-for-others. Sartre himself in his later work has been both more concrete and more positive. In his fiction, however, the problem of human relations tends to become entirely a political problem. Even when individual, it is the political commitment which is uppermost and which determines the nature of personal relations. De Beauvoir, on the contrary, while she has done some political writing, has been more concerned with the personally human. In particular she has been interested in the relations of men and women—that is, in love, in sex, and especially in the peculiar problem of what it means to be a woman in the twentieth century. *The Second Sex (Le deuxième sexe),*[2] although its conclusions have provoked a great deal of controversy, is unquestionably the fullest treatment of women and women's problems which has ever been written. In general it belongs to the sphere of psychology and sociology rather than that of literature, hence is beyond the scope of our present enterprise. Yet its analysis of the particular forms of bad faith dependent on sex lies back of much of de Beauvoir's fictional characterization and is pertinent to this discussion.

De Beauvoir is emphatic in her statement that woman has been too much sacrificed to the species. As wife and mother she safeguards the future but is offered little opportunity to live her own life in the present. At best there is an unfair exchange: woman is man's pleasure, man is —or is supposed to be—woman's justification for being. Somehow the human type has been identified with the masculine type. Woman as a member of "the second sex" has become the Other. De Beauvoir goes to great length to show that neither man-written history nor biology justifies equating distinctively feminine characteristics with stamps of inferiority. Woman is not made to be an object-other to a man-subject any more than any human being is born as absolute subject or absolute object. If we accept her premise, then we can easily see that bad faith will assume the form of denying the fundamental equality of the sexes for the sake of gaining some kind of false guarantee for one's own being. Bad faith will have the same basic structure whether it is masculine or feminine, but it will manifest itself in different ways. Masculine bad faith consists in regarding women only as women instead of as human beings. It may take the form of contempt, in which case women serve to bolster the male ego in much the same way as the Jew helps to guarantee the position of the anti-Semite. It may also appear in the guise of exaggerated respect such as we find in knightly circles during the Age of Chivalry or in pre-Civil War Southern United States. In this case woman is supposedly put on a pedestal even above man. But she holds this position at the cost of allowing herself to be determined entirely by the ideal which man has of her. As a person she has as much freedom or reality as a Dresden doll.

Today the man in bad faith looks with amusement at the antics of "emancipated women" in much the same way as he regards a dog which has been trained to do cleverly but awkwardly what a man can do better. As with the Jew in the eyes of the anti-Semite, the exploits of women are never a threat to him, for no matter how brilliant, they are still but the exploits of women. In his relations with individual women, such a man makes a sharp distinction. Most are objects for his use as liquor is there to quench his thirst or food to ease his hunger. With his wife or beloved mistress, on the other hand, he is persuaded that the woman is the center and meaning of his life. But actually what he so fondly possesses is simply a magic speaking mirror. Even the mirror image is not quite accurate, for what he seeks is not a true picture of himself. Rather he wants the woman to guarantee for him a permanent Self-for-Others, which he himself has fashioned and which the woman may assure him is the real "He" no matter what other experiences may come to contradict it. What he seeks in the woman is identification with himself. He wants to be sure of getting the reactions which he himself would like to have to all his actions, but he wants to feel that these reactions are freely given, hence reassuring. His project is not unlike that of the Sartrean lover, and of course this man believes himself to be genuinely in love.

De Beauvoir does not claim that all men have deliberately wronged women by allowing them only dependent being. On the contrary, she says that most men genuinely believe that women are happier this way and prefer to be protected and taken care of. This is partly rationalization in bad faith. As de Beauvoir says,

> It is not too clear just what the word *happy* really means and still less what true values it may mask. There is no possibility of measuring the happiness of others, and it is always easy to describe as happy the situation in which one wishes to place them (p. xxviii).

Yet she admits that many women prefer to be kept in a position where they do not have to worry about anything except how to please the one who is psychologically their master. It is an established fact that whereas most men dislike marrying a woman who might be more intelligent than they, most women desire not only equality but superiority in their husbands. Part of this may be women's desire to conform to what society has set up as conventional, but part of it must be due to willingness to be in the dependent position. De Beauvoir explains this situation by pointing out that there is a tendency in every human to flee from self-responsibility. This is, in fact, the core of bad faith. But to yield to this inclination is to refuse to face honestly what one is; it is to evade the responsibilities of being human. Man's worst crime against woman has been precisely this: "Throughout her life from childhood on, they damage and corrupt her by designating as her true vocation this submission, which is the temptation of every existent in the anxiety of liberty" (p. 721).

But women are not guiltless. There is also distinctively feminine bad faith. The most common form is a kind of narcissistic love of being an object. In this attitude the woman accepts the idea that her purpose in life is to persuade men to admire her and to look after her. But she herself becomes fascinated by the object which she has made of herself in order to attract them. Ironically, such a woman frequently becomes so self-absorbed and self-centered that she cannot provide the sense of identification which the man expects. At best she is merely a token of his prowess or wealth, like his Cadillac and his membership in exclusive clubs. He will soon look elsewhere to "find himself." More often she will work hard at the role of "perfect wife" but feels vaguely discontented as though her life has now by its very completion been cut off.

A second form of bad faith in women consists in accepting the view that men are really superior and then using it as an excuse for failure. An example here is the woman college professor who is always saying that men can do more publishing because they are stronger and have their wives to take over the responsibilities of running the home. Again, such women will pride themselves on what measure of success they have achieved, thinking that because in general men's professions are only grudgingly opened to them, it is enough to have done what they have. As de Beauvoir puts it, feminine talent has often been hindered by a "reasonable modesty." There are also minor pretenses to which particularly the intellectual woman is prone. De Beauvoir, for example, presents the amusing picture of the woman who is out on a date with an attractive man. She is afraid to appear to him as she really is for fear of not being "feminine." As a result she plays at being the simpering moron and becomes ridiculous.

> She makes mistakes like those induced by the menopause: she tries to deny her brain just as the woman who is growing older tries to deny her age; she dresses like a girl; she overloads herself with flowers, furbelows, fancy materials; she affects childish tricks of surprised amazement. She romps, she babbles, she pretends flippancy, heedlessness, sprightliness (p. 685).

Then in annoyance with herself she may suddenly give up the game and try in momentary hatred to prove her superiority to the male before whom she has humiliated herself. If only, laments de Beauvoir, men would be content to love equals and not slaves and would renounce the myth whereby femininity is identified with stupid passivity, then intellectual women could relax. "They would find themselves women again without taking so many pains, since, after all, that is what they are" (p. 686).

But the worst form of feminine bad faith is seen in the woman who wants both the privilege of equality with men and the privileges which have been granted to her as a member of the "weaker sex." Pointing to the too frequently attacked Mabel Dodge Luhan, whose attempt to win D. H. Lawrence has been denounced as fervently as though she were the only woman to have done such a thing, de Beauvoir says that she is an example of this last form of bad faith in that she urged the cause of equality between the sexes while using her own sexuality as a means of trying to dominate Lawrence.

De Beauvoir states that the liberation of women would actually mean the liberation of men as well, though many of both sexes are secretly afraid of this liberation. For it would entail a full confrontation of their freedom and its resultant self-responsibility. To dare to be a human being is the greatest challenge. The old myth of femininity admittedly would be lost. But de Beauvoir claims, with what seems to be obvious truth, that so long as men and women are physically different and so long as sexuality remains a basic bond between them, there can hardly be an uninteresting neutrality as the result of accepting both as human beings. Rather, she argues, a liberated companion can offer far more of interest and fascination to man than any animated mirror or pet cat.

Our examination of existentialist views as to what constitutes a life in good faith (sexual or otherwise) must be postponed until the next chapter. We have already encountered several instances of relations between the sexes in bad faith: Lucien's attitude toward his future wife is one example. The truth is that in the work of Sartre we find hardly anything else on the part of either men or women. Véronique in *Nekrassov* is an exception, but she is presented primarily as a Communist rather than as a woman. Ivich, Xavière's counterpart, seems at first not quite to fit the pattern. But in spite of sadistic tendencies, she—like Xavière— is an example of narcissism. Although she wants to dominate, it is always as a woman who fascinates men by making herself an irresistible object. She never at any time tries to set up a relation of equality with anyone. The best example from de Beauvoir's early works is Hélène in *The Blood of Others*. During the first part of the book she tries to evade all responsibility by making Jean Blomart almost literally her whole life. She does not mind being an object to him and prefers even his neglect or insults to living without him. But the result is that she makes him only the pole of her own emotion, her *raison d'être*. She not only does not know him as a person, but resents his having any interests in life except their own relationship. Jean feels pity for her and finally assumes responsibility for her because she seems unable to exist by herself. It is not love. At the end of the book, Hélène has learned to make decisions for herself. She works with Blomart rather than merely at making herself attractive to him. And for the first time he loves her.

Until now our discussion of human relations has been based largely on emotional bonds between individuals or on sex-determined attitudes. The larger issue of responsibility toward people in general we have touched on briefly in connection with the problem of bad faith in political attitudes. In *The Blood of Others* de Beauvoir's conclusion could be expressed in the formula: "We are each one of us totally responsible and wholly without excuse." Everyone is free to choose his course of action within the physical and social environment within which he finds himself. But by every act a person is changing the environment within which another will choose. The Other by his very existence forces us to be responsible for him, but he cannot use us as an excuse. Sartre's Orestes in *The Flies* presents almost the same position. He accepts the tension of freedom and refuses the way out offered by submersion in religious guilt and atonement.

In his analysis in *Being and Nothingness,* Sartre depicts human relations as inescapably associated with guilt; the guilt is existential but not due to any religious doctrine.

> It is before the Other that I am *guilty*. I am guilty first when beneath the Other's look I experience my alienation and my nakedness as a fall from grace which I must assume. This is the meaning of the famous line from Scripture: "They knew that they were naked." Again I am guilty when in turn I look at the Other, because by the very fact of my own self-assertion I constitute him as an object and as an instrument, and I cause him to experience that same alienation which he must now assume. Thus original sin is my upsurge in a world where there are others; and whatever may be my further relations with others, these relations will be only variations on the original theme of my guilt (p. 410).

People are guilty toward each other because they are constantly causing the internal hemorrhage of each other's world. Sartre (like Kant) feels that grammar reflects the existential situation: I cannot say, "I know I." I can never take a total objective view upon myself, and yet somehow there emerges in my relation with the Other a mysterious Me-object which seems to alienate me from myself. In a sense Sartre is stating in a new form that the coexistence of consciousnesses creates an inevitable conflict of claims or demands. Putting the same idea in positive form, William James once said that ethics arise from the moment that we have two loving souls upon a rock. Since, according to Sartre, the most basic need of an individual is to be able to move freely in a world to which his own subjectivity gives form and meaning, the existence of the Other offers violence to his freedom.

Another concept of guilt inherent in humanity is found in Albert Camus' *The Fall (La Chute)*.[3] There is, I believe, some question as to the extent to which we are meant to take the hero as a symbol of the human condition as a whole. But whether Clamence is all mankind or merely one human type, Camus has used him to draw a more devastating picture of bad faith than any we have yet examined. The basic problem in *The Fall* is not the relation of a man with any particular Other. It is rather the question: Is it possible for a human being to be really concerned for any Other? Or is man by nature so egocentric that the only love of which he is capable is love of self?

Camus calls *The Fall* a *récit*, and it is in fact a dramatic monologue by Jean-Baptiste Clamence, a famous Parisian lawyer who has voluntarily left his country and vocation to live in retirement in Amsterdam. For him (if not also for Camus) the setting is symbolic. Partly surrounded by the inclement sea, Amsterdam seems to be set in the midst of concentric circles reminding Clamence of the circles in Dante's *Inferno*. Thus here, as in Sartre's *No Exit*, the point is made that it is our everyday life which is hell and that we are inhabitants well suited to our environment. Clamence spends most of his time in a bar called "Mexico-City"; the whole *récit* is an uninterrupted sequence of one-sided conversations which he has with a Frenchman whom he meets there. The listener is not individualized except that Clamence refers to him as a lawyer and a man something like himself. But even this characterization is a bit suspect, for it is part of Clamence's confessed technique to size up his listener and then play upon real or fancied resemblances which the stranger bears to himself. The owner of the Mexico-City is the only other individual in the book, and—as characterized by Clamence—his symbolism is evident. Clamence calls him the Gorilla. He runs a bar for sailors from all over the world but makes it a point to speak nothing but Dutch and limits himself mostly to grunts. Obviously he represents totally unawakened, nonreflective man, even primitive man, in contrast to the overcultivated, unhappily introspective Clamence. The two offer us the same kind of Hobson's choice which Huxley gives us—the Brave New World or life among the savages on a New Mexico reservation. Clamence reveals himself partly through the narration of the events of his earlier life and the decision to which they led him and partly through his explanation of his present outlook and sense of mission. One feels that he is holding nothing back, not even the duplicity inherent in the very act of confession. But beyond all the introspection it is possible to see even more of bad faith than Clamence admits in himself.

The story is sparse in external events. Clamence had been so well known in his legal career that he has thought it necessary to change his name. He had been admired for his charm, his elegant and persuasive language, his altruism. His success with women was remarkable and he knew how to handle affairs so delicately that he avoided all scandal and all unpleasantness even in ending relationships (though in one case a cast-off mistress did later commit suicide). In order that his conscience might be completely clear, he specialized in defending the accused, thus remaining on the right side of the law and yet knowing that he had done his best for the unfortunates who committed crimes as the result of social pressures. In short he devoted himself so wholly to the good of humanity that he could enjoy with clear conscience the approval which the world bestowed upon him. He admitted to a need to feel superior which obsessed him to the extent of making him want to be even physically elevated. (He admired mountain climbing and skiing but could never understand the fascination of speleology or archaeology.) But since his sense of superiority was gained by adherence to a code forbidding all evil or petty actions, and since the public's admiration was won by the good deeds he did for others, he could smile at his self-satisfaction and in fact considered himself one of the elect, a man especially destined for happiness.

The turning point came one evening when, as he was standing alone at night on a bridge over the Seine, he suddenly thought he heard someone laugh. There was no one else there. The laugh came from within himself, a projection of the judgement which he unconsciously realized could be passed upon himself. One could call it conscience. One could call it the Sartrean Look, which may be present in the imagination even though no living Other is within sight. At any rate, Clamence heard the laugh more than once in the days which followed, and it had the disturbing effect of making him remember things which his great ability to forget had previously prevented from troubling him.

One disturbing memory was of the day when he became involved in a traffic jam. He had allowed himself to become provoked by a motorcyclist and actually descended to fisticuffs. Even worse, when a third person intervened and punched him, Clamence had let the blow go unreturned. The episode in retrospect was disquieting from two points of view: In the first place, he was bothered by the fact that he had not returned the blow and that he had allowed the fact to rankle and had spent several days indulging in revenge fantasies; this seriously threatened his view of himself as a man who could rationally control events or if necessary rise above them. In the second place, the mere fact that he had lost his temper and got involved in a street fight seemed to indicate that his being on the right side of the law was chiefly accidental. In a crisis he was as ready as anyone else to resort to violence and asocial conduct.

But the truly devastating memory was of another event. It had occurred on another midnight when he had to cross a bridge. He noticed a young woman leaning over the rail but paid little attention. A few minutes later he heard a splash and cries of fright.

> I wanted to run, and I did not move. I was trembling, I believe, from cold and from shock. I told myself that I must act quickly and I felt throughout my body an irresistible faintness. I have forgotten what I thought then. "Too late, too far . . ." or something of the sort (p. 82).

It is important to note one thing about this occurrence: Clamence does not act, or refuse to act, as the result of conscious reflection. If he had had time to consider that a life depended upon his action, it is probable that, consistent with the altruistic role he had chosen, he would have felt that he must save the woman if there was any reasonable chance of doing so. But at the same time he does not feel that the suddenness of it all is an excuse. Actually the fact that his refusal was more a reflex than a decision makes him blacker in his own eyes. For it seems to him that the impulse came from what is his deepest and most basic outlook on life. It is the real Clamence who has refused and only the play-acting Clamence who might possibly have acted if the situation had allowed for more reflection. At the time he had been able to repress his awareness of the event's significance. Later his not having bothered to read the papers on the days following seems to him an additional evidence of callousness. It might, however, have been an indication of an unacknowledged apprehension.

When the laugh forces Clamence to recall and re-examine that moment on the bridge, his failure to prevent the suicide not only serves as the death blow to his feeling of moral superiority but opens up the Pandora's box of reappraisals of all his acts and attitudes. He had always prided himself on being able to help people and then honestly forget that they were under obligation to him. Now he begins to realize that the truth is not that he had forgotten the obligation but that the people involved meant so little to him that he had forgotten them. He catches himself one day in a slip of the tongue. When someone thanks him for a favor, he says, "Nobody else would have done as much." Another time he gives assistance to a blind man and tips his hat—to the public. Gradually he discovers that at least in his case all altruism is but the obverse of a profound egocentrism. He is modest, kind, and helpful because he wants to have—both in his own eyes and in the eyes of others—the reputation of being humble and considerate. Every virtue, every noble act is one more stone in the monument of his own self-pride. He has throughout his life been possessed by one great love and one only—the love of self.

Clamence's first reaction to this new view of himself is to attempt what later he realizes is impossible; that is, to achieve innocence by acknowledging his guilt. But even this act is not born of true humility; it is a way of asserting superiority by putting himself on the side of the one laughing. At any rate he resolves to make people see him for "what he really is." He begins to include disquieting comments in his speeches and gradually loses his law practice. He turns to debauchery and there comes close to finding a temporary relief. The healing power of debauchery stems in part from the fact that in it a man makes no pretense to anything but self-satisfaction. It is partly too that it weakens one's physical powers and dulls reflection. Clamence in this connection makes the rather strange statement that in moments of extreme fatigue he seemed to have found the secret of existence. I wish that Camus had allowed him to enlarge upon his remark. What was the secret? That one must forget oneself in intense living, no matter what kind? That one must make oneself void of all desire? Or what? In any case after a night's sleep Clamence himself is unable to recall what it was that he had discovered. After a time debauchery provokes its own destruction: Clamence is too worn out to continue his systematic self-exhaustion. At least he no longer hears the laugh. He thinks that the crisis is over, that he has only passively to await old age and death. But then as he hopefully sets out on an ocean voyage, he sees some floating debris which reminds him of the girl in the Seine. The laugh comes to his ears once more. This time he knows that there is no escape. He gives up his career, goes to Amsterdam, and under an assumed name becomes, as it were, an Apostle of the Laugh.

As Clamence relates this narrative to his companion, we are listening to one of the sermons which it is his habit to preach to clients at the Mexico-City. Superficially his method and purpose are easy to define. By revealing the egocentrism which had underlain his own seemingly blameless life, he awakens in his companions the sense of their own deficiencies. Almost imperceptibly the self-portrait becomes first the picture of all humanity and then the listener's mirror. But when we try to determine whether Clamence's mission is in good or in bad faith, the situation is much more complicated. Clamence calls himself a "judge-penitent." Part of the time it seems that he might as well have used the words "a repentant judge," for one of the main themes of his sermon (and of Camus' writing as well) is the impossibility of judging innocently. So long as society allows the existence of suffering and poverty, all are guilty and nobody has the right to pass judgement upon anyone else. Moreover, who can fathom what a man really is? Hell, concludes Clamence, ought to be a place where everyone is classified once and for all with places assigned and no chance of explaining oneself. Clamence goads his visitor by asking him what kind of visiting card he would prepare for himself if he had to include with his name a permanent designation of his way of life. A cowardly philosopher? A Christian landlord? An adulterous humanist? Clamence himself derives a wicked sort of satisfaction by keeping in his possession a stolen painting called "The Righteous Judges." This was originally a panel belonging to a Van Eyck altar piece known as "The Mystery of the Lamb." By holding onto it he is symbolically illustrating the permanent separation of the judges and innocence.

Yet while he refuses to judge the specific acts of the people with whom he comes in contact, Clamence does not refrain entirely from passing judgement. He has chosen his title accurately, for he remains both judge and penitent. His self-accusations are accompanied by abundant condemnation of men in general. Future historians, he says, will find that one sentence is enough to sum up twentieth-century man: "He fornicated and read the papers." Man has lost himself in conformity and in organizations. The denunciation is not limited to men of a particular era. In general, says Clamence, men can afford to love only the dead, for toward them we need feel no obligation. But it is only the recent dead. The older dead we forget. True love for the living may occur once or twice a century; the rest of the time what passes for love is built upon vanity or ennui. Added to man's self-centered indifference to others are his actual crimes. Clamence refers in specific detail to pogroms, massacres, refinement of torture. But perhaps the most dismal truth about man is that he does not have the courage to make a whole-hearted choice of either right or wrong. We want not to be guilty and not to have to make the effort of cleansing ourselves. "Not enough cynicism and not enough virtue." Most of us belong with the neutral angels in the Vestibule to Dante's hell.

Clamence makes no pretense that he is himself exempt from this condemnation. If he were offered another chance to save the young girl, he would once more find that the water was too cold and persuade himself that "it was too late." But it is precisely in this identification that his conscious bad faith resides. He is well aware that by forcing others to accept the validity of his view of humanity, he is still asserting his old will to power. In fact he states that his self-accusation is for the explicit purpose of giving him the right to judge others. In making them judge themselves, he appears superior in that he has recognized the truth first and presented it to them. He acknowledges also that he is still using others for his own purpose. This admission occurs in connection with a curious passage on freedom. Clamence states that he recognizes his complete freedom and responsibility for his acts. If there were a God, then one could hope for pardon. But without God there is no way of atonement. "At the end of all freedom, there is a sentence." But there is one thing which he can do. By convincing others that all mankind is as guilty as he, Clamence feels less the weight of his own guilt and his solitude. This means of course that he is making others his instruments. "Whenever I can, I preach in my church here at the Mexico-City; I invite the good people to submit and to cast their vote humbly for the comforts of slavery, although I present it to them as the true freedom" (p. 158). The neat part of all this is that Clamence by admitting his whole procedure to be in bad faith can openly acknowledge the delight he takes in his work. "What ecstasy to feel oneself God the Father and to hand out definitive certificates of evil conduct and morals" (p. 165). Clamence insists that he is happy, and he hysterically challenges anybody to say that he is not. Yet he still hears the laugh, though rarely and from afar, and one feels that self-accusation and the project of evoking a guilty complicity with others are perhaps more deeply embedded in bad faith than his cynical introspection perceives.

In trying to achieve some definite appraisal of Clamence's pessimism and his "mission," the reader's conclusion will, of course, vary considerably according to his own religious position and according to whether he feels that Clamence's message (either from Camus' point of view or the reader's) is the true gospel. Clamence rejects religion completely. God does not exist, and the guilty cannot hope for grace. For Christ, Clamence feels a strange sympathy. The supposed son of God partook of human nature more profoundly than is allowed by Christian theology. He shared the burden of human guilt in that his life was a crime against others. Clamence, who has already declared that the man who really loves will sleep on the floor if he knows that his friend has no bed, claims that Jesus must have suffered frightful agony knowing that innocent children had been slaughtered because of him while his parents conveyed him into Egypt to a place of safety. It was for this reason, says Clamence, that he welcomed death, and he thought that at last on the cross he would be vindicated. But the agonized cry, "Why hast thou forsaken me?" was in very truth a cry of disillusion. Clamence maintains that he loves this "first Christian" but that few of Christ's followers have done so. This truth Jesus foresaw, says Clamence, and showed a sense of humor by establishing his Church upon the head of Peter, who he knew would deny him.

If we allow ourselves to be converted by Clamence's gospel of pessimism, we must admit that man is a fallen sinner without hope of redemption. Clamence uses the idea of a fall from grace to describe his own transition from the time when he believed himself to be specially destined for happiness to the day when he recognized his total guilt. In his own mind clearly his fall is to be identified with the state of original sin in which all men are hopelessly engulfed. But to what extent is Clamence also Camus? In the minds of some critics the two have been interchangeable. On this basis, Donat O'Donnell was, I believe, the first to suggest that such complete recognition of man's inadequacy and need for grace could only be followed by application for admission to the Catholic Church. But Camus has not become a Catholic. Neither has he committed suicide nor stopped writing. Nor can we say that in his later work he has restricted himself to writing only material of the sort which might be included in the sermons which Clamence delivered at the Mexico-City. One suspects therefore that Camus is not Clamence.

Philip Thody, in my opinion, has come closest to the truth in suggesting that while *The Fall* may have been in part a katharsis for Camus to rid him of certain personal obsessions, the portrait of Clamence is primarily satiric. Thody agrees with other critics that the assumption of the name Jean-Baptiste is significant but considers the judge-penitent a false prophet. He points out that the last name, Clamence, is equally important and clearly ironic; for it sounds almost like *clémence,* which means forgiveness or pity, exactly the quality which Clamence does not have. Thody feels that Camus is attacking those who make use of universal guilt feelings as a means of enslaving people. Camus, he believes, is speaking out against religious leaders who have dominated people by playing on their psychological needs, and against those intellectuals who have let their feelings of social guilt lead them to Communism.[4]

That Thody is right and that Camus intends Clamence to serve as a study in bad faith (more profound than that which the judge-penitent recognizes in himself) seems to be borne out by a statement which Camus made in an interview.

> I detest virtue that is only smugness, I detest the frightful morality of the world, and I detest it because it ends, just like absolute cynicism, in demoralizing men and keeping them from running their own lives with their own just measures of meanness and magnificence.[5]

It seems clear to me that Camus intended Clamence to represent both of the attitudes mentioned here: in his days of "grace" he personified complacent virtue; in his "fall" he is absolute cynicism. Clamence preaches the need for self-understanding and acknowledges in himself a calculating humility. Actually he represents a curious mixture of self-evasion and pride. He is too proud to accept the human condition for what it is. He prefers to hate all men (including himself) rather than to consent to live a life on relative terms. Because there is evil in men, he will admit to no magnificence. Although he is constantly confessing to a love of self, it is a false confession (and he himself has warned us that the confessor lies most when he is closest to the truth). Clamence does not in truth love himself any more than he loves anyone else, for love means accepting someone for the good that is within him and being able to pardon the evil that he cannot help. Clamence is forever showing that nobody is wholly worthy of admiration, but this is something quite different. Furthermore, the standards by which he is judging himself and others are never quite brought out in the open. Clamence professes to be non-Christian, but the values against which he measures himself seem to be derived from Christian ethics. To make self-abasement one of the greatest virtues and concern for self the worst of sins, to put the emphasis always on motive rather than act ("As a man thinketh in his heart, so is he"), to feel (as Clamence does) ashamed of loving this life for its own sake—if all this is not a species of Christian morality, what is it? In preferring to condemn himself in accordance with a system already established rather than to forge a new code for himself, Clamence is evading the freedom which he admits fills him with terror. When he hopes that the police will learn that he has the stolen picture and that they will come to arrest him, he is trying to escape from himself by letting someone else pass sentence. As surely as Daniel in *The Age of Reason,* Clamence seeks a kind of absolute via self-punishment; like Daniel he finds it easier to indulge in self-hate for what he is than to accept the challenge to become something else. It seems to me quite evident that Camus does not regard Clamence's conclusion as the correct one. Despair is no more an ultimate position for him than it is for Sartre and de Beauvoir—or for the Christian. Despair is a temptation, not a final resting place.*

Justin O'Brien, the American translator of *The Fall,* has said that a central purpose of the book is to criticize Sartre's existentialism.[6] Exactly what O'Brien meant by this statement I do not know. If it is true, it is so in only a very limited sense. One small episode is very probably a direct hit at Sartre. Clamence tells of the time during the war when he was elected by a group of fellow prisoners to see to the fair distribution of their small supply of food and water. He tried to apportion the rations, not in equal amounts but in proportion to the needs. One day he himself drank the water which might have gone to another. He excused himself by saying that as leader he had to stay alive and that the other man was dying anyway. Clamence (and almost certainly Camus)

---

* I had already written this interpretation when the *Atlantic Monthly* published Charles Rolo's article, "Albert Camus: A Good Man" (May, 1958) in which he quotes a statement by Camus concerning his intention in *The Fall.* The quotation supports my view without, I think, making it necessary for me to modify anything which I have said. "Europeans are no longer believers; they are agnostics or atheists. (I have nothing against that. I am more or less a pagan.) But they have retained their sense of sin. They can't unburden themselves by going to confession. So they feel the need to act. They start passing severe judgments, putting people in concentration camps, killing. My 'hero' is the exact illustration of a guilty conscience. He has the European resignation to a feeling of sin." Rolo points out, apparently with Camus' approval, that the name "Clamence" is meant to suggest the voice of the prophet *clamans (in deserto)* (p. 32).

regards the action as wrong. But there are several occasions in Sartre's novels and plays in which a leader sacrifices an individual for the sake of a cause. And in de Beauvoir's *The Blood of Others* Jean Blomart wants to go out on a dangerous mission and is dissuaded by precisely this argument—that as leader he must preserve himself for the good of the group. Taking the book as a whole, I think that O'Brien's interpretation would hold good only if we restricted Sartre's position to the analysis of human relations in *Being and Nothingness*. In his pitiless exposure of the weaknesses of humanity and his all-embracing denunciation of every human attitude as corrupt, Sartre in this one place is not unlike Clamence. If Sartre had not made it clear that there can be an ethics based on good faith, we might well conclude that he—like Clamence—had deemed it enough to hold up to human-reality the reflection of its irremediable corruption. But Sartre has not chosen to preach the futility of all action, and Camus knows it. The two writers are alike, I think, in believing that one must have the courage to live without perfection; *The Fall* and *The Flies* agree in so far as they both show that surrender to guilt feelings may be but one more form of betraying the human race.

Bad faith in human relations is based on any of three fundamental positions: One may attempt to deny the Other's freedom, to dominate and use him as if he had only a subordinate and inferior being; one may prostrate oneself before the Other so as to be relieved by him of the burden of one's own freedom; one may—in the name of an abstract perfection—prevent all loving relations between people by deciding in advance that nobody is worthy of them.

## 4. CONCLUSION

While listing the crimes of which men have been guilty, Clamence exclaims, "How many crimes have been committed simply because their authors could not bear to be in the wrong!" He goes on to tell the story of a man who was continually deceiving his wife although he found her perfect in every way. His sense of wronging her became so acute that finally the guilt was intolerable. "What do you think he did then? He stopped deceiving her? No. He killed her (p. 25)." This stark tale is identical with the central thread of O'Neill's play, *The Iceman Cometh*,[1] which was produced in the forties. I do not know that Camus borrowed the episode from O'Neill. As Clamence might point out, the horrible thing about the story is that it is universal enough so that two writers might easily think of it coincidentally. But the similarity is striking. In *The Fall* Camus shows how cynical self-accusation may itself become a means of self-evasion. *The Iceman Cometh* raises the question of whether it is possible for any man to live without bad faith in the form of some comforting illusion about himself.

Although there is some Freudian-style character delineation, this play more than any other of O'Neill's works is concerned with the human condition more than with the specific problems of a closely knit group of individuals. The characters are Hickey—a hardware salesman —and a collection of dead beats at Harry Hope's saloon and rooming house. As the group waits for Hickey to come and throw his annual party for Harry's birthday, it becomes obvious that they manage to exist together in a state of mild bickering by showing mutual respect for each other's pipe dreams and self-deceptions. Some of them—like the Captain and Jimmy Tomorrow—are always putting off applying for the jobs they are convinced they could have for the asking. Others—like Rocky and the two streetwalkers, Pearl and Margie—keep their self-respect by a careful choice of words. The girls are "tarts" but not "whores," Rocky is a "bartender," not their "pimp." And so on down the line. Finally Hickey arrives. He orders drinks for everyone but reveals to their dismay that he has become a teetotaler. Worse yet, he announces mysteriously that he has found peace by at last giving up his pipe dream and that he is going to force them all to prove that their talk is not all mere pipe dreams and illusion.

Of course everyone fails, and the whole structure of things collapses. Those who have been going to act find that they do not have the courage. Rocky and the girls call things by their real names, and good-natured friendship gives way to mutual hatred. Moreover, now that illusion is gone each member of the group not only sees himself as he really is but knows that this is how he appears to others. Mutuality is impossible, and the earlier easy bickering is replaced by cutting recriminations and actual physical attacks.

Hickey is alarmed and sincerely puzzled. In an effort to explain he consents to tell how getting rid of his own pipe dream had brought peace to him. All his life he had loved and betrayed his forgiving wife Evelyn. She never lost her belief in him, and he was convinced each time that he could reform. This time, he had felt, there would be a showdown. If he got drunk at Harry's party, it would be the end. But he knew that he would do as he had done every other year. And so he had killed

Evelyn to bring her peace, because he loved her and could not bear to go on hurting her. Since then he had felt such perfect peace that he no longer needed to drink, and he had wanted to relieve his friends of the burden of their pipe dreams too. In a kind of revery, Hickey recalls the moment after the killing.

> I felt as though a ton of guilt was lifted off my mind. I remember I stood by the bed and suddenly I had to laugh. I couldn't help it, and I knew Evelyn would forgive me. I remember I heard myself speaking to her, as if it was something I'd always wanted to say: "Well, you know what you can do with your pipe dream now, you damned bitch!" (p. 241).

For a moment Hickey and his audience recognize the truth, that Hickey had killed his wife because he hated her and that his peace had been the result of finally getting rid of the burden of guilt. But while it had been easy for Hickey in the new spirit of innocence to call the police and prepare to give himself up, he cannot face the revelation of what his true motives had been. He tries to call back the words. "Good God, I couldn't have said that! If I did, I'd gone insane!" Harry Hope is quick to pick up these words. Of course Hickey had been insane. All his actions during the past hours had been unlike the Hickey they knew. In fact everything which all of them had done had been just the result of playing along with Hickey's insanity. As the police lead Hickey away, the stage is already set for the group's recantation of any recent accusation of self or others. The pipe of dreams is lit once more.

But there are two exceptions. One of the roomers at Harry Hope's is Larry Slade, a disillusioned syndicalist-anarchist, who had been forced by Hickey to admit that under his guise of longing for death there was a cowardly craving for a few hours longer on any terms whatsoever. Larry is reluctantly harboring Parritt, the son of his former mistress. Parritt is lying low after the exposure of an anarchist bombing plot, as the result of which his mother is in prison. Larry feels that Parritt is appealing to him for help and tries to avoid responsibility. During Hickey's revelations, it becomes obvious that Parritt sees some kind of parallel with his own situation. He finally admits that it was he who betrayed his mother to the police, not because of disbelief in the Cause nor even for money but because her powerful personality was destroying his own freedom, and he hated her. Scornfully rejecting Hickey's way out, Parritt faces the truth and realizes that only by killing himself can he ever get free of his mother. Larry helps him to reach this decision and realizes that now for the first time his desire for death is real. O'Neill's conclusion seems to be that for people who have not lived up to their ideal of themselves, the choice is between bad faith and death.

*The Iceman Cometh* is a play about man; it is not merely the story of Hickey and his friends. It is a play, too, which puts uppermost the question of man's relation to himself; and it seems to say that there are brief moments at which a man is capable of recognizing that he is what he has chosen to be. O'Neill lets us see the precise point at which Hickey and the men and women at Harry Hope's deliberately reach for more self-deception in preference to the self-knowledge which tortures. Yet this is not an existentialist drama. O'Neill stays too closely to the old idea that once man's nature is made, all he can do is to remain as he is or die. There is no indication that a man may radically change himself.

On the other hand, although the works of Sartre, de Beauvoir, and Camus which we have studied have all shown us characters who have chosen to live in bad faith, no one of these authors believes that good faith is impossible. Man *can live* without illusions. His acceptance of himself as man and only man does not mean that he will give up all aspiration and simply repeat the dreary patterns of the past, stripped now of any hope of transcending them. The discovery of freedom is also the discovery of a future. And to discover a future means to determine a future.

# III. RECOGNITION AND ENGAGEMENT

## 1. TO LEAP OR NOT TO LEAP

ALTHOUGH SARTRE SAYS that the one common feature of the divergent branches of existentialism is the claim that existence precedes essence, it has always seemed to me that the bond between them is more a matter of mood than of any abstract principle. All existentialist writers offer—each in his own way—a challenge to conventional moral codes, a sense of urgency in matters of conscience, an interest in the private introspections of the individual. In addition, there are certain emotionally charged psychological concepts which are forever recurring, ideas scarcely to be found in other philosophies—anguish, dread, nausea, despair, the compulsive demand for passionate choice and total commitment.

One of the most interesting of these is the notion of the absurd. As early as the second century, Tertullian planted the seed when he said of the crucifixion, "It is believable because it is absurd; it is certain because it is impossible." Condensed in the formula, *Credo quia absurdum,* Tertullian's pronouncement has stood for the belief that only a God and a divine plan which surpass human reason to the point of seeming to contradict it are adequate for man's salvation. A God who conformed to human reason would be a God subject to human limitations. Kierkegaard wrapped the statement in more emotion but did not change its meaning. To him it is absurd, perhaps even blasphemous, to

hope that there could ever be any meeting between finite man and infinite God. The greatest absurdity of all is the doctrine that this union
was actually effected in Christ. Yet only such absurdity is commensurate
with the immensity of man's need and the grandeur of his desperate appeal. Naturally a person will not win salvation simply by deciding on
rational grounds that only the irrational can satisfy his heart's desire.
The Christian who makes the Leap in faith must at the same moment
actively believe that he is acting contrary to reason and that he is unworthy of the grace which will save him. Kierkegaard, of course, made
this Leap and bounced back to tell us of the joys on the other side.
Kafka remained all his life teetering on the brink, convinced that he
ought to jump but never able to decide in which direction. He seems to
have been a man who managed to live simultaneously in two of the
worst of all possible worlds. Among humanistic existentialists the concept of the absurd is of central importance, but it remains at the heart
of the data, so to speak; it is never transfigured so as to become in itself a promise of escape from the human condition. As with the religious
existentialists, the absurd retains a connotation of disproportion, of discrepancy. For Camus the absurdity of man lies in the fact that he makes
demands upon himself and on the world which would make sense only
if there were a certain God and a perceptible meaning in existence; and
yet he knows that there is no God and he can perceive no meaning.
Without God, man has a concept of sin; in a meaningless universe he
demands a meaning; his finite mind insists on pursuing projects whose
scope is infinite. These ideas are implied again in the work of Sartre
and of de Beauvoir, but they give special emphasis to the contingency
of man's being. Man longs to feel that his existence is necessary, is
"justified." But the notions of "justification" and "necessity" are in
themselves human concepts. Man's attempt to achieve absolute Being
can only result in the vain pursuit of the impossible in-itself-for-itself—
the "missing God."

We have seen that bad faith is an evasion of man's essential freedom.
The one who lives in bad faith refuses to face the truth of his existence
and pretends that someone or something other than himself is responsible for what he makes of his life. Obviously, good faith will demand
that a man honestly confront his situation and accept full responsibility
for his chosen mode of existence. But before considering how to lead a
life in good faith, or even whether it is possible to do so, we must face
another question: Will the man in good faith choose to live? If life is

totally absurd—i.e., without meaning—then perhaps the only answer in good faith is the refusal to live. There is but one truly philosophical problem, says Camus—suicide. For the humanistic existentialist the Leap in question is a leap over the precipice. If he decides not to jump, then his task is to consider how it is possible to attain a life which is significant in purely human terms. The Leap of faith in the direction of any supernatural refuge is forbidden from the start.

Camus has made the absurd the central theme of two plays, a novel, and a book of essays. In *Cross Purpose (Le Malentendu),* he draws our attention to the absurdity of things as exemplified in gratuitous human suffering and in the misunderstanding and hatred existing where there might "more naturally" have been love and mutual help. The characters of the play when confronted with the absurd seek neither to comprehend nor to transcend it; they simply despair. The plot is a variation on the prodigal son story. Jan, the returning son, is incognito; the only welcome prepared for him is that extended to the victim of a murder plot. The scene is laid in a gloomy, rarely frequented inn located in an out-of-the-way spot in central Europe. During the years since he ran away, Jan has lived happily and prosperously in the South. Having heard recently that his father has been long dead, he has come to see whether he can help his mother and sister, who are still maintaining the old inn. Yet while he tells his wife that the journey is undertaken because they perhaps need him and not because he has any need of them, it soon becomes clear that he feels compelled to return for more than altruistic reasons. At first he tries to explain that men have a duty as well as a need for happiness. Then he says,

> One can't be happy in exile or in forgetfulness. One can't always remain a stranger. A man has need of happiness, true. But he needs too to find out what he is [*sa définition*]. And I imagine that to find my country again and to bring happiness to those I love will help me in this (p. 27).[1]

Fearing the effect of too sudden a revelation and hoping obscurely that he can make his mother and sister love him for himself and gradually realize who he must be, Jan sends his wife to another hotel and prepares to register as a guest in his mother's inn. Meanwhile we have learned from the conversation of mother and daughter that they have in recent years adopted the practice of robbing and murdering unaccompanied wealthy customers. The motivating force behind this conduct is Martha's (the daughter's) passionate longing to escape to a southern land of sun and sea. Camus is remarkably successful in showing how this hope seems to Martha a promise of life and new birth, so much so that the mother's willingness to resort to desperate measures is quite convincing. Jan's obvious wealth offers to the pair the chance finally to accomplish their plan.

Camus exploits the irony of the situation to the fullest. When Jan attempts to establish some sort of friendliness with Martha, she rebuffs him with the statement that he is to receive exactly the treatment accorded to other guests, neither more nor less. He finally succeeds in arousing some warmth and eagerness in her by talking of his home in the South, but it is this reminder of the beauty of her land of hope which stiffens Martha in her weakening resolve to carry on with the murder. When Jan is almost ready to give up and go away without revealing himself, Martha offers the first unsolicited overture—the cup of tea containing a knockout drug. When the mother, who had secretly resolved to spare him, finds that he has already drunk the tea, she assures him that after all it had been brought by mistake. Jan falls into a drugged sleep, and the mother, now that the usual train of events has been started, finds it easier to let them continue; she joins with Martha in throwing Jan into the river.

Up to this point the tragic irony is akin to the Hardy variety. In spite of the unpleasant habits of the two women, one feels that but for the absurd trick of fate, all might have ended well. If the mother had arrived before Jan had drunk the tea, if Jan had revealed himself at the first sign of Martha's wistful longing for another life, they might all have gone south to swim and sun-bathe happily together. But the discovery of Jan's passport and consequently of his true identity not only influences future developments but throws a new light on past events. In the mother the sudden knowledge effects a bitter and yet somehow wonderful awakening. Although she had found it easier not to look at the victims, she discovered that after the first time even murder became a habit. Her hope that her daughter might have a better life was wistful rather than passionate. The only bond she felt with humanity at large was a fellow-feeling of compassion for the universal unhappiness of the world. When she learned of the number of suicide drownings in the river, she remarked to Martha that they were less cruel than life itself. Preparing to take "the stranger" down to the river bank, she feels—not in madness like the old women in *Arsenic and Old Lace* but with a dull sincerity—that she is bringing the man peace. Later the miracle of the love which has just shown itself after twenty years of silence and forgetfulness awakens the mother to her own emotions. She feels for her son an intolerable love and a grief so overwhelming that she cannot cope with it. The only solution is to join her son at the bottom of the river. To Martha this talk of crime and punishment makes no sense. She pleads with her mother not to sacrifice a living daughter to a dead son. The mother replies that she knows her feelings do not make sense, that the world does not make sense either. But she knows too that when a mother is no longer capable of recognizing her son, then her role in life is ended. "In a world where everything can be denied there exist forces which cannot be denied, and on this earth where nothing is sure, we have our certainties. *Bitterly.* A mother's love for her son is now my certainty" (p. 81). Martha's reaction is totally different. Instead of feeling remorse, she completely destroys any possibility of interpreting events as the ironic outcome of chance or malignant Fate, and declares that she would have acted in the same way even if she had known that Jan was her brother. This is certainly not just because she is unaware that Jan had come home for the express purpose of making his mother and sister happy. It is because she hates him for having had twenty years of the love and happiness of which she has been deprived. The fervor of her denunciation of him is also surely due in part to jealousy of her mother's love for Jan. Although there would be nothing to prevent her going away alone, her mother's rejection of her makes Martha realize that "in crime one is always solitary" and that now nothing can make her happy. She prepares to join the mother she had loved and the brother she hated.

But first Martha must talk with Maria, who comes in the morning to search for her husband, and it is here that Camus reveals the full breadth of the absurd. Martha freely tells her the truth, without apology and without pity. She resents the happiness which Maria has had in the past, but what really maddens her is Maria's belief that the calamity which has come to her is the exception in a universe where love and family ties and meaningful happiness are possible. Martha deliberately tries to drive Maria to despair by showing her that there is no hope anywhere in the world, "that no one is ever recognized."

> I cannot die leaving you with the idea that you are right, that love is not in vain, and that all this is an accident. For it is now that we are in the normal order of things. . . . Try to realize that neither for him nor for us, neither in life nor in death

is there any homeland or peace. . . . We've been swindled, I
tell you! What good is this great craving for being, these yearn-
ings of our soul? Why cry out for the sea or for love? It's
laughable. Your husband knows the answer now—that house
of horror where we will at last lie close to one another (pp.
97-98).

Martha goes on to say that when Maria too comes to realize how death
is the answer to all of man's hopes and questions, she will find in retrospect that even her present, personal pain is happy by contrast. "But
know that your grief will never equal the injustice which has been done
to man!"

Martha concludes by counseling Maria to struggle to attain the insensitivity of whatever force is responsible for man's creation.

Pray to your God that he may make you like a stone. That is
the happiness which he chooses for himself, the only true happiness. Be like him. Make yourself deaf to all cries. Become
one with the stone while there's still time. But if you feel that
you're too much a coward to enter into that blind peace, then
come to join us in our common house (pp. 98-99).

Maria cannot accept the idea that life is totally meaningless; she follows
Martha's advice and prays—but for help.

O God, I cannot live in this desert! . . . Have pity on me! Turn
your face toward me! Hear me, Lord, and give me your hand!
Have pity on those who love each other and are separated
(p. 99).

At this point the old servant, who has not previously spoken, suddenly
appears and asks Maria if she has called. Maria appeals to him with
almost the same words she had addressed to God. He responds with
one word, the last of the play—"No."

In *The Stranger,* which Camus wrote after he had finished the first
writing of *Cross Purpose* but before he presented it to the public, the
hero Meursault finds an old newspaper clipping reporting as an actual
event the plot of *Cross Purpose.* The account is stripped of everything
which makes the story significant. The son conceals his identity just as
a kind of joke *(par plaisanterie),* and Meursault feels that he somewhat
deserved what came to him. But he thought about the story a lot and
concluded, "In one way it was improbable. But in another it was quite

natural." ² Just what seemed to him improbable and what natural is not explained. But knowing that Meursault is *par excellence* Camus' hero of the absurd, we may perhaps make an accurate guess. The improbability would lie in the initial situation. From a rational point of view (which is only halfway the point of view of the absurd), it would seem unlikely that we would find both a son who chose to hide his identity and a mother and sister ready to murder a hotel guest. Yet on the other hand it is natural that those separated for so many years would find no special bond between them if their common memories were suppressed. Life provides no automatic, self-evident ties of affection even between the nearest of kin. In a universe without transcendent meaning, why should we be surprised by this incident where only the hidden factors make the event remarkable?

In *Cross Purpose* the general character of the absurd is already sketched out—the existence of suffering and injustice among men who will in any case find that death makes futile all their projects, the deaf impersonality of a world in which man constantly searches for a reason to explain and justify his struggle but can find none. Yet while Jan, Martha, and Maria all try to find a way out and fail, the play is not without the suggestion that there might be a solution. Jan speaks of the love which may flower if one has the slow patience to tend it. Moreover, he and Maria have both known happiness in the South. True, Jan had felt it was not enough and had sought something more. Yet even if we say that his relative, human happiness had not satisfied him, it was not that it had not been real or that he had not wanted to go back to it. His journey north had been in part to find some assurance that he belonged and was necessary (a futile hope so far as this play is concerned), but it was partly too because he wanted to share the happiness he had with those he felt to be akin to him. It is perhaps not going too far beyond the play's intent to see in Jan's return the attempt of a man who had achieved inner peace but who could not enjoy it so long as others are still suffering.

While I think that it would be doing violence to the play to soften any of Martha's bitter summing up of life, yet Camus in the years following has not continued to offer stony insensitivity and a miry bed as the only two alternatives. Maria cries out that she cannot live in this desert, but later in *The Myth of Sisyphus* Camus stated in so many words that his intention was "to see if thought could live in these deserts." Although we are not yet ready to examine his conclusions, we may note that even in *Cross Purpose* the sun-drenched land of what obviously is his native Algeria stands as a hope and symbol of a life in the here and now which is rich, intense, and *humanly* rewarding. There is another hint of escape in the final words of the mother. Although she feels that even her new-found certainties are absurd in a senseless world and although her emotional awakening leads her to suicide, she dies not because of the barrenness of life but because of a new vision of a richness she has herself destroyed. She is akin to de Beauvoir's heroine of *The Blood of Others,* who learned that life takes on meaning at the moment when one finds something one is ready to die for.

*Caligula* * is more obviously a philosophical play than *Cross Purpose.* Here the encounter with the absurd comes at the beginning; it determines events instead of being revealed by them. The actual Caligula is represented by the ancient historians as having suddenly gone mad as the result of an illness. Apparently convinced of his close kinship with the Olympians (not too surprising an obsession in a man' whose ancestors had been made gods by an act of the Senate), Caligula manifested all the arbitrariness of divine will; he inflicted public ridicule on important members of the court, killed and tortured both his enemies and those who supposedly were close to him, forced all Rome to recognize his favorite horse as a consul and a member of a priestly college. In Camus' play, Caligula's strange conduct begins after the death of his beloved sister, and the Court believes that it is her dying which has driven him mad. In a sense they are right. But it is not exactly the loss of Drusilla which matters to Caligula. So far as she is concerned, he is tormented less by regret than by the discovery that grief does not last. The essential point, however, is that he has discovered as a living truth the fact that "men die and they are not happy." Martha had tried to persuade Maria of this same truth by words. Caligula tries to teach it to all of Rome through his actions. He makes public appearances in which he assumes the form of the various gods so that he may show the world how easy it is for man to play the ridiculous roles of these illusory beings. By his capricious cruelty he tries to force the Romans to question their easy optimism and to see the universe as the imper-

---

* *Caligula* (1938) was written before *Cross Purpose* (1943) but was produced a year later (*Caligula,* 1945; *Cross Purpose,* 1944). I have chosen the nonchronological order for discussion both because it is possible that Camus may have revised the plays before their production and because the logical development of the two is such that *Cross Purpose* seems to me less precise in its message than *Caligula.*

sonal, even hostile environment which it really is. Some of his acts are a bit more pointed. He refuses to enter into war because he values human life more than military triumphs. But he justifies the number of his murders by saying that he had merely supplied some of the dead which would have been furnished by an epidemic. He explains his apparently random choice of victims by remarking that it doesn't matter in what order men die since all must die sooner or later and since all are equally guilty (presumably because they all either cause or accept the fact of the suffering of other men). At other times he emphasizes that he is but following to its logical conclusion either his own special insight or the prevalent beliefs of all men. His arbitrary murders are the reflection of the capricious destruction inflicted by nature. His decision to proscribe the wealthy men of the state and confiscate their property is but the natural consequence of the view that the most important thing in the Empire is the national treasury.

Caligula is finally assassinated by a group of conspirators under the leadership of Cherea, who understands the Emperor too well to hate him but who feels that Caligula must die for two crimes: because he has put despair into the heart of the young and because he has stripped life of meaning, without which man cannot live. In spite of Caligula's perception of the absurd and his resolve to force others to realize it, he is not yet the "absurd hero." At the end of the play he says, "I have not found the right way. I have failed. My freedom is not the good one." And Camus has stated that Caligula was wrong in not respecting human life. Yet we should be wrong, I think, to conclude that Caligula is wholly an unsympathetic character serving as the antithesis of attitudes which Camus would approve. Caligula is contrasted with Scipio and Cherea, and it is true that they give voice to views which parallel to a degree those found in Camus' essays. Thus Cherea makes people and things important. He argues that if we are going to live in this world, we must plead its cause. And Scipio declares that he loves Caligula for what he was before the recent crisis.

> He was good to me. He encouraged me, and I know by heart some of his words. He told me that life wasn't easy but that there were religion, art, love to support us. He said over and over that the only mistake was to cause suffering. He wanted to be a just man (p. 117).

Yet Cherea persists in thinking that life has some sort of basic meaning, and Scipio exults poetically in a feeling of harmony with nature.

They have not transcended the absurd but have been unwilling or unable to confront it.

In spite of Caligula's failure he embodies in his conduct two attitudes which Camus recognizes as legitimate and makes a part of the positive dialectic of the philosophy of the absurd. First of all, there is the idea that a man frees himself only at that point at which he recognizes that the world has no importance, that the truth of the world is that it has no truth. Closely allied with this view, though not identical with it, is the statement that it is indifference which rekindles love in the heart of the man who has once known the world's absurdity. Secondly, there is the suggestion of philosophical revolt which becomes important in Camus' later work apropos of politics as well as personal self-realization. Throughout the play Caligula seeks to capture the moon as a symbol of the impossible. He pursues the impossible for the very reason that it is impossible. He has a need for the impossible because "things as they are do not seem to me satisfactory." We must not dismiss Caligula's desire as a mere whim of his madness. He realizes at the end that he will not have the moon and that all his efforts have merely resulted in referring him back to himself and the knowledge of his failure. Yet it is Camus' fundamental principle that man's grandeur and possible happiness lie in his refusal to give up his desire for the impossible. If man is to save himself, he must never cease to revolt against the limits of his condition at the same time that he refuses to pretend that they are not there.

Despite these slight suggestions of a positive position, *Cross Purpose* and *Caligula* serve primarily as data to document the absurdity of man-in-the-world; they do not provide any clear statement as to the proper attitude which we are to adopt confronting the absurd, nor do they contain any examination of the absurd as a philosophical concept. For the philosophy of the absurd we must turn to *The Myth of Sisyphus*, where Camus presents for the first time his "logic of the absurd" *(un raisonnement absurde)*. The philosophical premises and reasoning established in this book (1942) are as basic to Camus' work as methodological doubt was to Descartes. In 1955, in a preface to an American translation of it, he writes, "After fifteen years I have progressed beyond several of the positions which are set down here; but I have remained faithful, it seems to me, to the exigency which prompted them." Essentially *The Myth of Sisyphus* raises the question of whether the man who refuses to lie to himself will say "yes" or "no" to life itself; later works consider the problem of how to live the life one has chosen.

Camus begins, "There is only one really serious philosophical problem: that is suicide. To judge whether life is or is not worth the trouble of being lived is to answer philosophy's fundamental question." The problem becomes acute at that moment when one confronts the absurd. Such confrontation is like an awakening; and unless one deliberately closes one's eyes again, something of importance is bound to result. One goes on inevitably to suicide or to recovery.

Camus is nowhere more closely linked with traditional existentialism than in his description of the sudden upsurge of the absurd in our experience. Explicitly stating that he is making here no claim to originality, he offers a nonexhaustive enumeration of ways in which the feeling of the absurd may suddenly overwhelm one. Care or anxiety (of which Heidegger makes so much) is at the root of all these experiences. But one may view them also as the sudden perception by consciousness of a void or "nothing" in its existence. It is as though in the drama of life, the stage set should suddenly topple over. The occasion may be merely an abrupt detachment on the part of consciousness apropos of the daily routine.

> Get up in the morning, the streetcar, four hours at the office or factory, eat, streetcar, four hours work, eat, sleep—and Monday, Tuesday, Wednesday, Thursday, Friday, and Saturday in the same rhythm—this path is followed easily most of the time. But one day the "Why?" rises up and it all begins in that weariness tinged with astonishment (p. 27).

Or the absurd may coincide with that "revolt of the flesh" with which a man suddenly feels himself situated in time. A person may one day reflect on the fact that he is thirty years old. He places himself in time.

> He recognizes that he is at a certain point on a curve which he admits that he must traverse to its end. He belongs to time and by the horror which grips him he recognizes in time his worst enemy. Tomorrow—he was looking forward to that tomorrow when with all his being he should have rejected it (p. 28).

Again we confront the absurd when we face the alien density of the world. If at any moment we put aside the familiar associations with which we generally cloak the world about us, if we strip the universe of the human uses and significance which we have put upon it, then the world becomes itself again, hence it escapes us. It is no longer and in no way whatsoever "human." We are alone in a universe with which we have no communication, nothing in common. Similarly, we stand baffled before the nonhuman aspects of human beings. In what way can that physical reflection in the mirror be "I"? Human actions, if denuded of the unifying theme of our own reflection, are senseless, stupid, absurd.

> A man is talking on the telephone behind a glass partition; we don't hear him, but we see his unintelligible dumb show: we wonder why he is alive. This uneasiness before the non-humanity of man himself, this incalculable fall before the image of what we are, this "nausea" as a contemporary writer calls it—this too is the absurd (p. 29).

Finally, there is the fact of death and the feeling which it induces in us. Before the ineluctable end of our destiny all is rendered ultimately useless, all efforts, all ethics. There is additional absurdity in the fact that everyone lives as if he did not know the truth about death. And this is inevitable, for there is in reality no experience of death. Experience implies that which is lived and made conscious. But we can have no consciousness of our own death, and the deaths of others are somehow not quite convincing. We cannot transfer our awareness of their absence into the comprehension of our own nonexistence. These themes—man's facticity, man's inability to grasp, as if from within, the nature of the In-itself, man's anguish before the mystery of Self and his own mortality —are found everywhere in the literature of humanistic existentialism.

Camus' intellectual appraisal of the notion of the absurd (as contrasted with our simple experience of the feeling) is once again more an elaboration and restatement of the existentialist position than a new point of view. In part, Camus is interested in pointing to the inadequacy of reason. Apropos of his own discussion of the absurd, he states at the outset that true knowledge is impossible but that we may understand the absurd *practically*. Part of Camus' general criticism of the inadequacy of reason is based on observation of the limitations of thought as evidenced in the structure of Aristotelian logic. But primarily he is interested in the discrepancy between the demands of reason and its inability to satisfy them. In particular he is concerned with the question of *meaning*. Men spend their lives seeking coherent unity and meaning in the universe, but this does not mean that the unity and meaning exist. Reason may *describe* nature but cannot explain it. Moreover, Camus will not accept the way out offered by religious existentialists who, according to him, have made of the very failure of reason, a reason for believing in something beyond reason. To the man who will not forget his confrontation with the absurd, "reason is vain and there is nothing beyond reason" (p. 55). The *cogito ergo sum* for the logic of the absurd is comprised in one clear statement:

> I do not know whether or not this world has a meaning which transcends it. But I am aware that I do not know this meaning and that at the moment it is impossible for me to know it. What can a meaning which is outside my condition signify to me? I can understand only in human terms (p. 73).

But the absurd does not reside in the meaningless universe. By itself the world is not absurd; it is neither rational nor irrational, it is simply unreasonable. Nor is the absurd a quality of man alone. The absurd arises when man confronts the irrational with all of his nostalgic longing for happiness and reasonable unity. "The absurd is born of that confrontation of the human appeal and the unreasonable silence of the world" (p. 45). It is "the lucid reason setting its own limits." It is "sin without God."

Facing the absurd, Camus asks whether the man in good faith can live without appeal to transcendent meanings. "I want to know whether I can live with what I know and with that alone" (p. 60). In searching for an answer, we must follow along its grim path the relentless logic of the absurd. We must allow nothing of transcendent meaning or hope. We must forever keep before us that absurd which unlike Eurydice dies only when one looks away from it (p. 76). For a kind of first principle, Camus points out that people commonly make the mistake of assuming that if life has no meaning, this is equivalent to saying that life is not worth living. Actually, he argues, the idea of meaning and that of worthwhileness are quite separate. Although Camus does not put it in these terms, it seems that the common assumption contains a surreptitious shift from general to particular and from concept to value judgement. The fact that the universe does not reveal itself as permeated with objective meaning does not mean that I—or any other individual—will find my (or his) life of no value. There is a hidden second step in the statement as it is usually made; this is the assumption that if life has no meaning in relation to the universe, an individual life can have no meaning for the one who lives it. But it is precisely this which is in question; it cannot be assumed. Almost too easily Camus arrives at his first consequence for the logic of the absurd. We have asked, he says, whether life had to have a meaning in order to be worth living. But suddenly we find that it will be all the better lived if it does not have a meaning. His argument rests on the premise that to live an experience is to accept it fully. Now awareness of the absurdity of life causes us to know that life *is* without *meaning;* therefore to accept life fully one must live with constant awareness of the fact that life has no meaning.

Such acceptance is not resignation but *revolt,* the first of three positions consequent to confrontation with the absurd. This revolt is not a refusal to accept the absurd but a decision to live keeping it constantly before one. It is "the assurance of a crushing destiny without the resignation which ought to accompany it." If we remember that the absurd springs from the encounter between human demand and the unresponsive universe, we can see that a man may assume either of two attitudes toward it: He may simply suppress the demand, in which case he will commit suicide, which means consenting to the irrational as surely as if he took the Leap in faith. Or he may insist on sustaining the demand of consciousness without pretending that it is satisfied; in this case he will be like the condemned man, the extreme opposite of the suicide, who asserts his right to live even as sentence is passed. He maintains an awareness of death and yet rejects it. This is revolt, "which gives to life its value." "For the man without blinders, there is no finer spectacle than that of the intelligence at grips with a reality which surpasses it" (p. 78).

Revolt, while obviously it appeals to Camus, is merely a position which is both possible and consistent with his view of the absurd. There is as yet no reason why it is obligatory. Camus supports his case for living with two other consequents. The first of these is freedom. Any hope of eternal freedom such as is promised by various theologies is cut off from the start. Aside from the fact that the absurd man, relying only on what he knows, has already rejected God, Camus feels that human freedom and an all-powerful God who would support it are mutually exclusive. The old argument has never been refuted: either God is all-powerful and responsible for the evil of the world as well as its good, in which case we are not free; or we are responsible and he is not all-powerful. But leaving God out of it, the absurd man has demanded a conclusion which is based on the certainty of death; and this means automatically that freedom is temporally limited. If freedom exists, it must be a mortal freedom. But such freedom, Camus argues, the absurd man possesses more than anyone else. People are accustomed to think of freedom in terms of ability to accomplish a chosen aim against a background of established meanings. But actually, in so far as the world has a fixed purpose within which a man fulfills himself, he is enslaved by it. "To the extent that he imagined a set purpose for his life, he conformed to the exigencies of a goal to be attained and he became a slave to his freedom" (p. 81). In this passage Camus does not restrict himself to universal meanings which might confine a freedom. Even a self-imposed meaning which one deliberately chooses as a unifying theme for action, while it may make life more valuable, nevertheless hampers freedom.

> To the extent that I hope or that I worry about a truth which would be my own, or about a way of being or of creating, to the extent that I order my life and thereby prove that I admit that it has a meaning, I erect barriers between which I confine my life (p. 82).

The man who has awakened to the absurd and who means to live out his condition most fully refuses to take his freedom seriously. The more he is without a future and without hope, which is in itself a bond, the more he is really free. And this increases his *disponibilité*. This word, which appears frequently in existentialist literature, is usually translated "availability." It indicates a readiness to respond to new possibilities, to look on all projects with a disinterest not tainted with indifference.

> The divine *disponibilité* of the man condemned to death before whom the walls of his prison open on a certain early dawn, that incredible disinterest with regard to everything save the pure flame of life—death and the absurd are here (one can feel it clearly) the principles of the only reasonable freedom: that which a human heart can live and prove by its own experience (p. 83).

This brings us to the third consequence of the logic of the absurd—*passion*. Recognition of his mortal freedom renders a man indifferent toward the future but all the more passionate to drain off the full intensity of present experience. "The present and the succession of presents before a soul which is at every moment conscious—this is the ideal of the absurd man" (p. 88). Two ideas are involved here: first, the notion implied throughout the book, that anything which man finds good or valuable or in any way significant must be so in and through consciousness. Absurdity is the product of consciousness confronting the world; but so are revolt, freedom, and passion "for the pure flame of life itself." Awareness is what matters; there is ultimately no deeper satisfaction than man's conscious and deliberate consent to the full intensity of experience, no matter what its quality. As a corollary to this position there follows the view that for the absurd man, what counts is quantity of experience. But lest we think that this is to introduce into the logic of the absurd a scale of values, hence the view that after all life is meaningful, Camus hastens to assure us that the fact of death means that no man is in control of the quantity of experience which his life may have. Therefore, we are forbidden any look toward the future which might result from an ethics of quantity. Once more we are brought back to the realization that it is intensity of experience in the present which matters.

> Thus I derive from the absurd three consequences which are my revolt, my freedom, and my passion. By the sheer activity of consciousness, I transform into a rule of life what was an invitation to death—and I refuse suicide (pp. 88-89).

Camus decides to accept the "wager of the absurd" and to declare worth living this life which has no meaning. At this point it may seem that he reverses Socrates' statement to Crito and says that it is not the good life which counts but only life itself. But the criticism is not quite justified. Even at this early stage Camus has introduced two qualifications: The absurd man is stubbornly honest, and he seeks the fullest possible awareness of all that is involved in whatever he experiences. These restrictions by themselves are heavily consequential. For the man who rejects all illusion, who is totally aware of all that his situation comprises, and who has neither hope nor fear for the future—such a man appears to be already well on the road to some kind of sainthood. Admittedly the atmosphere of the absurd still retains some of the dry dust of the desert, and it is well that Camus has not been content to remain on this level.

At this point it may be interesting to compare Camus' conclusions with those of William James, who wrestled with the same problem in his essay, "Is Life Worth Living?" [3] * James divides his discussion into two parts. In the first section he lays down the same conditions as Camus. Can life be worth living if we limit ourselves to only those things which we know, rejecting any hope of higher purpose or meaning? What can we say to the man intent on suicide for merely metaphysical reasons? James gives three reasons for living. The first is simple pugnacity; and although James offers it in terms reminiscent of the homely inspirational works of the early twentieth century, pugnacity is in essence hardly distinguishable from the absurd man's revolt. The second is curiosity. Many a man, says James, would set down the glass of poison long enough to see what the postman might have brought. Inelegant as the idea may be as here stated, it contains in embryo the view that man's deepest satisfaction is the simple process of fulfilling his desire to know and understand. It is roughly equivalent to Camus' feeling for the value of consciousness itself. We have met it specifically in de Beauvoir's *She Came to Stay* when Françoise refused to sever her painful relation with Xavière because she felt sustained and swept on by "an impersonal curiosity so violent that it had all the warmth of joy." James' third appeal is to our sense of honor, our feeling that we ought to contribute something to a world in which other beings have already given so much to make possible and to enrich our existence. None of the existentialists uses this argument in quite the same way as James. But we shall see later that each of them ultimately finds individual freedom and happiness impossible and worthless without the simultaneous recognition of others' freedom and respect for it.

In the second part of his essay James is radically different from Camus. Pointing to the phenomena of mysticism and other unusual and apparently inexplicable psychic states, he asks why we should be forbidden to assume that there *may be* conscious experiences of a sort now unknown to us, and why it is impossible that further development of human capacities should not reveal that there is a higher meaning

---

* In fundamental outlook there is a certain general resemblance between pragmatism and existentialism. Both put strong emphasis on action, on the relative or subjective quality of truth and of ethics; both extend their interest to problems usually associated with psychology rather than philosophy; both (e.g., John Dewey) have sought application of their philosophy to contemporary social problems. There are, of course, striking differences as well. Pragmatism is on the whole much more optimistic, has much more tendency to appeal to "common sense." James (unlike most pragmatists) attempts to provide a basis for "rational faith" in theism of a sort not consistent with either religious or humanistic existentialism.

to life after all. James is careful not to offer any hypothesis as to the nature of this meaning, for his point is that the meaning, if there be one, must be such that at the present stage of human development we could not perceive it as meaning. But it is quite clear that for him personally one of the greatest reasons for living is the challenge that there *may be* a higher significance to life, and that if there be, it is only by exerting all our efforts that such a purpose can be brought into perceptible existence.

It is very important to distinguish James' position from that of religious existentialism. The latter leaps illogically from the recognition that the world is not rational to the idea that in this very irrationality man will find his salvation. Moreover, while its proponents speak of God as wholly transcendent and as having no common measure with man, they generally go on to discuss the myths of a particular religion as if they were in some way a revelation of God's nature. Finally, religious existentialists almost without exception hold that the Leap in faith must be accompanied by a willingness to renounce the claims of one's individual personality. If we are to become one with the All, we must be ready to be nothing in ourselves. But James makes no such assertion.* He insists only that where all is at present uncertain, the infinite future and human effort may just as well turn out to reveal significance as more of the meaningless. Actually it is the very lack of certainty which for James makes the challenge so exciting. In another context he writes,

> I have often thought that the best way to define a man's character would be to seek out the particular mental or moral attitude in which, when it came upon him, he felt himself most deeply and intensely active and alive. At such moments there is a voice inside which speaks and says: *"This* is the real me!" . . . Now as well as I can describe it, this characteristic attitude in me always involves an element of active tension, of holding my own, as it were, and trusting outward things to perform their part so as to make it a full harmony, but without any *guaranty* that they will. Make it a guaranty—and the attitude immediately becomes to my consciousness stagnant and stingless. Take away the guaranty, and I feel (provided I am *überhaupt* in vigorous condition) a sort of deep enthusiastic bliss, of bitter willingness to do and suffer anything, which translates itself physically by a kind of stinging pain in-

---

* Not in the essay which I am discussing. Elsewhere, especially in explaining his "over-beliefs," he comes closer to the ideals of Western theology.

side my breast-bone (don't smile at this—it is to me an essential element of the whole thing!), and which, although it is a mere mood or emotion to which I can give no form in words, authenticates itself to me as the deepest principle of all active and theoretic determination which I possess.[4]

The interesting thing about James' conclusion is that while it is a position which humanistic existentialists firmly reject, it is one which is not really inconsistent with their own point of vew. The premise of Camus' logic of the absurd is simply the statement that the universe reveals no higher meaning which man can at present understand. But whether there might be a meaning which future man could comprehend Camus does not pretend to know. Seemingly he is not interested in investigating the hypothesis. Sartre and de Beauvoir appear to have adopted the view that the universe is ultimately and forever irrational; yet their claim that human nature is not fixed ought to allow for evolutionary changes in man's understanding. It would be straining things to the breaking point if we were to ask humanistic existentialism to adopt any specific hypothesis regarding a higher meaning for things. Yet I can see nothing in its principles which would forbid man to postulate the *possibility* that by his efforts he might help to bring about a situation in which other men would find more compelling reasons for living. It would, of course, remain up to the individual whether this hope for future men would or would not make his own life more rewarding to him. For within the limitations of humanistic existentialism, man can find no reason to hope that he may in any way escape his own death or any guarantee that the human condition will be improved with or without his efforts. If there be a higher meaning, it is by definition one which present man could not understand if it were pointed out to him. Camus, Sartre, and de Beauvoir have all apparently found the hypothesis of any significant change in the power or achievements of consciousness too slight a hope on which to base any plan of action or *raison d'être*. We are referred back to the absurd man's first question: Can thought live in these deserts where the universe is unresponsive to man's deepest demands? Can I live without appeal to anything beyond the human as I know it?

But this question of meaning is a delicate and slippery thing. And more than anything else, it revolves around the problem of time. We have seen that Camus in *The Myth of Sisyphus* limits the life of the absurd man to the intense experience of a succession of presents.

Camus severs his absurd man from the future for two reasons: first, because the knowledge of the inevitability of death fatally undermines all far-flung projects; second, because adherence to any fixed and extended purpose limits the freedom which is one of the gifts of confrontation with the absurd. In so far as it is possible for a man to live wholly in the present moment, we may say that his life may have value, but Camus is right in declaring that it does not have meaning. "Meaning" signifies at the very least a reference to something beyond the immediate sensation. But is it possible for a consciousness to live entirely in the present? Sartre and de Beauvoir say "No." The Being of the For-itself is such, says Sartre, that we can never say of it that it is, but only that it is-about-to-be. The present, like the flying arrow, which never is at point A, B, etc. but is always in process of passing over A, B, etc., exists only as the moment at which a person decides the way in which he is going to use his past experience to determine the nature of his project for the future—or more accurately his pro-jected future. We cannot isolate or live any one instant by itself any more than we can explain the movements of a tennis player without reference to the anticipated motion of the ball. Thus the For-itself exists *for* and (in a sense) even *in* the future. It is because the For-itself not only may but must live with the future always open before it that a consciousness may give meaning to its life.

Of course Sartre (and de Beauvoir) must qualify their view. Since in the most ultimate sense each person is isolated and can experience nothing beyond his present life, they are unalterably opposed to the idea of sacrificing a present generation for some abstract, far-off future. It is the relatively near and in part foreseeable future which allows me to give significance to my life. Moreover, one of the sources of anguish is the individual's realization that in his designs for the future, he can never be sure—even assuming that the plans objectively turn out as intended—that the Self who meets them will view them in the same light as the Self which initiated them. As Sartre somewhat poetically puts it, I make a rendezvous for myself down there in the future, but I do not know who will turn up to keep the appointment. This means that even the personal purpose which I have elected to bestow upon my life is at every moment subject to question. Thus while I may create a unifying theme to serve as a meaning for my existence, it remains so by virtue of my constantly renewed determination. In a sense for Sartre as for Camus, life is a succession of presents—though for Sartre each present is nothing more than the opening of a new door onto the future.

As a matter of fact, Camus too has modified his original radical position. In the first place, the present of which he speaks is never an isolated moment but rather what consciousness organizes into a unit of experience. Furthermore, if we look beyond *The Myth of Sisyphus*, even if we strictly exclude anything from Camus' later development of the philosophy of revolt (which adds the social dimension), we find him speaking of giving meaning to a life as a whole. In 1945 he wrote,

> I continue to believe that this world has no higher meaning. But I know that something in it has meaning and that is man; for he is the one being to insist on having a meaning. This world has at least the truth of man, and our task is to provide him with reasons to justify him against destiny itself. There are no reasons other than man, and it is he who must be saved if one wants to save the idea which one forms of life.[5]

Life makes no sense, but it is ours to make sense of. Traditionally the popular, and often the philosophical, view has been that unless there is a definite, supernaturally imposed pattern in the structure of things, a specific form within which human life is to develop, then existence is not only a tale told by an idiot but something intolerable, to be avoided entirely or foolishly squandered. But if one confronts a blank canvas, there are other alternatives beside committing suicide or throwing mud at it. One can (William James) set about scraping the surface and hope to find a painting underneath. Or one can set about painting a picture which will be personally gratifying.

At this stage of our discussion, that is as far as we have progressed. Lacking a transcendent pattern, the individual is free to impose upon his life a pattern which is meaningful to him. Later we shall see that for construction or for full appreciation of any satisfying pattern, there must be some degree of communication with our fellow creators. But we are not yet ready to consider the problem of committing our freedom in the interests of others. The humanistic existentialist has resolved not to take the Leap—neither the Leap toward faith nor the fatal plunge over the precipice. He will live, and he will live in good faith. But how? Since man never lives wholly apart from others, the problem of accepting the responsibility for one's own freedom and that of respecting the freedom of others cannot really be separated. Nevertheless, for purpose of discussion, we may distinguish between the literature which is primarily concerned with the individual's attempt to make his life significant in his own eyes and that which is interested in examining programs for action once the social commitment has already been made. Let us consider then first the absurd man, who is resolved to live meaningfully in a life without meaning, and then the freedom which deliberately engages itself in a world where the only real limit to freedom is the existence of other freedoms.

## 2. THE ABSURD MAN

Despite the intricate argument in Camus' logic of the absurd and despite the highly introspective quality of the characters whom we have met up till now in the literature of humanistic existentialism, one does not have to be a philosopher in order to confront the absurd and to live a life in good faith. The fictional hero who comes closest to fitting Camus' description of the absurd man is the central character of *The Stranger,* Meursault, an unassuming office worker in Algiers, not overly given to reflection. That he is also a man in good faith is indicated by Camus' only half-ironic statement that Meursault symbolizes "the only Christ of which we are worthy."

The first half of the book consists of Meursault's matter-of-fact account of the events following immediately upon the news that his mother has died at the Old People's Home. He goes to the funeral, where he experiences more physical discomfort and embarrassment than grief. That same weekend he meets a girl whom he had known some time before and found attractive, and they spend the night together. During the days which follow, Meursault grows increasingly attracted to Marie. Meanwhile, a fellow lodger, Raymond, confides in Meursault that he is involved in a serious quarrel with his mistress, an Arab girl, and with her brother, who has threatened him. Meursault agrees to help in any way he can. On a Sunday morning he and Marie go along with Raymond for a beach party with two of Raymond's friends. The Arab whom Raymond fears comes up to them suddenly with some of his friends. There is a fight in which Raymond is hurt. Meursault takes Raymond's revolver so as to prevent him from starting out to shoot his assailant, and he goes for a walk by himself along the sea. Suddenly he meets the Arab. The man draws a knife and Meursault shoots him. The second half of the novel concerns Meursault's imprisonment and trial. The law reconstructs events in such a way that he is declared guilty of premeditated murder. All that remains is for Meursault to decide what attitude to adopt in the face of his imminent execution.

Even upon superficial reading it is evident that Meursault is not being tried for having murdered the Arab. Had that been the case, a plea of self-defense would have resulted in a few years' imprisonment at the most. What the prosecuting attorney dwells upon is not the details of the murder but Meursault's apparent indifference at his mother's funeral and the callousness of a man who could begin a love affair on the very next day. When Meursault's own lawyer asks whether his client is on trial for having killed a man or for having buried his mother, the prosecutor replies that the relation between the two facts is "profound, moving, and essential." "I claim that when he buried his mother, this man showed he had a criminal's heart" (p. 136). Camus has said apropos of *The Stranger,* "In our society any man who doesn't weep at his mother's funeral runs the risk of being condemned to death." [1] So much is evident to any thoughtful reader, and when the book first appeared, many critics did not see much beyond this satiric intent. They were inclined to find in Meursault a very ordinary man, something of a drifter, who was pitiably caught in a trap of prejudice and circumstantial evidence and who attained a measure of dignity only by his ultimate defiance of both death and his judges. In an attempt to correct this point of view Camus provided an explanation which gives greater stature to Meursault and which may enable us to see how he fits the requirements of the absurd hero. Evidently Camus intended to portray in Meursault not a poor individual who irritated society but a man who seriously threatened it. He is condemned because he will not play the game. And this is the explanation of the novel's title. "In this sense, he is a stranger to the society on whose outskirts he wanders, living his own private, lonely, sensual life." But in what way does he refuse to play the game?

> The answer is simple: he refuses to lie. Now, lying is not only saying what is not. It's also saying more than *is,* and in matters of the human heart, more than we feel. We all do this every day, in order to simplify life. Meursault, contrary to appearances, does not want to simplify life. He tells the truth, he refuses to exaggerate his feelings, and immediately society feels itself threatened. For instance, he is asked to say that he is sorry for his crime, according to the conventional formula. He answers that he experiences more annoyance on its account than genuine sorrow. And this nuance condemns him.

> So, for me, Meursault is not a mere drifter but a poor, naked human being, in love with that sun which casts no shadows. He is far from being completely without sensibility; a profound

passion, though a tacit one, moves him—a passion for the absolute and for the truth. The truth at stake is as yet only negative, the truth of being and feeling. But without this truth, no conquest over oneself and over the world will ever be possible.

Seen in this light Meursault is a man willing to die for the truth and the comparison with Christ is at least intelligible.

This disconcerting honesty is revealed especially in Meursault's relations with people close to him. Toward his mother, his conduct had been sensibly dutiful but never sentimental. Although the prosecuting attorney tried to cast aspersion on a man who would put his mother in a public institution, the director of the Home pointed out that Meursault was not in a position to look after her himself and that she was much happier in the Home. It was the realization that now it would actually be a wrench to her to leave there which had kept Meursault from visiting her often—this plus the fact that it would have meant going to considerable inconvenience and giving up his Sundays. It is apparent that Meursault by a kind of nonreflective quantitative calculation balanced the pleasure bestowed by his visits against the discomfort involved and decided it was not worth it to make the trip frequently. The same sort of matter-of-fact appraisal appears in his conduct after his mother's death. Sitting beside her body, he wonders whether his smoking would imply any disrespect to her and decides that it could not possibly make any difference. For the rest, he simply acts by his immediate impulse. Since he is not hungry, he refuses the suggestion that he go out for dinner, but he accepts a *café au lait*. He admits that he does not know just how old his mother is. He says that he does not wish to look at her (a refusal which he does not try to explain even to himself). Throughout he refrains from (or more accurately never even thinks of) conventional expressions of sorrow. During the following week Meursault's conduct is not perceptibly different from what it was before the funeral. Since his mother had not been a part of his daily life, why should her death change anything? On the other hand, alone in the evening he finds himself "for some reason thinking of Mother." And on many occasions he recalls something which she had said and evaluates a situation from her point of view. Even though they "had not talked with each other very much," there apparently had been a degree of comfortable unanimity.

Did Meursault love his mother? Or more particularly, had he felt grief at her funeral? When Meursault's lawyer puts the question to him, he finds it difficult to answer because he is not accustomed to reflect upon his emotions. Nevertheless, he tries to reconstruct his past feelings and says first that he had certainly been very fond of his mother but that he realizes this does not mean much since "all healthy people had more or less wished for the death of those they loved." Disturbed by the lawyer's agitated response, Meursault goes on to explain that his reactions are always in large part determined by his physical state and that on the day of the funeral he had been numb with fatigue and lack of sleep. Yet he concludes very seriously that he would have preferred it if his mother had not died. It is not only Meursault's lawyer who would be disconcerted and shocked by such a statement. One may easily imagine Kafka pronouncing judgement and condemning Meursault, not for his conduct at the funeral, but for his willingness to live content with so weak a bond between himself and the person with whom he had for so long shared his life. But this is not the point. Camus is not arguing that it is desirable for human beings to be so close to indifference, but that in a world where this is the truth about most human relationships, Meursault is, in Socratic fashion, ahead of those who pretend that things are other than they are.

Camus is subtly skillful in showing how Society echoes Meursault's conduct even while it hides the fact from itself. For example, he is condemned for showing no signs of violent grief. But it seems entirely natural to the warden that the close associates of Meursault's mother should be kept apart from the coffin so that they may not be upset by the sight of it. The reason implied is that the knowledge of their own death in the probably close future would be too painful. But there is also the suggestion that if the coffin is not there to remind them, the fact of their friend's death will not be greatly disturbing. At the time of the funeral Meursault is made to feel embarrassed because he does not know his mother's age, and the admission is made into a point against him at the trial. But when in response to his employer's question, Meursault (to avoid more embarrassment) replies, "She was about sixty," the employer looks relieved and feels that the whole matter is closed. The amenities having been observed, it is obvious that he does not care whether a person somewhat advanced in age dies at one time or another. At the trial a witness from the Home, who says that Meursault's mother sometimes complained of his neglect, adds that it was the usual thing for inmates to complain about their relatives. Everything points to Meursault's having brought to light a truth about human indifference and self-preoccupation which Society does not want revealed and which it generally covers up with sentimental platitudes about undying mother love, filial devotion until the grave, a "natural" love for our fellow human beings, etc. That the people witnessing the trial dimly comprehended that Meursault was being sacrificed to protect them from the truth about themselves is indicated by the attitude of those listening when the death sentence is pronounced. The young journalist averts his glance. Meursault looks at the faces of the crowd and thinks that he can read upon all of them a feeling of sympathetic respect. Here the idea is merely suggested; later we shall see in the work of Sartre and Jean Genet the full development of the notion that Society bears toward the condemned the religious veneration merited by the sacrificial scapegoat.

Meursault's attitude toward Marie is illuminating in another way. As one might expect, he never analyzes the appeal she has for him so as to classify it as sensual, spiritual, or a proportioned mixture of the two. He simply desires *Marie,* and desire is stimulated and delighted by her body, her appearance in the red and white dress, her individual tricks of gesture and facial expression. At their second meeting there occurs the conversation which has been quoted perhaps more often than any other passage in the book. "When she laughed, I wanted her again. A moment later, she asked me if I loved her. I replied that the question really didn't mean anything but that probably I didn't" (p. 54). Yet a little later he tells her that he is perfectly willing to marry her if she wishes; and still later, after watching her fitting in gracefully with Raymond's friends and helping with the party lunch, he considers very seriously the desirability of their getting married. In prison after the murder it is memories of Marie which comfort, and separation from Marie which most torments him. It is when he learns that she will no longer be allowed to visit him that he first grasps the full reality of his being in prison and feels that his life has been brought to a dead end. At the close it is the image of Marie's face, "golden like the sun and alight with the flame of desire," which personifies for him the life he so desperately hates to leave. But if he wanted to marry her, if he values her more than any other single person or thing in his life, if it is of her he thinks when he tries to summon up the image of a happiness he has known and lost, why will he not call it love?

We may find the clue in a passage in *The Myth of Sisyphus* where Camus is discussing Don Juan as one type of absurd hero.

> We give the name of love to that which binds us to certain beings only by means of a reference to a certain collective way

of seeing for which books and legends are responsible. But I know of love nothing but this mingling of desire, of tenderness, and of intellect which binds me to a particular being. This compound is not the same for another person. I have no right to give the same name to all of these experiences (p. 102).

Camus goes on to say that Don Juan multiplies what he cannot unify; that is, knowing the absurdity of love, which (over and over again) exists by virtue of feeling itself eternal in the face of inevitable death and change, Don Juan deliberately wills to make his life a repetition of intense, short-lived joys. When one of his women exclaims, "At last I have given you love!" he replies, "At last? No, but once again." His revolt takes the form of living each love as a unique and absolute experience without his ever losing sight of the fact that it is a love which exists in the present only. Don Juan lives a succession of presents— rebelliously, freely, passionately—all in the erotic key. If at the end his body betrays him and he finds that he has almost literally outlived himself, his mocking derision, which has been with him from the start, makes the inevitable end a deliberately chosen fate, not a punishment externally inflicted. Meursault is not a Don Juan. He is lacking in the reflective detachment necessary for such deliberate restriction of living to a single repetitive theme. But I believe that the passage quoted apropos of Don Juan explains Meursault's unwillingness to tell Marie that he loves her. He cannot find in his feelings for her that collective, self-evident meaning which literary loves seem to have in common. Moreover, it is also Meursault's habit to live a succession of presents. Faithful to his actual being and feeling, he is accustomed, by inclination rather than philosophical conviction, to live as fully as possible all that the immediate moment offers. In the interest of present experience he refuses a hollow future which he cannot foresee. He will make no commitment to love, which (literary conventions insist) is nothing if it does not believe itself eternal.

It is usual for common sense to despise the man who lives primarily in the present. He is likely to get into difficulties (as does Meursault), and he is generally considered selfish. But Camus makes us see such a one in a new light. In the first place, Meursault's preoccupation with the immediate experience increases that *disponibilité* of which we spoke earlier. Although he is bored and finds it difficult to listen to people who mouth conventional observations which they themselves do not understand, he is wholly absorbed in anyone with whom he is in real contact. Over and over we find him using the word "interesting." He gets involved with Raymond because he finds him interesting. Although rumor says that Raymond is a pimp, this does not matter to Meursault since that aspect is totally outside his relation with Raymond. Again, Meursault is interested in the eccentric habits of his neighbor Salamano, a man who has evidently transferred to an ugly dog his earlier habit of mistreating the wife whose death made his existence seem utterly empty. On one occasion Meursault spends time following an elderly woman who had piqued his curiosity by her odd behavior at his restaurant. At the trial he forgets his anxiety about the verdict in his interest in the way both attorneys are conducting his case. When this interest is directed toward others, it means that he makes himself wholly "available" to them. And if the result is that they expect from him some sort of commitment, he is willing to put himself at their disposal. He is ready to marry Marie. He consents to help Raymond in his intrigue. While he cannot see why Raymond wants to pin down their relation by a verbal declaration that they are "pals," he offers no objection and even goes so far as to support Raymond's statement to this effect at the trial, although the admission is dangerous to his case. In short, his relation to other people turns out not to be real indifference after all. Interest is also concern. Moreover, especially with Marie, Meursault seems to give the lie to any claim that human relations must necessarily be in bad faith. I can find no trace here of the wearisome frustration of Sartre's subject-object conflict. Meursault does not seek in Marie either a means of guaranteeing his own subjectivity or a way of evading self-responsibility. He does not use her in order to attain happiness. He is happy to be with her because she is as she is. In prison, even as he wishes that he might be with her, he reflects that it would be only natural and proper that she should forget him and take someone else as her lover. Such feelings (whatever we are to call them) would hardly satisfy a woman expecting the poetry and passion of Romeo or Othello. We can understand why Marie should feel that she perhaps loved Meursault for his "queerness" but that she might eventually come to hate him for it. But the distinctive quality of Meursault's attachment to Marie is that it is based on an absolute respect both for her and for himself as free individuals. As such it allows a measure of selflessness. For while he makes no pretensions of living only in and for her, he feels that her freedom to live contentedly in the future is far more important than any duty of loyalty owed to him. Their relation while it lasts makes life more valuable for each of them; but it is not parasitism or even symbiosis.

In pleading for the death sentence for Meursault, the prosecuting attorney tried to show that his "criminal" conduct at his mother's funeral and his murder of the Arab were inextricably connected. The ironical fact is that while the lawyer's reasons were wrong, his conclusion was right—as Camus has carefully shown. Meursault had tried to explain to his own lawyer that at the time of the funeral he had been so stupefied by fatigue and by the heat that he was only half aware of what was going on. Much later when he is asked why he killed the Arab, he can only reply, "Because of the sun." In his first account of the event Meursault says,

> The sun was burning up my cheeks, and I felt drops of sweat collect on my eyebrows. It was the same sun as on the day when I buried my mother and—like then—my forehead especially was paining me, all my veins pounding together against my skin. I couldn't stand that burning any more, and so I took a step forward (p. 86).

As it turns out, he quite literally kills the Arab because of the sun. Meursault had no personal hatred for him and considered the incident closed when Raymond was wounded. It was quite by chance that he still had the revolver. Although he had grasped it as a precaution when he saw the Arab draw the knife, there was a moment when he realized that he might safely withdraw without action. But the pounding in his head, the pitiless glare of the sun, which brought tears to his eyes at the instant when the accumulated sweat rolled from his eyebrows and filmed his vision—this, combined with a sudden blinding flash of light which leapt from the moving blade of the Arab's knife to sear Meursault's eyeballs in an outburst of pain, caused everything to reel before him. With his whole being strained to the utmost, Meursault felt that the sky was raining fire down upon him. His taut grip on the revolver tightened still more; the trigger gave way and abruptly shattered the peace of the sun-drenched beach and the calm balance of Mersault's existence. In the sudden release of tension and without knowing why, he fired four more shots at the Arab's inert body.

Naturally the jury cannot accept Meursault's explanation. They much prefer the prosecutor's theoretical reconstruction of events. It is easy to believe that a man who apparently lacks the normal emotions and sense of decency would deliberately carry out a premeditated murder—even if the motive by itself appears weak and unconvincing. But to believe that a man might commit a murder without *being* a criminal is both difficult and dangerous. There is a disturbing quality about Meursault's account of the event. In one way, since his act was nonreflective, since he had all to lose and nothing to gain, since it was all apparently the result of yielding to the intolerable pressures of a particular moment, he seems to be curiously innocent, hardly responsible. We have an extreme case of what we observe every day—the fact that all our decisions, actions, even our conscious reflection, are effected within a situation in which the facticity of our physical bodies plays a major role. But if we are tempted to say that Meursault's act was determined and that he was not responsible for it, we realize immediately that this is not determination of the usual sort. The doctrine that a man is determined by his heredity or environment is in many respects a comfortable and optimistic one. We may salve our own consciences by the thought that we are willing to do our part to help better the conditions of the poor, the handicapped, and the feeble-minded; we believe that every asocial act has a cause and that by altering the environment likely to produce such causes we may prevent crime and rehabilitate criminals. But Meursault's act is not the kind to be explained by heredity or by environmental conditioning. Despite the prosecutor's pleas there is nothing in Meursault's previous life to suggest that he would ever get involved in a crime of passion. In fact the moment of the murder stands out as an abrupt cleavage between all the even tenor of his past and that which is to follow. Meursault's response to the sun and the flash of the knife demonstrates rather the terrifying freedom of the human being, who may at any given instant feel himself cut off from everything which has preceded, and who may then do what nothing in his past life or habitual reactions would ever have foreshadowed. Meursault's act suggests the frightening possibility that any one of us might under certain pressures perform an action which we consider absolutely criminal and without any of the accepted criminal motivations. We feel that in his place we might have done as he did, but we cannot feel ourselves to be criminals either now or in the imagined circumstance. Thus if we say Meursault is innocent, we seem to undermine the whole structure of the serious law by condoning a murder for a triviality, "because of the sun." But if we condemn him, we are condemning ourselves. It is far easier to let ourselves be persuaded by the prosecutor and conclude that Meursault was preparing himself for the murder as he sipped *café au lait* beside his mother's coffin. The problem of Meursault's guilt and motives apropos of the murder is, after all, a secondary one. The real issue is whether a society can allow the existence of a man who seems to deny the seriousness, the permanence, and the classifiable predictability of human emotions. When the examining magistrate hears Meursault's calm denial that he believes in God, he exclaims, "Do you want my life to have no meaning?" Is it conceivable that this menace to society should not be guilty?

In his cell Meursault naturally spends more time in reflecting than had been his custom earlier. Realistically, Camus has him employ the homely, simple language appropriate to a person unused to philosophical subtleties. At first he discovers for himself the profound reality of his mother's statement that a person can get used to anything (a principal theme of Dostoyevsky's *House of the Dead*). Then he finds himself dwelling on another of his mother's sayings to the effect that nobody is ever absolutely and completely miserable. In this he is akin to Tolstoi's Pierre (in *War and Peace*), who learns that the limit of suffering is quickly reached and that in extreme circumstances the slightest improvement, the simplest pleasure, the very changes of the day or season may bring a joy as intense as only the greatest moments bring in our usual life.

After his condemnation Meursault thinks considerably about the sentence and the impending execution. It seems to him that there is a discrepancy between the absolute judgement itself and the ordinary quality of the people who pronounce it. And he feels that it would be somehow more fair if a man were given a slim fighting chance instead of being obliged to join with his judges in hoping that the machine will work effectively the first time. He does not fear death itself, but he finds it difficult to lose the habit of thinking like a free man; and he unashamedly dislikes the thought of never experiencing again the peaceful happiness of life as he had known it. Consequently, he lets himself hope that his appeal for a pardon will be granted. He rejoices each dawn when it is evident that at least on this day the execution will not take place. Then the Curé makes an unsolicited visit, and it is in the course of their conversation that with a sudden burst of passion Meursault awakens to a new awareness of himself and of life, an intense consciousness in which the logic of the absurd and the poetry of profound revolt are marvelously intermingled. The interview had begun like so many others with Meursault's tedious debate about his right to deny God's existence, and then it had drifted on to the question of an afterlife. Meursault admitted that it was natural to wish for another life after death but that this was of the same order as other impossible wishes, like "wishing to be rich, to swim very fast, or to have a better formed mouth." He says that the only kind of afterlife which would mean anything to him would be a life in which he could remember this one. The Curé, less angered than grieved, tells Meursault that with his poor blind heart he cannot see that the priest is on his side, and he promises to pray for Meursault. At this point something in Meursault seems to explode as forcibly as the revolver beneath the burning sun. What exasperates him is that the man is so positive.

> You see, he was so certain about everything! And yet not one
> of his certainties was worth a single hair from a woman's
> head. He was not even sure of being alive, since he lived like
> a man already dead. As for me, I might appear to be empty
> handed. But I was sure of myself, sure of everything, sure of
> my life and of that death which was going to come to me
> (pp. 168-169).

In the tirade which follows we see the full conscious revolt of the absurd man. Since the only certainty is death, there is but one privileged class, those who are still alive. Sooner or later all are condemned. So what does it matter whether he, or for that matter the Curé, is to die after being condemned for not having wept at his mother's funeral or for some other reason. The ugly dog belonging to Meursault's neighbor Salamano was as important before the dark chill of the future as Salamano's wife. From "the long range point of view" all human activities are equal—all are of no importance whatsoever. Meursault's rush of anger seems to wash him clean, to strip him of hope, to render him indifferent. But this indifference has nothing in common with despair or renunciation. Feeling cut off from hope and from the future, he is free to "cultivate the pure flame of life itself." For the first time he can understand why his mother on the brink of death had seemed to start to live again, had played with the idea of taking on a fiancé. Absurd she may have been, but she was not pathetic, and nobody, including Meursault, had the right to weep for her. Now on the edge of doom he feels perfectly free, ready to start afresh but liberated from the demands of hope and from the "meanings" which society had tried to force upon him.

> Before this night heavy with stars and constellations, for the
> first time I opened my heart to the tender indifference of the
> world. Finding it so like myself, so fraternal even, I felt that
> I had been happy and that I was still happy (p. 171).

Earlier Meursault had been ready to weep at the thought of how the people in the courtroom hated him. Now he concludes,

> To finish it all off and so that I may feel less alone, I have only to hope that there will be a great crowd of witnesses on the day of my execution and that they will greet me with shouts of hate and derision (pp. 171-172).

Meursault's strange happiness must not be confused with pantheism or with some sort of natural mysticism. He does not feel that he is one with the universe or seek to lose himself in it. Yet his joy in life itself (both here at the end and in his earlier quiet existence before the shooting) is inseparably connected with his delight in the beauty of the world and in his physical contact with the sun and sea. That these feelings of Meursault are also those of Camus is evident if we look at a series of lyrical essays by Camus, written at various times in his life, short pieces which give one the impression that they have been felt rather than thought—though with Camus thought and feeling seem to move together. To me, at least, it seems that in Camus ideas and emotions reinforce one another, whereas with Sartre and de Beauvoir emotions are constantly being subjected to reflective analysis for justification or rejection and in any case for classification. One might quote almost at random from Camus' essays, but it may be particularly rewarding to look at passages from "Wedding at Tipasa," written in 1939 before *The Stranger* and "Return to Tipasa," dated 1952. The earlier essay is a paean of earthly joy, a "wedding with the world." Camus augments its pagan quality by using the names of the ancient deities: "In the spring Tipasa is inhabited by the gods, and the gods speak in the sun and in the scent of the absinth." [2] But as an enlightened pagan, he points out that these are not the Mysteries of Demeter and Dionysus but of the earth itself.

> At Eleusis it sufficed to be a spectator. Here too I know that I shall never come close enough to the world. . . . And I understand here what is meant by "glory": the right to love without limit. . . . When I throw myself down among the absinth plants and let their scent enter into my body, then—against all my preconceptions—I shall be conscious of attaining a truth which is that of the sun and which will be the truth of my death as well (pp. 18-20).

Yet this ecstatic communion with nature is not for Camus a transcending of the human state but a recall.

> I love this life with abandon and I want to speak of it without reservation: it makes me proud of my condition as a human being. Yet people have often said to me: There is nothing in that to be proud of. Yes, there is something: this sun, this sea, my heart leaping with youth, my body with the taste of the salt still on it, and that immense setting where tenderness and glory meet in the yellow and the blue. It is to conquer all this that I must exert all my strength and resources. Everything here leaves me intact; I abandon nothing of myself; I don no mask. It is enough that I learn patiently the difficult art of living which well equals all their knowledge about life (p. 20).

Years later Camus comes back to Tipasa. Thinking of his earlier visits, he reflects that at that time he partook of a kind of innocence which left him unaware that a morality existed. Now he knows of its existence and feels himself incapable of living up to its demands. Anxiously he wonders whether Tipasa will manifest to him the beauty he had found there as a young man. Very gradually the beauty of the place reveals itself to him as before, and he finds himself able to give the same response.

> I found here once more the ancient beauty, a young sky, and I could measure my good fortune, understanding finally that even in the worst years of our madness the memory of this sky had never left me. . . . There the world began anew in a light which was always new. O light! It is the cry of all the characters of ancient drama as they confront their fate. This final recourse was also ours, and I knew it now. In the middle of the winter I learned at last that there was in me an invincible summer.[3]

To Camus the appreciation of external beauty and the bodily pleasure of physical existence in a world where there is such beauty are inseparable. Earlier in the same essay he writes,

> To renounce beauty and the sensual happiness which is attached to it, to serve exclusively the cause of the wretched—this demands a nobility which I lack. But after all nothing is true which forces one to exclude. Beauty by itself ends in a

simper, but justice isolated from it ends in oppression (pp. 149-150).

Camus goes on to say that if justice is to to be kept from shriveling up to a bitter, dry pulp, men "must keep intact within themselves a freshness, a wellspring of joy." If they are to struggle for the good of humanity, they must first learn "to love and to marvel" as they confront the splendor of the world.

Such passages if taken by themselves might suggest that Camus is closer to romanticism than existentialism, and it is true that the demand that nature furnish strength and comfort reminds one of the later, romantically inclined Heidegger "letting the object be" that it may "speak to him." We are far removed in spirit from Sartre's confrontation with the natural world as "an instrumental hierarchy of possibilities." Some critics, indeed, have tried to see Camus' logic of the absurd as a unique and aberrant excursus away from what would otherwise be a consistent evolution of his thought from the early essays, with their love of physical life and communion with nature, to the later philosophy of revolt in which this tenderness toward the world is extended to a concern for human justice and solidarity.[4] I cannot agree with this view. In the first place, Camus himself, as we saw, has stated that he has remained true to the fundamental requirements of the logic of the absurd. Furthermore, there is evidence even within the essays that Camus' delight in the world accompanies and perhaps even partly stems from the belief in the total indifference of the world. In "The Minotaur," a half-descriptive, half-poetic evaluation of life in the North African city of Oran, he concludes his picture of desert and sea with words which might easily have come from *The Myth of Sisyphus*. "Here are opposed to each other magnificent human anarchy and the permanence of an always equal sea." [5] And a few pages later in terms startlingly reminiscent of Sartre, he makes it clear that the longing to be identified with the absolute universe of suns and stones is a temptation. "There is in every man a profound impulse which is neither one of destruction nor of creation. It is merely the impulse to be one with nothingness." The absurd man, Sisyphus, Meursault, all feel free to love the world and even to sense a kind of alliance with it at that moment when they realize that they—like it—have no higher meaning in the over-all structure of things. What Camus seems to say is that the hope of some controlling purpose which would make this life other than it appears to be is tantamount to taking away all significance from this life as we know it. For such hope is equivalent to resignation, and we have seen in *The Myth of Sisyphus* that the decision to live is a revolt, the very opposite of renunciation. Camus epitomizes his position in "Summer in Algiers." "If there is any one sin against life, it is not perhaps so much to despair of life as it is to hope for another life, hence steal from this one its implacable grandeur." [6] We must not classify Camus as pantheist or romantic. There is in his work neither deification nor personalization of nature. Meursault, drawing himself up proudly side by side with the unapproachable universe, fraternal only in its indifference, is as far removed from Faust "in forest and cavern" as Kierkegaard is from Aquinas.

In "The Enigma" (1950), Camus, once more recalling the wonder of his youth in North Africa, asks, "Whence comes the absurdity of the world? Is it this splendor or the memory of its absence?" [7] Is man absurd because, as a creature who lives by meaning and unity, he can yet love so intensely a world which has neither? Or does the absurdity consist in his spending most of his life in a struggle which removes him from this ecstasy?

This question, implied rather than stated, is treated with particular delicacy and sensitivity in a late short story by Camus, "The Unfaithful Wife" *(La Femme adultère)*.[8] The heroine, Janine, has accompanied her husband on a difficult business trip among isolated Arab villages high up in the desert. The biting cold and desolation, the unfriendly reserve of the Arabs, whose language she could not understand though she had heard it spoken all her life, make her feel more acutely the bleakness of her own existence. She realizes that she and her husband have never loved each other or at least that they have never known the joyous love which can live and express itself in full sunlight. They have clung together because they feel a mutual need for being loved and for protection against their secret fear of death. In the late afternoon Janine and her husband climb to the top of a fortification from which they can look out far over the southern desert. The vast expanse, the silence, the light, which as dusk approaches seems to change from crystalline to liquid, slowly untie the knot which "the years and habit and boredom" had tied tight in her heart. Even the nomads in their tents, men she had never seen till now, demanded and absorbed her passionate attention. Living from time immemorial there close to the earth, they were men "who possessed nothing but served no one, wretched and free sovereigns of a strange kingdom." Suddenly it seems to Janine, who has come here by pure chance, that she had been promised this kingdom which now would never be hers save for this fleeting instant. With infinite, tender sadness, she feels that at this moment the course of the world has stopped. From now on "Nobody would grow older, nobody would die. Everywhere henceforth life was suspended, save in her heart, where at the same moment someone wept with pain and astonished wonder" (pp. 32-33).

Late at night while her husband is sleeping, Janine returns to the summit. Borne up by some obscure hope that to look out again toward the south may deliver her from her fear of death before the time of dying has come upon her, she stands silently and tensely, opening herself to the night.

> After so many years during which she had run madly, to no purpose, fleeing before her fear, now at last she came to rest. At the same time it seemed to her that she found her roots again, the sap surged afresh in her body which was no longer trembling. . . . Then with an intolerable sweetness the waters of the night began to fill her, submerged the cold, rose little by little from the dark center of her being and overflowed in continuous waves until they reached her groaning mouth. A moment later the entire sky stretched above her as she lay prostrate on the cold earth (pp. 40-41).

Janine goes back to the inn and silently slips into bed without awaking her husband. But a moment later he arouses, gets up to pour himself a drink from the bottle of mineral water, and hears her sobbing uncontrollably. In answer to his question, she can only stammer, "It's nothing, dear, it's nothing at all."

There is undoubtedly a deliberate juxtaposition of symbolism between the "waters of the night" which rolled over Janine like a flood of peace and the bottle of sterile water which satisfies the purely physical thirst and safeguards the health of her husband. The title of the story is accurate. Janine has won from the desert night a fulfillment which her husband has never been able to give her. From his point of view her midnight vigil may well be called adultery. But it would be a mistake, I think, to look on the story as being primarily a study of human relations. Undoubtedly Camus has deliberately contrasted Janine's sensitivity with the materialistic outlook of her husband. And he is commenting on the pathos of a union where two people are bound together by their common need for protection against their fears, without ever knowing the joy of love. But Janine's weeping is for the lost splendor of the world, which she has known for a fleeting instant, which she feels that she will never find again.

The work of D. H. Lawrence is rich in incidents of this sort, passages describing the sense of spiritual fulfillment wrested from physical contact with the things of nature. One of his short stories, "Sun," offers a particularly striking parallel. Here the heroine, Juliet, who has never felt quite alive with her rather conventional American husband, is spending some time away from him, living in an Italian village. She forms the habit of going daily to an isolated spot where she lies naked beneath the sun. Gradually she begins to feel at peace with herself, feeling strangely fulfilled as though the sun had taken carnal possession of her. At this point, however, Lawrence's story diverges radically from Camus'. Juliet has become intensely aware of an unspoken attraction existing between her and an Italian peasant. She wants to go to him, to bear his child. "He would have been a procreative sun bath to her, and she wanted it[!]." [9] Unfortunately, Juliet's husband returns too soon and decides that he also will walk naked in the sun. "But he smelled of the world, and all its fetters and its mongrel cowering." Juliet is resigned but recognizes that now she will never know the only human relationship which might have been the still more intense counterpart of her liaison with the sun.

Other works of Lawrence tell us what that coming together would have been—a deep union of blood consciousness which, Lawrence insists, binds and enriches without impairing the integral, individual selves. Obviously for Lawrence the ultimate meaning of life is found in his particular concept of sex, merely the most intense manifestation of a profound contact which, on a level far deeper than that of the reflective consciousness, a man may establish between himself and nature and other human beings willing to acknowledge this "blood brotherhood." But Janine does not seek out the Arabs in their tents; nor does Camus feel that it is important for her to have any further encounter with a French soldier who had been attentive to her on the bus or even to think of him again. Sex may be a momentary refuge or escape from the world's absurdity but does not cancel it out. While there are admittedly sexual overtones in her nocturnal communion with nature, Janine's basic need is not simply for a better, more sensitive lover. Yet her tears suggest that somehow her experience of the present beauty of the world is not enough. Is it only that the ecstasy cannot be sustained? Apropos of Meursault too, Camus' statement that he is the only Christ we *deserve* suggests that loyalty to the intensity of immediate being and honesty about one's feelings—while a necessary starting point—are not the highest destiny for the man who has confronted the absurd and decided to live in spite of, or even because of, the fact that life has no higher meaning. Meursault could find life worthwhile and live without anguish or anxiety because of a certain innocence. But leaving aside the question as to whether such a life is better or worse, it is impossible for one who has lost his innocence. As Camus says in "Return to Tipasa," neither beauty nor justice can live apart from the other. "There is beauty and there are the humiliated." Meursault had learned "not to expect much of people," and the result was that he respected their right to live as they pleased and made no demands on them. But once we have begun to reflect on the condition of men in general and in particular circumstances, once we have been engaged in events which shape the lives of others, we can no longer ignore them any more than we can ignore our physical response to our natural environment. Then we find that sensuous-aesthetic enjoyment is not enough to fill even our succession of presents. The door is open to other people, and we must decide whether to invite them in or how we may keep them out. Revolt takes on a social dimension.

But before we consider the absurd man-in-the-world, we must look at other existentialist attempts to give meaning to life on an individual basis. Not everyone is as responsive to sea and sun and desert as Camus. Furthermore, Camus has said that the ways in which one may accept the challenge of the absurd are many and varied. In *The Myth of Sisyphus* (in addition to Don Juan, whom we have briefly considered) Camus has sketched out three such lives, those of the writer, the actor, and the conqueror. As it happens (probably not intentionally) each of these has been portrayed in novels by Sartre and de Beauvoir. It is these which we must examine next.

## The Writer

*Nausea (la Nausée)* [10] purports to be the intimate journal of a young intellectual, Antoine Roquentin, who has come to the city of Bouville to complete his historical study of the Marquis de Rollebon. So far as external events are concerned, very little happens in the novel. Roquentin strikes up a reserved acquaintance with various of the city's residents; he is mildly concerned when one of them gets into difficulties and he makes feeble efforts to help; he has a reunion with his former mistress and learns that the affair is irrevocably over. Meanwhile he has become increasingly dissatisfied with his research and finally decides to give it all up and leave Bouville. But the real interest of the novel (and Sartre is remarkably successful in giving the illusion of rapid movement and even of suspense) is in the inner life of Roquentin. The account of his efforts to comprehend existence and to give meaning to his life might be subtitled "First Steps Toward Existentialism." Its origin is almost surely autobiographical, just as the veritable flavor of Bouville and the vignettes of its provincial residents are certainly echoes of Sartre's experiences during the years when he taught at a lycée in Le Havre.

While *Nausea* lacks the positive sense of social responsibility which is so prominent in Sartre's later work, it is scathing in its condemnation of the city's "leading citizens," endowed at birth with "sacred rights" to protect them throughout their lives in the Serious World. The most damning portrait, however, is not of the wealthy bourgeoisie but of the ineffectual Humanist, "the Self-taught Man," who is educating himself by reading through all the books of the local library in alphabetical order. The Self-taught Man is stupid and socially inept; his love for mankind is disastrously expressed in his timid caress of a young boy's hand in the library. Roquentin feels that the Self-taught Man's sentimental love of humanity is not realistic and not genuine. It serves as a vague and undemanding religion which reassures him and effectively prevents him from making any effort at really constructive thought or action. In his later work Sartre has many times indicated that action for the benefit of mankind is the natural and legitimate way in which to engage our freedom, but he is always particularly careful to distinguish this position from what seems to him a foolish belief in the universal goodness of mankind; he is even more opposed to the idea that one may justify one's life by simply replacing the mystic's love of God with the love of one's fellow men. Such humanism seems to him simply a manifestation of the sentimental fallacy. The Self-taught Man loves everyone because he loves no one. He does not even love himself, for he uses his false sentiment to hide from himself the possibilities of his own freedom.

At one point the Self-taught Man refers to an American book called "Is Life Worth Living?" The reference is probably to the James essay. The Self-taught Man's interpretation of it is not accurate, but the position he presents is vaguely Jamesian even if not derived from this essay. He says of it,

It concludes in favor of voluntary optimism. Life has a meaning if we really wish to give it one. First of all we must act, throw ourselves into some enterprise. Then if later we reflect on it, the die is already cast; we are committed. I wonder what you would think of that, Monsieur (p. 148).

What Roquentin thinks is that this is exactly the sort of lie which the people around him are constantly telling themselves. Once again the position criticized is so close to Sartre's later one that it is important to distinguish. The legitimate existentialist view holds that life may be meaningful (i.e., valuable, significant, true to the facts of man's "human condition" and situation) only if one is willing to engage in action where everything is at stake and without any guarantee either of outcome or of any essential "rightness." Actually one has to engage in such action in any case (though one may try to disguise the fact), for no action is really guaranteed and a refusal to act is itself a commitment. The difference between this program and that suggested by the Self-taught Man lies both in the awareness which accompanies the action and in the reasons for self-engagement. Back of the doctrine of "voluntary optimism" (at least as it is presented here) is the implicit assumption that personal content at any price is the original mainspring of all action. One acts for the sake of becoming so involved in an enterprise (*any* enterprise) that it becomes impossible to detach oneself from it and evaluate an action save in the terms offered by the enterprise itself. It is a deliberate attempt to plunge so deeply into the Serious World that one forgets it is not the real one. Existentialism, on the other hand, allows that all actions are equivalent *sub specie aeternitatis,* or more accurately, it claims that there never is or will be any possibility of bringing an impersonal transcendent point of view to bear on them. But it argues that our encounter with freedom must never be forgotten. Freedom can be lived only through action. To act is to assert that one prefers one end rather than another. Thus for the existentialist, engagement is not for action's sake alone but for the ends proposed. Instead of desiring to benumb his reflective consciousness by his activity, the existentialist demands the clearest possible awareness of the relation between intent, result, and the conduct which unifies them.

Roquentin, however, is not yet concerned with the problem of engaged or committed freedom. As he contemptuously rejects the too-easy answers of the sentimental humanist, he reflects that he is not really concerned with the problem of whether or not life is worth living. But he is preoccupied with two related problems: how to escape the waves of nausea which from time to time come over him without warning, and how to find in his life events which he may think of as "adventures." Roquentin's experience with nausea is an enlargement of that encounter with Being-in-itself which we have met before, especially with Lucien in *The Childhood of a Boss*. Unlike Meursault and Janine, the fictional characters of Sartre and de Beauvoir are never content to derive solace from contemplating the indifferent universe. Theirs is a purely metaphysical confrontation. They are not concerned primarily with finding out how life may have value in such a world but with understanding the nature of Being and Existence. They try (unsuccessfully, of course) to achieve an insight into reality which is not merely a human view of it but which somehow provides an explanation intelligible in human terms. It is actually the extent to which they succeed rather than their ultimate failure which produces intense nausea and anguish. Roquentin starts out by feeling that nausea is something which he encounters—as one might meet an illness or a depression, both of which would in a certain sense come from the outside even though they are inner states while one actually lives them. Later he finds that this is not so. Nausea is not something which he can learn to avoid; he *is* nausea. Existentialist nausea is not, of course, the simple symptom of an upset stomach which precedes vomiting. But neither is it a wholly psychic state. It is that physical feeling and the awareness of the feeling which make up our consciousness that we *are* our bodies. In intensified form nausea leads to vomiting, which as a symbolic expression is the keenest representation of our revulsion at the inescapable contingency of our human condition. In one of the most frequently quoted passages of the book Roquentin describes the sickly sweet feeling which comes to the fore in those quiet moments at which we try to savor our bodily existence and concentrate on being what we are whenever consciousness is denied any object save itself in its own facticity.

> I exist. It's sweet, so sweet, so slow. And light. You'd say it hung there in the air all by itself. It stirs. Everywhere there are little gentle touches which melt and pass away. All soft and gentle. Water wells up in my mouth. I swallow it, it slides down my throat, it caresses me—and now my mouth is full of it again. I have in my mouth forever a little pool of whitish water, lying hidden, brushing my tongue. And this pool is Me. And the tongue. And the throat is Me (p. 131)

As Roquentin contemplates existence—his own or that of objects in the world—it reveals a disquieting quality of being both inevitable and unjustifiable. Against the background of Being, which simply *is,* so fully that one cannot even ask the reason for its being without presupposing that it already is, against this undifferentiated plenitude it seems that there is no room to seek reasons or justification for particular beings. Roquentin finds no reason for his hands being just as they are and no other way. Why should they not suddenly become something else? Yet again objects, whether his own body or things out there in the world, have a sort of passive resistance which makes them be absolutely what they are, offering as it were a meaning which one cannot read. The root of the chestnut tree exists so absolutely in its own complete fullness that one cannot really think about it; and yet since there is no reason for it to be a root of a chestnut tree, it is absurd. The same is true of Roquentin. Since he exists as a particular consciousness, he not only is continually aware of the body across which he is conscious but he cannot stop being conscious; he must forever think, think, and think about thinking. In a kind of "horrible ecstasy" Roquentin senses the obscene fullness of existence, which is "an imperfection," "a sagging" *(fléchissement)* of Being. Existing things have no reason for being, they are neither necessary nor meaningful. And yet they are there. They are *de trop,* and he, like them, is *"de trop* for eternity."

Roquentin contrasts this pointless, superfluous existence with that of mathematical objects. A circle, for example, is not absurd or *de trop* inasmuch as it can be explained as the rotation of a straight segment around one of its extremities. Of course a circle doesn't exist. But then consciousness does not exist quite in the manner of other objects. An individual consciousness in so far as it is particularized exists contingent to a particular body. But consciousness is never a fullness; it is that "hole in being" without which we could not even say that Being *is there.* Roquentin as a consciousness tries to find whether he may, in the midst of this existence which is *de trop,* carve out for himself the kind of being which the circle possesses. This pursuit is his search for "adventures." Early in the novel he reflects that he has missed in life the one thing which he considers most valuable. It is not a specific thing such as love or glory or money. Nor is it that he "has never really lived"—in the vulgar sense of that saying. He has traveled widely, has known at least one intense emotional relationship, has taken part in exciting events. In fact, for many years he had convinced himself that he knew well the wonderful moments which go to make up adventures. Now he realizes that he had been lying. The only adventures he has known have been in books. The events related there might have happened in real life, and the episodes of his own history could furnish material for books. But there is a difference. The incidents of his life have not taken place in the same way as the adventures in books, and it is the manner of their happening which he holds so precious. What would be necessary, he reflects, would be that an event should have *form*, that it should possess a real beginning and that the end when it came should appear as the inevitable conclusion of that beginning. In a real adventure the beginning would never pass unnoticed. One might be walking along idly, with no particular thought in mind and suddenly think, "Something has happened!"

> No matter what: a light rustle in the shadow, a thin silhouette crossing the street. But this trivial happening is not like others: suddenly you see before you a great form, its outline lost in the fog. And you say to yourself, "Something is beginning" (p. 57).

In the adventure one appears to be swept along in an inevitable sequence of instants, every one of which is uniquely precious, to be drained dry and willingly let go only because of one's impatience for that which is yet to come. The end comes sharp and clear. "The adventure is over, and time resumes its slack routine of everyday." A person would consent to die or to lose a fortune or a friend if he might only live the experience over again in exactly the same way. "But an adventure does not begin again nor can it be prolonged." An adventure comes to pass with its beginning announced like the first notes of a piece of jazz; it moves with steady beat and inevitable progression to the final chord. Roquentin thinks of a popular song he particularly likes and exclaims, "What heights couldn't I reach if *my own life* might become the subject of a melody!"

We can see that the "adventure" resembles, but is not identical with, Camus' "succession of presents." There is the same intense immediacy, the same absorption in living an event for its own sake. But for Camus the moment becomes significant by seeming to be cut off from time, whereas for Roquentin the experience demands an aesthetic form which depends upon the unification of successive moments within time's larger flow. Roquentin does not realize his hope of living through a complete adventure, but he does occasionally get the *feeling of adventure*. He concludes that the situation itself really has nothing to do with determining whether or not an adventure is to ensue. It all depends on how the instants are linked together, and we tend to attribute to content what actually belongs to form. What happens in an adventure is that we feel the irreversability of time.

> We see a woman, we think that some day she will have grown old, only we don't *see* her growing old. But at a particular moment it seems to us that we do *see* her grow old and that we feel ourselves growing old along with her: this is the feeling of adventure (p. 80).

To Roquentin the feeling of adventure and the feeling of nausea are opposites, and he seeks the one in order to escape the other. Then when he learns the truth, that he *is* nausea, he knows that there can be no adventures. He cannot live isolated and meaningful pieces of experience along with the constant awareness that he and all other existents are *de trop,* unnecessary. Time is nothing more than a haphazard relating of events without significance.

It is in this frame of mind that Roquentin prepares for a reunion with his former mistress, Anny. Unlike most of the women in Sartre's fiction, Anny is more forceful and philosophically sophisticated than the hero. She is almost a Diotima to Roquentin. If we are to say that he represents an earlier Sartre, then surely Anny is the (perhaps purely imaginary) older woman in Sartre's life. In their relation years before, Anny had always shown herself particularly skillful in evoking the feeling of adventure. "She knew how to make the most of time." It was, for instance, her habit when Roquentin was with her for a brief visit, to fill most of the interval with manufactured quarrels and petulance. Then during their last hour she would cancel it all by a gesture of deep affection so that in rare, silent communion, he would sit holding her hand, feeling in bitter joy each moment passing by. Now when he meets her again, Roquentin finds Anny for the first time willing to explain why, each time they met throughout those years, she expected him to sense without explanation the role she had assigned him and to play it as if in a theatre. She lets him know, too, why it was that he always disappointed her. It turns out that Anny had pursued a dream of "perfect moments" to match his pursuit of "adventures." With her too the quest had its origin in books; as a child Anny had looked at the full-page illustrations in her books and decided that each must have been selected to represent some especially "privileged situation." Later she found in her life "annunciatory signs" (the *feeling* of adventure), and she sought the "privileged situations" out of which she might create the "perfect moments" as the artist seeks the material for the work of art which is to come. But to Anny such creation was not gratuituous like the artist's but was required by her sense of moral demand. It seemed to her necessary that at certain times she and everyone around her sense that the situation was exceptional and impose the proper order upon it. That the order was an aesthetic one is indicated by Anny's example.

> There was a king who had lost a battle and who had been taken prisoner. He was there in a corner, in the camp of the conqueror. He saw his son and his daughter pass by in chains. He did not weep, he said nothing. Next he saw one of his servants pass by, he too in chains. Then the king began to groan aloud and to tear out his hair. . . . You see, there are times when you must not weep, you would be foul if you did. But if you let a log fall on your foot, you can do what you like —whine, sob, jump up and down on the other foot. What would be stupid would be to be stoical all the time. You would exhaust yourself for nothing (p. 193)

But Anny has discovered at last that there are no perfect moments, and this rather than his clumsiness is the reason why Roquentin has always failed her. What prevents them is not that people are too imperceptive to play their roles properly or that there are always trivial distractions. It is primarily that Anny cannot really believe in what she is doing. She cannot feel that her actions will have fateful results. More important, she has discovered that the great emotions on which the perfect moments depend simply do not exist. She had formerly believed in the reality of a great love or hate which would come like a tongue of fire to rest on her head and lift her out of herself. Now she knows that emotions are not pure or overwhelming; they are nothing but herself, they are like a piece of dough rolled thinner and thinner, and Anny wonders how people ever came to make distinctions and invent names for them. As an actress she had believed for a time that she might create perfect moments histrionically, but she succeeded only for those on the other side of the footlights. And so she gave up acting. As Roquentin hears all this, he is first excited over the realization that apart they have been traveling together and arriving at the same destination. But Anny will have none of it. She insists that they do not mean the same thing and that he has not found her. Sartre seems to imply by this that encounters with existence, since they are not intellectual, cannot be conceptualized and compared. In any case, Roquentin is at a loss when Anny asks him what he would propose to do about it all. He realizes that like her he has "outlived himself." They are both solitary and cannot help each other. Sartre is not yet ready to develop the idea of a solidarity which may spring from the very fact that we know each other to be isolated. Roquentin feels that Anny has returned only to take away all hope. He is alone and free with a freedom that is "a little like death."

By now it is clear that if there is to be any solution at all, it must be an aesthetic one. During his conflict with nausea and while he awaited the meeting with Anny, Roquentin had been finding it increasingly difficult to continue his research into the life of the Marquis de Rollebon. More and more he realizes that the written record, even the Marquis' own letters, means nothing in itself. How can he tell when the Marquis is lying to others or to himself? All Roquentin can do is to impose his own order upon these past events, but this order remains outside the events themselves. At times he has the feeling that he is doing a work of pure imagination and that he would be better off writing a novel about Rollebon. In a novel, he feels, the characters would be more believable or at least more entertaining.* Later he reacts more violently. Concluding that the past does not exist, except in so far as a living person chooses to sustain and determine the present meaning of past events, Roquentin feels that he has made the Marquis live at his own expense.

> M. de Rollebon was my partner: he needed me in order to be, and I needed him in order not to feel my being. I furnished the raw material, that material which I had to resell, which I didn't know what to do with: existence, *my* existence. . . . I had ceased to be aware that I myself existed. I no longer did exist in myself, but only in him. It was for him that I ate, for him that I breathed. . . . I was only a means of making him live; he was my reason for being, he had released me from myself (p. 131).

This decision immediately preceded the "horrible ecstasy" of Roquentin's encounter with the In-itself. By the time he sees Anny, he has given up his work on Rollebon, he knows there are no adventures. After his interview with her, he prepares to leave Bouville but with no

---

* Evidently Sartre has not continued to hold these ideas about biography. In developing his theory of existential psychoanalysis, he claims that it may be profitably applied to achieving more accurate biographical studies. Cf. his own *Baudelaire*.

clear idea of what he will do. While he waits for train time, he stops in at his usual café and listens for the last time to the record of a popular song which had in some way always comforted him and sometimes given him the feeling of adventure. Until the record started to play, all that he felt was a dull undercurrent of nausea overlaid with a slightly more painful messy suffering. But suddenly there were the four notes of the saxophone, and the melody began.

> Some of these days
> You'll miss me honey.*

Roquentin feels ashamed. "A glorious little suffering has just been born." It is a pure suffering, an ideal suffering (une souffrance-modèle), a suffering which has nothing in common with the diffuse slackness of existing things. The melody is complete, perfectly contained. And it is not contingent. It does not depend on the plastic disk, for to break the record would not be to destroy the melody, which would live on by itself. It is its own explanation as the circle is explained by its center and rotating segment. "It does not exist, for there is nothing about it which is de trop; everything else is superfluous and de trop in relation to it. The melody is" (p. 224). Now Roquentin realizes that what he has wanted all along is simply this—to be. But Being is denied him. Then he thinks about the Negro woman who sings the song and about the composer who wrote the music. It probably wouldn't make any difference to them, he reflects, to know that in the seventh largest city of France someone was thinking about them. Yet Roquentin feels that if he were in the composer's place, he would be happy. The composer and the Negro woman are saved. Like the dead or like the heroes of novels, "they have been washed clean of the sin of existing, not completely, to be sure, but as much as any man can be." The song is the adventure, the perfect moment. One can think of how the composer tried to write it, of its beginning in his ear and mind, of its completion as he set it down. Or one can imagine the Negro woman approaching the studio, bestowing upon the song a sensory permanence. "And why not I?" asks Roquentin. Why should people not later say of him, "He

---

* In view of Sartre's stress on the importance of the rhythm in this selection, he should have got the words accurately. (He quotes them in English.) They should be,

> Some of these days
> You're gonna miss me, honey.

("Some of These Days" used by special permission of copyright owner, Jerry Vogel Music Company, Inc., New York 36, N. Y.)

was sitting in a café when . . . ." The novel concludes with Roquentin's reflections on the type of book he will write in order that he may, in part, justify his existence by inserting in the midst of its flux a little bit of gemlike Being. It must not be history or biography again, for "an existent cannot justify the existence of another existent." It will probably be a novel.

Actually, of course, it will be—and has been—*Nausea.* There is something a little touching in this self-revelation on Sartre's part. Ironic, too, for Sartre's later theory of an "engaged literature" resulted in his being criticized for being too neglectful of posterity. But here in *Nausea* we see him, no less than the poet in Plato's *Symposium,* turning to artistic creation as a means of winning immortality; for what is the thirst for immortality if it is not the hope of escaping the contingency of immediate existence? Sartre is of course following in a long tradition when he sees art as the imposition of form upon a formless flux. Nevertheless, it is important to distinguish his intent from that of traditional theories. For Plato great art offered a beauty which was a veritable glimpse into eternal Truth. The function of art was to aid the soul to realize its origin and ultimate destiny. The Forms were not imposed but revealed. Even for Schopenhauer, although existence itself is only the blind, meaningless struggle of the Will for survival, still the Ideas are real, the true forms within which the tragic struggle manifests itself. Art satisfies and comforts because it is Truth. But whereas both Plato and Schopenhauer think of form as already existing and merely made manifest in a new, particular setting, Sartre stresses that there is no form except as it is newly created in the work of art. By his choice of a simple popular song, he makes it even more clear that he is not confusing the artistic process with revelations of eternal verities.

Sartre's position is closer to that of John Dewey, who claims that the work of art arises when the artist imposes an arbitrary form upon experience, breaking the continuum of means and ends by creating a unity in which particular means and ends seem to exist for each other, cut off from a wider past and future. But Dewey is unlike Sartre in stressing the continuity of artistic experience and experience in general. It is Dewey's view that everyday experience frequently produces at least a low level of artistic experience in so far as we succeed in feeling a unity within the continuum, exactly what Roquentin would call an "adventure." To Sartre the background of absurdity and nausea prevents our achieving such unity except in art. At least in *Nausea* Sartre claims that art satisfies exactly in so far as it gives us what is not in life rather than showing us existence as it is. Such a view is on the surface inconsistent with Sartre's later insistence on the social responsibility of the author and clearly represents an earlier stage of his thought.

Here, as in Camus' early work, the problem is narrowly focused on the individual's personal encounter with the absurd. It is as though each writer felt that every man must by himself try to come to grips with the problem of individual existence before he is even in a position to raise the question as to what will be his relations with others. Of the two, Camus is the more radical in his view of a literature of the absurd. As though to dash Roquentin's hopes to the ground, Camus says explicitly in *The Myth of Sisyphus* that we must not try to see in the work of art a way of escaping from the absurd, for it is itself an absurd phenomenon. Yet he defines the function of art in words that Roquentin himself might have used. "In this universe the work of art is man's unique chance to maintain his consciousness and fix its adventures. To create is to live twice" (p. 130). For Camus the essential thing is that the absurd writer must never forget that his work is gratuitous, must never let it create the illusion of there being a higher meaning after all. Knowing that his works are ephemeral like himself, he will perpetually remind himself that finally they do not matter; like Rimbaud he will be prepared to give them up.

But bleak as this pronouncement undoubtedly is, the literature of the absurd is not a literature of despair. In an essay written in 1950, Camus points out that even the pronouncement that everything is meaningless is a meaningful statement. To refuse even a relative meaning born of man's ephemeral relation to the world in which he finds himself would mean to suppress every value judgement. But to decide to live is to assert a value. A true literature of despair would be a silent literature, and this is a contradiction in terms.[11] Thus literature is a form of revolt as much as Don Juan's loves or Meursault's "succession of presents" or the initial refusal to commit suicide. The ultimate goal of the absurd creator is not to explain; it is simply to describe. Such description is in no way a mere recording. It is free creation, limited only by the one fact of the final destiny which is death. The knowledge that literature is meaningless to the universe does not render it without meaning within its own sphere.

> There remains a world of which man alone is master. What bound him was the illusion of another world. The outcome of his thought is no longer renunciation but the abundant flow of

images. It plays its games—in myths, of course, but in myths with no profundity save that of human suffering and like it inexhaustible.

Moreover, absurd literature is in truth creative, for its author, "valuing the pure flame of life itself," wants to bring into the world more and more life. Since he cannot have unity, he seeks diversity. An absurd literature rejects illusion and the hope of ultimate meanings in existence; what it offers is the opportunity of seeing how life as it is may be valuable.

Both Camus and Sartre, in so far as they consider aesthetic creation as a means of making life more significant for the writer, seem to feel that the most satisfying creation is fiction. This may be in part the explanation of why both men have sought to present even their most abstract ideas in the form of novels and plays. In each case the reason seems to be that in a world where existing beings have no discernible meaning behind them, the purest form of creation appears to be that in which created life is justified within the form which perfectly contains it. Society seems through the centuries to have agreed that the imaginative writer deserves a special place among those whose products are fruits of the mind. Plato may have banished the poets and dramatists for having merely imitated life, but this is a recognition of the fact that what they offered was life itself and not an explanation of it. If Sartre is right in saying that each man, while wishing to remain pure consciousness, at the same time desires most ardently that as a free consciousness he should be nevertheless absolutely defined, his own *causa sui,* then it is small wonder that every man secretly desires to write a novel or drama, thus putting his life into a book. I suspect that most people if offered the choice would be Tolstoi rather than Toynbee, Shakespeare more than Kant, Dostoyevsky and not Descartes. If Plato still seems the greatest of philosophers even to many non-Platonists, this is perhaps due to the fact that the philosopher who banished the poets made of his ideas the highest poetry. When we can decide once and for all whether the *Symposium* is a metaphysical treatise or a drama, then we shall have explained Plato. With pure philosophy, with history, with "scholarship" of any sort, the work stands before us for judgement, to be rejected as false or incorporated in that growing but still narrow body of information which we treat as our "practical absolute." But with the creatures of art, we cannot judge them in the same way. We may admire them or treat them with contempt. We may believe them to move freely or to be secretly motivated behind the scenes by their creators. But they are neither true nor false. As with all existents, we can only say of them that they are there.

## The Actor

Anny gave up acting because she could not herself believe in the "perfect moments" which she was creating for her audience. For Camus, on the other hand, the actor's life is a legitimate type of revolt in the face of the absurd, and for Sartre the actor playing his role is a symbol of our human condition. Camus stresses the ephemeral quality of the actor's goal. Although from the point of view of, say, Sirius, literary works are equally transient, nevertheless the writer may comfort himself with the idea that at least his achievements may outlive their creator. But if we except the cinema artist, who, like the singer on Sartre's record, is in this respect comparable to the author, then the actor's endeavors are truly limited to a few brief hours. He may repeat his moments of glory but he cannot render them enduring. Thus the actor more than anyone else has chosen to live out the absurdity of his condition by intensifying it rather than seeking to evade it. From the point of view of an ethics of quantity, he can hardly be surpassed, for he lives out in compressed, intensified *form* the diversified experiences of many lives. Moreover, while he concentrates always on appearances, the actor cannot avoid in part becoming and remaining what he has been. In picking up his glass in the bistro, he uses the gesture of Hamlet reaching for the cup. He shows us, says Camus, how thin is the line between what a man is and what he wants to be. There is in all this a kind of miracle, an absurd miracle, for the body, that same body which seals man's absurdity by setting limits to his experience, this concrete here-and-now body, transforms the actor's physical fate. It becomes an instrument for conveying knowledge to the audience and to himself. Through his body he escapes his time and place, his past and future, his very personality. Small wonder that the Church condemned these men and women who were not satisfied to live but one life, and who on many occasions showed their defiance by choosing to live a comedy in preference to eternity.[12]

Sartre's study of an actor is found in his play, *Kean*. This is an adaptation of an earlier comedy, *Kean or Disorder and Genius,* written by Alexandre Dumas and first acted in 1836.[13] Sartre has kept the main outline of Dumas' plot and much of the conversation, though in fairness to Sartre it must be said that in this play he has shown himself capable of writing light drawing-room repartee which is at least equal to that of the original. *Kean* is the story of the English actor, Edmund Kean, who finds himself involved in a double triangle: he is in love with Elena, the wife of the Danish Ambassador. Elena seems to return Kean's love, but this does not prevent her from being flattered and interested when she perceives that she has attracted the marked attention of the Prince of Wales. Meanwhile, Kean has been placed in a peculiar position by Anna Damby, a young heiress who has run away from her fiance and placed herself under Kean's protection, thus to a degree compromising them both. She has taken this drastic step partly because she wants to become an actress under Kean's tutelage, partly because she is in love with him. Kean, both pleasantly impressed by her daring and exasperated by her persistence, consents to make her his protegée but refuses her suggestion that they should be married, Anna to provide the order to protect the disorder of Kean's genius. After a series of misunderstandings among all parties, things come to a head when Anna takes the heroine's role in one of Kean's special performances. Elena (especially in Sartre's play) is jealous and has forbidden Kean to perform with her; Kean has requested the Prince of Wales to give up his pursuit of Elena and not attend her in the box. As they perform, Kean pays little attention to the scene on the stage and watches Elena and the Prince. Finally, he breaks from the Shakespearean drama entirely and hurls reproaches at the Prince. There is the inevitable scandal, and Kean's friends try to protect him by declaring that he was taken by a sudden fit of madness. Later Elena comes secretly to see Kean. His joy is soon turned to disillusion when he finds that she merely wants to recover tokens and letters which might compromise her. His plea that she elope with him she rejects entirely. There is a bit of excitement when it seems that Elena may be caught by her husband in Kean's rooms, but the Prince of Wales suddenly arrives on the scene, effects Elena's escape, and allays her husband's suspicions. Alone with Kean and Anna, the Prince offers Kean pardon if he will consent to leave England. Kean, who by now has realized that it is Anna who is worthy of a real love that is more than play-acting, prepares to go to New York with her so that they may work in the theatre together.

In Dumas' version the love story is a real romance. Kean genuinely loves Elena until he discovers her shallowness, then recognizes true worth in Anna. But everything is complicated by the different social positions of the members of the triangle. What seems primarily to interest Dumas is the undefined status of the actor. Elena feels that it is glamorous to carry on a flirtation with a famous actor but would not dream of entering into any serious or permanent relation with one. The Prince of Wales has put on a show of being Kean's friend and companion, and Kean had believed that in their friendship the difference in rank was nullified. But when the Prince refuses Kean's first serious request, Kean perceives that what he took for friendship was merely condescension. At the disastrous performance of *Romeo and Juliet,* he cries out that he is not Romeo but Falstaff—no, not even Falstaff but a punchinello. Dumas' Prince of Wales redeems himself. He recognizes the justice of Kean's rebuke and tries to repair things by his kindness at the end. When he sees Kean and Anna about to leave together, he understands and is delighted that all has turned out so well.

Sartre retains and broadens the social implications. There is the same uneasiness in Kean's relations with Elena and the Prince. Kean is constantly speaking of himself as a bastard, taking his illegitimate birth as a symbol for the fact that he has no established place in society, that because of his spending his life acting roles, the world does not know whether he is himself or the characters he plays. In his stage denunciation of the Prince, he holds the public responsible as well.

> Kean has died, dead in his youth. Quiet, Assassins! It is you who have killed him! You, who took a child that you might make of him a monster * (p. 166).

Nevertheless, the principal themes of the two plays are not the same. Dumas was concerned with the difficulties of a man whose profession brought him in touch with the upper classes, who enjoyed his art without respecting his trade. Sartre is interested in this problem too, but only in passing. What he really sets out to investigate is the psychology of the actor as an actor (never forgetting, of course, that an actor is a particular man who acts). Those changes Sartre has made in the play are all designed to bring out the dilemma of the man who plays a role until he does not know how to distinguish himself from the roles he plays. And Sartre raises the question as to whether anyone (not only the actor) can be distinguished from the roles he chooses. In Sartre's play, Kean is perpetually contrasting the emotion he acts on stage with

---

* Sartre makes this sentence the theme of his biographical study of Jean Genet. In the case of Genet, too, Sartre stresses the idea that his illegitimate birth was one reason for his choosing to be an outsider to society. Francis Jeanson in his book, *Sartre par lui-même,* maintains that Sartre, though born quite legitimately in wedlock, has chosen to live the role of the bastard in the social world.

that which he experiences in the wings. As Othello he can rage, gesture, modulate his voice appropriately to the perfect words which give form to his jealousy and despair. When he is Kean the sharpest blow finds him sinking back weakly in his chair and murmuring, "You have hurt me very much." Worse than this, he cannot tell whether what he thinks are his real reactions are genuine or merely part of another role. Even when (as Othello) he publicly rebukes the Prince from the stage, he is not sure whether he is expressing *himself* at last or merely playing the greatest role of his career, "the actor who risks his life by the dramatic assertion of a subject's rights before the false friend-sovereign." Or perhaps he merely thinks that Elena and the Prince are Desdemona and Cassio. That his speech carried something of the flavor of a public performance is suggested by the reaction of the Prince, who is not really hurt or angry. He remarks (in the tone of voice one assumes to congratulate an actor on his performance), "He was simply wonderful!" On the other hand, inasmuch as Kean had seemingly ruined his own career, what he had done appeared to be not a gesture but a veritable act. Reflecting on the episode afterward, Kean finds it impossible to decide. But the crisis has nevertheless resulted in new insight. Kean feels (at least for the moment) that he will never be able to act again.

> In order to act, you have to take yourself for somebody else.
> I took myself for Kean, who took himself for Hamlet, who
> took himself for Fortinbras. . . . Fortinbras didn't take himself
> for anybody. Fortinbras and Mr. Edmund are of the same
> kind: they are what they are and say what is (p. 175).

Realizing that throughout his career he has been playing the part of The Great Actor away from the footlights as thoroughly as he played Hamlet in the theatre, Kean resolves simply to *be* himself, Mr. Edmund. But one further step is necessary. Who is Mr. Edmund? Only what Edmund Kean decides to make him. Rather subdued, Kean decides that at least he can "imitate the natural until it becomes second nature."

In the final resolution of the emotional entanglements Kean shows that even as an actor he has learned to distinguish between roles which are in bad faith and acts which are in good faith. The final scene between Kean and Elena (unlike that in Dumas) is high comedy. At first Kean earnestly begs her to elope with him and is bitter at her refusal and her insincere attempts to justify it. Then suddenly, as Elena, disappointed at his simple tenderness, begs him to express his love in the grand words he knows so well, Kean steps back in horror. He realizes that she is in effect prompting him, giving him his cue. He informs her that she must play out the comedy alone, and the rest of the scene depicts his very funny efforts to show her that she does not believe anything of what she is saying. By pretending actually to abduct her in the romantic style she had demanded, he convinces her that she is only acting. At the end of the scene Elena and Kean, really friends for the first time, can join in an accomplice giggle as they hear the suspicious Ambassador storming outside. Elena remarks, "He still thinks he's in Shakespeare!" In his explanation to Elena, Kean had pointed out that because of their special situation the two of them and the Prince of Wales had all tried to live simply as the reflections of what they saw in the eyes of the others.

> We are all three victims. You were born a girl; he was born too high, I too low. The result—you enjoy your beauty through the eyes of others and I discover my genius in their applause. As for him, he is a flower. If he is to feel himself a prince, he must read it in his subjects' faces. Beauty, royalty, genius— one and the same mirage. You are right. We are only reflections. We all three live on others' love and we are all three incapable of loving (p. 199).

Of the three it is only the Prince of Wales who fails to gain any new insight. When he arranges for Kean's safe departure from the country, he is acting partly out of concern for Kean; he is also insuring the removal of a rival. When Kean with singular lack of perception shows himself entirely willing to leave and admits that he is not in love with Elena and perhaps never has been, the Prince feels tricked. It is evident that he had merely paid court to Elena because Kean's desire for her had made her seem desirable. What the Prince wishes is to have the admiration of Kean, whom all England admires as the nation's greatest actor, and yet show himself superior to Kean by taking away from him the admiration of the woman Kean desires. It is Anna who quickly perceives what is happening as the Prince, knowing now that it is she whom Kean loves, suddenly begins to pay her compliments. Becoming in her turn the prompter, she tells the Prince that Kean is still passionately in love with Elena but is pretending otherwise to save his pride. Kean reluctantly obeys the cue and plays the comedy through.

Both Dumas' and Sartre's *Kean* end with the offer of Kean's prompter, Solomon, to go along with Kean and Anna and help them in their theatrical career in New York. Dumas had never raised the question as to whether Kean would continue his acting career if allowed to do so. Sartre's Kean, however, had stated that he could never act again since he could not find the real Edmund Kean who might pretend that he was someone else. He had suggested to Elena that as Mr. Edmund, he might take the jewels which admirers had given him and use them to start a trade as a jeweler. Yet now we find him prepared to go on as an actor after all.

Sartre offers no explicit explanation of Kean's change of mind, but I think the reason is easy to find. One line which occurs in both plays has a special significance in Sartre's because of the particular way he has set up the situation. Solomon says that Kean and Anna will need a prompter "if you two are going to go on playing *la comédie.*" There is no reason to think that Kean will henceforth play only Shakespeare comedies. Dumas undoubtedly used *comédie* in its more general meaning of "drama," perhaps with satiric overtones appropriate to the immediate situation. But I think that for Sartre the specific meaning of the word is important. For the future Kean will be playing comedy even if he continues to do Othello, Romeo, and King Lear; for he will know now that he is only acting. He will never again make the mistake of thinking he is Othello or for that matter that he *is* the great Kean. He will no longer feel it necessary to play himself in the tragic manner. If now Kean knows who he is, it is not that he has found a real and stable person with genuine traits against whom he can measure the play-acting. He knows now that he is only what at any time he experiences and feels and chooses to do. But he has learned to be guided by those emotions he actually feels instead of persuading himself that he feels what would be conventionally expected. He can distinguish between the Kean who finds delight in the spirited charm of Anna Damby and the Kean who would turn all women into Juliets. Chastened and subdued as the real emotions are, they satisfy as the grand pretense does not. Henceforth tragedy will be for those on the other side of the footlights. We can see how far we have come from Anny (in *Nausea*), who gave up acting because she could not forget herself in her role. Kean finds the possibility of good faith of more value than "perfect moments." At the same time Sartre makes it clear that from a certain point of view Kean, like every person, is playing a role. For since man is free, since his being is simply that which from moment to moment he decides to make it, whatever he decides to make of himself has validity only as the role he has chosen. Good faith consists in recognizing this fact. There is, however, a difference between this fundamental role played against the background of Nothingness which everyone bears at his heart and the role which attempts to deny this Nothingness. This is, we might say, the difference between acknowledging and not acknowledging the author of the script. If Kean produces as Kean what is really Shakespeare, it is moral plagiarism.

## The Man of Action

For another absurd type Camus chooses the conqueror. But the conqueror in our age is no longer the triumphant general. He is the man who, knowing that there are no victorious causes, has a fondness for lost causes. "Conquerors know that action in itself is useless. There is only one useful action, that which would remake man and the earth. I shall never remake man. But one must act 'as if.' " [14] In his portrayal of the man of action, Camus is very close to Sartre's and de Beauvoir's treatment of action in good faith. In each case there is no illusion of there being any ultimate, absolute end. One acts in the interest of relative ends and a limited future. But one commits oneself as fully as if the struggle were for an eternity. The goal is always man himself. As Camus puts it, every revolution, beginning with that of Prometheus, is against the gods; it is man's assertion of right against his destiny. But we can fight this battle only in the historical context. One might say that Dr. Rieux in *The Plague* is a conqueror in this sense. For he spends his life struggling against disease (injustice and oppression on the allegorical level) even though he knows that death is the final conqueror, no matter how many times his medical skill may postpone the defeat.

The novel which most specifically and fully discusses the question of ambitious or idealistic action and mortality is Simone de Beauvoir's *All Men Are Mortal (Tous les hommes sont mortels).*[15] In this de Beauvoir has reversed the terms: the hero is no longer a man confronting the absurd discrepancy between the aspirations of his consciousness and its mortality. Instead we have Raymond Fosca, who in Carmona, Italy, in the thirteenth century is offered an elixir which would make him immortal. He tries a few drops of the liquid on a mouse; he "kills" the animal, watches it come to life again. Then, wholly unable to understand the horror and fear of his wife who watches him, Fosca confidently drinks the potion. With the invulnerability he gains from it, he is able to make himself master of Carmona and to bring the city to heights of fame and power which it had never known before. But gradually he realizes that the great gift is a curse. It cannot help him to save his wife from dying of the plague. It wins him only hatred from his son, who dies cursing his father for keeping the rule in his own hands and not handing it on to him as a naturally aging father would have done. From then on, Fosca knows that he cannot use his strange power to do things for those he loves. If he deprives them of the opportunity to risk their lives, he takes away all that makes their lives meaningful. Over the centuries Fosca meets again and again the same obstacle: it is only when he is intimately associated with someone, only when he loves deeply enough to desire the other's mortal happiness as keenly as if it were his own that he feels himself really alive. But such a relation demands truth on both sides, and Fosca learns that the truth immediately destroys whatever human bond he has established. One woman whom he loves shrinks from him because she feels that he belongs to another species, that he is not a man but a strange creature whose touch would be frightening and repellent. His closest friend grows to hate him, knowing that Fosca will see the realization of what they are working for, while he has given more of himself than Fosca and will never see the outcome. When in the eighteenth century Fosca meets Marianne, the woman who means more to him than any other has meant, he tries to keep the secret from her. So long as she does not know, they are happy. Although Fosca is tormented by fear of her learning the truth from an enemy of his who knows it, even this anxiety adds value to his life, for he feels vulnerable, that he at last has something to lose and to fight for. The threat of time (her time) makes the single days precious. But inevitably Marianne finds out, and she feels that their life together has been a lie. Where she gave herself, he could only lend; what was a life commitment for her was a mere accident for him. There is no way for him to convince her or anyone else that he loves or passionately believes in any person or thing. How can one prove belief or passion when there is nothing one can risk? The promise to love forever is merely laughable when forever is really forever. Fosca remembered Marianne longer and more vividly than his other women. But gradually as everything around him changed, there was nothing to sustain his memories of her. It was not so much that he forgot Marianne as that she had slipped out of the world. He remembered a name, events, a face, but not Marianne.

Before she died, Marianne begged Fosca to devote his existence to the service of mankind, both for his own sake, that he might feel himself alive as a man among other men, and for the sake of mortal men so that his immortality might be used for their benefit. During the centuries Fosca had gone through many changes in his attitude toward his responsibility for others. At the start his personal ambition was hardly distinguishable from his desire to exalt Carmona. But immediately after drinking the immortal draught he found himself out of step with the city's inhabitants. At first he lived too much in the future, demanding impossible sacrifices from the present generation in the interests of the one to come. Later, as he saw the futility of all the wars and shifting alliances between the Italian states, Fosca tried to isolate the city; and the citizens complained that history was passing them by. At last he decides that Italy is too small. Feeling that hope for the future rests in Maximilian, he succeeds in attaching himself to the Hapsburgs and becomes the power behind the throne for Charles V of the Holy Roman Empire. It is Fosca's ultimate goal to make himself the ruler of the universe, and he intends to use this power to force men to organize the world for their own highest good. In every way he fails. Charles' campaigns in Europe do not turn out as planned. Fosca visits the Spanish conquests in the New World and is sickened at the misery and suffering which the Spanish have caused there to no purpose. Deciding to renounce all ambitions for himself, he reflects that the universe does not exist. The universe is always elsewhere, in the depths of the future. The universe is nowhere. There are only men, men forever divided among themselves. Talking it over with Charles, he says,

> One of the heretic monks we condemned to the stake said to me before he died: "There is only one good—to act according to one's conscience." If that is true, it is useless to want to dominate the earth; one can do nothing for men; their good depends only on themselves (p. 213).

Fosca never abandons this point of view. He does not take up politics again. In his private life he tries at first to help those with whom he comes in contact. Then as he finds it impossible to establish any enduring relation with people, he grows embittered and deliberately uses his wealth and experience to ruin person after person, thus showing his contempt for the trivial mortals who reject him. Under Marianne's influence he mellows again and aids her in her idealistic educational enterprises in the century of enlightenment. Still under her influence, he aids her great-grandson and his associates in the early proletariat struggles of the nineteenth century, spending some years in prison as the result of his revolutionary activity. But at the very moment when their cause seems to have triumphed, he leaves them; the gulf between them and him is too great. He cannot help projecting himself far into the future, from which point of view every victory is doomed to turn into a defeat. What good to have raised Carmona when Italy itself was going to fall? What good to engage in any particular struggle for human freedom when the battle will have to be fought over and over again? He cannot take seriously the enterprises of those who "from the moment of birth begin to die." He can understand the reply of his mortal companion, that "between birth and death there is a life," but it is not meaningful for himself. His associates can enjoy absolute victories over particular evils, and the future cannot take away the moment of triumph. But he has not wept and risked all for this victory, hence he can never make it his. Because for him there is no price, he can buy nothing of value.

Sometime between the mid-nineteenth century and the present time Fosca has learned the Indian secret of inducing a deathlike trance which renders him incapable of feeling. Most of his time is spent in this state. The story of his earlier experiences is given us by Fosca himself, who is recalled to living once again by the efforts of Regina, an actress. She is a woman who represents an extreme form of the subject-object conflict which we have met in the work of both de Beauvoir and Sartre. She is extraordinarily ambitious but makes a dramatic gesture which destroys her chances of a successful career, all for the sake of demonstrating her complete freedom as a sovereign consciousness. When she learns Fosca's secret, she is excited at the idea of achieving a kind of vicarious immortality by being loved by an immortal, and she demands that he tell her the complete account of his past. Throughout his story there are breaks in the narrative, showing Regina's increasing distress. At the end she too rejects him. She cannot bear the idea of seeing her life reduced to nothing beneath the gaze of an immortal. But the damage is done. After he has gone, she acknowledges that she has been beaten. "In horror, in terror she accepted the metamorphosis: a gnat, a bit of foam, an ant—until her death." But Fosca's is the more horrible nightmare. He envisions himself ages hence still living on an earth from which all mortal life has departed; there he will be in a dead world beneath the pitiless white light of the moon, he alone save for the one creature against whom he had committed his worst crime, the mouse who had shared with him the elixir of immortality.

To me, there is no piece of existentialist literature more depressing than *All Men Are Mortal*. I am sure that de Beauvoir did not mean the effect of the book to be wholly negative. Her intention no doubt was to show that it is by fully accepting the human condition that one may achieve happiness, that mortality instead of being a destructive limitation is what makes it possible for life to be significant. She has certainly shown quite effectively the utter horror of a life which, while still finite in scope, would be unending in time. The unpleasantness of knowing that one *must* die pales into nothing beside the possibility of knowing that one absolutely *could not* die, no matter what the circumstances. But the most pessimistic thing about the novel is what also seems to me an aesthetic flaw, no matter whether one considers the book as a philosophical myth or as science fiction. This is the fact that Fosca does not seem to learn anything from his experience. He begins to take the point of view of eternity, which obviously de Beauvoir considers to be deleterious, as perhaps it is; but he never grows in wisdom. In the eighteenth century he sets up his own laboratory and is seemingly in advance of the scientists of his age, but he is disillusioned rather than excited by his discoveries. It is no good for man to learn about nature, he decides; in order ever truly to understand, man would have to get outside his own condition. But is not this the whole point? Especially for an immortal, would not the overwhelming question be to see whether perhaps the barriers to human happiness might be broken down? Like all the existentialists, de Beauvoir insists that there is no such thing as a fixed human nature, and this means that no one can save men collectively against their will or solve their inner problems for them. But if human nature is not fixed, then how is one justified in saying that the future can be nothing more than repetition of the same limited successes and ultimate failures of the past? Midway in the book Fosca, like Caligula, uses the moon for a symbol of the impossible. He feels that he stifles on the earth and that his only hope would be to pierce the heavens. Then why not try it?

De Beauvoir wrote this book in 1946. We should not, of course, expect her to foresee moon expeditions any more than we should try to explain her use of the mouse as an anticipation of the decision to include mice in outer space investigations. In any case, she would probably say that mere extension of man's geographical sphere would not necessarily change his psychological or metaphysical possibilities. It is true, of course, that Columbus' discovery of America, consequential as it was, did not result in a millenium. But is there any reason to think that space travel, which is at least possible, would introduce only quantitative changes in man's life? Existentialism emphasizes the lack of guarantees. Does this give it the right to predict the future? I find it hard to imagine that anyone would ever accept immortality on condition that the present state of things should never significantly change. But suppose that one were offered Fosca's elixir without guarantee, negative or positive. If anyone could be found with the courage sufficient to accept the offer, it ought to be someone who puts a high value on man himself, who believes in an open future, who advocates passionate commitment and readiness to take risks and to live without assurances. It ought, I believe, to be an existentialist.

Fosca as an immortal could not interest himself in mortal projects. One must act in time, and he and those around him were moving in two different temporal dimensions. He learned, however, that for mortals life could have meaning for the individual only if he deliberately committed his freedom in the interests of others. Here, as everywhere in the literature of the absurd, we find that man cannot for long go on living by himself. Others *are there*.

## 3. ENGAGED FREEDOM

"On the far side of despair hope begins." Out of the awareness of our mutual solitude is born a sense of human solidarity. The question of social and political commitment more than any other issue reveals a large area of disagreement among humanistic existentialists, but they are unanimous in believing that each man's recognition of human interdependence emerges from his lonely, personal rebellion against the human condition.

Camus' political philosophy was first presented in 1951 in *L'Homme révolté (The Rebel),* the book which precipitated the abrupt and much too public break between him and Sartre. Before entering upon the critical discussion of historical revolt and revolution which comprises the bulk of the treatise, Camus attempts to bridge the gap between Sisyphus and Prometheus, between the man who decides to live for himself against the universe and the rebel who chooses to die that his fellow men may live better. In the same way that we could say that the problem of *The Myth of Sisyphus* was suicide, so the basic question of *The Rebel* is murder, "logical murder" performed in the name of a political ideal. In the earlier pages the question of whether murder can be justified amounts to asking whether we are in any way obligated to respect another's right to live. Referring back to his earlier study of absurdity, Camus points out that the absurd attitude regarding murder leads to a contradiction. On the one hand, we have to recognize that if there is no meaning and if we can assert no ultimate value, then "everything is possible and nothing has any importance." We may choose between cultivating indifference or participating in the game of power where human lives are counters. In either case there is no justice or injustice but only masters and slaves. But although the *feeling* of the absurd allows this conclusion, the *logic* of the absurd calls for a different sort of reasoning. As we have seen already, the first result of this dialectic is the rejection of suicide; the absurd man asserts human life as the one necessary good, for without life there cannot be that confrontation with the absurd which gives the "absurd wager" its support. But once we have rejected the position of total negation, then logical consistency demands that we extend the principle where it naturally applies. If human life is good, then the life of the Other is good as well as my own. Murder cannot be condoned if suicide is condemned. We cannot—in logic—justify murder and reject suicide. The absurd man will accept (not approve) killing if it appears as a natural fatality or if it is a crime of passion. He must inevitably rebel against "a logical crime." Like methodical doubt, the logic of the absurd cannot give us positive answers for the problems of our time. "But like doubt, it can, by turning back on itself, direct us toward a new investigation." [1] Its *cogito ergo sum* is revolt.

Up till now we have considered revolt simply as the individual's decision to go on living in the absence of any higher meaning; we have not yet examined its inner structure and total significance. Camus now presents a paradox: The moment a man revolts, he is asserting the existence of something more important than his own life. Like the absurd man, the rebel pronounces a No which is not a renunciation. Such a No is inevitably accompanied by a Yes. If a slave says "so far and no farther," he is asserting a limit; he is at the same time affirming that there is something beyond that limit which he wishes to preserve. If a person risks or prefers death to loss of freedom, for example, he is thereby attaching a higher value to his freedom than to his life. He asserts that something in him is worth preserving at all cost. So far, we are but slightly beyond the position presented in *The Myth of Sisyphus:* the rebel is willing to sacrifice his bodily existence for an idea, but it is still *his* idea, his own spiritual life, as it were. Now Camus goes one step further. He claims that in the act of rebellion a man transcends his individuality. If he demands All or Nothing, he is recognizing a good which goes beyond his own individual destiny and he is subordinating himself to it. "He acts therefore in the name of a value which is still unclear but which he feels, at least, is one which he shares in common with all other men" (p. 28). This leads Camus to a view which is quite contrary to one of the most basic principles of existentialism (as a technical philosophy). "The analysis of the conduct of revolt leads us to the suspicion, at least, that there is a human nature, as the Greeks believed there was and contrary to the postulates of contemporary thought" (p. 28).

It is hard to see just what Camus means by this. Sartre has pointed out that the concept of a human essence or fixed pattern of human nature must be supported by a belief in God or at least in some higher, more than human force or purpose. Take as an analogy Henry Ford and his automobile. One can pass judgement on a car as fitting or not fitting the requirements of the perfect Ford, by comparing it to the factory blueprint originating with Mr. Ford. But without a Creator, without God, there is no blueprint, no pattern, no point of view by which to judge or predict. Camus has never been willing to assume either God or transcendent meaning. What then is this human essence which for him seems to precede our individual existence? And how can a person *know* it? Or if Camus would object that it is not a matter of knowledge, how can one perceive this common essence on any level of experience which Camus may have in mind? I cannot see how within his premises there can be anything more than our sympathetic awareness of the factual similarity of our own finite being and that of others, a realization of those common physical and psychological factors which go to make up what Sartre calls the human condition. But Camus explicitly denies that we are dealing with any kind of "psychological identification." He points out that on many occasions we may revolt at seeing others subjected to treatment which we are willing to accept for ourselves, that we may even rebel against injustice done to people who stand for the very things against which we are revolting. Thus we need all humanity as a ground for the values the rebel chooses to defend. "In revolt man surpasses himself in others and from this point of view human solidarity is metaphysical" (p. 29). Whether Camus is right or wrong in using the term "metaphysical," there is no denying the fact that man can and does determine and sometimes sacrifice his own concrete, personal experiences in the interests of the well-being of specific men or mankind, whose joy or sorrow he can only experience vicariously through sympathetic imagination. Camus goes on to say that this feeling of human solidarity is inextricably bound up with the human species' increased awareness of itself in the course of its long adventure. Yet he certainly does not hold to the idea of any collective mind. Humanity becomes increasingly conscious of itself and its potentialities only as individual men become more conscious of themselves and of humanity. Finally, it seems to me, Camus does make the bridge between individual and social awareness a psychological one. His present reasoning, while a further development, is still faithful to the conditions laid down for the logic of the absurd. The absurd man, Camus reminds us, suffered in solitude as he encountered the absurdity and apparent sterility of the world. His first step out of his isolation comes at that moment when he realizes that all other persons feel this same sense of strangeness and estrangement, that the whole human race "suffers from that distance between itself and the world." Once I realize that I am not alone in facing the absurd, I am drawn out of my isolation. I can no longer feel that the confrontation is a lonely one even if I should wish to do so. My rebellion against my personal situation is transformed into a revolt against the human condition. "I revolt, therefore we are" (p. 36).

In this conclusion Camus comes remarkably close to the position of Sartre and de Beauvoir. Camus says that what makes us feel our common kinship with others is the realization that we are all struggling against a common foe—the absurdity of a universe which by itself furnishes no reason for living. Sartre (de Beauvoir's position is much the same) says that a sense of solidarity may arise from our awareness that we all suffer from the same lonely solitude. In his social philosophy, however, he makes a distinction between our sense of solidarity as victims—the Us-object—and that which we experience as doers of action in common—the We-subject. On the concrete, social level, he claims that the We-subject never exists except in that delicate, unstable situation which arises for short periods when, for example, a group traveling together in a bus witnesses a funny incident, or when we all follow the same signs in a railroad station, or in specific tasks demanding teamwork (cutting down a tree or rowing a boat), or in certain solitary activities when we obey directions for employing a tool (in America the universal use of package directions for everything from assembling a hi-fi set to opening a bag of peanuts). The Us-object, though not a permanent structure, is much more stable. It may, of course, exist as an evanescent moment, as when two lovers are suddenly confronted by a third person (the theme of *No Exit*); but it may equally well come about when an oppressed class (the workers in an unjust capitalist society or unpopular national or racial minorities) feel themselves to be objects before the oppressors' subjectivity. Then there may be born a solidarity which leads to action. If the revolution is successful, however, the Us-object disintegrates and is not replaced by a We-subject but by a community of individuals cooperating for their mutual profit without ceasing to think of themselves each as independent subject.[2]

I think that Sartre is probably right here. At first thought it would seem that if there is an Us-object in the face of oppression, there must be an accompanying We-subject. But it is true that practically nobody thinks of himself as being a member of the bourgeoisie, a white, or a Gentile until he suddenly feels that he is put on the defensive, thus becoming actually part of an Us-object. For example, the Republican who, after a Democratic landslide, publicly prayed in a nonpolitical meeting that God would "give us strength to bear the reversal of our hopes." The one seeming exception might be small hate-groups like the secret anti-Semitic societies in this country or the Ku Klux Klan. But while each member of the group tries to feel that he is one with the unanimous crowd, and even though his need of a victim is for the purpose of guaranteeing his position as subject, nevertheless what emerges is not a bona fide We-subject. For as Sartre pointed out earlier, the very fact that the anti-Semite seeks to make an object out of the Jew in order to *secure* his own position as subject means that he is actually trying to make a possession—i.e., an object—out of his own subject-being. What he desires is a pseudo-subjectivity which he may proclaim as an especially privileged Being. This is proved by the fact that what he wants of his companions is not that he may join with them in a freely chosen cooperative project but that he may become a kind of object to the hypostatized unanimity of the mob. On the other hand, if we try to apply Sartre's distinction to the more fundamental revolt which Camus had in mind, there is a difficulty. Are we to give the name of We-subject or Us-object to that sense of solidarity which springs from the rebel's sudden awareness that his solitary struggle has become part of mankind's revolt against the human condition? In so far as it stems from a common threat, one might be tempted to say that it is an object-state. But we feel immediately that this cannot be right. Man can never be an object to the impersonal universe; his resolve to live in spite of and in the very face of absurdity is the quintessence of subjectivity. Although there is no reason why Camus' work should be forced to fit Sartrean categories, it seems to me that the rebel's first movement in the direction of others must certainly be equated with the birth of a We-subject.

Actually, I believe that Sartre has implied the existence of a We-subject on many more occasions than his theory would seem to warrant. In part, at least, the bridge between the individual and the social philosophy of existentialism was not so much evolved through abstract dialectic as it was forged out of the violent events of World War Two and the French Resistance. In an essay entitled "The Republic of Silence" Sartre points out that the first result of the Nazi terror was that each man was forced to arrive at a new understanding of himself. There was no longer any easy escape into the Serious World. Faced with the degrading Nazi propaganda, and forbidden to speak out, every man and woman in France knew that "each accurate thought was a conquest," every word and gesture was a commitment, every act a conscious choice by which a man showed what he had decided to make himself. Above all, everyone knew that on any day he might be put to the ultimate test.

> Thus the basic question of freedom was posed, and we were brought to the verge of the deepest knowledge that man can have of himself. For the secret of a man is not his Oedipus complex or his inferiority complex: it is the limit of his own freedom, his capacity for resisting torture and death.[3]

Sartre has written two works which are primarily concerned with the psychology of persons facing torture and death; they are a short story, "The Wall" *(Le Mur),* and a play, *The Victors (Morts sans sépulture).* Although neither of these is as positive as Sartre's essay, it is interesting to observe the difference in tone between "The Wall," published in 1939, and *The Victors,* which came out in 1946 after Sartre had taken an active part in the Resistance and had known the threat of torture and death if not the actuality. "The Wall" is reminiscent of Camus' *Cross Purpose* in that it underscores the tragic absurdity of a world in which good intentions or even acts of heroism end in gratuitous disaster. It is the story of Pablo Ibbieta, a prisoner of the Fascists in the Spanish Revolution. With two other men he spends a night in prison, knowing that he is to be shot in the morning. When his companions are led away to the firing squad, Ibbieta is offered the chance to save his life by giving information concerning the whereabouts of one of his friends. More to amuse himself than anything else, he sends the officer off on what he believes to be a wild goose chase. A little later the man returns, and Ibbieta learns that he has accidentally caused his friend to be captured. The story ends as he sits back and laughs so hard that tears come to his eyes.

Even allowing that there is something hysterical about this laughter, we must not explain it simply as indicating the breakdown of a personality. Ibbieta laughs because the fact that his choice of death rather than betrayal has produced the same result as deliberate betrayal would have done seems to him now simply of a piece with the whole structure of things in this crazy universe. What Sartre stresses in this story is not the solidarity of those who know that they must die, but the gulf which separates them from those who still feel that their lives are important. Ibbieta recognizes that he and his fellow prisoner have somehow the same look about them, and he hates it. He prefers to torture himself with the thought of his loneliness. He recalls his mistress, remembering how, as they looked at each other, something seemed to pass from one to the other. Now, he thinks, if she were to look at him, the look would stay in her eyes. He is alone. Later when he refuses to save his life by giving information, he honestly cannot find his motives for refusal. He no longer feels either love or friendship; the cause of Spanish freedom no longer seems real to him. Nothing is important, and this is perhaps the reason why he will not give in. To admit that it made a difference who should be stood up against the wall and shot would be to deny the insight of the last twenty-four hours. Having tasted his own mortality, he will not struggle for a trivial reprieve. Ultimately he is willing to face death and torture rather than to give up a certain idea which he has of himself. At the same time, his laughter at the end is a mockery of the whole human endeavor. There is a kind of complicity in it, but it is a travesty of the We-subject, not a genuine revolt.

In *The Victors* the scene is laid in Occupied France; five Resistance workers have been captured and are awaiting their turn in the torture chamber. Again the question at stake is whether or not they will try to save their own lives by betraying their leader. But this time the leader, Jean, is there in prison with them, although their captors do not know his identity and are merely holding him until they can check on some things he has told them. There is every reason to believe that he will go free if his companions keep silent. Once more Sartre stresses the gap between the near-dead and the living. Lucie, Jean's mistress, does not betray him in the torture chamber; but when she is with him afterwards, she finds that they have nothing in common, that he is a stranger to her. The only personal kinship she can still feel is directed toward a fellow prisoner who, although he too had refused to give information, is humiliated by the knowledge that he could not keep himself from screaming.

Thus where Ibbieta had resented the common likeness which imminent death had painted on the features of the condemned, *The Victors* reveals a sympathy, almost a tenderness, springing up among those who have known the ultimate loneliness in which each man probes the limits of his pride and weakness. But there is more to it than this. In "The

Wall" Ibbieta held out because of a kind of personal pride; even as he decided that human projects were of no importance, he showed himself willing to suffer any extreme rather than allow that the person who made that decision could be manipulated. In the final sense he asserted the integrity of the individual, but this same pride prevented him from seeing his friend's capture as cause for anything but sneering cynicism at all human aspirations. Lucie and her companions know such arrogance too, and it is largely this which separates them from Jean. But at the end they show themselves willing to sacrifice even this pride for something which transcends them. One of the prisoners has a plan whereby they can probably persuade their captors to think that the body of another dead comrade is Jean's. The others do not want to accept his suggestion because it will seem to the torturers that they have won. Yet at last they consent, partly because the desire to live asserts itself despite all, mostly because they think that if they escape, they will be able to warn others of their associates and prevent their capture. Thus they sacrifice for others what Ibbieta valued so highly that he was willing to risk all to maintain it. As with Ibbieta, their plans miscarry, for the man in charge breaks his promise and has them shot after they have "confessed." But there is no suggestion here that Sartre thought the sacrifice simply absurd, and even the torturers are shamed.

In "The Republic of Silence," Sartre, though without reference to *The Victors,* states what I believe he would consider to be the positive social message of the play. After describing the utter loneliness of the Resistance worker who had to act and to suffer alone in this army where one but rarely saw his comrades, he goes on to say,

> Yet, in the depth of their solitude, it was the others that they were protecting, all the others, all their comrades in the Resistance. Total responsibility in total solitude—is not this the very definition of our freedom? This being stripped of all, this solitude, this tremendous danger, were the same for all. . . . Each of them, standing against the oppressors, undertook to be himself, freely and irrevocably. And by choosing for himself in freedom, he chose the freedom of all.[4]

It is easy to see how in the army of the Resistance each one chose the freedom of others in choosing his own. For even if under the influence of torture a man should elect relief from pain or the promise of life at the price of betraying a comrade, still he was thereby choosing only life or painlessness, not freedom. Sartre, however, has tried to find a philosophical bridge between the social and the individual which would be the abstract equivalent of the link emerging at a specific moment in history. In a popular lecture afterward printed under the title *Existentialism Is a Humanism (L'Existentialisme est un humanisme),* Sartre tried to explain how he could consistently poke fun at the humanist in *Nausea* and yet maintain that in an important sense existentialism is itself a humanism. We have met already in our discussion of *Nausea* Sartre's objections to the humanism which makes a kind of religious cult of man. In its more serious form, Sartre believes that this worship of mankind may result in a fascism which saci.fices individual men to the concept of Man which is held by a certain group. In a less dangerous but foolish manifestation, such a humanist will identify himself with a few great men, feeling that he personally is responsible and to be honored for whatever achievements particular members of the human race have accomplished. The kind of humanism which Sartre is willing to claim for existentialism does not take human nature as something already given, but as something which is perpetually being made. As he defines it in one passage, it sounds completely individualistic. It is the recognition that man is never closed in on himself, that each person exists by a continual process of choosing himself across a multitude of concrete projects, these choices and these projects, of course, being made within a human world. An "existentialist humanism" reminds man that he himself is the only lawmaker and that "in his forlornness he will decide for himself." Yet man (even individual man) will fulfill himself, not by turning in upon himself, but by seeking outside himself particular goals which will be to him a liberation and a fulfillment.[5]

Elsewhere in this same discussion Sartre goes a step further. Every man, he says, exists in an organized situation in which he is already engaged; thus, every choice which he makes is a choice involving mankind.[6] This remark seems to mean two things. First, it is a more abstract statement of the idea which we met in de Beauvoir's *The Blood of Others:* since each person chooses as he freely decides but within a concrete situation whose form depends on choices already made by others, everyone is totally responsible and everyone is wholly without excuse. There is a second, more universal application. Although there is no human essence determining man in the sense that the potentialities of the seed determine the plant, still it is possible at any given moment to say what men within the historical situation have made of mankind. To paraphrase William James, "When the last man has had his last say," then some outside observer could pronounce what human nature had been; but even this pronouncement would not be a judgement as to what man might have been, but merely an abstraction of what in actual fact he had shown himself to be. In so far as men share in common a "human condition" in contrast with inanimate things or animals on a lower level of consciousness, judgement may be passed on what men collectively have made themselves. To this extent each man by his own individual choices is showing what he considers man to be, is helping to define what man will have been.

> When we say that man chooses himself, we mean that *each one* of us chooses *himself,* but at the same time we mean too that in choosing himself each one chooses all men. In fact there is not one of our acts which, in creating the man we wish to be, does not thereby create an image of Man as we judge he ought to be (p. 25).

Sartre points out that the limitations of the human condition have both an objective and a subjective side. They exist factually, they are abstractly the same for all men; while they vary in detail according to time and space, etc., they are easily recognizable. But in their significance they are wholly subjective, for they have meaning only as lived. Consequently, although our common human condition does not mitigate the ultimate isolation of our individual experience, it does enable us to understand the projects of other men. Thus we may rightly speak of a universality of man. "I establish the universal in choosing myself" (p. 70). In one of the most constructive applications of this idea, Sartre points out that each individual is personally responsible for the historical events of his nation and epoch. Looking at the past, we may say even of the most obscure, those whose names have long been forgotten, that they helped each one to make possible those generalizations with which we designate periods as having had a special *Zeitgeist:* [7] "In the Middle Ages, man was on the whole content to accept the place in the universe which the Church allotted him and the social status into which he had been born." Or "In the first fifty years of the United States men were restlessly pushing on to new frontiers, scornful of newly acquired stability and anxious to wrest a still greater empire from the wilderness." For us in the present we cannot evade responsibility even for those things which we say we haven't wanted and would never have chosen. The war which comes is my war. The oppression [8] which exists is my oppression. States are nothing but the men who make them up; the public is only the sum of private individuals. An obvious objection here is that perhaps one has actively worked to avoid a specific situation. In that case it seems that Sartre would have to admit that one was not morally responsible for its coming into being. He would insist, however, that one is responsible for it so long as one continues to accept it without resistance.

Ultimately, I think, in any discussion of solipsism and the social, we are brought back to de Beauvoir's simple statement: "Others are there." To ignore them is impossible. The moment I encounter another's Look, there arises my Self-for-others. My attitude toward my Self is affected by my awareness of the Other's judgement as surely as my choices are formed out of my situation in time and space. It is only through the mediation of the Other that I can know who I am. Theoretically it might be possible to imagine myself as having been a Robinson Crusoe since birth, in which case I should not need to evaluate myself as possessing certain human qualities in contrast to others. But since in actual fact I never have nor could have been in such a situation, I must of necessity subject myself and realize that others subject me to the same kind of critical appraisal as I make of others. Thus the existential nature of the person is such that my relations with myself are colored by my relations with others and I cannot avoid being involved with others in the very heart of my being. Even in bad faith I never fully believe the lie which I tell myself. I cannot be at peace with myself if I know that I am what I despise others for being. Conscious that the Other lives in a world as subjectively intense as my own, I cannot shut off from my imagination awareness of his suffering; and what one imagines, this in a certain way one experiences.

De Beauvoir more than Sartre has elaborated on the implications of our psychological (one might even say metaphysical) inter-dependence. In *The Ethics of Ambiguity* she says that an existentialist ethics is not solipsistic since it holds that "the individual defines himself only by his relation to the world and to other individuals." [9] This, of course, is a logical consequence of the basic assumption that consciousness in itself is a nothingness and could not exist without objects of which to be conscious. In another essay, *Pyrrhus et Cinéas,* she points out that respect for others' freedom is not an abstract rule but a first condition for the success of my effort. [10] Actually I can never force another's freedom. Even in extreme sadism, I can only affect the body. But to the extent that I try to surround another freedom with factual limitations, I am cutting off my own possibilities by limiting the opportunities for self-transcendence which the other might offer me. Furthermore, by a logical step comparable to that which we found in Camus' discussion of the rebel, I cannot separate my attitude toward a particular life from that which I hold toward life in general. If I convince myself that the Other's life is nothing more than that of an ant, then I affirm that the human adventure as a whole is nothing more than the story of an anthill.[11] De Beauvoir does not any more than Sartre believe that there is a given human essence gradually being realized. We cannot say that on the basis of his mere existence another man *is* my brother. "But if I weep over him, then he is no longer a stranger to me. It is my tears which decide." [12] Once we have chosen a pro-ject of ourselves which includes another, we can never make a further choice in which he is not somehow there.

In one more way, de Beauvoir emphasizes the positive side of human relationships. Through another I extend, if I do not escape, my own finitude.[13] I may find it meaningful to engage in projects whose realization only others may know, and my ability to feel in imagination their comfort or joy extends the horizons of my own experience. Existentialism no less than Christianity stresses the infinite value of every human soul. This is not because a person is valuable to a God or by the measure of any supra-personal evaluation. It is rather that there exists *no* objective standard of measurement. The subjective existence of each person is absolute and unique, allowing no final basis for comparison. The world in so far as it is something other than undifferentiated fullness exists only for a consciousness. Thus each person's world is a totality, existing for himself alone and allowing no comparison with the world of another. If, then, another has need of me, my existence is to this existent absolutely justified. On the other hand, one must beware in this matter of helping others. If we try to determine their lives even beneficently, this is an attack on their freedom and they have no reason to be grateful to us. The only time that we can really act for another is when he expects something from us and we give him precisely what he asks.[14] This last doctrine de Beauvoir somewhat modifies in *The Ethics of Ambiguity*. An easy evasion for bad faith is to claim that some oppressed groups are content with what they are, hence we have no obligation to awaken them. Her reply here is that such people have not chosen their condition out of all the possibilities potentially open to them. If we refrain from showing them that other choices exist, we are attacking their factual freedom as surely as if we put them in prison.[15]

There is still one related question which we have not posed directly. Granted that I need to respect the freedom of others in order fully to realize my own, granted that I *am* free and that good faith demands

SELF-ENCOUNTER / 229

that I recognize the fact and reject the Serious World of absolute values, is there any reason why I should be obliged to prefer good faith to bad? Whether oppressor or oppressed, do I have any obligation to recognize all possibilities and continually reassert my free choice of what I will be or do, rather than to assume that my destiny is controlled by external forces and let myself drift along comfortably and unheroically? Both Sartre and de Beauvoir have brought up this question. On one level the answer is "No." If I prefer bad faith, nobody can bring in any external reason to show that I "do not have the right" to continue in it. On the other hand, such an attitude is dishonest. If a person wants to be dishonest, let him be so. But let him not try to justify himself in the name of truth or logic. Obviously, however, both Sartre and de Beauvoir (Camus too) believe that a life in good faith is in some final way *better* than its opposite. Whether or not it is simply because it is most of the time pragmatically expedient, human beings seem to place a high premium on truth for its own sake. On specific occasions they may try to reap the advantages of depriving others of a truth which they themselves possess; they frequently delude themselves into thinking that something is true which would be more pleasant to them than what the truth actually is. But very few would consciously and deliberately choose not to know a truth available to them even if they knew it would make them unhappy. Although none of the existentialists, so far as I know, has gone deeply into the matter, it seems that there are psychological grounds as well for rejecting a life in bad faith. Where there is pretense, there is bound sooner or later to be disillusion and conflict. If one stays in prison to avoid the evils of the world, he will miss the good as well. Perhaps dissatisfied Socrates does not really understand the spurned pleasures of the satisfied pig, but the man who tries to live like the pig will not find them satisfying.

Once we grant that the best life for man is a life in good faith, a life in which he does not hide from himself the reality which he is, a life in which he will assume the responsibility of his freedom, then the fact that we both need others and recognize a duty toward them is inescapable. Upon this assumption two new questions arise: What kind of bond can exist between two individuals in good faith? What sort of political commitment is appropriate for a person in good faith—both generally, and specifically in the mid-twentieth century?

Turning first to private relationships, one would expect to find somewhere in existentialist literature an examination of the possibility of genuine love in an intense relation between man and woman. Somewhat surprisingly there is nothing of the sort in the work of either Camus or Sartre. Love affairs, yes. But they are largely mere sexual incidents. This is not to say that these writers have provided absolutely no examples of love in good faith. Presumably they approve of the relationships existing between Meursault and Marie *(The Stranger),* between Anna and Kean, and between Goetz and Hilda (in *Lucifer and the Lord).* But even in these the love theme is secondary to another philosophical question, and there is little exploration of the psychological aspects. De Beauvoir has given us more. In *The Mandarins* [16] she has, as it were, written a novel to order for our discussion. The remark is not entirely facetious. It is like de Beauvoir to pose just the sort of question which we have raised and then write a novel in reply to it. The remarkable thing is that she can so often produce a genuinely artistic work on this basis. In my opinion, *The Mandarins,* despite its philosophical and even propagandistic intent, is the most successful of her novels. It seems more a creation in its own right and less a commentary on Sartre (though as I pointed out earlier, it is entirely possible that what pass for Sartrean principles are in part the result of discussion with de Beauvoir). What is even more important, the characters in *The Mandarins* are three-dimensional, are alive and interesting for themselves, not merely for the ideas which they represent.

*The Mandarins* pursues two themes, not so much simultaneously as alternately. Third-person passages in which Henri is the central character alternate with first-person passages supposedly written by Anne Dubreuilh. Although the two are in the same close circle, Henri being the friend and political associate of Anne's husband and eventually marrying her daughter, nevertheless the inner lives and basic conflicts of the two are quite separate. Henri's problem is primarily a political one; we are given enough of his private life and emotional involvements to make him seem real and individual, but essentially he represents the existentialist intellectual trying to find the right path, looking for solutions to the national problems of post-war France. Anne, a psychiatrist, is sympathetic with the social commitments of her husband and Henri; from time to time she finds herself questioning the validity of her work in view of the peculiar nature of world affairs. But fundamentally her problem is a personal one: how to accept the fact that she is on the verge of growing old, how to adjust to the demands of the various relationships existing between her and members of her family and even more particularly with the American writer with whom she falls in love.

Reserving Henri and politics for later discussion, it may be rewarding to examine de Beauvoir's remarkable and completely feminine treatment of women in love.

Anne's relation with her husband, Robert, plays a special and rather curious part in the novel. In a way it is present implicitly whatever else happens, and it may even be said to dominate the action, since any important decision on Anne's part is directly or indirectly determined by it. Yet it is less carefully developed and there is less time given to analyzing it than is bestowed on any of the other relationships. The explanation, I think, is that de Beauvoir had the feeling that she had analyzed this quiet conjugal love for us already. And indeed she had. For to anyone who has read *She Came to Stay* it is evident that in so far as their feelings for each other are concerned, Anne and Robert are simply Pierre and Francoise after ten years of peace with Xavière. In *The Mandarins* de Beauvoir has all but dropped the thin disguise which she used in *She Came to Stay* and let it be quite obvious that Robert is Jean-Paul Sartre. Robert is a famous professor at the Sorbonne. It is as his student that Anne first meets him; gradually they become friends and lovers, finally husband and wife. As passion cools and as Robert becomes involved in political activity (in writing rather than in action), their personal demands on each other are superficially less but their roots, so to speak, grow more tightly intertwined. That their love has been, and still is, profoundly satisfying is indicated in a prolonged revery in which Anne recalls earlier events and reflects on the present situation.

> It's a wonderful stroke of luck if when you're twenty years old you receive the world from the hand you love! It's wonderful luck to find your exact place in it. And Robert managed to do another remarkable thing—he protected me from loneliness without depriving me of solitude. We shared all things in common; yet I had my own friendships, my private pleasures and worries. If I liked, I could pass the night resting tenderly against his shoulder or as tonight I could remain alone in my room like a young girl. I look at these walls, at the rays of light shining under the door. How many times have I known this sweetness—to go to sleep while he is working within reach of my voice? It's been years now since we felt desire for each other; but we were too tightly knit together for the union of our bodies to have any great importance. In giving it up, we had, so to speak, lost nothing at all (p. 47).

Anne (and clearly de Beauvoir too) remarks on more than one occasion that passion and desire cannot live on, once the body which has inspired them has grown too familiar. This view, while probably more often true than the proponents of romantic love would like to admit, is profoundly shocking to the American myth of a passionate love which finds its eternity in, and only in, a life span of exclusive matrimony. If de Beauvoir intends that every lasting love in good faith must inevitably fit the pattern of the Dubreuilh marriage, she is too extreme and assumes that it is too easy. On the other hand, she is very successful in showing that for Anne and Robert the situation could not be different. With Robert the difficult thing to understand is how he could ever have been absorbed by a passionate and deeply emotional involvement. Even Anne apparently can hardly believe it, and she occasionally wonders with a trace of melancholy if Robert would have loved her and found her important to him if their first meeting had not happened to be at a time when he was comparatively free of public commitments. It seems clear that at most Robert is the type of man who, having once known intense emotion, would be quite content to chalk it up to positive experience and be happy henceforth with the knowledge that understanding and devotion were ready at hand if he should want them. Although we are told that he has occasional extramarital affairs, we never learn any of the details, and Anne is certainly right in not being disturbed about them. It seems unlikely that Robert's sexual excursions could mean anything more to him than a brisk walk in the fresh air.

As for Anne, she understands so thoroughly that Robert *is* the ideas he works with and the political projects he sponsors or initiates that she loves him for what he believes and does, and she savors the intimacy of his moments of human discouragement. If occasionally she is faintly embarrassed at being married to "a public monument," the feeling springs not from impatience with Robert but annoyance at the public's attitude. At the same time she is not completely happy. Although she does not want to change anything between herself and Robert, she nevertheless has the feeling that she has lost herself in her double role of successful psychiatrist and wife of a famous man. "To survive means to be always making a new beginning." In her fear of destroying the satisfying pattern of existence which she had created, she had gradually walled herself in until now she began to feel stifled. When her daughter taunts her with moving through life with white kid gloves, Anne rebels. Going out to dinner with a new acquaintance, she accepts his invitation to go to his room. But the night is a failure. It is not that Anne feels scruples about Robert. They have agreed that each is to seek personal fulfillment in whatever way he desires, and she does not now particularly think of him. But she and the other man are both trying too much "to make love out of their heads." She cannot love a man's sex without loving the whole man or at least feeling that he is one who could be her friend. This stranger, who appears almost hostile, seems to have nothing to do with her even in his passionate embraces. The episode is in line with de Beauvoir's discussion of the distinctive and complicated nature of feminine sexuality and the impossibility for most women, at least, to separate completely the physiological aspect of sex from the emotions. (It is interesting to contrast her view with the quite different theory of Sartre, following Stekel, to the effect that frigidity in women is usually or always due to bad faith—a woman frequently denying to herself that she has experienced the pleasure which actually she felt). Anne does not dwell on the incident, but she fears regretfully that her habit of detachment has perhaps made it impossible for her ever to know passion again. She realizes why her past seems suddenly to belong to some other being. "It is because now I am another person, a woman thirty-nine years old, a woman who is conscious of her age" (p. 78). But being in good faith, Anne does not take this realization as an excuse for slipping into the Serious World and playing the part of an aging woman no longer responsible for choosing her way of being. Instead she resolves that it is more than ever necessary for her to get away and find some new life in which she may live for herself outside the roles in which she had been submerging herself. She accepts an invitation to go to America for a Psychiatric Congress and lecture tour.

In Chicago Anne meets Lewis Brogan. In this romantic interlude author, as well as heroine, seems to enjoy a kind of emotional holiday. For once it is feeling which predominates instead of mind and will. Tenderness, longing, and foreboding, joy and ecstasy, pain and despair are all portrayed simply as they exist, coming naturally into being and as inevitably passing away. The love affair is at once unique and universal as all loves are; it does not give the impression that it has been described to prove a point or to justify a theory. It is simply lived and ultimately outlived. Its significance is only that it can be, that it is and has been—absolutely. Midway in such a love Anne learns that when one mortal heart feels that it has found another, "the measure of my life may just as well be a single smile as the whole universe. To choose one or the other is equally arbitrary." At the moment she even feels (in flat contradiction to existentialism) that she has no choice! The Anne who loves Lewis in America is not out of harmony with the Mme. Dubreuilh we have known in Paris. Even though with her and Lewis there is no question of "making love out of their heads," what first attracts them to each other and makes the complete physical-emotional union possible is that community of tastes and interests which is listed as first prerequisite in all "advice to the lovelorn" columns. The two of them share the same political views, like the same food, enjoy the same magazines; they are similar in their sense of social responsibility, choosing to live ascetically in Chicago's Bohemia and going to out-of-the-way "native" inns on their trip to Mexico. Within this unanimity there is a notable absence of the subject-object conflict which de Beauvoir made so much of in *She Came to Stay*. Although Anne feels that in Lewis she finds a great need satisfied, that she comes alive again both as a woman and as herself, there is no indication that for either of them love is an escape. It is a love which springs from the abundance which they have to give to each other and which by the very giving is increased. Anne senses in Lewis none of the sexual hostility which she had perceived in other men. In love in good faith there is evidently no "second sex."

At the same time, de Beauvoir is subtly skillful in distinguishing between masculine and feminine reactions even in an "equal love." Gradually it becomes increasingly apparent that it is Lewis who determines the emotional mood of the day, who will lay down the ultimatum, who finally brings an end to the affair. Anne, although she is fully happy only during the time that she is with Lewis, never forgets that love is not all that there is in life. Their relation is such that she feels self-fulfilled, not lost to herself or merged so closely with Lewis that she can exist only through him, and this means that she cannot forget or ignore her own personal responsibilities in Paris. Lewis more or less recognizes the fact and loves her the more for it. Yet at the end he will not accept a love which is not a total commitment. Unwilling to settle for a few weeks each summer, he is sullen at Anne's refusal to get a divorce and come to the United States permanently, although he admits grudgingly that he would never consent to live abroad for her sake. At last he decides that a year-round love with part-time satisfaction is not worth the price. He determines not to let himself love, and Anne finds to her despair that, for Lewis, to will not to love is the same as not loving.

The description of the weeks which follow Anne's realization that she has come to spend the summer with a man who no longer loves her is, in my opinion, one of the high points of contemporary writing. Whether de Beauvoir is portraying Anne or Simone, she displays an extraordinary gift for the sensitive expression of complicated emotions and creates a character of amazing depth. Naturally these are weeks of dull, sodden misery. Anne weeps so constantly that the reader almost joins with Lewis in wondering impatiently how she can cry *all* the time. But they are not tears of self-pity. The contrast between anticipation and reality, the realization that she must reconstruct treasured memories now she knows that Lewis had secretly been resenting her even in their earlier happiness together—all this makes the horror of the first fatal moment constantly spring up afresh. But even when most abject, her suffering is not pathetic, and she never fails to struggle for a certain objectivity. She flares up in anger when Lewis, after what she falsely takes for a reawakening of tenderness, proceeds to make love to her perfunctorily and impersonally, as if she were a mere pick-up, and with complete disregard for what their relation has been in the past. She resents his cavalier assumption that despite the change in him she can spend a cheerful summer with him, enjoying casual good times on the shore of Lake Michigan along with a group of his friends. Yet she realizes that in truth she has no complaint; Lewis was right in saying that you can't give the same love to someone who is only half yours as you would to someone who is yours completely. Lewis would have liked them to make one life for themselves; she had insisted on two lives which should only at certain intervals come tangentially together. She cannot blame Lewis, and she is sympathetically aware that he too has suffered, both earlier, when he struggled not to love her, and now too when he wounds her by showing a hostility which comes from his own inner conflicts. When the time comes for her to return to France, Anne is beyond tears and despair. She expects and hopes for nothing and arrives in Paris to face once more the problem of how to begin to live again.

Throughout the novel, both in Anne's narration and in the third-person passages, de Beauvoir uses another woman in love to serve as a foil to Anne. This is Paula, Henri's mistress. Structurally Paula plays much the same part in *The Mandarins* as Elizabeth did in *She Came to Stay;* that is, she represents a woman caught in an unhappy love which has been in bad faith from the start. But Paula is even more seriously ensnared in her self-deception than Elizabeth. At the beginning of the liaison, she had already won considerable acclaim as a popular singer and had every reason to believe that she was started on a spectacular rise to fame. But against Henri's protests she insisted on giving it up "for him" and making a vocation out of her love. As time goes on,

Paula is less in love with Henri than with memories of their earlier passion, and he is frankly bored. Paula has by now so completely become nothing but the woman she believes she has seen in the adoring eyes of Henri that she is incapable of existing except as an object whose being would be supported by his love. As he gradually tries to break away from her, she refuses to believe what he says, tries various methods to prove that he is as dependent on her as she is on him. When he finally declares that the affair is over and walks out on her, she is unable to accept the reality. Since she can no longer lie to herself and maintain her usual relation to the facts of the outside world, she simply severs all connection. After scenes of violence and threats of suicide, Anne, who as friend and psychiatrist had been trying in vain to help during the previous months, finally succeeds in sending her to a hospital for psychiatric care. When they meet six months later, Paula is "cured," but Anne can feel no joy in contemplating her.

What happens at this point is, I believe, unique among novels with a psychoanalyst for protagonist. Throughout the novel it is implied that Anne's professional work is within the Freudian tradition; there is no suggestion, for instance, that she is interested in existential psychoanalysis or that she has been trying to develop any new general theory of her own. Yet her concept of the goal of psychoanalysis and its value was perhaps a little unorthodox. She had chosen psychiatric work because she wanted to help people.

> Oh, I never thought that one could present someone with a prefabricated salvation from the outside. But often it is foolish little things which keep people from being happy, and I wanted to help them get rid of these hindrances (p. 47).

Her goal was never mere "adjustment."

> My purpose was not to procure for my patients a false sense of inner comfort; if I sought to free them from their private chimeras, it was in order to render them capable of meeting the real problems which arise in the world. And each time that I succeeded in it, I considered that I had done a useful work (p. 58).

Such had been her attitude earlier when she still believed that every responsible person had his part to play in a history which was slowly leading humanity toward happiness. In the post-war society she no longer believed in "that beautiful harmony" and wondered more and more frequently about the value of adjustment in an unjust world. To what could she rightly ask her patients to adjust? In the usual novel involving a psychoanalytic cure, the subject is liberated; he learns for the first time to live freely and creatively. It is hardly going too far to say that he is born again. Paula too talks of finding herself, but Anne is not convinced.

> Paula was cured—no doubt of that. But her voice, her gestures, her expressions evoked in me the same embarrassed discomfort I felt when I looked at those artificially young faces which the plastic surgeon refashions out of old flesh. She would probably until her death play the role of a normal woman, but it was an endeavor which hardly predisposed her to sincerity (p. 494).

To Anne it seems that Paula has not found herself but rather been persuaded to give up the endless process of self-pursuit and take refuge in conformity to the Serious World. In Paula's case the new fictions by which she lives may be in truth life-saving remedies, but Anne finds her "adjustment" as drastic an expedient as a prefrontal lobotomy, which saves the patient from insanity by allowing him to live at a reduced intellectual and sub-emotional level. Paula herself reveals a slight nostalgia for the earlier intensity, bitter as it had been, but for the most part she is distressingly ready to put into trivial social projects all the earnest enthusiasm which she had earlier devoted to her singing and then to the drama of her love for Henri. She explains to Anne that analysis had uncovered the "reason" for that ill-fated love. As a child of four she had unconsciously held herself responsible for the death of her infant brother, of whom she was violently jealous. In her relation with Henri she had felt obliged to play a masochistic role, identifying him with her brother. Now she is freed from him, though by way of over-reaction she is somewhat resentful and feels that he had taken advantage of the situation. Her determination to enjoy herself now has almost the flavor of a plan for revenge. Anne has used this kind of explanation with her own patients and recognizes its value.

> Yes, in order to save Paula it was necessary to despoil her love, even in the past; but I thought of those microbes which can be exterminated only by destroying the organism on which they feed. Henri was dead for Paula, but she herself was dead too. I did not know this stout woman with sweaty face and bovine eyes, who sat there beside me swigging down her whisky (p. 496).

Anne (if, as seems likely, she shares at this point the opinions of her existentialist creator) does not precisely doubt the truth of her colleague's hypothesis, but she feels that it is not the whole explanation, and that if it is taken as a final, decreed evaluation, it becomes a device in bad faith. Even at best it is an example of the genetic fallacy. Granted that Paula's jealousy and guilt concerning her brother had existed as defined, it was still Paula who chose to maintain them in the pattern of her later life. Moreover, the theory fails to account for and tries to deny the particular quality of the love which Henri too had shared in the first years, the joy, the ecstasy, the richness which to Paula had been more precious than any taste of artistic success or promise of fame. Anne feels like weeping over this dead love which after being for ten years the meaning and pride of Paula's life must now be recast as a shameful sore. "I would rather die of suffering," she thinks, "than thus sneer at my past and scatter its ashes to the wind."

During the weeks after her separation from Lewis, Anne sternly prevents herself from following the example of either Paula mad or Paula adjusted. She forces herself to recognize that the affair is over; she will not try to kill the abortive love which she still feels, but neither will she resist the cure which already she realizes time is bringing. Her feeling is a subdued echo of the words of another woman writer who was especially interested in analyzing the passions she lived through intensely but truthfully—Edna St. Vincent Millay.

> After all, my erstwhile dear,
> My no longer cherished,
> Need we say it was not love,
> Now that love is perished? [17]

Ultimately Anne's life is linked all but fatally with Paula's unhappy one. On the day that she found Paula ready to kill herself Anne took from her a small phial of poison. She put it in the bottom of her glove box, intending to throw it away later. Just before the close of the novel we find her wondering if she had kept it with a premonition that she might have use for it in the future. Anne is not considering suicide because of Lewis, or at least not directly so. In part her depression is specifically feminine. As a woman she knows that she has reached the age at which she is no longer immediately the object of masculine interest and admiration. There is not much chance of her finding again the absorbing passion she has known with Lewis. Her sexual life is not necessarily over, but she must face the fact that in the years to come the eliciting and enjoyment of desire will become less and less an important part of her existence—and this regardless of whether or not she wills it so. In a broader sense Anne's is the despair which seizes men and women alike at that moment at which it becomes apparent that the future is not infinite, that those hopes of youth which have not been fulfilled may very likely never be fulfilled, that the great moments of a life may well be those of the past rather than those still to come. For the first time Anne *feels* the imminence of death. She looks at Robert and sees in him already the traits of an old man. Suppose that at the outside he still has twenty years. What use to struggle for those twenty years? It seems to Anne now that death is the only truth. Grasping the tiny phial, she seems to free herself from death as a threat by making her own death depend on herself alone. Should she assert the truth of death by drinking the liquid or should she declare all these thoughts a mere depression and nervous crisis by resolving to begin again? That is the real question—beginning again. Long before this, Anne had recognized that there is nothing which can't be outlived, and that if life is lived in good faith, one must be constantly willing to start over again. But she had known too that there are moments when one thinks that one would rather die than seek for courage to mend oneself again. This is her position now. She realizes that she can build a new kind of life if she will try, a life which will offer its own unique projects with its possibilities for eager struggle, failure, and reward. But within her, like unburied ghosts, her dead pasts cry out to her—the little child Anne "who believed in paradise," the young girl who "thought that ideas and books and the man she loved were immortal," the mature woman who loved and was loved by Lewis. How can she bear to carry them with her into the slow birth of another being? Why not give them peace?

For a time, Anne consented to her death but without moving. Then she heard voices from the garden, and suddenly the living Others *were there*. She had felt that Robert and the rest of the family did not really need her. Perhaps—abstractly—they did not. But since she had once existed in their lives, she could not cancel herself out. This death which she had been contemplating—it was her death, but it was they who would have to live this death. She could not inflict upon them such a burden of agony and remorse. Moreover, by their mere presence, they seem to pull her toward them. And if they have been strong enough to snatch her away from death, perhaps they will be able to help her to live again.

Either one drowns in indifference, or the earth is-repeopled. I have not drowned. Since my heart continues to beat, it will indeed have to beat for something, for someone. Since I am not deaf, I will once more hear myself called. Who knows? Perhaps one day I shall again be happy. Who knows?


In the work of Camus and of Sartre there are several passages in which a friendship is the subject of the same kind of careful and sensitive presentation as de Beauvoir employs in her portrayal of love. In each case the relationship is treated as important for its own sake as an absolute experience. But each one, too, significantly reveals something about the nature of the more general social commitment which the two authors hold. In one of his most moving short stories, "The Growing Stone" (*La Pierre qui pousse),* Camus shows how a man who has felt himself an exile finally wins a place for himself in the kingdom of men by an act of personal friendship.*

D'Arrast, a French engineer, has come to Brazil where he is about to direct the building of a dike for the small community of Iguape. There he is received with ceremony and exaggerated expressions of gratitude by the leading dignitaries, but the majority of the people stand aloof. His request that he might be allowed to look inside one of their houses is finally granted but with unfriendly reserve. Meanwhile, he sees a miracle and learns of a strange vow. The miracle took place in a sacred grotto. Some fishermen had once washed there a statue of Jesus which had come mysteriously from out of the sea. Ever since that day there was a rock in the grotto which kept thrusting itself out a little farther. At an annual festival the people would come and break off pieces of it with a hammer, but it kept on growing. D'Arrast hears of the vow from one of the natives of Iguape. He was a ship's cook and had vowed one time when he was in danger that if Jesus would save him, he would carry a huge rock and march in the sacred procession to the church. Tomorrow is the day when the vow must be fulfilled. Sensing in d'Arrast a sympathetic interest and feeling that d'Arrast, whom he insists on calling "Captain," somehow represents a higher authority, the cook asks his help. Tonight there will be the dances in honor of St. George, and

---

* In Camus' volume of short stories, *Exile and the Kingdom,* all of the stories treat in some way the theme of man's exile from the rest of the universe or from mankind. "The Growing Stone" comes at the end of the book and seems to me the only one of the stories which suggests that the Kingdom can be finally reached.

he fears that he may forget his vow and let himself be sucked into the excitement of the ceremonies and join in the dancing. If he does, then he will not have the strength to carry the rock in the morning. Will d'Arrast promise to prevent him from dancing? D'Arrast is touched and strangely disturbed by the request, even more so when the cook leads him to admit that he also had once felt like making such a vow though he had not been able to do so. The cook leaves him with the words that if d'Arrast will help him keep his promise to Jesus, it will be as though he were somehow making and keeping a promise of his own. That night d'Arrast attends the dances. He is overpowered almost to unconsciousness by the intense, primitive emotion; but he does not join in the dancing nor is he asked to do so. Neither can he prevent the cook from dancing, and d'Arrast finally leaves, exiled and discouraged. The next morning he comes to watch the procession. The cook is there with the rock, but his strength rapidly fails him and he falls to the ground. D'Arrast quickly joins the procession, straps the rock upon his own shoulders, and moves forward. But when he gets near the church, he does not go inside as expected; instead he takes the much longer march to the cook's home and puts the rock in the center of the room, half buried in the cinders and earth of the hearth. The cook and his family return, sit around the stone in silence. Then, with the joyous feeling that his life was beginning again, d'Arrast sees that the cook's brother has moved aside to make room and hears the words, "Sit down here with us."

The meaning of the story is unmistakable. So long as d'Arrast merely offered his technical skill, he won gratitude, but not friendship. But by carrying the rock, he showed himself able to respond to the cry which is addressed by one heart to another. It is his *disponibilité* which counts, not his training as an engineer. The stone is still the old stone of Sisyphus, but this time two men have carried it together. Sisyphus, by embracing his task deliberately, was able to love his rock and the indifferent universe of which it was a part. D'Arrast, by making the cook's vow his own, finds his place among men. The title of the story, "The Growing Stone," is—probably deliberately—ambiguous. Does it refer to the rock in the grotto or to the one which came to rest in the cook's home? D'Arrast had not joined in striking the grotto rock with a hammer, and he had carried the other rock to a destination not intended in the vow. Clearly there is an interplay of human and divine in these symbols. By carrying the rock as far as the church and then going in a different direction, d'Arrast indicated that he respected the cook's intent but that he could not join with him in religious belief. Human effort, especially joint human effort, must be directed toward man himself. The stone which truly grows is that which resides as the center of men's love for one another. It is perhaps not going too far to say that d'Arrast himself is halfway a Christ figure. When he first arrives in Iguape, the chief of police tries to subject him to the usual nuisance regulations for foreigners and says that the passport is not in order. Without investigating the matter, the judge sends the chief off to prison and says d'Arrast is to name the punishment. Eventually d'Arrast is able to get him pardoned as a special favor to him and in his name. Thus d'Arrast has power over life and death, and the chief of police, who had been punished for treating d'Arrast as he would have treated any other man, is extravagantly grateful for the grace bestowed upon him. The parallel with original sin and divine grace is apparent. The cook had appealed to d'Arrast for help against his own weakness in yielding to temptation. When the cook shows that he cannot save himself, d'Arrast takes the cook's burden (the sins of the world) upon his own shoulders. But from here on he rejects the role. He does not enter the church but stays among the humble. As "a Christ for our time," d'Arrast is better qualified than Meursault. But Camus does not believe that in serving man rather than God, any man has the right to say that he has become God.

In "The Growing Stone," d'Arrast enters into community with men by a symbolic act of personal sympathy and understanding. In *The Plague,* two men are drawn together in a rare experience of friendship by their awareness that, each in his own way, they are fighting against the same disease. In taking care of the sick, Dr. Rieux has been closely associated with Tarrou, who has organized the citizens into groups of emergency workers. Late in the course of the epidemic they take an "hour off for friendship," and Tarrou explains what the plague symbolizes to him and the motives which lead him to fight so hard against it. The pattern of his life has been determined by one thing—his horror of legalized murder. As a boy he was not the self-tormenting kind and cherished no ideal of asceticism or devotion to noble causes. But at seventeen, he accompanied his father, a prosecuting attorney, to court one day and heard his successful plea for the death penalty against the defendant. Tarrou never forgot the man in the box, sitting there scared and horrified "like an owl frightened by too bright a light." It seemed to Tarrou that the society in which he lived was based on the death sentence and that in seeking to tear it down, he would be fighting against murder. Hence he joined a political group (not named by Camus) which was dedicated to the ideal of setting up a better society. He realized that their program for action occasionally resulted in condemning certain people to death, and he found it hard to accept the fact. But his companions persuaded him that these few had to die in order that there might be a world where for the rest of time there would be no death sentences. And remembering "the poor owl" in the courtroom, he forced himself to go on. Then came the day when he first saw a man killed by a firing squad. Suddenly he realized that during all those years when he sincerely believed that he was fighting against the plague, he too was one of those who had the plague and was spreading its contagion. His associates continued to provide reasons, often impressive reasons, to justify the occasional sacrifice of some men in the name of salvation for all men. But Tarrou replied that the men of the courts too had their reasons to justify the death sentence, and they based their arguments on the same appeal to necessity and *force majeure*. If once you admit that some men are to be sacrificed for the good of others, why should you draw the line at one place rather than another? Such is the logic of our life that one cannot act without running the risk of killing or letting someone be killed. We are all infected with the plague. Worst of all, it is the microbe which is natural. Health, integrity, purity are products of the will and can be maintained only by unrelaxing vigilance and constant tension. Hence in this world where all are more or less sick, those who are weary unto death are the men who struggle in vain to recover. Tarrou concludes that there are only pestilences and victims; by refusing to side with the pestilence one may at least be an "innocent murderer," doing the least possible harm to men and occasionally perhaps even a little good. Thus in the face of evident evil, such as the epidemic which has struck the city of Oran (or the Nazi Occupation), Tarrou will do what he can to help the victims, but he will not take part in political action which infects at the same time that it seeks a vaccine. That this course may result in leaving to others the task of making history Tarrou is uneasily aware. But he feels that his own path for attaining peace must be sympathy, his morality comprehension. He does not believe in God, but his vital concern is to learn how one can become a saint. "Can one be a saint without God? That is the only real problem I recognize today." [18]

There is much of the veritable Camus in Tarrou's attitude. Camus has on many occasions spoken out against the death sentence and has defended his position at length in *Reflections on Capital Punishment (Réflexions sur la peine capitale)*, a book containing another essay on the same theme by Arthur Koestler. In addition, Tarrou's position holds in essence the principal idea of *The Rebel*—that the revolution which takes away men's freedom for the sake of absolute justice is no better than the unjust despotism set up for the purpose of securing the unlimited freedom of a few. There are certain absolute limits which one cannot trespass in the name of any ideal without thereby corrupting that ideal from within. It seems to me that Camus is never more existentialist in spirit than here where he has recognized a point of difference between himself and the proponents of existentialism as a technical philosophy. The idea of absolute limits, of course, is tied up with the idea of a human nature or essence, for to say that there are limits which men must observe is equivalent to declaring that there is a human value which all men can recognize and share. To this extent, I suppose, Camus is holding that essence precedes existence after all, and is thereby in this respect an essentialist and not an existentialist. But the limit which he claims is universal only in the sense of the Kantian Kingdom of Ends: it rests on the assumption of the absolute value of the human person. Camus stands shoulder to shoulder with the existentialists in opposing the real essentialists—Christian, Hegelian, and Marxist—whose doctrines of original sin, the Absolute Idea, and economic determinism all subordinate the individual to a historical process which is in some part outside him. Furthermore, if we are to take seriously existentialism's claim that ultimately it is the individual who counts and that no power of reasoning is adequate either to justify or to explain him away, then Camus is more existentialist than either Sartre or de Beauvoir. It is they who attempt to justify their decisions by rational calculation. Tarrou declares that he is not concerned with argument; what he remembers is "the poor owl" in the defendant's box and the man with the hole in his chest falling down before the firing squad.

Nevertheless, Tarrou is not identical with Camus, and there are suggestions within The Plague that perhaps his way is not entirely the right one. In his preoccupation with trying to be a saint, there is just a slight suspicion of Clamence (in The Fall). Tarrou acknowledges some slight doubt of himself as he compares his own endeavor with the work of Dr. Rieux. In his first serious conversation with Dr. Rieux, Tarrou had asked him abruptly if he believed in God. Rieux answering in the negative, Tarrou then inquired why, since he did not believe, Rieux showed such devotion. Rieux replied that if he believed in an all-powerful God, he would leave the business of healing the sick to him. As it was, he felt he was "on the right path of truth in struggling against creation as he found it."

Since the order of the world is ruled by death, may it not perhaps be better for God if we do not believe in him and fight with all our strength against death without lifting our eyes toward the sky where He sits in silence? (p. 147).

Tarrou feels that Rieux is right to go on fighting his war in which no victory can be lasting. And the doctor in turn is sympathetic with Tarrou's desire to fight the plague—in the broadest sense of the term. But for his own part he feels that men are rather good than bad.

But they are either more or less ignorant, and this is what we mean by virtue or vice. The most hopeless vice is that of the ignorance which believes that it knows all and that it is authorized to kill. The murderer's soul is blind, and there is no true kindness or noble love without the clearest possible understanding (pp. 150-151).

This is a strange half-Socratic half-humanism. Having declared that he does not believe in God, Rieux then postulates some kind of supracontrolling force to the world. It is as though he were picking up the idea implied in one passage in *The Myth of Sisyphus,* that there just possibly might be a meaning to things but that it certainly is not one which is significant for man in his present state. Therefore, even in the interests of this possible something, the best man can do is to struggle against the death and meaninglessness which certainly are the structure of the human condition as he knows and lives it. But while vice is ignorance, it does not follow that virtue is knowledge. The blindness of the murderer, the clear-sightedness of the innocent, have nothing to do with intelligence quotients and very little to do with intellectual development. Rieux' virtue is akin rather to the "comprehension" mentioned by Tarrou. It requires not only constant vigilance in anticipating the full consequences of our acts but the highest possible consciousness and deepest sympathetic awareness of the full experience and potentialities of others and of ourselves. It involves our living to the fullest the possibilities of human solidarity without ever forgetting the final bitter isolation of individual subjectivity. Yet while Rieux and Tarrou follow parallel lines, as it were, their paths are not the same. Tarrou is struggling to obtain an impossible innocence. Rieux says, "I feel more solidarity with the victims than with the saints. I seem to lack the taste for sainthood. What interests me is being a man" (pp. 279-280). To which Tarrou replies, "Yes, we are searching for the same thing, but I am less ambitious."

Camus has stated in an interview that he prefers Rieux' attitude as "a human, strictly human possibility" to Tarrou's spiritual quest for sainthood.[19] This is in harmony with Camus' rare modesty as well as with his unflagging and realistic fight against the plague of our times. Yet in *The Rebel,* which holds much the same relation to *The Plague* as *The Myth of Sisyphus* bears to *The Stranger,* Camus' doctrine of pure revolt shows an interweaving of ideas derived from Rieux and Tarrou both. The rebel realizes that for him the only alternative to the acceptance of oppression and injustice is a "calculated culpability." He will not work in the name of any party or principle which seeks to justify murder as an expedient, but he realizes that in life today one cannot act—or even refuse to act—without risking or consenting to the death of others. Therefore he cherishes—like Tarrou—the hope that he may be an "innocent murderer." But the greater emphasis on action and the specific nature of this "calculated culpability" suggest Rieux more than Tarrou. "If revolt could found a philosophy, it would be a philosophy of limits, of calculated ignorance and of risk. The man who cannot know everything cannot kill everything" (p. 357). Here again we find a connection between right conduct and clear-sightedness. But this time it is the rebel's Socratic knowing that he does not know which makes him realize that he cannot treat living men as expendable for the sake of men yet to be born. To put it in terms appropriate to Rieux, the doctor would perhaps administer a serum to a sick man in a calculated risk which would result either in certain death or in recovery. He would never consent to forcing men to be guinea pigs for an inoculation still in the experimental stage. Furthermore, the rebel, like Rieux, realizes that in preferring to serve Man rather than God he must not make the mistake of trying to become God. He remains faithful to his original principles, willing to abide by the primary rule of today: "Learn to live and to die, and in order to be man, refuse to be God" (p. 377).

Perhaps the truth of the matter is that Tarrou and Rieux represent two aspects of Camus himself: On the one hand, there is the thirst for purity of heart and the feeling that it is wrong to compromise with any society or with any party which permits the sacrifice of individuals for the good of the majority; on the other hand is the realization that preoccupation with one's own innocence and retreat from the world form one more way of consenting to the evils which already exist. If men are to be saved, there must be rebellions; but if the revolutionary movement is not to destroy both men and principles, it must preserve the rebel at its heart. In *The Plague* the two ways are symbolically reconciled. Rieux and Tarrou recognize their differences, but each of them sympathetically comprehends what the other wants; each feels that the other man's path is right for him. After their long talk in "the hour for friendship," they decide to go for a swim, agreeing that while one must fight for the victims of the plague, still if one lives only for that, there remains no reason for fighting. At the lonely shore Rieux feels a curious happiness and reads in the face of his friend, too, "that same happiness which forgot nothing, not even murder." In a moving passage, Camus describes the feeling of peaceful strength and unanimity which comes over them as they swim side by side "with the same rhythm, the same vigor."

> Dressed again, they started back without either one having uttered a word. But they were one in heart, and the memory of this night was sweet to them. When from far off they saw the plague watchman, Rieux knew that Tarrou too was telling himself that the disease had granted them a short reprieve and that was good, and that now they must go back to work again (p. 282).

In Sartre's novel sequence, *The Roads to Freedom,* there is another friendship, which in some ways offers a striking parallel to that of Rieux and Tarrou. This is the account of Brunet and Schneider, which is related partly in the closing chapters of *Troubled Sleep* and partly in an episode called "A Strange Friendship" *(Drôle d'amitié).* The latter appeared in two installments in the 1949 volume of *Les Temps modernes* and is an excerpt of what was to be the final volume of the tetralogy. From a literary point of view, the story of Brunet and Schneider is quite different from the Rieux-Tarrou friendship. It involves much more of struggle, of misunderstanding and reconciliation; it is developed slowly in fine detail with all the complexity of a complicated love affair. But what makes the parallel so startling is that Sartre in these two characters, even more than Camus in *The Plague,* sets forth the conflict which is evident in all of his later works and which unquestionably resides in his basic thought.

Toward the end of *Troubled Sleep* Mathieu falls in battle, and Brunet quietly slips into the role of central character. Unlike Mathieu, he does not choose to die for nothing but allows himself to be taken prisoner so that he may work for the future. Brunet is a Communist and considers himself to be so completely one with the Party that he thinks and feels only with and for it. Schneider, however, whom Brunet meets in the prison compound in France, perceives that there is in Brunet more idealism and tenderness for men than he would like to admit, and he is for this reason attracted to Brunet. When Brunet sets about organizing a secret Communist core among the prisoners, Schneider tells him that he recognizes him as a Communist from pre-war pictures and that he would like to work with him. Schneider explains that he himself is not a Communist but that he has always sympathized with their work and would like now to be one with them. As they work together, they seem to stand for opposite types of Communists: Brunet represents the totally committed Party man who disapproves of individual acts of generosity, who insists on absolute discipline, who would force men to work for what he believes to be their ultimate good whether this is their own choice or not. Schneider, on the other hand, is always alert to the immediate suffering of those around him and thinks in terms of individuals rather than collectivities. If there are extra rations which cannot be equally distributed, Brunet is willing to accept them, along with other Party leaders who have extra responsibilities, hence are—in Party terms —more valuable to the common cause. Schneider refuses to receive anything which any of his companions are denied. When they are transferred from their temporary camp, Schneider openly shares the men's hopes that they will be kept in France and perhaps released. Brunet admits that he prefers the rigors of a German camp so that the men will realize once and for all that the war is really on and that the enemy must be opposed to the bitter end. Yet when the troop train unmistakably heads for Germany, Brunet and Schneider work together, not only to prevent the men from behaving rashly, but to make the moment as easy for them as they can. In the stalag the two are almost happy as they train the men in preparation for the day when with Russian help the Nazis will be defeated and the prisoners released to take their part in the fight for a better world. In their private relation there is a kind of tenderness, nothing homosexual, but a deep personal concern such as Brunet had never felt before, either for his associates or for the oppressed he sought to help.

Then one day a new detachment of French prisoners comes in, and Brunet finds among them Chalais, a Party leader who had had contact with other Communists from outside the prison in Occupied France. Chalais' arrival upsets everything. In the first place, he tells Brunet that Schneider is a proven traitor to the Communist Party. He had been a card-carrying Communist, known by the name Vicarios, the editor of a leftist paper in Algiers. Then in September 1939, he renounced the Party in protest against the Russo-German Pact. Chalais adds that later Schneider gave information against certain of the Party to the governor general. And the Party had issued a warning against Schneider to all its workers. Understanding something of the Party's usual practice in dealing with "traitors" and feeling that, despite this startling revelation, he still knows Schneider's character, Brunet does not quite believe the accusation of betrayal. But "to die and to leave the Party are one and the same." He is shocked, he feels cheated, personally betrayed. Confronted by Brunet, Schneider neither denies nor excuses himself except to explain that he had realized his work with Brunet could not last and that he had joined them because he was "fed up with being alone." When Brunet brings up the charge of informer, Schneider asks incredulously if Brunet could possibly believe it. Brunet, against his inner convictions, replies, "I believe everything which the Party says." Schneider gazes at him intently and then leaves with the words, "My poor Brunet!"

Schneider-Vicarios is not exposed to the others but transferred to another barracks where he will not be associating with the comrades. During the weeks which follow, Brunet, though he cannot avoid painful memories of Schneider, forces himself to remain separate from Vicarios. But the voice of the traitor is within himself. Chalais is the type of Communist Brunet had vainly tried to be. Completely Party-centered, he has only scorn for the stalag's non-Communist socialists. Brunet, who has come to admire many of them, is irritated by Chalais' air of being a physician for dead men. The traitor inside protests and says, "Poor fellows, they suffer from death in the soul!" From Chalais, Brunet learns that the Party line has changed and that the work which he has been doing is all wrong. This is, of course, the period between the fall of France and Russia's forced entry into the war in 1941. Brunet had been teaching that the workers should reject the armistice and declare themselves still at war. The new directives explain that the forces of the Free French are allied with the bourgeois democracies in a war for imperialism. Party members cannot support them. The Soviet Union is sending materials to aid Germany with the idea that when all the belligerent nations are exhausted, it is she who will dictate the peace. Brunet at first challenges Chalais, saying he too speaks for himself and not the Party; but he is silenced and sickened by Chalais' proof, a copy of the Communist Party newspaper, *"Huma,"* which the Nazis had allowed to be openly printed in Paris, thus showing their gratitude to the only group which had supported the Pact. Hard as all this is for Brunet to swallow, he makes the attempt, trying to believe that the Party cannot be wrong and that it must be acting for reasons he cannot know. But he and Chalais find it difficult to convince the men whom Brunet has trained. They take the attitude that Brunet is still their leader and that he is being silenced or persuaded against his better judgement by superior authority. The only recourse is for Brunet to be somehow discredited. Moved in part by political motives and in part by jealousy of Brunet's popularity, Chalais suddenly reveals to the Communist prisoners the true identity of Schneider. Two of the men go out to attack Schneider, and Brunet, knowing full well that it is a trap, defends him, thus proclaiming himself as a champion of Party traitors and not to be trusted. Within the stalag Chalais has won.

Feeling that there is nothing else to be done, Brunet resolves to join Schneider in an attempt to escape from the camp. They get civilian suits from a prisoner who works in a camp store and start out at night to make a break. Earlier Brunet had tortured himself with the thought that if the Party was right, then he was wrong and terribly alone, but that if the Party was wrong, if Schneider was not a traitor, then all men were alone. There seemed no way out. At any rate, thought Brunet, the two of them were alone, and in this very isolation they resembled each other. Now as they walk together in the darkness, everything seems strangely resolved. Brunet no longer goes round in circles trying to find in the man beside him first Schneider and then Vicarios. From now on he is still Vicarios, no question about that, but in defending him, Brunet rightly or wrongly has chosen him as a friend. "Brunet was happy because Vicarios was walking there beside him. From time to time he stretched out his hand and touched him; and from time to time he himself felt the touch of a hand" (p. 1035). And a few minutes later as they are ready to clear the barbed wire, "He began to count. At forty-five he placed his hand on Vicarios' shoulder and felt the strong fingers which grasped his wrist. He was deeply stirred; they were the fingers of friendship" (p. 1037). But this love is destined to die newborn. In the dash for safety they are fired on, and Schneider is wounded. Brunet tries to urge him on to cover, but he cannot make it. He tries to carry Schneider, and Schneider repulses him. As Brunet pleads with him, Schneider will only say, "It's all your fault. The Party has done me in." Brunet sits there in total despair, holding the dying Schneider close to him.

This absolute suffering no human victory could ever efface. It was the Party which had killed him. Even if the U.S.S.R.

should win, men were still alone. Brunet bent forward and buried his hand in Vicarios' soiled hair. As if even yet he could save him from horror, as if two lost men could at the very last minute conquer solitude, he cried out, "To hell with the Party! You are my only friend" (p. 1039).

But Schneider is dead, and the Germans are now very near. Brunet rises and goes to meet them. "His death has only just begun." *

This interlude is to me as deeply moving as anything to be found in the whole of Sartre's work. But it is curiously indecisive. While the events themselves proceed to their denouement with tragic inevitability, none of the basic problem is resolved. The intense emotion which is suggested in the closing pages (a warmth of feeling which no snippet of quotations can convey) certainly suggests a close human relationship such as one would never deem possible on the basis of Sartre's analysis of human relations in *Being and Nothingness*. In their own way these moments of tenderness are as absolute as the suffering of which Brunet speaks. And yet Schneider seems to destroy them by his last words. Although he uses the plural pronoun in the words "It's all your fault," referring to Brunet and the Party together, nevertheless he makes no exception of Brunet; and he dies with a look of unbearable hatred in his eyes. Thus we are left wondering whether Sartre does or does not believe in the possibility of an enduring personal relationship which is in good faith. On the political level things are still less resolved. In spite of all that had happened, Brunet, as they were on their way to escape, told Schneider that he would never leave the Party. His last lament might suggest that, like Camus, he was renouncing any murder which condoned the sacrifice of individuals. But I think we must take his words as the despairing cry of a human being in agony rather than as a political *volte-face*. Brunet at the end is reminiscent of Ibbieta realizing that in the face of death even the cause for which he was dying no longer meant anything to him. The two really fundamental questions are

---

* Apparently Brunet does not die, and he will ultimately be able to work for the Party again. Similarly Mathieu, although most critics have assumed that he died in *Troubled Sleep,* is destined to be only severely wounded. Prof. Robert Champigny, on the basis of an interview with Sartre, comments on the fate of the main characters in the unpublished—and probably unfinished—fourth volume of *The Roads to Freedom.* "On his return to France, Brunet was to discover that his line of action in the prisoners' camp was again congruous with the Party doctrine. Mathieu was to find at last an opportunity for committing his treasured freedom thanks to the Resistance. Still intent on cultivating abjection and perversity, Daniel was to become a collaborator, then kill himself." [20]

left hanging in midair: At what point does realistic action become mere expediency sacrificing ends for means? Can the intellectual who believes in human freedom and in truth work with a party which, albeit in the name of an absolutely just future, suppresses both?

In comparing the social and political positions of Sartre and Camus, one may increase the density of the problem by bringing in the multiple arguments eulled from their political articles and their fiction, but I do not believe that the lines of difference have ever been more clearly laid down than in their treatment of these two episodes. It is significant that in each story the friends who represent divergent attitudes neither clash head on nor finally merge. But it is easy to see too that for Camus there is ultimately established a kind of unity in difference, the balanced tension of the bow, whereas in Sartre the conflict finally rends the two friends asunder and destroys at least one of them. Camus has gradually worked out a political philosophy and stuck to it. Sartre, both in his life and in his writing, has fluctuated, seeming now to stand with the early Brunet, now with Schneider. It is probably significant that Camus—like Schneider and unlike Sartre—joined the Communist Party in his early twenties. For a short time he worked as a propaganda agent among the Arabs in Algeria, then shortly afterwards left the Party, primarily out of disgust at the Soviet Union's opportunistic withdrawal of its support from the Arab cause.[21] Apparently he has never regretted his decision. If Sartre as a young man had made a comparable commitment to the Communists, it is very possible that his later career would have followed an entirely different course.

Of the two, Camus' position, though no easier to live, seems to me less difficult to comprehend. As presented in *The Rebel,* his philosophy is one of limits and of moderation. It certainly does not advocate passivity. "In the world as it is today only a philosophy of eternity can justify nonviolence" (p. 354). But for the rebel, if violence occurs, it is not legitimized. It is the result of calculated risk and personal responsibility, and one may resort to any violence only as an extreme limit which is opposed to another extreme of violence. "The authentic action of revolt will consent to take up arms only for institutions which limit violence, not for those which codify it" (p. 360). Just as the philosophy of revolt seeks a dynamic mean between violence and absolute nonviolence, so it holds that justice and freedom must find their limits in each other. So too the real and ideal must neither one be pursued at the expense of the other. To justify action and systems in the name of *what is* denies man's transcendence and enchains him to the material world. But to force men to live their solidarity only as a "we shall be" is to destroy the first principle of human solidarity, the "we are" on which the philosophy of revolt is founded. The rebel must be like the artist, who squarely confronts reality without escaping from it. Revolt is uncompromising as to means but will accept approximation in achieving its ends. It lives in the relative and abhors absolutes. The difference between Camus and Sartre is epitomized in their distinctive ways of defining the concepts of revolt ( = rebellion) and revolution. To Sartre, revolt is purely negative. It is a movement of opposition which cannot be defined in positive terms since it does not move toward new definite values. Politically it is abortive because it does not achieve or even envision a total, concrete society and hence cannot successfully incorporate itself in history. Individually, it is the attitude personified in the subject of Lindner's study, *Rebel without a Cause.* Revolution, on the other hand, is a realistic program of action directed toward definite ends, moving with the course of history, which it directs and modifies. Camus does not wholly disagree with these definitions, but his evaluative interpretation of them is entirely different. Revolutions he distrusts because in their attempt to inject ideas into history and to reshape the world to fit a theoretical structure, they are likely to shove mankind into a kind of Procrustean bed. If revolutionists are to succeed, they must have power; and to get it they kill both men and principles. Revolt, on the other hand, is an incoherent but specific impulse which remains faithful to its origins; it is less a program for action than a testing stone against which all conduct—action or passivity—must be measured. Revolutions tend to justify all in the name of *efficiency.* Revolt seeks rather to be *effective.*

> When the end is absolute—that is, historically speaking, when one believes it to be certain—then one can go so far as to sacrifice others. When it is not, one can sacrifice only oneself in a struggle where the common dignity is at stake. Does the end justify the means? Possibly, yes. But what will justify the end? To this question which historic thought leaves dangling, revolt answers—the means (p. 361).

When in 1952 Sartre and his friend Jeanson violently attacked *The Rebel* in *Les Temps modernes,* they accused Camus of trying to stand aloof from history, of refusing to make a choice in the post-war world on the ground that the issues were not sufficiently clear. His criticism of Marxism and Stalinism they interpreted as a way of playing into the hands of reactionaries. Camus' doctrine of limits and relative action they took as a willingness to compromise with the status quo and to retreat into the ivory tower. The attack was unfortunate and unfair. Sartre and Camus have certainly disagreed on the policy of supporting the Communist platform, but Sartre too has refrained from any ultimate commitment to the Party and finally broke with it completely at the time of the crisis in Hungary. It is Camus who has proved to be the more uncompromising and Sartre who would find it more difficult to justify his past actions as being consistent with his philosophy of freedom. Camus is reluctant to support any specific party, but this does not mean that he has remained politically inactive. He has written indefatigably in support of issues in which he believes—trade unionism, the right to free expression of one's beliefs, the evil of capital punishment, a program for the realization of a "relative Utopia" which would abandon present-style nationalism and frontiers in favor of a more satisfactory international democracy.[22]

Camus has seldom made his strictly literary works overtly political. Frequently he will take what would seem to be the larger issue and use it as mere background for a poignant vignette of the everyday reactions of persons caught in the conflict. Thus, for example, in his short story called "The Silent Men" (Les Muets),[23] the scene is laid in a coopers' shop where the men have returned after an unsuccessful strike. The employer makes overtures to them, pleading with them to let bygones be bygones, saying that perhaps another time he can arrange a better settlement. The men say nothing at all, not even when two of them are called in for a private interview. In the afternoon they learn that the employer's daughter has fallen seriously ill, and they hear the sound of the ambulance which takes her to the hospital. Later the employer comes to the workroom again and stands on the threshold. The men turn toward him as if to speak. They feel the need to say something but cannot. The employer goes away. Presumably he realized that the silence this time was a different one, but there is no telling. On the political level the story resolves nothing whatsoever, but it is a strangely moving portrayal of men who are drawn together by the simple fact of suffering; of how their common humanity outweighs their differences as one man to another; of the strange inhibitions which prevent men from expressing their real feelings when most they want to.

In another story, "The Guest" (L'Hôte),[24] the setting is Algeria with its background of conflict between French and Arabs. Once again Camus neglects political implications and examines the intricate web of personal relations arising from one slight incident. The central character is Daru, a schoolteacher, French, but born in Algeria. At the opening of the story he is isolated by a blizzard in his small schoolhouse high up on a plateau. A gendarme comes from a nearby village bringing an Arab who has killed a man in a family quarrel. The gendarme begs Daru to take the man into custody, to keep him overnight and deliver him the next day at a police station a few miles farther on. Daru is most reluctant but finally consents. At night he takes no measures to secure the Arab and secretly hopes that the man will escape. In the morning the prisoner is still there, and they start out together in the direction of the police station. But having gone part way, Daru stops. He gives the Arab a package of food and some money and explains to him that the road toward the east will take him to the police station; another one, just perceptible from where they stand, will take him south to the desert where nomads will give him shelter. Daru leaves him. A little later he looks back and sees the Arab walking slowly in the direction of the prison. Back at the school he finds a note on the blackboard. "You have turned in our brother. You will pay." The story ends with the words, "In this vast country which he had loved so well, he was alone."

If there is any political message in "The Guest," it is simply the sad observation that the present situation is so terribly wrong and confused that even those French residents of Algeria who love its people do harm and meet misunderstanding in their very effort to help. But I do not think that Camus was primarily concerned here with political allegory. Like so much of his work the story points at once to the grandeur of man and to his tragedy. Daru feels so great a human sympathy for the unfortunate that he cannot hand the Arab over to the police even though he knows that by his promise to the gendarme and by civil law he is bound to do so. The Arab responds by choosing prison rather than an escape which would save his life but perhaps bring trouble on his benefactor. Against this willingness of two men to sacrifice themselves for each other is set the total misunderstanding on the part of the Arab's relatives. Nothing could illustrate more perfectly Dr. Rieux' statement that while men are on the whole rather good than bad, they are all either more or less ignorant.

There is one work by Camus which is definitely political. This is *The Just (Les Justes)*,[25] a play which serves as a literary illustration of one section of *The Rebel*. In his study of historical revolutions, Camus declared that the only revolutionists who had remained faithful to the original principle and values of revolt were a small group of Russian terrorists whom he calls "scrupulous" or "fastidious" murderers *(meurtriers délicats).*[26] These men and women, living about 1905, were entirely different from Dostoyevsky's "Possessed." They believed that their society must be destroyed but without their ever glorying in the destruction. On the contrary, they recognized that if they were to bring in the kingdom of love and justice, violence was unavoidable, but they did not thereby justify it. Murder for them was both necessary and inexcusable. They demonstrated its impossibility and its inevitability by choosing actions in which they paid with their own lives for the lives they took. In *The Just* Camus chooses these historic personages for his characters, and he weaves into the conversation remarks which they are supposed to have made. As in all existentialist literature, the emphasis is not on historical realism but on the ideas and emotions which are called into question. The plot, based on an actual event, is simple. Kaliayev is planning to throw a bomb at the Grand Duke. He has the opportunity but holds off because he sees the Duke's niece and nephew are in the carriage with him. Later, when the children are not there, Kaliayev has another chance and throws the bomb. The Grand Duke is killed. Kaliayev is arrested and hanged. The important thing for everyone in the play is to arrive at a proper understanding of the nature of Kaliayev's deed. To him the act has not been a crime, and he will not renounce it even for the promise of a pardon. In fact, renunciation or even pardon without renunciation would in his eyes remake the act as murder. It is his death which will justify it. If he does not die, then his action becomes an inexpiable bloody deed of violence. His mistress, Dora, understands this and begs at the end that she may throw the next bomb so that she, like Kaliayev, may soon attain in death the innocence which she craves but cannot know so long as she lives.

Between Kaliayev's first hesitation and the later successful assassination there is a scene in which Camus confronts Rebel and Revolutionist. Kaliayev has come back to his comrades after the first abortive attempt. Dora understands and approves his decision. The revolutionist Stepan does not. They must choose, he says, between sentimental charity, which only seeks to heal the suffering it sees before it, and the revolution which is going to remove all evils, present and future. Because Kaliayev spared two children today, millions of Russian children will die of hunger in the years to come. The revolution will triumph on the day when they decide to forget children. He loves the people, Stepan declares, and regards no act as forbidden so long as it serves the people's cause. None of the others will accept this argument. Love, they maintain, does not wear this visage, and many of their comrades have died explicitly to show that there are some things which are not permitted. Dora sums up the less absolutist and more humane position of revolt.

> Yanek [Kaliayev] consents to kill the Grand Duke since his death can bring nearer the time when Russian children will no longer die of hunger. This already is not easy. But the death of the Grand Duke's nephews will not prevent any child from dying of hunger. Even in destruction there is an order, there are limits (p. 73).

Stepan insists that there can be no limits for those who believe in revolution, a doctrine which Camus constantly emphasizes. But Kaliayev will not give in. He has determined to give his life to overthrow despotism, but he sees in the words of Stepan the annunciation of another despotism which, if it is ever brought into being, would make of him an assassin by the same acts by which he sought to establish justice. Moreover, if men are to live, they must have more than justice; they must know as well love and innocence. Kaliayev as the spokesman for revolt speaks to Stepan in the spirit of Aglaia in *The Idiot*. "You have no tenderness, nothing but truth, and so you judge unjustly." [27]

If now we leave Camus and turn to Sartre, we find a quite different type of problem. Camus' doctrine of revolt is, as a theory, complete and definite. The literature which reflects it is concerned, like the theory itself, with elucidating the principles which one ought to adopt for social and political action. We do not find in Camus' fiction any attempt to relate this philosophy to *specific* decisions which one may have to make as a political or military leader in today's world. Hence the question of consistency in practical application does not arise. On the other hand, Sartre's primary purpose in several works has been specifically to show how theory and practice come together in harmony or in compromise. Hence we not only meet the question of consistency, but we must decide whether Sartre's way of applying his philosophy perhaps results in a modification of the original position.

Sartre has never worked out the theoretical details of his political thought as fully as Camus has done in *The Rebel*. In 1946 he presented in *Les Temps modernes* two articles which sought to explain the philosophy of revolution as the existentialist saw it in contrast to Marxism.[28] At this time I think it could be said without unfair oversimplification that Sartre approved the Marxists' aims without subscribing to all of their methods or to their concept of history. Sartre's philosophy of revolution is based on the premise that all men are by nature free. We can see this truth, he claims, in the very fact that men are capable of recognizing oppression as distinct from other kinds of afflictions. Matter cannot oppress matter. One rebels against men or gods but not against storms and earthquakes. The guiding ideal of revolution should be respect for the freedom of all men and the factual liberation of all. Revolution does not aim at bestowing upon certain minorities privileges which have previously been denied them. It must be in the name of all men and for the good of all. Sartre's ideal revolutionary looks on any society as merely a human fact which he may accept or try to change. History is the record of human action past and present. It is not controlled by any outside force, and it does not lead to any inevitable outcome. The revolutionary looks at it from the point of view of the future and in the light of the particular future end which he proposes. Thus thought and action are inextricably interwoven. Action reveals reality and at the same time is a modification of reality.

Sartre has summarized the essentials of a philosophy of revolution in a sort of credo comprising four basic principles. First, Man is unjustifiable and his existence is contingent. No Providence has designed his being, nor was he himself ever free not to exist or not to be free. Second, since there is no external justification for individuals, this means that no collective order which men may establish has any privileged claim to "rightness"; men may at will surpass any such order in the direction of other orders. Third, the system of values prevalent in any society reflects the social structure of that society and tends to preserve it. Fourth, as a natural consequence, men may always seek to go beyond an existing set of values toward other new values which are anticipated and even invented by men's very effort to pass beyond the present society.

Much of this is a restatement of Marxist theory. The Marxists also, of course, claim that the revolution is for the deliverance of all mankind, that the ultimate goal is a classless society without exploitation, oppression, and social conflict. Sartre is with Marx too in holding that it is among the workers that such a revolution must be initiated, that only the working classes are in a position to extend class solidarity to include the whole human race. Marx had pointed out on more than one occasion that the values and criteria for judgement by which opponents criticized his ideas were themselves products of bourgeois efforts to preserve the existing state of affairs. Nevertheless, the differences between Marx' and Sartre's theories are at least as striking as the similarities. Marx was able to see that in the course of history many socialistic and revolutionary groups had become reactionary by the process of turning idealistic and relative aims into absolute principles. Nevertheless, he and his followers envisioned the establishment of the classless society as a permanent, ideologically perfect state. The Sartrean philosophy of revolution allows for a continual transcendence—always in the direction of greater freedom and an open future. Even if the ideal of maximum freedom for all could be realized by one generation, it would have to be reformulated by the next—in order to remain freedom. Moreover, the belief that men are free leads Sartre to reject completely what he calls the "materialist myth." Men are not things. They are not subject to determinism by obscure forces of history. Economic determinism is just as much a myth as determinism by heredity or environment. A person cannot be defined just by his class; individual members have individual reactions. Most important of all, no results of men's actions can be guaranteed, neither their actual working out, nor their effect on other men, nor the judgement which the future will pass upon them. For all these reasons, men must not be sacrificed either to a mystic idea of the State or to a vague Utopian future.

Such in essence were Sartre's ideas on revolution in 1946, when he was comparing his position with theoretical Marxism only. But a philosophy which calls for constant action in the real world is seldom, if ever, asked to make a decision involving the possibilities foreseen by nineteenth-century Communist theory. Urging that we must choose within the world as we find it and not hold out for an ideal situation in which the issues are clear cut, yet believing equally firmly that we must never accept any existing value system as absolute, Sartre has fluctuated, seeming first to emphasize one side of this paradox and then the other. Like Camus he believes that we must accept a "calculated culpability," but he seems to have found more difficulty than Camus in determining at what point action meets the limit which, if trespassed, bestows upon an act a meaning opposed to what it originally intended. Sartre's faith in human freedom has led him politically so far to the Left that on many occasions he has spoken approvingly of the Communists as being the only party really interested in furthering the cause of the workers. Consequently when he speaks of the "engaged writer," there is a storm of protest from persons who take the term as applying not to a writer concerned with social issues but to one working for the Communist Party, hence not free at all.

It is true that Sartre has on occasion praised the Party; it is equally true that at other times he has denounced it. But his pronouncements pro or con have always been those of an outsider, and they have been explicable in terms of the specific question at issue. More times than not he has been in agreement with the position of the French Communists apropos of domestic policies. He has frequently criticized American "imperialistic" aims. Yet when Russia attacked Hungary in 1956, Sartre not only condemned "absolutely and unconditionally the Soviet aggression"; he declared that it would never be possible under any circumstances whatsoever to resume relations with the present leaders of the French Communist Party.[29] Throughout the decade preceding this decisive break, Sartre appeared to feel every so often that perhaps he really ought to join the Communists, but his strong conviction that the writer must be free to write the truth as he sees it prevented him from taking the final step.

Somewhat ironically, Sartre's statement that exactly this was his position was made in a radio speech which in this country was generally interpreted as meaning that he would soon join the Communist Party. In 1952 he spoke of the Party's distrust of intellectuals who wanted to work with the Communists but on their own terms and reserving the right to criticize or to break away. Sartre used the name "slimy rat" for these people and said, "You can trust me in this. It is a slimy rat who speaks to you." [30] The expression is interesting for more than its vividness. In *Being and Nothingness* Sartre has written a brilliant analysis of slime and sliminess, taken both literally and metaphorically. Slime represents a "substance between two states," the "agony of water," a deceptive substance which is not quite one thing nor the other. It represents symbolically a dreaded state in which a person wants to launch forth a free project of himself into the future but feels himself caught back by invisible chains from the past. Sartre's designation of himself as a "slimy rat" indicates that he recognized that he had been trying to maintain an untenable position. The fact that he never tried to make himself other than a "slimy rat" is proof that he accepted the tension between the need for commitment and the necessity to remain intellectually free. He has gone on committing himself with regard to specific issues, but he has withdrawn more and more from association with any group demanding surrender of one's freedom of thought. In all of this he has never retracted his most positive expression regarding the duty of the writer, the statement which he made in *What Is Literature?* in 1947.

> If at present I am asked whether the writer in order to reach the masses ought to offer his services to the Communist Party, I answer no. The political policy of Stalinist Communism is incompatible with the honest practice of the literary profession (p. 280).

Thus the writer who is to show us the possibilities of free men must be himself free; but he must learn like everyone else how to commit his freedom. With Sartre the process has not been smooth or easy. In his fiction the struggle is clearly recorded.

Very early in his career Sartre was at pains to distinguish the free choice of action within a situation, which existentialism postulates, and the *acte gratuit* of which Gide and the Surrealists made so much. This "gratuitous act" is an act of pure caprice, an act with no motive other than the wish to demonstrate that one can perform such an act. For the Surrealists, the perfect example of the *acte gratuit* is the man who for no "reason" decides to fire a revolver at random in a crowd. In one of Sartre's earliest short stories, "Erostratus" *(Erostrate),*[31] Paul Hilbert decides to do precisely this, though in a superabundance of freedom he intends to kill six men, not merely one. The story can hardly be taken as a serious consideration of the *acte gratuit* versus *liberté engagée.* Hilbert is presented as a sex pervert, a *voyeur,* who cannot bear any physical contact with others and who is equally incapable of any psychological intimacy. He hates humanity and intends to kill for the sake of protesting against the humanism which he feels has invaded every corner of modern life. He is motivated also by a desire for publicity, wanting to imitate the Greek Erostratus, who set fire to the great temple at Ephesus in order that his name might not be forgotten. But everything goes wrong. He cannot maintain the calm which he had intended. He fires at the same man three times out of panic, loses his way, and has to take refuge in a café lavatory. At the last moment, he cannot find the courage to commit suicide and he lets himself be arrested. The whole episode is a travesty on the *acte gratuit.* Hilbert's miserable crime is anything but that. But there is nothing in the story to suggest that Sartre was interested in developing his own concept of a free act. The study of Hilbert's twisted personality is excellently done but might very well have been written by a traditional Freudian rather than by the man who was going to outline the basis for a psychology of freedom in his "existential psychoanalysis."

It was in *The Flies,* published four years later (1943), that the concept of engaged freedom first appeared in drama. There, we may recall, Orestes learned that so long as he remained aloof, his freedom meant nothing, had no value. It was only when he deliberately committed it in the service of the people of Argos that he began to feel that he was really alive. In *The Flies* Sartre argues that freedom is meaningless unless it has a content. In *The Roads to Freedom,* the first two volumes of which came out in 1945 and the third in 1949, Sartre works with the same theme in developing the character of Mathieu. One might say that Mathieu has learned all of the theory of existentialism without ever quite knowing how to put it into practice. In contrast to Daniel, he tries to live in good faith; unlike Brunet, he dwells on his conflicts, tries to see things from every possible angle, thinks instead of acting. Two frequently quoted passages reveal the decisive stages of his development. The first comes toward the end of *The Reprieve*. Mathieu is standing alone on a bridge. In a long inner monologue he sees himself in relation to the rest of the universe in much the same way that Roquentin confronted the In-itself, realizing his own absurd contingency and the nauseating superfluity of existence. Mathieu finds himself not as Nausea but as freedom (the two, of course, are not really opposed to each other).

> Inside, nothing, not even a puff of smoke, there is no *inside,* there is nothing. Myself: nothing. I am free, he said to himself, and his mouth was dry. Halfway across the Pont-Neuf he stopped and began to laugh: liberty—I sought it far away; it was so near that I couldn't touch it, that I can't touch it; it is, in fact, myself. I am my own freedom. He had hoped that one day he would be filled with joy, transfixed by a lightning-flash. But there was neither lightning-flash nor joy: only a sense of desolation, a void blurred by its own aspect, an anguish so transparent as to be utterly unseeable. . . . He was alone on this bridge, alone in the world, accountable to no man. "I am free *for nothing,*" he reflected wearily. . . . And yet he must risk that freedom (pp. 362-364).

Mathieu drifts on into the war, doing each day what seems to be demanded of him but without ever really committing himself, following generally the pattern of morality conventional for the circle in which he moved. Then comes the fall of France. In a small town, deserted by their officers, Mathieu and the other soldiers await the inevitable arrival of the Germans. Finally they come, and at last Mathieu decides to act. He could easily let himself be taken prisoner; resistance will accomplish nothing. Nevertheless, he takes up a position in a tower and fires on the Germans below. I'd give anything, he thinks, just to hold on for fifteen minutes!

> This was revenge on a big scale; each one of his shots wiped out some ancient scruple. One for Lola, whom I dared not rob, one for Marcelle, whom I ought to have ditched, one for Odette, whom I didn't want to screw. This for the books I never dared to write, this for the journeys I never made, this for everybody in general whom I wanted to hate and tried to understand. . . . He was firing on his fellow men, on Virtue, on the whole world: Liberty is Terror. . . . He fired: he was cleansed, he was all-powerful, he was free.

> Fifteen minutes.[32]

Mathieu has at last given his freedom a content. But it is a question whether we should call this an engaged freedom. His act amounts to suicide and a suicide which is for nothing just as his earlier freedom was for nothing. Moreover, the whole episode smacks of resentment and a small boy's rebellion rather than philosophical revolt. Mathieu is protesting against his former refusal to choose, but it seems impossible that this final choice is really the right one.

During the years 1948 and 1949 Sartre seems to have felt with particular acuteness the need to present the problem of political commitment in concrete terms. This is the period of "A Strange Friendship" where, as we have seen, Sartre shows sympathy—if not full approval—for Schneider, the Communist who broke with the Party when it showed itself ready to sacrifice ideals and truth for expediency and lies. Two other works raise the question of the proper relation between means and end: *Dirty Hands (Les Mains sales)*[33] and *In the Mesh (L'Engrenage)*.[34]

In *Dirty Hands* Hugo, an intellectual, idealistic Communist, confronts the Party leader, Hoederer, who for reasons of political expediency is pressing for an alliance with the Party's enemies. Hugo has been commissioned by other Party leaders to kill Hoederer, whom they consider to be a traitor. Hugo finally shoots him but at a moment when Hugo himself is not quite sure whether his motive is personal jealousy or the moral belief that Hoederer is wrong and will destroy the Party by placing expediency above principle. After a term in prison, he is released and learns that the Party has now adopted Hoederer's policy and regards him as a hero. Hugo faces a clear choice: he can adopt the official view and say that his deed had been simply an act of passion; or he can claim that his motivation had been political, in which case he will be acting contrary to the Party's decision. He chooses the latter alternative even though he knows it will mean death at the hands of the Communist agents.

When the play (under the title *Red Gloves*) was produced in New York, American critics hailed it as unmistakably anti-Communist. Sartre was considerably annoyed by this. He declared that it was Hoederer's point of view with which he sympathized, not Hugo's.

> Hugo has never been for me a sympathetic character, and I have never considered that he was right in relation to Hoederer. But I wanted to represent in him the torments of the kind of youth who, in spite of feeling the kind of indignation which is properly Communist, never succeeds in joining the Party because of the liberal education which he has received. I didn't mean that such young people are wrong or that they are right. In that case I would have been writing a propaganda play. I simply wanted to describe them. But it is Hoederer's attitude which alone seems to me sound.[35]

I suspect the truth is that at the time when he wrote *Dirty Hands,* Sartre himself was finding it hard to choose between the two points of view and consequently has written a play in which the arguments on each side are of about equal weight. It is easy to see how one could pick out evidence for either interpretation. The fact that Hugo's decision is made with the knowledge that he will die for it gives to his act a heroic cast; consequently one is inclined to feel that his creator must believe him to be right. Yet even here there is an ambiguity. Hugo states that he still feels that Hoederer was wrong and that, whatever may have been in his mind when actually he pulled the trigger, sooner or later he would have had to kill a man who lied to his comrades and who would perhaps bring about the corruption of the Party from within. But at the end the reason he gives for refusing to say that he committed the murder for personal reasons is that he wants Hoederer's death to retain a certain dignity, so that this man whom he had come to understand and to love may not seem to have died by chance in a trivial quarrel over a woman. In the earlier conversation between the two, Hugo puts up a strong defense for the idea that one must not condone evil means in the name of noble causes, that a party which consents to use its enemies' methods has sunk to the level of those whom it opposes. But the effect is considerably weakened as Hoederer points out that whereas he is willing to lie for the ultimate good of the Party, his policy is at least one which will save many lives. Hugo is willing to sacrifice individuals in the name of lofty principle; it is ideas he loves, not men. Hugo refuses to soil his hands but is all too ready to put on the red gloves of bloodshed. The argument that clean hands are a luxury which those dedicated to human welfare must forego is so forcefully presented that one is not surprised that Sartre himself has not always appeared able to resist it.

*In the Mesh* is to my mind the most cynical of Sartre's political plays. It is a scenario or screenplay tracing the rise and fall of a dictator in a small, unidentified country. As the scene opens, we discover that a successful popular revolution headed by François has just put down the tyrant, Jean Aguerra. François holds a trial so that the inevitable execution may seem to be an act of justice rather than murder. The majority of the play consists of a complicated series of flashbacks in which various people, including Jean himself, reconstruct past events.

We learn that Jean had never desired personal power for its own sake. He had decided very early to fight against oppression, and he learned quickly that he could get nowhere without force. Yet he did not resort to violence willingly. His first important social efforts were directed toward persuading a group of workers to give up a hopeless strike which could only result in useless suffering. When he failed and when the strike was broken by troops, then he decided with a few others that the only recourse was a revolution against the government. The movement grew rapidly but not without violence. Jean says,

> At the outset I had decided to struggle with violence, but I hoped I should only use it against our enemies. And then I realized I was caught in a mesh, and that in order to save the cause one was sometimes obliged to sacrifice the innocent (p. 115).

The turning point came on the day Jean killed a friend under the mistaken impression that the man was a traitor. From that day on, Jean felt estranged from his friends and hated himself, but he continued to make what sacrifices the cause demanded. At length the revolution was successful. The Regent was sent into exile, and Jean held the highest office, presumably a kind of provisional dictatorship. His party had fought particularly for three things: the nationalization of the country's oil industry with the accompanying improvement of the workers' conditions, freedom of speech, and the election of a parliament. No sooner had Jean taken office than he received a visit from the Ambassador of the country which held most of the oil concessions. The Ambassador warns Jean that his government will regard any attempt on the property of their nationals as a *casus belli;* moreover, there are thirty-five of the government's divisions stationed along the frontier. Bitterly, Jean realizes that he has no choice in the matter; his country is too small to survive a war and keep even a modicum of independence. By maintaining the status quo a few more years, there is a chance that their neighbors will fight each other with a resultant change in their own governments. The important thing now is to keep the nation at peace. This first compromise undermines all the rest of the program. He cannot allow a parliament to be elected, for he knows that the first thing it would do would be to nationalize the oil. He has to suppress the freedom of the press so that public opinion will not be stirred up sufficiently to force his hand. Finally, he realizes that the one thing he can do to build up the country's economy is to impose upon the nation a speedy mechanization of agriculture. The peasants resist; Jean orders the police to intervene, and the result is burned villages and mass deportations. Jean still believes that he is right but he understands and sympathizes with those who refer to him as "Aguerra the tyrant."

Throughout the early years Jean's best friend had been a journalist, Lucien, who was willing to work with the party but on condition that he take part in no violence. Lucien believed that no victory was worth the loss of a single human life. Jean could not agree with him, and yet he recognized that without people like Lucien, there was danger that the revolution would betray itself. At first he was willing to regard Lucien as the party's conscience, but once he was in office everything changed. Lucien could not understand Jean's seeming betrayal. Jean could not allow Lucien to continue attacking his measures in public editorials. Finally, when Lucien refused to be silent, Jean reluctantly had him imprisoned. Just before Lucien's death, Jean visits him. Although the play does not make it quite clear why Jean could not have given the same explanation years before, nevertheless he does at last succeed in making Lucien see just how he had been forced to take the actions for which he was so hated. He concludes,

> "And what have you done? What is the use of babbling about justice if you don't try to bring it about?"

Lucien looks at Jean almost in despair.

"Why do you say that to me? Do you want me to die in despair?" . . .

"Don't you think I'm in despair myself? I've taken everything on my shoulders. All the murders . . . even your death. And I loathe myself."

Lucien lifts a hand and takes Jean's. "Jean, I think I understand you."

Jean lifts his head and Lucien asks him almost anxiously: "Do you think it was a crime to want to remain unsullied?"

"I . . . I don't think so. I think there have to be men like you and men like me. We've done everything we could, Lucien, and both of us have gone the limit" (p. 125).

Jean asks if Lucien could acquit him. Lucien replies, "You did what you could." After this last flashback, we return finally to the courtroom. François, the new dictator, will not accept the report of Lucien's verdict. Jean is sentenced and led out to execution. The play ends as François, now ensconced in Jean's office, is talking with the same Ambassador. We hear him say gloomily, "We shall not touch the oil fields."

*In the Mesh* might well be taken as a documentation for Camus' distinction between rebel and revolutionist. It seems clear that in 1949 Sartre's sympathies were more with the revolutionist than with the rebel. One feels that he is not happy about the situation but that he accepts it as necessary, much as he consents to live without a belief in God or in any suprahuman guarantee for our value systems. In fairness to Sartre, however, it should be pointed out that all his revolutionists sincerely believe in the ultimate good toward which they are struggling and for which they seem at times to sacrifice too much. The idea that personal integrity and high principles may be bought at too high a cost is not limited to Sartre's work or to ideological conflicts. It is, for example, the central theme of Cozzens' *By Love Possessed*. It would be no more just to accuse Sartre of generally condoning expediency, lies, and political murders than to reprimand Cozzens for counseling lawyers to embezzle.

In the early fifties, before the Soviet action in Hungary, Sartre brought out two more plays which were set against a political background. Neither, however, advanced or significantly modified his position. *Luci-*

*fer and the Lord,* which we considered for its metaphysical and religious implications, can be read just as well as a political allegory. Goetz, its hero, as the bastard son of a noble and a peasant, shifts from the camp of the aristocrats to the side of the peasants but without feeling that he is really accepted by either side. Thus he represents in a fashion the intellectual who tries to make himself a worker, like Hugo in *Dirty Hands.* It does not seem to me that the outline of the conflict in political terms ever emerges very clearly. Sartre claims that the play shows that so long as he tried to follow an Absolute—either Good or Evil—Goetz succeeded only in destroying human lives. This is true on the metaphysical level, but it is difficult to see how it works out politically. At the end Goetz resolves to give up both personal despotism and the saintly doctrine of nonviolence. This is a compromise, no doubt. But as he puts this resolution into practice by taking his stand with the socialists, his first act is to kill the captain who tries to prevent him from taking command. It seems to me that we are still in the spirit of *In the Mesh,* where ends take precedence over means to the extent of sacrificing human life to a cause. This may be realistic action, but I cannot see that Goetz has entirely forsworn absolutes.

In *Nekrassov,* the correctness of the Communist position is implied but not examined. The plot concerns a confidence man, Valéra, who meets up with a journalist, Sibilot, who is in danger of losing his job if he doesn't find a sensational story to satisfy his editor. They concoct a plan to save both of them; Valéra, who is being pursued by the police, will pose as the Russian Nekrassov, pretending that he has fled the Soviet Union, and will write a series of "confessions." What follows is a hilarious satire directed against the reactionary press. Much of it is a just criticism of the irrationality which too often is found among opponents of Communism and would have been quite pertinent in the days of McCarthyism in the United States. But the implication that the Communist press would be entirely free of this sort of thing leaves the play one-sided. At most, it is a highly amusing farce, and one can sympathize with the remarks of those critics who felt that a great philosopher and the author of *The Flies* might well have spent his time on something more significant.

Sartre has produced no fiction since his action at the time of the Hungarian affair. His most significant pronouncement since then is perhaps his introduction to *The Question,*[36] the account by Henri Alleg of his torture at the hands of the French paratroopers in Algeria. Sartre's introductory essay is not narrowly political. It condemns the French colonial policy, but it is more concerned with the broader implications of the fact that a democratic government would condone the use of torture. During the Occupation, Sartre says, every Frenchman asked himself, "Will I be able to hold out if they torture me, or will I talk?" Now everyone should ask, "If my friends, fellow soldiers, and leaders tear out an enemy's fingernails in my presence, what will I do?" "Torture is senseless violence, born in fear," says Sartre. It seeks to persuade a man that he is not a human being; it results in well-nigh annihilating the human quality of those who administer it. The time has come for us to realize that exploitation, racial hatred, and the torture which they employ are all bent on destroying man himself.

> The victim and executioner merge into the same figure, a figure in our own likeness. In fact, in the final extremity, the only way to avoid one role is to accept the other (pp. 15-16).

How one may aid the victims without merely putting the present executioners in their place remains the important question. We may hope that Sartre will try to answer it.

Simone de Beauvoir has been closely associated with Sartre in political action. Like him she has never become a member of the Communist Party, although she has on many occasions supported it on certain issues. On the whole her position has been rather more consistent than Sartre's, and I do not believe that one can fairly charge her with being willing to sacrifice individuals to principles or principles to expediency. In 1945 her play *Useless Mouths (Les bouches inutiles)*[37] raised the question which she was to treat again in *All Men Are Mortal:* Are the officials of a city justified in saving the future of that city at the cost of the happiness of its present inhabitants? The city in question this time is Vaucelles, which is under siege. There is hope that ultimately the King of France will come to the city's aid, but meanwhile the food supply is giving out. The Council decides to reserve the food for its fighting members. The useless ones, the women and children and old men, will be driven outside the city walls. Steps are actually taken in preparation for this drastic measure, but at the last moment one of the members of the Council declares that he can no longer support the decision. This is partly because he, like several of the others, cannot bear the hatred and estrangement which have replaced the earlier love existing between them and "the useless mouths." And it is partly that further thought has raised the whole question of the validity of the abstract concept "utility" as a criterion. "Useful" to whom and for what? One member of the Council still argues that they must not condemn the whole city to death for the sake of sparing half of it, that at all cost Vaucelles must live. But another retorts that Vaucelles is nothing. What matters is the pact which has existed among its citizens, and this is what they are about to destroy. The inhabitants will gladly risk their lives on behalf of their wives and children; they are ready to die for the community. A death freely chosen is not an evil. But if they condemn the old, the women, and the children, they are stealing from them their privilege of choosing to die as well as depriving them of their lives. If they reject half the population, if they kill love and confidence, they will not save the city. They will no longer be a city but only a horde of creatures. The Council is persuaded. The entire population prepares to march together out of the city for whatever fate awaits them. In this play de Beauvoir decidedly prefers men and women to political systems. It is significant that a Communist critic, Pol Gaillard, analyzed the situation and came up with the conclusion that de Beauvoir had made the wrong decision and shown partiality against the characters who did not share her views.

In *The Mandarins* Henri and Robert engage in a public political dispute which is obviously inspired by the Sartre-Camus break in 1952. What brings matters to a head is the question of whether or not they ought to publish in their leftist-non-Communist newspaper certain new information about the existence of illegal prison camps in Russia. Henri feels that unless they oppose oppression wherever they find it, they are betraying their cause. Robert argues that though he deplores the fact of the camps, they cannot afford the risk of seeming to indict the Soviet regime as a whole. Robert, more strongly than Henri, believes that they will get nowhere unless they can work with the Communists, and is obviously willing to make concessions. There is bitter estrangement. Henri feels that Robert has sold out and is half ready to believe the rumor that he has secretly joined the Party. Ultimately the situation is resolved and the two men are reconciled. Robert never quite admits that he was wrong about the camps; he does, however, confess to Anne at one point that while he would like to see the Communist cause triumph, he could not live in a Communist world. And he finds later on that he, as well as Henri, gets into trouble with the French Communists as soon as he tries to make decisions independently. At the end of the novel the two of them are starting in on a new project—the launching of an independent weekly, which will try to take the lead in guiding the responsible intellectuals caught in the confused situation of post-war France.

De Beauvoir is consistent in *The Mandarins* in sticking to the idea that the intellectual must not relinquish his freedom of thought or seek to suppress the freedom of others in his efforts to find right solutions for his country and to help improve the lot of mankind in general. Nevertheless, the one idea which keeps cropping up throughout the novel is that in the mid-twentieth century, France is no longer a major power; the real issue is between the United States and Russia, and ultimately the choice which the French must make, both as individuals and as a nation, will be the decision as to which of the two countries to support. To an American it is startling, to say the least, to have de Beauvoir state casually that of course in this case one would choose Russia. Whether or not she would say it now, since Hungary, I do not know. In searching through *The Mandarins* to see what it is which she particularly resents about America, I find the answer in her firm conviction that in every crisis arising anywhere from Spain to the Far East, the United States has supported the forces of reaction. There is both exaggeration and truth in her claim. What strikes me as surprising, however, is not so much de Beauvoir's objections to our foreign policy as her refusal to judge us by anything except our mistakes. Toward the Soviet Union and toward the government in China she takes the attitude that there is much that is wrong but that we must be ready to excuse it for the sake of the good which has been accomplished and for the ideals in the name of which these governments have been established. To us she seems unwilling to extend the same charity.

Conduct in good faith, whether on an individual basis or in politics, is based on the recognition that all men are free. Each one is totally responsible and wholly without excuse. But if we are to accept this premise and these conclusions, we must look more deeply into the nature of the human person. On the whole, the psychology of the last hundred years has seemed to indicate that men's actions are determined. If humanistic existentialism is to justify itself, it must provide a psychological interpretation of man which shows that he is capable of free choices. It is now time for us to examine the psychology of freedom.

# A Psychology of Freedom

PART THREE

A Psychology of Freedom

# I. EXISTENTIAL PSYCHOANALYSIS

In any study of the human being as such, it is difficult to say where philosophy ends and psychology begins. This is particularly true for existentialism. For while it asks once again the old metaphysical question (What *about* man and his place in the universe?), it is even more interested in the inner state of the individual who feels he must ask the question and in his emotional reactions to the answer he discovers or invents. In the work of Sartre, too, the psychological is never quite forgotten even where the ontology is most abstract. Toward the end of *Being and Nothingness* we are informed that there will be, as end-products of that work, a new ethics and a specific psychology. The ethics has not yet been written. Suggestions for an applied psychology are presented in the chapter, "Existential Psychoanalysis."

Sartre's psychoanalytical theory stands midway between his philosophy and his literature. If in a sense it is a consequence of the philosophy, it is at the same time an explicative cause of the literature. Much as Sartre may object to the "theatre of characters," the fact remains that the protagonists in his fiction are people and not personifications. They may experience anguish and nausea; they may illustrate patterns of bad faith or point the way to a life in freedom. But we do not find a volatile character representing the For-itself who has ambivalent feelings toward a phlegmatic figure resembling the In-itself, the two of them maintaining a relation based on deception in the land of Bad Faith, but separating forever when For-itself learns the truth about things through the aid of a hypnotist named Freedom. We are worlds removed from John Bunyan and not even on the same continent with Dante. But if these fictional beings are going to appear to us as real persons making existentialist choices, then the link between abstract concepts and concrete manifestations must be a psychology.

In "Existential Psychoanalysis," Sartre explains how we may hope to understand the life history and personality structure of the individual person. Whether or not other psychologists accept the theory as valid for actual therapy, the explanation at least provides us with the clue to understanding the behavior of Sartre's own creations. To examine existential psychoanalysis after reading Sartre's literature is like looking behind the scenes of a marionette theatre, not that the characters have behaved like puppets, but that we now see the means by which their actions were made possible. When contemporary writers say that they are not interested in psychology, they mean that the portrayal of an individual personality with all its complexities and intricate development is not their chief concern. But any literature which sets out to explore human possibilities (and what literature does not?) presupposes a psychology of some sort. There is naturally no reason why all humanistic existentialists should feel bound by the principles of Sartrean psychoanalysis. Yet while the theory holds good specifically only for Sartre and for de Beauvoir (who would disagree merely in details), it serves as justification in a general way for any literature of situations which gives first place to the freedom of the individual person.

It is important for us to understand just what Sartre intended existential psychoanalysis to be. It makes no claim to be a therapy. It is not meant to pass for a fully developed psychoanalytic method to be substituted for the analysis now practiced. "Existential psychoanalysis has not yet found its Freud," Sartre has said, and this is not mere modesty. The Freud of existential psychoanalysis would be an analyst who would clothe the present skeletal structure with empirical evidence. What Sartre has given us is the outline of the theory for a method. Anticipations of the method, he says, can be found in certain particularly successful biographies, and he has attempted to provide two of these in his studies of Charles Baudelaire and Jean Genet.

The term "psychoanalysis" is not ill-chosen. Although Sartre has attacked some of the most fundamental of Freud's positions, nevertheless the new theory is in the psychoanalytical tradition. Many Freudian insights are retained intact; still more are kept *en bloc* but placed in a new setting. An existential psychoanalysis without Freud as its predecessor would be inconceivable, and Sartre implicitly acknowledges the fact when he presents his own theory largely in terms of those points wherein it agrees and those wherein it disagrees with the work of Freud and his successors. Following his procedure, we may consider first the similarities.[1]

He points out first that

> Both kinds of psychoanalysis consider all objectively discernible manifestations of "psychic life" as symbols maintaining symbolic relations to the fundamental, total structures which constitute the individual person (p. 569).

Sartre and Freud are together in their opposition to the Behaviorists in so far as the latter try to explain human conduct as mere response to stimuli. No psychoanalysis will attempt to explain any human reaction solely by the immediate stimulus. Even a seemingly inexplicable outburst of hostility, for example, or the sudden inability to meet a comparatively easy problem is meaningful if we can relate it to the person's basic outlook on life. For Freud the explanation may be present in an unresolved Oedipus complex or something of the sort. Sartre will seek it in a man's fundamental choice of his way of being. For both writers the subject to be analyzed must be viewed as a totality, not a bundle of unrelated drives or tendencies or habitual reflexes.

Second, neither psychoanalysis accepts what Sartre refers to as "primary givens," the "great explanatory idols of our time—heredity, education, environment, physiological constitution." * The Freudian libido is nothing before or in addition to its fixations; it is but "the permanent possibility of fixing anything whatsoever upon anything whatsoever." For existentialism, of course, man is nothing before the original upsurge of his free consciousness. Any type of psychoanalysis holds that it is an error to think of man as being like a board of switches which may be manipulated independently of each other and by external agents. But it would be just as incorrect to allow that a person may be born with a ready-made disposition, as a substance with patterns for future development already imprinted. The most flagrant example of this error is *The Bad Seed,* the novel by William March, in which the granddaughter of a murderess develops "inevitable" homicidal tendencies and murders

---

* In comparing existential and "empirical" psychoanalysis, Sartre makes no attempt to distinguish between ideas which were peculiarly Freud's and those which belong to later orthodox Freudians. Thus Sartre's second point of agreement, for example, would probably be acceptable to most present-day Freudians; Freud himself gave rather more weight to hereditary and constitutional factors than Sartre indicates.

three people while she is still a child—all this in spite of having a family and an environment in no way conducive to such a character and even without anyone's being aware of the girl's ancestry.

Third, both kinds of psychoanalysis "consider the human being as a perpetual, searching historization." Each man has made of and for himself a life history composed of the relations which he has sustained with the physical and social environment. The analyst's subject is not an isolated interior personality but a person living in the world, and his total situation must be taken into account.

> Psychological investigations aim at reconstituting the life of the subject from birth to the moment of the cure; they utilize all the objective documentation which they can find; letters, witnesses, intimate diaries, "social" information of every kind (p. 569).

A further point brings the relation to Freud still closer. "What they aim at restoring is less a pure psychic event than a twofold structure: the crucial event of infancy and the psychic crystallization around this event." Sartre does not really explain this point in his theoretical presentation. It is surprising that he does not do so, for the statement is not clear except in the light of other Sartrean contexts, not included in *Being and Nothingness*. The reference to Freudian doctrine is obvious enough. Two principles are involved. There is first Freud's claim that the libido may remain "fixed" at any of the three stages which precede full "genital" sexuality. If the child remains at the oral, anal, or phallic level, he does so as the result of intense emotional involvement with one or both parents, and his later relations with people are going to be determined by the original Oedipal conflict. Bound up with this view is the concept of "repetition compulsion," by which Freud means that a person is compelled by his instinctual tendencies to continue in the patterns which he has early established and to repeat throughout his life the experiences (whether pleasurable or painful) of his early childhood. Both the idea of libidinal fixation and the repetition compulsion involve a strict determinism. They are so integral a part of Freudian psychology that it is difficult to see how one could accept them without going along with the rest of Freud's theory. But it is still more difficult to see how Sartre could fit them in with his view of man as pure undetermined consciousness. The answer is that Sartre does not agree with Freud on either point. For Sartre the decisive event of infancy or childhood is only incidentally if at all connected with sexual development and the Oedipal situation. It may be any moment whatsoever which brings to the child an awareness of himself as an individual in a particular relation to the world around him. In Sartre's study of Baudelaire, the crucial event is the remarriage of the poet's mother when he was seven years old. Sartre treats the incestuous attachment as significant—without it the remarriage would not have been critical—but he regards the resultant Oedipus complex as only one manifestation among many of a still more basic orientation. In the case of Jean Genet, the crisis in childhood has nothing to do with emotional involvement with any individual, but centers around the moment at which Genet is caught stealing and is made to feel that in his very nature he is inescapably a thief, doomed to permanent exile from the society of "the good." Moreover, in Freud's view, once the direction of the libidinal drives is firmly established in the id, it is practically impossible for a person ever to escape from the repetition compulsion without the aid of an analyst. For Sartre, the individual consciousness is never completely the prisoner of his habits or illusions and may by its own impulse break through the barriers which it has itself established.

Sartre's final point of agreement with empirical psychoanalysis is the refusal "to admit that the subject of analysis is in a privileged position to proceed in these inquiries concerning himself." We do not take at face value the patient's own account of himself, his symptoms, or his history. The Freudian does not trust the patient, for he believes that no matter how sincerely the subject may want to help in furthering the analysis, he is hindered by determinant unconscious motivations. He lies continually without even being aware of it. For Sartre, the nearest equivalent to the unconscious is bad faith. But obviously, in order for bad faith or illusion to be possible, and if analysis is to be helpful, there must be some distinction in the subject's levels of awareness. Sartre differentiates between being conscious and knowing. I cannot, according to him, have an experience without being aware of what I am experiencing. In a general way I am conscious even of my symbolic actions and the resulting satisfaction or pain resulting. If I tell myself that I am acting for one reason when in reality my motive is quite different, I am not really unaware of my "rationalization." But I refuse to focus on the motive which embarrasses me or which does not fit into the picture of myself which I am trying to create. Moreover, the fact that I am conscious of all that I do does not mean that I fully comprehend the relation between my present act and all those which have gone before—even though they are not wholly forgotten. In short, my consciousness is largely on the nonreflective level. Knowledge demands reflection. Self-consciousness I have always; self-knowledge demands both deliberate effort and intellectual acumen. To the degree that I have in my earlier life chosen to live nonreflectively, to let myself be fascinated and absorbed by the objects of my own consciousness, I will find it difficult to establish the necessary connections and the significance of those choices which I have made in the past and by which I am now determining my future. The task of the existentialist psychoanalyst is less that of the guide who points the way to hidden treasure and more that of the teacher who tries to make the student see the connection between two ideas which are already before him. Both psychoanalyses will treat the patient's introspective data as documentary evidence but also as facts which still need interpretation.

This does not mean, of course, that self-analysis is impossible. Karen Horney in her book *Self-Analysis* shows how within a modified Freudian approach the neurotic who is not too deeply disturbed may effect a practical psychoanalysis of himself. The existentialist with his radical view of freedom has an even easier basis for self-readjustment. But in each case, as Sartre points out, the point of view taken is that of the Other. In so far as I achieve self-knowledge, I am making myself an object of reflection, and examining my own history as if it were that of someone else. Neither the analyst nor I myself can capture a pre-reflective subject. What is known is always an object-self, though my subjectivity and my future choices will undoubtedly be affected by this Self upon which I have directed my attention.

To explain the similarities between traditional and existential psychoanalysis has been in part to point to the differences between them. Looking now at the disagreements explicitly rather than by implication, we find that Sartre has initiated five basic departures.

First of all, Sartre rejects the libido theory. He feels that it is a mistaken oversimplification to try to explain all psychic manifestations in terms of instinctual drives, which would be to reduce man to his biology. Furthermore, a libido or a will to power is not primary.* It "constitutes a psycho-biological residue which is not clear in itself and which does not appear to us as *being beforehand* the irreducible limit of the investigation." Sartre objects that both the usual analysis and most so-called "psychological biographies" have failed to carry their search far enough.

---

* The "will to power," of course, is a reference to Adler, not Freud.

Even things so fundamental as modes of sexuality, libidinal fixations, or a will to power need an explanation which is meaningful in relation to the particular individual considered. To accept any of them as primary is to forget the person himself. What Sartre proposes as the true, self-evident irreducible is the original free impulse by which a person has chosen in one way rather than another to relate himself to Being. This choice *is* the person inasmuch as it provides the basic unity on the ground of which he forms all subsequent desires. Sartre refers to this primary thrust as "the unification of an *original project,* a unification which should reveal itself to us as a *nonsubstantial absolute.*" [2] In a sense this "nonsubstantial absolute" is identical with freedom itself. But it is a particular freedom which is in process of making itself. It is a person's decision as to how he is going to write his history in the world. At first thought, it might seem that the choice of Being would be an even more abstract and general irreducible than the libido. Sartre, however, argues that the choice as actually made is both particular and concrete; that is, when we are considering a real subject, we can (if the analysis is successful) discover the initial choice as it was revealed by concrete behavior apropos of a specific event, and we will read the results of the choice in the subject's later projects in the everyday world. The choice is abstract only in the way that we might say (to furnish Sartre with an example) a man's intention to go to New York is abstract. If we observed him packing, buying a ticket, riding on the train, and getting off at Grand Central Station, we could state that these activities were meaningful only in the light of the unifying intent of going to New York. But there is nothing abstract about the intention itself, which in fact could not exist without a pre-outlining of the concrete conduct involved or without a total situation comprising the existence of New York, the location of the man's present residence, his relation to people and projects there, etc. Pursuing this example further, it is easy to imagine an investigation of this man which would reveal that he was in general fond of traveling, that he had a varied career behind him with radical changes in occupation, that he had been engaged in both unhappy and successful love affairs with unlikely women, that he had three times changed his political party, and that his earliest memory was of an episode in which he simultaneously realized his existence as a separate person and recognized with a sense of power that the wood about his house was not an enclosure to fence him in but a call to adventure, the stuff of his freely chosen projects.

Sartre's second disagreement with Freud is equally radical. Existential psychoanalysis rejects all determinism—biological, psychological, environmental. Freudian theory is deterministic in two ways: First, the conscious self or ego constantly functions with only partial awareness of what it is doing; to a greater or less degree it is dependent on the pre-conceptual libidinal drives or instincts. To this extent the person is driven by forces whose nature he cannot possibly know. In the second place, Freud's picture of human development (both collective and individual) may be described as mechanistic-evolutionistic.[3] For the individual this means that although his life is an historical process, it is an unfolding rather than free growth; the changes are more in content than in psychic structure. The basic patterns have been established within the first years of childhood, and the individual tends to live by repeating the earlier experiences in accordance with the concept of repetition compulsion. From this point of view, one might take "depth psychology" as a term referring to an actual limitation. It is as though one built one's life only vertically, limiting each new experience to what could be supported on the original structure. Rejecting this psycho-biological determinism entirely, Sartre pictures a life as expanding horizontally as well as vertically. One may, by investigation, discover the original movement, but there is nothing which prevents a person from changing his direction. There still remains the question of environmental or social determinism. For Freud, except for the immediate family, which plays such a large part in determining the nature of the Oedipus complex, sibling rivalry, and the like, society as a conditioning factor is of subordinate importance. It is significant largely as its regulations encourage or put obstacles in the path of the libidinal drives. The presence or lack of such limitations may, of course, have an effect on mental health; they cannot be discounted entirely. Yet the pressure they exert is largely external; they do not (save, once again, indirectly through the family) mold infantile sexuality or determine the fixation of the libidinal drives. In any case the question for Freud is hardly an important one, for in a generally deterministic system, environmental conditioning may be easily assumed to be present in varying measure according to whether the biological and psychological factors are more or less decisive. But for Sartre, who insists vehemently that it would be meaningless even to ask what a particular person would have been like if he had lived at another time or in another place, there arises a real problem. He himself has said that he finds no difficulty in holding that every man is wholly conditioned by his situation and yet remains "an irreducible center of indetermination." [4] In our examination of existentialist literature, especially in de Beauvoir's *The Blood of Others,* we have seen this paradox worked out in such a way as to show that each of us is totally responsible for helping to create the world within which others must make their choices, but that each is wholly without excuse as regards the actions which he himself has chosen. Throughout this discussion the concept of man's freedom has been present as an underlying assumption. We have seen this freedom made manifest in a multitude of concrete choices, and we have examined the various ways in which men may try to escape or deny their freedom. But we have not yet met the question head-on as a metaphysical problem. It is time for us to do so now. Is Sartre consistent? Is it possible for man to be free and socially conditioned at the same time? Just what is this freedom with which the existentialists are forever confronting us?

Sartre claims that the main cause of the futility of the usual arguments between advocates of free will and proponents of determinism is the fact that neither side has an adequate concept of the nature of an "act." They dispute as to whether or not a man's act must of necessity have a cause. But this, says Sartre, is nonsense. By definition an act must have a goal or purpose, and this means that there is a reason for it. An act not intended to accomplish something would not be an act at all; it would be mere random movement or at most purely involuntary motion like our usual breathing or the beating of our hearts. But while the determinists are right in maintaining that there can be no act without a cause, they are wrong in holding that the cause is something external to freedom itself. A cause or motive or reason is not something which appears ready-formed and from some external source. Out of the host of tasks to be done which are constantly offered to me by the things of the world, I freely choose and constitute a certain one as the motive for an action. Although the probability that I will act consistently with my behavior on comparable occasions is exceedingly high, my doing so depends upon my being content with my life as it is. Even such an elementary act as watching out for cars when I cross the street depends on my ever-renewed or suddenly abandoned view of life as worth the effort of living. We will not then waste time wondering whether or not a particular act has a cause. It is caused, but it is I who have determined the motive behind it. Without the decision of a consciousness there would be neither act nor cause and effect, but only a simple succession. Of course the fundamental question has not yet been answered. Am I *really* free in constituting my motive for an act? Am I *really* free even in choosing whether or not I want to go on living? Or am I the victim of my physiology, my psychological past, and the environment which fosters or thwarts my projects? And once again, what is freedom?

To begin with, Sartre emphatically declares that freedom is not a synonym for power. To be free does not mean that one *can* do whatever one wants to do. Things in the world and the actions of other people offer resistance. But obstacles do not prevent freedom; they are what makes freedom possible. If wish were synonymous with fulfillment, then there would be no distinction between dream and reality. Moreover, a freedom without material or logical limitations would be infinite; and since man himself is finite, it would no longer be a *human* freedom. If freedom is to be meaningful at all, it must be a freedom to choose, and choice demands alternative possibilities which limit each other. The resistance of the world outside us is the material out of which freedom forms its projects. Sartre goes into infinite detail to show that whatever may be my facticity (my factual limits of time, space, physical strength, external events about me), it is I who determine its significance, its meaning for me, and its place in my life. If I have been born in an isolated village, I may make of this fact a motive for conforming to the mores of village life so as to win the approval of the rest of the villagers, I may make it an excuse for lethargy (What chance is there in a place like this?), or I may make of it an incentive to prove myself "better than my surroundings" and get to New York or Paris. Similarly with the possibilities offered me by time: I may fit myself comfortably into what the present society offers me, I may rebel against it in nostalgic longing for the past, or I may seek to change it in the interests of a better future. Even my physical characteristics are neutral qualities until I constitute them as potentialities of one sort rather than another. Frail health may inspire me to struggle pugnaciously to prove that I can be an athlete despite all (whether this goal is *actually* attained or not has nothing to do with my freedom of choice); it can invite me to reflection and artistic creativity; it can provide me with an excuse predisposing me to expect and even ask for failure. The same type of reasoning applies with regard to nationality, sex, the social position of one's family and so forth.

To many people this sort of argument appears true enough but evasive. The real question appears to be whether having once responded to my environment in a particular fashion and having formed a character or personality, I am any longer free to change my point of view. Will I not of necessity be impelled to want certain things and not be free to want other things? But what impels me? The past? But I am constantly remaking my past. I cannot undo what I have done, but I can declare that my act was done rightly or wrongly, that I will make of it either an aberrant impulse or a pattern which I shall continue to follow in the future. The past is meaningful only in terms of the significance I give it in the present. Then am I impelled to want certain things simply because when I want them I am one person rather than another? This is probably true, but Sartre might easily ask, "Is there any reason to require that freedom should include the possibility of wanting to choose what one does not want to choose?" Such a demand—that a person should be capable of choosing what nothing in his outlook or situation would make desirable—conceals within it a fallacy. It assumes that one *is* already a certain being and then *possesses* as a thing the freedom to choose to be something else. But freedom is not something one has; it is what one is. "Freedom is existence," says Sartre, "and in it existence precedes essence." [5] If at any time we consider a human being—even a child—he is a being *in situation*. Although a consciousness is nothing other than a power of focusing and reflecting upon objects, nevertheless we may legitimately speak of it as *a* consciousness. Unless it is conscious *of* something, it is nothing at all. And the moment that consciousness is aware of anything, it constitutes a situation. For it is always a consciousness of particular objects, and its awareness of these is accompanied by a nonreflective background of awareness of a particular body through which this consciousness can establish relations with a world which it can *affect*. A freedom not in situation would, once again, be a nonhuman freedom—if indeed it would be freedom at all. Yet while a consciousness can never make a choice which is not related to its present situation, perceived across a particular body and interpreted in the light of past experience, Sartre insists that consciousness is never identified with its objects. They are still objects, and it may choose at any time a new way of relating itself to them and them to each other as it projects itself into the future.

For evidence of this freedom, Sartre appeals to each man's experience. I encounter my freedom in anguish, he says, an anguish which grips me whenever I suddenly realize that in my projects in the world the one unsure element, the one thing I cannot grasp nor predict, is my Self. There is anguish in the present when I sense a vertiginous appeal in the chasm far below and realize that nothing prevents me from jumping over the precipice even though "I" do not want to die. There is anguish before the past when I realize with agony at my heart that the good resolutions I made yesterday have no authority to hold me back unless I freely choose today to remake them. And there is anguish before the future as I make plans which will involve a Me whom I cannot forsee—as the soldier fears not so much the enemy in the coming battle but that Self who may suddenly turn coward under fire.

Thus though Sartre offers also as illustrations the phenomenon of religious conversion and the moments of sudden insight and shifts in orientation which play such an important part in literature, we find that in the final analysis freedom is not a proposition to be proved but a fact to be experienced. It is not a human essence, for it is the lack of essence, a pure existence which *is* and which makes its objective history by its choices in the world. As for the human condition (the facts which all men share in common, having a body, facing inevitable death, etc.), these are the material without which a *human* freedom would not be possible. In one sense Sartre has simply chosen one horn of the dilemma. Before the past we generally feel that our acts *have been* determined. But in the present the *feeling* of freedom is our greatest certainty. Sartre, of course, adds that the determinism which we see in the past is the result of our present reinterpretation and organization. When the past was the present, there existed only many possibilities, pointing in various directions, among which our consciousness had to choose those which later we would stamp as a pattern. It is particularly difficult to prove the fact of freedom because proof (by definition) implies that there is something fixed. It is remarkably comparable to the difficulty of pinning down at once the position and velocity of an electron. On the other hand, determinism, without presenting the same logical difficulty, is equally impossible to prove. It seems easy for the analyst to point out to the patient that he has been the victim of unconscious forces. But what determines whether the knowledge presented to the patient will cause him to accept the facts and to modify his reactions or, on the other hand, to resist the information and continue in the same path? Somewhere the conscious ego has to choose to assert itself and change direction. Sometimes, too, there are "spontaneous cures," where a person without the aid of outside help can break the bonds of childhood patterns. Perhaps he has met with new types of experience which threw a different light upon his past conduct. But how was he able to see it? There seems to be hidden even within Freudian theory an unpredictable power of decision which is indistinguishable from that freedom which the existentialists identify with consciousness itself.

Sartre's third disagreement with Freud is really inseparable from his rejection of the libido and of determinism. This is his refusal to admit the existence of an unconscious and the corollary view of the psyche as made up of ego, id, and superego. This position is, of course, demanded by Sartre's philosophy. If consciousness is nothing but the power of effecting a nihilation, a withdrawal from the rest of Being, naturally it cannot contain any hidden contents. Consciousness is wholly translucent. The belief in freedom also requires the rejection of the unconscious, for man is not free if he is determined by what, on principle, he cannot know. Yet while Sartre's convictions on freedom and the nature of consciousness are firm enough to lead him to reject the unconscious on this basis alone, he has not been content to do so. His specific objections are presented in connection with his discussion of bad faith. The Freudians, he claims, have failed to understand the mechanism of any sort of self-deception, and for this reason they have introduced the unconscious. If there is a separation between id and ego, then we can have a lie without a liar. For I (the conscious person who speaks to you) stand in the same relation to my id as I would to an Other. I say what appears to me to be true; if it is false, it is because I have been misinformed or at least have failed to understand the communication which came to me from the id. For "I" am my ego, but "I" am not my id. Only a third person as interpreter can ferret out a truth which will be the same for id and ego alike. Sartre claims that aside from any question as to whether such an explanation fits the facts, it simply raises the same problem again on another level. In a deliberately ridiculous painting of the landscape of the psyche according to Freud, Sartre pictures the censor as a national frontier with customs, passport office, currency control, etc. to check on all who wish to pass from the territory of the id into the conscious ego. But if the censor represses all impulses which would be dangerous to the equilibrium of the conscious life, and if it allows passage to those which are harmless or well disguised, then, Sartre argues, the censor is in bad faith; that is, the censor is conscious of the true meaning of the id's attempts at communication but makes itself be unconscious of them (from the point of view of the ego). Thus the problem of self-deception or of a lie to oneself is as much alive as ever. This situation exists especially, Sartre claims, when the analyst encounters "resistance" in the patient. At a certain stage in the analysis, when the analyst and patient are close to the crux of the neurosis, the patient frequently begins to make matters difficult—breaking appointments, falsifying his dreams, generally not cooperating. Where does the resistance come from? It cannot be the work of the ego, for the patient consciously wants to be cured and has come for this express purpose. It cannot come from the id, for this is always trying to make its

true wishes known. Therefore it must be the censor which for some reason prevents the ego from being conscious of the reason for the actions
to which it is impelled by the id. The censor *must* be conscious in order
to know what to repress.

One argument proposed in opposition to Sartre's position is that the
drives in the id are pre-conceptual and that thus it is, on principle, impossible for either censor or ego to be conscious of them. This reasoning,
which seems to imply that consciousness is synonymous with reasoning
and conceptualization, does not seem to me an effective reply. Moreover,
the *raison d'être* for psychoanalytical therapy is the firm conviction
that with the proper encouragement the patient may be able to relive
his earlier experiences and, by making them conscious, escape the consequences of earlier libidinal fixations. If this is to happen, there must
occur at some point a breaking through the barrier between id and ego.
Whether or not we call this the overcoming of the censor's resistance,
there has certainly resulted a conceptualization of pre-conceptual material.

In addition to the fact that Sartre feels that Freud does not solve the
problem of self-deception, he argues that the hypothesis of the unconscious produces a new difficulty. The Freudian theory demands that
there be a psychic unity of such a kind that an act performed on the
conscious level may symbolically satisfy unconscious demands. Now in
order to delude the censor into letting the drives pass, the impulses of the
id must be conscious of themselves as likely to be repressed, hence
needing to be disguised. On the other hand, if the symbolic satisfaction
or thwarting of these drives is to produce such intense emotion in the
ego, it seems that consciousness must have at least some obscure comprehension of the meaning of its conduct. If ego and id are separated
from each other, then the relation between the symbolic act and its
motive is like that of sympathetic magic. The concept of the unconscious,
"due to the fact that it breaks the psychic unity, cannot account for the
facts which at first sight it appeared to explain." [6]

Last of all, Sartre objects to Freud's assumption that certain symbols
have a fixed meaning for all people; for example, that in dreams or in
symbolic acts a pincushion always stands for the breast and the faeces
are the equivalent for gold. In all fairness it must be said that Freud
himself was willing to modify this view in certain cases and that most
of his followers have used the principle so flexibly as to have denied it
practically. It is easy to see that Sartre could not possibly hold to it.
If each person is unique and free, then the symbolic significations of

objects for him will be determined by their place in the particular ensemble of meanings which he has established in his individual life history. They will, in other words, be manifestations of that basic choice which the analyst is seeking. Existential psychoanalysis still more than Freudian must adapt itself to the needs of each patient; moreover, since the free choice of consciousness may be revoked, the method may have to be radically altered even in the course of one analysis.

Such is existential psychoanalysis as Sartre sees it in relation to Freudian or empirical psychoanalysis. For the libido Sartre has substituted an original choice of Being, a particular relation between consciousness and the rest of the world; in place of determinism he postulates the free upsurge of consciousness in a situation established by that consciousness in the world; the separation between consciousness and an unconscious is gone, but a distinction between mere awareness and knowledge allows for illusion and self-deception; instead of assuming a universal symbolism to which theoretical psychoanalysis has provided the key, the existentialist analyst must seek the clue to symbolic conduct in the basic choice which is the goal of his investigation. This last position of Sartre's might seem to introduce a vicious circle: if the particular acts are meaningful only in the light of the original choice, and if the original choice is to be sought by analysis of the empirical acts, then where is one to start? Actually, however, Sartre's position is not different here from that of any analyst who has rejected Freud's universal symbolism; it simply means that the analyst must confront the concrete behavior and attempt to explain it in the light of a unifying and reasonable hypothesis until the reactions of the patient himself show that the scientific guess has been the correct one.

The rest of Sartre's presentation of existential psychoanalysis is largely concerned with pointing out its connection with Sartre's philosophy as already presented or, more specifically, establishing those general principles upon which he feels any psychology must be based. The fundamental precepts of his theory he sets forth clearly and succinctly.

> The *principle* of this psychoanalysis is that man is a totality and not a collection. Consequently he expresses himself as a whole in even his most insignificant and his most superficial behavior. In other words there is not a taste, a mannerism, or an human act which is not *revealing*.

The *goal* of psychoanalysis is to *decipher* the empirical behavior patterns of man; that is, to bring out in the open the
revelations which each one of them contains and to fix them
conceptually.

Its *point of departure* is *experience;* its pillar of support is the
fundamental, pre-ontological comprehension which man has
of the human person. . . .

Its *method* is comparative. Since each example of human conduct symbolizes in its own manner the fundamental choice
which must be brought to light, and since at the same time
each one disguises this choice under its occasional character
and its historical opportunity, only the comparison of these
acts of conduct can effect the emergence of the unique revelation which they all express in a different way (pp. 568-569).

Sartre adds that the criterion of success for the psycho-analysis
will be the number of facts which its hypothesis permits it to
explain and to unify as well as the self-evident intuition of the
irreducibility of the end attained. To this criterion will be
added in all cases where it is possible, the decisive testimony
of the subject (p. 574).

To most people, Sartre's hope that psychoanalysis may happily conclude with a choice that is self-evidently irreducible will probably appear
as naively optimistic as Descartes' fond expectation of founding a philosophy upon "that which is so self-evidently true that nobody could possibly doubt it." To Freud, after all, the libido and its complex were
irreducible. Sartre, however, argues that the choice of Being is ultimate
in that it is synonymous with the For-itself's projection toward the In-
itself, which, as the very existence of the For-itself, is that which makes
it *this* For-itself and not any other or an undifferentiated pan-psyche.
After this it comes as something of a surprise when Sartre, after so
strongly emphasizing the uniqueness of every human project and the
contingency of the original choice, next proceeds to show that ontology
must furnish information concerning behavior patterns and desires, and
that this information will provide the basic principles of existential psychoanalysis. He hastens to explain that this does not mean that men
share in common an over-all pattern of abstract desires. But

concrete desires have structures which emerge during the study of ontology because each desire—the desire of eating or of sleeping as well as the desire of creating a work of art—expresses all human reality (p. 575).

Ontology as the study of both human and nonhuman Being can aid psychology in two ways: first, by illuminating the nature of desire as such, pointing out what it is that all empirical desires have in common; second, by revealing to us the potential meanings of the objects of desires—i.e., of the things in the world.

Like Plato in the *Symposium,* Sartre points out that desire is always a lack. One desires only what one does not already have. Thus consciousness as a lack of Being is the same as desire, and what it desires is Being-in-itself. Another way of putting it is to say that man, confronting the world, desires in one way or another to appropriate the world or to relate himself to the objects in the world. Man may desire to *do* or *make (faire)* something in the world, to *have* something in the world or to *be* something in the world. But *doing* or *making,* Sartre claims, is *having.* If I create a book or painting or a symphony, this is because I want it to exist through me, to be mine even as it is an expression of myself to others. All activity can finally be reduced to projects of appropriation—eating, sexuality, even the pursuit of knowledge. For all involve bringing into play a particular relation which objects or other people sustain through, and only through, myself. Sartre goes into great detail to illustrate this point. His most interesting discussion has to do with games and sport. To play a game is to realize the human condition symbolically, as we saw in connection with Sartre's discussion of the Serious World. A person who fully accepts the existential tension recognizes that he binds himself by rules which he himself has consented to setting up, that the only meaning in life is the act of living it. Yet aside from this metaphysical implication, Sartre claims that there is in specific games always a project of appropriation—beyond such obvious things as the desire to prove my superiority over others, improve my self-esteem, etc. In sport I possess the in-itself by transforming it from mere worldly environment into the supporting element of my action. In this sense sport is creative like art. In skiing, for example, I force the snow to produce its potentialities of cohesiveness and support, qualities which only my action calls forth. Activity involving sliding leads Sartre to the unusual conclusion that water skiing is the ideal limit of aquatic sports! Here is the passage:

Sliding realizes a strictly individual relation with matter, a historical relation; the matter reassembles itself and solidifies in order to hold me up, and it falls back exhausted and scattered behind me. Thus by my passage I have realized that which is unique *for me*. The ideal for sliding is a sliding which does not leave any trace. It is sliding on water with a rowboat or motor boat or especially with water skis, which, though recently invented, represent from this point of view the ideal limit of aquatic sports. Sliding on snow is already less perfect; there is a trace behind me by which I am compromised, however light it may be. Sliding on ice, which scratches the ice and finds a matter already organized, is very inferior, and if people continue to do it despite all this, it is for other reasons (p. 584).

Perhaps one of these "other reasons" is a person's desire to brand the in-itself with his own mark so that it may never be quite the same for those who follow after. Or possibly for nonexistentialists it is merely the desire for exercise at more than one season of the year.

But all these projects of appropriation, these desires of possessing objects in the world—what are they? They are, claims Sartre, projects of being. Things which I possess either actually or symbolically are extensions of myself. As witness of this fact, Sartre points to the frequent practice of burying a dead man's possessions along with him, and to the popular belief in haunted castles and in ghosts, which as degraded lares are "layers of possession which have been deposited one by one on the walls and furnishings of the house." What I have is a part of me, and yet it is not quite the same as myself. It is mine but not me. From this point of view Sartre says that while the object continues to be an independent being-in-itself, nevertheless, since it is supported in its being by the relation which I establish with it, and since it is thus a part of myself, the result is that in the object I am the foundation of my own objective being. I am—symbolically—the in-itself-for-itself which, as we have seen, is the unattainable ideal back of all of my projects. Thus for Sartre every desire and its accompanying project is one more manifestation of the way in which a man has chosen to *be* in the world, expressed by his way of appropriating the world. If we want to know what a person is, we must study the nature of what concrete activities he has chosen. This involves not only our trying to find out what the person thinks is the aim of his behavior, but what possibilities are offered by the behavior itself.

In his effort to show that the ultimate goal of each existential psychoanalysis is a choice that is not abstract but rich and particular, Sartre produces a rather surprising theory with regard to the possibility of establishing intrapersonal human meanings for the objects in the world. His procedure here is not entirely original. Following in the tradition of Husserl and the phenomenologists, Sartre thinks of things as revealing themselves in successive appearances, or *Abschattungen* (literally, "shadings"). When we perceive an object, we do not grasp it all at once but bit by bit according to the way we direct our attention or "intention" toward it. On our side we may say that we experience successive perceptions of a thing and then by combining them construct the total object as it is for us. But it is equally correct to think of the thing as revealing itself in successive profiles or glimpses. Even with Husserl it was possible to speak of attaining to the "essence" of the object as perceived. But Sartre goes farther, influenced chiefly by Gaston Bachelard, who developed the theory that it is possible to effect a kind of psychoanalysis of things. For Bachelard this undertaking consisted largely of discovering the qualities which objects allowed us to project into them. Sartre makes the thing itself the object of investigation and believes that we can discover what aspects of Being it is capable of revealing in its *Abschattungen*. In short, we must seek in things "the *ontological meaning* of qualities." He does not say by this that human meanings are actually *in* material things or their qualities, but they are there as potentialities to be revealed in the same way that in wood a person can realize the potentiality of the table, whereas he cannot do so with the scent of a rose or with steam. If we can discover these metaphysical purports in things, we have a precious aid for psychoanalysis. For things are the objects of desire; if we know what these objects mean, we are farther along in understanding the meaning of the desire and the basic project of the person. Thus, to take foods for an example, if we know what is the meaning of oysters, sauerkraut, and liver, we will find it significant that a man dotes on or is nauseated by oysters, sauerkraut, and liver. His hobbies, his favorite color, the cloth he prefers for his suits, all will be so many clues to lead us to the inner "person."

This theory seems to me to be of very limited use. It is probably meaningful if a person prefers violent or subdued color tones, conventional or unusual furnishings; it is perhaps significant if someone is absolutely mad about food usually considered taboo or is nauseated at the mere thought of eating any internal organ. A person's taste or distaste for onions and garlic may tell us something about his social attitudes. But while his fondness for mashed potatoes, for stamp collections, for straw hats, and for loud perfume are all very likely explicable and even revealing as a part of his individual history, it is hard for me to understand that there is a possibility of finding in these things an objective significance not limited to the particular person considered. How could any analyst (or group of analysts) ever be sure that what he discovered was really the *objective* meaning of a thing and not his own private symbolism? Worst of all, if we allow that Sartre is right, are we not back in the center of a more radical universal symbolism than Sartre objected to in the work of Freud?

As illustration of his method Sartre presents his famous analysis of the quality "slimy" *(le visqueux),* a strangely poetic description which effects in the reader the same fascinated ambivalence as the slimy itself. He deliberately chooses a quality which in everyday experience has application to the human sphere as well as to the material. We speak of "a slimy handshake"; we know people who are slimy. Sartre's point is that we have something more here than a metaphor resulting from the comparison of two separate experiences.

> It is impossible to derive the value of the psychic symbolism
> of "slimy" from the brute quality of the *this* and equally im-
> possible to project the meaning of the *this* in terms of a *knowl-*
> *edge* of psychic attitudes (p. 605).

Sartre's point is that the objective structure of the slimy is such that it offers a particular symbolic potentiality which each individual may realize in his first intuition of the slimy. In his description, Sartre gradually moves from the recordng of physical qualities to observation of just how one experiences these qualities. "The slimy" is a category which includes things like honey or jam, which we would ordinarily call "sticky," but not "the gluey" and not a thick nonsticky material such as a purée. As such, it is a "substance between two states"—not quite a liquid, but never quite achieving the solid state which it constantly promises. In slime there is an hysteresis, a retardation of the expected result, or an effect after the event; it is like "the haunting memory of a metamorphosis." It possesses, too, a tactile fascination. It does not run quickly from my fingers or stick to them like a paste; it rolls off slowly in long strands as though my fingers were extending themselves to be one with the substance I had tried to possess. Slime is not wholly elusive like water, and yet one cannot really grasp it.

> The slimy is *docile*. Only at the very moment when I believe that I possess it, behold, by a curious reversal it possesses me. . . . Its softness is leech-like (p. 608).

I am somehow compromised by the slimy.

> It is a soft, yielding action, a moist and feminine sucking, it lives obscurely under my fingers, and I sense it like a dizziness; it draws me to it as the bottom of a precipice might draw me. . . . In one sense it is like the supreme docility of the possessed, the fidelity of a dog who *gives himself* even when one does not want him any longer, and in another sense there is underneath this docility a surreptitious appropriation of the possessor by the possessed (p. 609).

Already, I think, we can see the relation between the slimy as a quality of matter and the slimy as manifested in certain people. If a man is slimy—or oily—we feel that he is never quite what he seems to be on the surface. Yet our reaction is not the same as that which we would have toward proven dishonesty. Although insincerity is frequently associated with sliminess, it is not a necessary component. Often in fact our repulsion toward a slimy person is mingled with a pitying realization that "he means well." The person who is slimy combines a certain elusive quality with a demand upon us. We feel compromised because he seems to involve us in a way that we ourselves have not chosen. Whatever we say he accepts, but subtly transforms it in the very act of accepting. His fluid adaptation to each of our moods makes it impossible to brush him off. We feel vaguely in the wrong and blame him for it. He clings to us, and the feeling of wanting to wash our hands after contact with such people is additional proof of the close association between physical and psychic qualities which Sartre is arguing.

What is the meaning of all this? Encounter with the slimy, according to Sartre, suggests to us the great fear, the anti-value which men sense in themselves just as they live by the impossible ideal of the In-itself-for-itself. What would satisfy consciousness' deepest longing would be the power of so dominating and absorbing the In-itself that it wholly possessed the In-itself but without destroying it; consciousness wants to be conscious of *having* the absolute Being of the world but without becoming the world. The symbol offered by the slimy is exactly opposite, an image in which consciousness would be utterly engulfed by the In-itself, where it would be just conscious of not being free to think its own thoughts. Sartre compares this state to the "psychosis of influence" where the psychotic feels that his own ideas are prevented from expression and he is forced to produce those suggested by an external agent. The possibility revealed by slime is that of "a poisonous possession." The slimy threatens consciousness with what Sartre might have termed a living death and what he does call "the revenge of the In-itself, a sickly sweet, feminine revenge." It is inevitably associated with the sugary and especially with that "indelible sweetness, which remains indefinitely in the mouth even after swallowing." The death of the For-itself, which is symbolized in the destruction suggested by sugary sliminess, is perfectly imaged in the death of the insect which is attracted to the pot of jam and drowns in it.*

If such really is the objective meaning which the human being derives from the slimy, then Sartre is right in claiming that a psychoanalysis of things can be extremely helpful to the analyst. If we know what slime means, then when we know that our patient is attracted or repulsed by slimy things, we are further along the road to understanding him. But I myself find it difficult to believe that the average person's reaction to the slimy is even nonreflectively the same as that of the existentialist philosopher. The fascination of Sartre's description undoubtedly results from the fact that it touches in us that which we share in common. But I am inclined to think that its brilliance lies rather in its insight into the nature of ambivalent feelings and the reasons back of our physical-psychological comparisons, not to mention the fact that any reader who has got this far in *Being and Nothingness* is bound to be overwhelmed by the amazing precision with which the image fits the Sartrean concept. Yet perhaps we should go just a little farther. There is in all of us a constant tension between our pride in ourselves as free consciousnesses and our longing to be rid of the burden of individuality. To lose ourselves is at once our greatest fear and most seductive temptation. It is possible that our dislike of having something sticky cling to us and our occasional impulse to thrust our hands into it does, after all, serve as an image of this fundamental ambivalence. Moreover, I think the image suggests the horror of a conscious engulfing rather than mere annihila-

---

* It is a shame that Sartre apparently did not know of Boston's famous molasses flood. In 1919 a molasses factory exploded, the molasses poured into the streets, and a number of people were drowned. Such a death strikes me as the perfect finale for the hero of an existentialist novel.

tion, which might seem to be a sort of peaceful surcease. Voluntary submersion in quicksand or the like is an uncommon method of suicide. Even Antigone finally hanged herself rather than await death buried alive in a tomb.

One point of special interest in connection with Sartre's analysis of slime is the presence of terms suggestive of still further overtones, either more "metaphysical purports" or little glimpses of associations peculiar to Sartre's own emotional reactions. Specifically, for instance, what does he mean by a "moist and feminine sucking," "a sickly sweet feminine revenge"? We could, of course, simply dismiss such expressions as indicative of a basic resentment of women. Certainly such an implied. comparison of women with either the slimy or the In-itself is inconsistent with his view of the character of *all* human consciousness and with the belief that one chooses the way to live one's sex just as much as any other physical characteristic. We meet the same problem more directly in connection with the one other example which Sartre gives of the psychoanalysis of things—his treatment of holes.

The analysis of the fascination which holes exert on children is of particular interest since the Freudians have made so much of it. According to Sartre, there are two types of conduct involved, that of filling up holes and that of poking through them, but it is only the first which he discusses. Sartre agrees with Freud that there is no such thing as an "innocent" child and that many material objects in the child's environment are significantly related to his sexuality.

> But we do not understand by this that a sexual instinct already constituted has charged them with a sexual significance. On the contrary, it seems to us that this matter and these forms are apprehended in themselves, and they reveal to the child the For-itself's modes of being and relations to being which will illuminate and shape his sexuality (p. 612).

For the Freudian the child's interest in holes is explained either by prenatal shock (or birth trauma), which Sartre rejects as simply too fantastic for serious consideration; by a presentiment of adult intercourse, which he argues is empirically unjustifiable; or by anal sexuality, which he rejects on the basis that the child's experience comes first and that since the anus as an erogenous zone is not provided with tactile nerve endings, the child cannot at the start experience himself "as a hole." The explanation which Sartre presents is that the hole offers itself as a nothingness to be filled, which is a symbol of the ontological condition of the For-itself in its relation to the world. "A good part of our life is passed in plugging up holes." Ultimately the placing of a finger in a hole so as to have it become one, so to speak, with the surrounding area, is symbolically to make oneself a lack of Being in order that Being may be there. Even when the child sucks his fingers, he "seeks again the density, the uniform and spherical plenitude of Parmenidean being" (a suggestion I myself cannot take too seriously). Sartre continues with a few more words on sexuality.

> The obscenity of the feminine sex is that of everything which "gapes open." It is an *appeal to being* as all holes are. In herself woman appeals to a strange flesh which is to transform her into a fullness of being by penetration and dissolution. Conversely, woman senses her condition as an appeal precisely because she is "in the form of a hole." This is the true origin of Adler's complex. Beyond any doubt her sex is a mouth and a voracious mouth which devours the penis—a fact which can easily lead to the idea of castration. The amorous act is the castration of the man; but this is above all because sex is a hole (pp. 613-614).*

But if Sartre has nothing more to say on the subject of feminine sexuality, de Beauvoir has said a great deal—in *The Second Sex,* which is for all practical purposes an application of existential psychoanalysis to the particular problem of the psychology of women. Her over-all point of view is not different from Sartre's; her criticisms of Freud are the same as his, and like him she is content to accept many of the insights of traditional psychoanalysis as true and not inconsistent with her own theories. But whereas Sartre either makes no distinction between male and female sexuality or limits himself to comments referring only to the actual structure of the respective sex organs, de Beauvoir is interested specifically in the way in which a woman's total situation is modified by her sex and by the attitude of men in general toward her. De Beau-

---

* The Freudians too, of course, have connected sexuality with eating as a form of filling up. In his "Collection of True Psychoanalytic Tales" Robert Lindner in *The Fifty-Minute Hour* tells the story of a girl who suffered from fits of compulsive eating carried to extreme and dangerous lengths. She was cured after Dr. Lindner discovered that the eating was the symbolic expression of her unconscious desire to be pregnant by the father she both loved and hated. It would be interesting to hear Sartre's explanation of such a case. He would probably claim that Laura was rejecting her being as For-itself and trying to form herself into the ideal In-itself-for-itself, though how he would relate this aim to her specific situation I cannot imagine.

voir's criticism of the usual psychoanalytical theories apropos of women is much too much extended and detailed to allow more than a very superficial summary here. She has two fundamental objections: Freudian doctrine places too much emphasis on biological determinism and too little on social conditioning; Freud and his followers have considered and classified all female conduct and attitudes solely in relation to the male.

Quoting Freud's statement that "The libido is constantly and regularly male in essence, whether it appears in man or in woman," de Beauvoir says that this leads Freud to regard the feminine libido as if it were "a complex deviation from the human libido in general." With this basic premise, it is only natural for him to give great weight to "penis envy" and the accompanying "castration complex" as determining factors in feminine neuroses and even in "normal" women. Once the male libido is equated with the human, a woman cannot help feeling that she is lacking, if not actually mutilated. In opposition to this view, de Beauvoir argues that the supremacy of the male is something which Freud either takes simply for granted or seeks to explain by a fantastic myth based on an imaginary anthropology. The collected evidence for "penis envy" is itself suspect, not that it does not exist but that it does not prove what it is taken to prove. If the possession of a penis is something to be coveted, this is not because of what the organ is in itself but because it is a symbol for privileges which are granted to the male in a patriarchal society. Adler recognized this in part, but de Beauvoir objects that he too considers women only as they are content to accept their inferior status or rebel by trying to act like men. Thus if a girl climbs trees or plays marbles, Adler would say that she is "imitating" the male; de Beauvoir argues that the little girl perhaps merely likes to climb trees and play marbles. Contrasting her position with that of traditional psychoanalysis, de Beauvoir says,

> The psychoanalyst describes the female child, the young girl, as incited to identification with the mother and the father, torn between "viriloid" and "feminine" tendencies; whereas I conceive her as hesitating between the role of *object Other* which is offered her, and the assertion of her freedom.[7]

Most of the prevalent ideas as to what constitutes "womanhood" and femininity de Beauvoir rejects as so many trappings of the Serious World; they are pseudo-absolutes which instead of actually determining what a woman is or should be, serve as protective defenses for men and women alike against the terrifying responsibilities of free *human* individuality. As for the physical elements of sexual differentiation, de Beauvoir regards these as being—like all other physiological or physical structures—the material within which a freedom chooses itself and makes itself a history.

> Woman is a female to the extent that she feels herself as such. . . . It is not nature that defines woman; it is she who defines herself by dealing with nature on her own account in her emotional life (p. 38).

As with Sartre, we are ultimately referred to the human person's free choice of Being.

In *Being and Nothingness* Sartre makes it clear that existential psychoanalysis does not yet exist either as a method or as a fully perfected theory. He is content to have shown that such a psychoanalysis is possible and to have provided the groundwork. On this basis it is hardly fair to test Sartre's theoretical principles by asking how they would actually apply to the problems commonly confronted by psychoanalysts. One cannot expect Socrates to provide a systematic defense of the Platonic doctrine of Ideas. At the same time it is legitimate, I think, to raise one general question: Someone might say that Sartre's theory of consciousness would perhaps enable us to explain the life and personality of a "normal" person or even of the neurotic. But is there not a special difficulty posed by actual psychosis? Is not existential psychoanalysis by definition rendered impotent in the face of mental disturbance produced by disease or brain damage? And in the case of deliriums —when the patient is convinced that he is someone else—or of multiple personality, is it even conceivable that such a situation could exist unless we assume an unconscious? So far as I know, Sartre has not confronted these questions directly, though he has remarked that in the case of a delirium, existential psychoanalysis, because of its insistence on the concrete, unique situation of the patient, is in a better position to know why he has imagined himself to be Napoleon, for example, rather than Martin Luther.

While it is admittedly dangerous to state how Sartre *would* reply to these questions, it is permissible, I believe, to detect what possibilities are suggested to meet the difficulties and still remain consistent with Sartre's theory as already laid out. The problem of brain damage is no more of an obstacle to Sartre's theory than to any other. Consciousness does not exist except in combination with factual limits of some sort. To the degree that a man is conscious, he organizes his environment as a situation; within this situation and in terms of this situation he freely chooses his actions. With respect to psychoses in which the patient seems to live entirely divorced from reality, Sartre would no doubt argue that the patient has deliberately chosen to live in a world constructed in accordance with his own requirements instead of in the "real world." The patient's choice of Being is one which makes no distinction between physical object and fantasy object, or, more accurately, one in which the patient has chosen to regard as invalid any evidence conflicting with the sort of experiences he has marked out for himself. Unable to change the environment as it is for the majority of people, he has chosen to change himself in relation to it. The distinction between consciousness and knowledge holds for the psychotic as for other people; the difference is that the self-deception is so thoroughgoing that it is nearly impossible for the psychotic (without help) to get back to the reality he has previously rejected. That even here a free consciousness may sometimes assert itself is shown by the occasional "lucid intervals" of psychotics, who seem to grasp nonreflectively that something is wrong even when they will insist firmly on the truth of each separate delusion.* The case of multiple personality especially interests me since I think (perhaps rashly) that existential psychoanalysis is particularly well equipped to deal with it. In his discussion of human relations, Sartre pointed out that in relations with other people there arises a Self-for-others, a Self which I know that I am for the other, but which I can never quite grasp. But of course I am never just one Self-for-others; I am a Self for each Other whom I meet, and this Self may seem to change from one experience to the next. We have seen in our examination of existentialist literature that one way of trying to understand and to guarantee one's Self is to try to see oneself as being absolutely this Self which one is for others. But if a person's task of grasping what he really is should be complicated by feeling either that he was one Self to one group and a different Self to another or that the Self he was in general for others was not the Self he seemed to be to himself, then it would be easy to see that

---

* On one occasion when I was speaking on existential psychoanalysis, one of the members of my audience offered an interesting anecdote: Two psychiatrists were idly speculating as to what form of psychosis they would prefer if they knew they would inevitably suffer from one. One man said he thought he would prefer paranoia. Some time later he became actually ill with paranoia. I do not pretend that the incident proves that one chooses one's psychosis, but the story is suggestive.

the attempt to *be* one's Self-for-others might lead to feeling that one *was* more than one Self. The famous cases of multiple personality, such as Sally Beauchamp or the many-faced Eve, seldom involve a total dissociation between the selves. No recourse to an unconscious is demanded. It is sufficient and better to postulate that a particular consciousness has willed to identify itself with successive images of a Self fashioned upon the evanescent Self-for-others. Existential psychoanalysis would maintain that the multiple personality exhibits another, more extreme example of man's desire to *be* absolutely that which his freedom is continually in process of making itself be.

Since Sartre has stated emphatically that the analysis of individual character complexity is not his main interest in literature, we would not expect him to fill his fiction with studies of neurotic or psychotic personalities. (The fact that unfriendly critics believe existentialist literature to contain nothing else is beside the point.) It is significant that the three examples of such psychological studies which can be found in his work are all in an early collection of short stories, *The Wall (Le Mur),* which appeared in 1939. We have already considered "Erostratus," which is rather conventional in treatment. In "The Room" *(La Chambre)* insanity is the main theme. But Sartre has chosen to tell it from the point of view of the wife who watches her husband fall more and more under the influence of a fatal mental disease. The description of the wife's desperate efforts to share even her husband's delirium, and her anguished decision to kill him before the person she has loved is completely gone, are portrayed skillfully and poignantly, but we learn little of what Sartre believed to be going on in the consciousness of her husband. The only suggestion that Sartre might be taking a different approach to the subject of psychosis than is traditional occurs in several conversations between the two when it seems suddenly that the husband has been making up some of the stories to trap his wife, that he only partly believes in the visions which torture him. But this situation would not be impossible within a Freudian framework.

In "Intimacy" *(Intimité),* on the other hand, Sartre is already working on the premise that behavior usually explained by recourse to the unconscious may actually be a phenomenon of bad faith. In his criticism of the hypothesis of the unconscious, Sartre quotes Stekel to the effect that in his study of neurotic frigidity in women, he found, every time he could carry his investigations far enough, that "the crux of the psychosis was conscious." According to Stekel, the women in question were made frigid by their marital infidelity. Because of their guilty knowledge, they tried to hide from themselves consciousness of the pleasure which actually they experienced—"in order to prove to themselves that they were frigid." [8] This theme Sartre develops via his rather unpleasant heroine, Lulu. She is married to a man who is impotent, but she is not very unhappy about the fact, since this allows her to dominate their relationship and boss him about as she pleases. Meanwhile she has a lover and all goes well until the day he asks her to go away with him. Then Lulu is utterly miserable. Since she will not admit to herself that she really enjoys the sexual relation she shares with the lover, the thought of being with him more permanently is not much of an incentive for leaving her husband. And she really loves the immature, almost childlike relation which the two of them share at home. At last, by a quite magnificent web of self-deception, she "inadvertently" manages to give her husband the address of the hotel where she is staying with her lover. The husband has friends come to intervene. Lulu "is persuaded" to return home, and writes her lover that she will meet him for their usual rendezvous the next day.

Freudian psychoanalysis is involved directly in only two of the existentialist literary works which we have examined: Sartre's *The Childhood of a Boss* and de Beauvoir's *The Mandarins*. In each instance psychoanalysis is made to serve as a device in bad faith to help the subject evade self-responsibility. The fundamental principles of existentialist psychology are implied throughout all of the literature of Sartre and de Beauvoir. They are applicable in large part, I believe, to the work of Camus, since he, no less than the other two, holds that men are free and responsible. For the specific application of existential psychoanalysis as a method, we must look not at the fiction but at existentialist biographies. Before considering examples of these, however, we should raise one other problem: Is the psychology of freedom entirely without connection with other psychology (save for the obvious debt to the Freudians)? Must it stand alone as mere theory? Or can it find support for some of its theoretical positions in the conclusions of certain contemporary analysts who have departed more or less from the Freudian tradition?

# II. HUMANISTIC EXISTENTIALISM AND
# CONTEMPORARY PSYCHOLOGY

---

IN SPITE OF THEIR REVOLT against pedantry, Sartre, de Beauvoir, and Camus in their serious treatises have all written with careful concern for the abundance of scientific and scholarly work preceding them. Sartre in particular has scrupulously indicated the relation between his ideas and those of psychologists to whom he is indebted or with whom he sharply disagrees. The list includes the early psychologists, of course, (Freud, Adler, Janet) and many of the later ones (e.g., Stekel, Lewin, Dembo, Piaget, Alain, and especially Bachelard). My purpose, however, is not to trace influences either upon or from Sartre, nor am I attempting a technical appraisal of his psychology as compared with that of his contemporaries. Rather I should like to show what is possibly a purely coincidental parallel between Sartre and certain psychologists now influential in America and to indicate briefly Sartre's relation to those continental psychologists who may be loosely grouped as phenomenological psychiatrists or existential psychologists. My intent is not to effect an evaluation of Sartre which would accurately "place" him in the scientific world. But it seems to me that our examination of the literature of humanistic existentialism will be more meaningful if we view the psychology upon which it is based in an over-all perspective a little broader than the comparison with strict Freudianism which Sartre himself has made.

One may find minor points of similarity to existential psychoanalysis in the work of almost any psychoanalysts who have not stuck rigidly to the Freudian tradition. For significant parallels in fundamental outlook (along with important disagreements) we may consider the work of Erich Fromm and Karen Horney. So far as I have been able to discover, Sartre has never mentioned either Fromm or Horney. Fromm makes one interesting reference to Sartre in a footnote in his *Man for Himself*, which was published four years after *Being and Nothingness*.

> I have used this term *existential* without reference to the terminology of existentialism. During the revision of the manuscript I became acquainted with Jean-Paul Sartre's *Flies* and his *Is Existentialism a Humanism?* I do not feel that any changes or additions are warranted. Although there are certain points in common, I cannot judge the degree of agreement since I have had as yet no access to Sartre's main philosophical opus (p. 41).[1]

In *The Sane Society* (1955) Fromm paralleled Sartrean terminology still more closely; but if he had read more of Sartre's work in the meantime, he has not seen fit to mention the fact. On the other hand, there is at least one indication of possible influence in the other direction— or else of use of a common source. Fromm and Sartre both choose to illustrate a person's first awareness of individual self-consciousness by an example taken from Richard Hughes' *A High Wind in Jamaica;* Fromm in *Escape from Freedom* (1941) and Sartre in *Baudelaire* (1947).[2] Aside from all question of influence and dependence upon similar authorities, the comparison between Sartre on the one hand and Fromm and Horney on the other is particularly appropriate for several reasons. All three have written books addressed to the general public as well as to specialists in their own field. All are concerned with the particular area in which philosophy and psychology are inextricably interwoven. Sartre as a philosopher has laid the basis for a new psychological method; Fromm and Horney as psychologists have developed the philosophical implications of their views and offered a new interpretation of man. All three hold that psychology must not be divorced from ethical considerations, that it may properly be concerned with the normative as well as the descriptive. All question the concept of mere "adjustment" as the legitimate goal for the analyst and feel that there is such a thing as a "pathology of normalcy." All emphasize sociological rather than biological conditioning and are greatly concerned with what Sullivan calls the "psychology of interpersonal relationships."[3] We may sum up all this by saying that the Fromm-Horney school proposes a study of the human being in situation—which is precisely the central focus of existentialism.

Turning specifically to Fromm, I find a most striking parallel with Sartre in Fromm's concept of man's alienation from nature and the related view of the ambivalent character of freedom. Already in *Escape from Freedom* Fromm had declared that "human existence and freedom are from the beginning inseparable," and he pointed out that as in the Biblical myth of the Garden of Eden, human history began with an act of choice. Man's first encounter with freedom is negative; it is "freedom from," not "freedom to." Man's expulsion from Paradise was in truth the beginning of his war with nature. He was free *from* complete subordination to nature, but not yet free *to* use his powers so as to live well apart from her. For by his self-consciousness, which is identical with his power to choose, man is removed from the oneness with nature which the other animals enjoy. He lacks their instinctual guarantees; he must determine his own destiny both as an individual and as a species. His grandeur is at the same time his crushing fate. Freedom is opportunity, responsibility, insecurity. Lacking the courage to struggle to develop their inner resources in new ways, or prevented by society from developing the potentialities which they recognize in themselves, most men find the burden of freedom intolerable and seek to lose their individuality by submersion in systems developed by others and passed off as absolute (Sartre's Serious World). Later, in *The Sane Society,* Fromm speaks of birth in negative terms.

> The fact that man's birth is primarily a negative act, that of being thrown out of the original oneness with nature, that he cannot return to where he came from, implies that the process of birth is by no means an easy one (p. 27).[4]

Meanwhile in *Man for Himself* Fromm had related man's anguish before freedom to a dichotomy in his nature, and he pointed out that man's intellectual and scientific progress as well as his loneliness were to be explained in terms of man's "filling in" the lack which he felt in himself.

> He is driven to overcome this inner split, tormented by a craving for "absoluteness," for another kind of harmony which can lift the curse by which he was separated from nature, from his fellow men, and from himself (p. 41).

Only the word "Nothingness" or "For-itself" is necessary to make this passage veritably Sartrean. Fromm goes on to develop as "existential dichotomies" what Sartre would call components of the human condition. These are three paradoxes which have all one way or another received special attention from the existentialists. There is first the fact that man's life is inalterably permeated with the idea that he must die, and yet death is not compatible with or intelligible to the experience of living. Second, there is the discrepancy between man's infinite potentialities and the finitude which from the start confines his actualities within an infinitesimal compass. Finally, Fromm stresses the paradox inherent in man's ultimate isolation and solitude and his need for relatedness. For Fromm, as for humanistic existentialists, there is never full communication between men; yet no man can come to know himself apart from other men nor develop his powers without them. In contrast to the "existential dichotomies," Fromm adds the "historical dichotomies." These are not contradictions inherent in the human condition, but rather those contradictions in men's existence which are man-made and potentially solvable. Examples of these are the institution of slavery in ancient Greece when many men believed in equality thoretically but could see no way of achieving it practically. A modern example given by Fromm is "the contemporary contradiction between an abundance of technical means for material satisfaction and the incapacity to use them exclusively for peace and the welfare of the people." In discussing the dichotomies, Fromm points out that people often deliberately or unknowingly confuse the two kinds. Thus such things as the inevitability of war or class distinctions are treated as absolute givens because they are advantageous to some and because those who suffer from them cannot see any solution and so assume there is none. The parallel with existentialist thought in this connection is obvious. We have met it over and over again in our discussion of bad faith.

These ideas all imply a certain view of human nature. Here Fromm is closer to the existentialists in theory than in practice. He denies that there is such a thing as a fixed human nature in the Hegelian sense or even in the common sense of the maxim, "You can't change human nature." At the same time he denies that human nature is infinitely malleable, for he recognizes that such an admission would be equivalent to saying that men can be manipulated without limit, which would be to deny all human freedom. This is exactly the existentialist position. There are many occasions, however, when Fromm in spite of his theory implies that there are certain human values which are absolute, and such a view demands that human nature also must be in some way fixed. Here he is closer to Camus than to Sartre. Yet it must be admitted that Sartre and de Beauvoir too assume a sameness of human reactions to certain basic needs even though they do not postulate it as part of their theory.

Fromm's famous "orientations" have no specific, one-for-one equivalents in existentialism, but the general idea back of them is certainly comparable to the formulated theories of Sartre and de Beauvoir. Fromm contrasts his view with Freud's by saying,

> The fundamental basis of character is not seen in various types of libido organization but in specific kinds of a person's relatedness to the world. In the process of living, man relates himself to the world (1) by acquiring and assimilating things, and (2) by relating himself to people (and himself) (p. 58).[5]

Sartre says the same thing in other words by stressing the idea that man comes to know himself and makes himself by means of the way in which he organizes the things of the world into a kind of instrumental hierarchy with himself as center of reference, and by the particular pattern of subject-object relations which he adopts with regard to other people. The specific orientations which Fromm discusses (receptive, hoarding, exploitative, marketing, and—in contrast to the others—the productive), in so far as they are *total* life-adaptations, come close to the existentialist original choice of Being. Though one should not press the parallel too closely, it is not inaccurate to say that the nonproductive orientations are similar to patterns of bad faith and that the productive resembles "good faith." The productive orientation demands that one adopt a truthful and rational outlook and that one spontaneously develop his own unique potentialities rather than conforming to external authoritarian standards, this process being limited, however, by the recognition of the right of other persons to do the same thing. Similarly, existentialist good faith requires that a man assume full responsibility for his life, recognizing his freedom to make of it what he will, relentlessly rejecting self-illusion and wishful thinking, and, once more, voluntarily restricting the external scope of his free acts by respecting the freedom of others. Especially interesting in this connection is Fromm's "market personality" (not identical with, but reminding one of, the "other-directed person" of *The Lonely Crowd*). The man with the "market personality" lives "as you desire me," always trying to make himself into the semblance which he feels his associates expect and admire, changing from group to group almost with the shifting styles of the season. Fromm's sketch of such persons is exactly equivalent to Sartre's description of those who try to be their Self-for-others instead of accepting the responsibilities of Being-for-itself. There is also the moving passage in *Being and Nothingness* in which Sartre discusses society's inclination to try to imprison men within the social roles which they have chosen, to make of a waiter only a waiter rather than a man who waits on tables, a soldier only a soldier, and so on. And most men, Sartre says, are only too happy to *be* the part they play.

Finally, we may note that basically, although Fromm is rather more optimistic than the existentialists, he shares their fundamental outlook on life. The resemblance is not always obvious on the surface. In his popular works Fromm is rather too willing to compromise with common opinion in order to put his ideas across without stirring up resistance and hostile criticism. Consequently he will employ familiar precepts about the necessity of faith, of belief in the love of God and the like, without always making it clear that he is using his words in a sense quite other than the traditional one. But Fromm's real point of view is unmistakably humanistic. In *Escape from Freedom* he says, "There is only one meaning of life; the act of living itself" (p. 263). In *Psychoanalysis and Religion* he points out that frequently religion itself may be an obstacle to the attainment of religious values, and he questions whether the retention of old symbols to express new ideals may not lead people to treat the ideal as an absolute reality which can be grasped once and for all. Nevertheless he concludes:

> There need be no quarrel with those who retain the symbol God although it is questionable whether it is not a forced attempt to retain a symbol whose significance is essentially historical. However this may be, one thing is certain. The real conflict is not between belief in God and "atheism" but between a humanistic, religious attitude and an attitude which is equivalent to idolatry regardless of how this attitude is expressed—or disguised—in conscious thought.[6]

In *The Sane Society* Fromm brings his brand of humanism still closer to that of existentialism by pointing out that man's greatest needs and passions do not spring from his biology but from "the very peculiarity of his existence." "There lies also the key to humanistic psychoanalysis. . . . The most powerful forces motivating man's behavior stem from the condition of his existence, the 'human situation' " (p. 28). On the other hand, Fromm has not restricted himself to psychological description and sociological analysis; he has also (particularly in *The Sane Society*) offered many specific suggestions for social changes which he believes would result in enabling more people to live productively. Fromm's political views are decidedly socialistic. They are not as radical as those of Sartre and de Beauvoir. They do not so evidently spring from the agonies of the conscience and from a personal love of humankind as do the ideas of Camus, nor are they as modestly presented. Yet in his non-totalitarian socialism and in his belief that society as a whole must be responsible for the well-being of all and at the same time must respect the individual potentialities of every man, Fromm is not unlike the Camus of *The Rebel*.

Turning now to Karen Horney, I think we need not make a completely separate case, since many points of similarity between her views and existential psychoanalysis are those which she shares with Fromm. But we may note certain parallels peculiar to her theory. Jack L. Rubins in 1954, in a review of the English translation of *Existential Psychoanalysis,* pointed out a general similarity between Horney and Sartre. Stressing especially a similarity in their notions about the nature of the Self, he says quite rightly that bad faith may be considered as a theoretical explanation of "the clinical concept of duplicity and alienation." But he makes two serious mistakes. In contrasting Sartre's theory, which he finds pessimistic, with Horney's optimistic one, he says that Sartre's individual "has no conscious responsibility for himself, or for decision. He cannot hope to grow beyond the limitations he may find and even accept in himself." This interpretation is, of course, totally wrong. Good faith demands that one acknowledge one's reactions and conduct and talents for what they are but never that their significance is fixed. Even worse, Dr. Rubins writes,

> "Being-in-itself," with its "original upsurge" toward freedom, is in many ways similar to our Real Self with its directive tendency of growth. And while Sartre does not mention neurosis or health, his "Being-for-itself" and "Being-for-others" roughly make up what we might call the neurotic or actual self.[7]

Obviously Dr. Rubins has failed to understand that it is the For-itself which freely decides what the Real Self is to be and that Being-in-itself does not upsurge into anything—or even into Nothing since it is the For-itself which is responsible for that too! Nevertheless it is possible to find a parallel which does fit the facts. Sartre points out that in everyone there exists a consciousness which is capable of recognizing its free potentiality to make of its life what it will; in addition, there may be another form of this same consciousness, consciousness which has put itself in bad faith and persuaded itself that it is not responsible for its acts and that it must behave according to prescribed lines of conduct laid down by its inherited nature, the demands of its past, its personal environment, etc. Roughly equivalent to these are the two Selves which Horney describes: the Real Self, comparable to a consciousness which acknowledges its freedom, and the Neurotic or Actual Self, the consciousness in bad faith, which allows itself to be wholly dominated by its neurotic trends.

There are four other general resemblances between Sartre and Horney. First, Horney, more than most psychiatrists working in the Freudian tradition, recognizes the impossibility of genuine detachment on the part of the analyst; she urges that since the analyst will not be perfectly objective under any circumstances, he should be willing to make some self-commitment in his effort to help the patient. (Obviously Horney would never allow this to go to the point of deliberate manipulation without respect for the patient's right to self-determination.) Sartre and all existentialists would agree here, for the impossibility of an impersonal, totally objective point of view is one of the most fundamental of existentialist principles. Second, the neurotic trends of which Horney speaks may be contradictory to one another, although taken together they constitute what seems to the subject a "safe" orientation toward the world. Similarly, as we shall see in his biographies of Baudelaire and Genet, Sartre too maintains that the basic choice of Being may involve an impossible contradiction though this does not prevent the person's making of it a *modus vivendi* throughout most or all of a lifetime. Third, Horney in her psychoanalysis gives far greater attention to the ego than is traditional with Freudians. She refuses to see the ego either as the mere servant of the id or as its detached supervisor. Whereas the Freudian analyst will largely limit himself to helping the ego become aware of repressed material, Horney insists that to help the patient change the attitudes of the ego itself is part of the essential task of the therapist. This position is at least an advance in the direction of Sartre's insistence that we must consider man to be wholly conscious, though Horney's position is by no means as radical a departure from the hypothesis of the unconscious as is Sartre's. Finally, Horney criticizes Freud's concept of transference as being too "mechanistic-evolutionistic." [8] She feels that the patient's attitude toward the analyst is seldom if ever the simple result of the patient's substituting the analyst for whatever person had served to polarize the infantile reactions responsible for the later disturbance. Horney holds that the transference is merely one manifestation among many of the subject's basic orientation toward the world, that his attitude toward the analyst will probably be more intense because the analysand feels that his whole way of life is brought into question; but for that very reason his conduct in relation to the analyst will bring into play exactly that behavior which he is accustomed to manifest in all of his personal relations. This is precisely the position of existential psychoanalysis, which views every act and attitude, however trivial, as part of the complex symbolic structure which makes concrete the underlying choice of Being.

Nevertheless I do not wish to stress unduly the parallel between the Fromm-Horney theories and existential psychoanalysis. In the first place, there are vast areas in which there is no overlapping even by way of disagreement. Sartre says nothing about the many strictly clinical problems which interest the other two, and this is as it should be, since Sartre is a philosopher and theoretical psychologist. On the other hand, Fromm and Horney are uninterested in the purely philosophical speculations which make up such a large part of Sartre's work. If we include other existentialists, the variety of approach is still more apparent. In addition, there are distinct points of disagreement even in fundamental attitudes toward the same problems. Perhaps most important is the question of the unconscious. Horney, as we have seen, gives greater emphasis to the ego than has been customary among psychoanalysts, and she remarks that only very rarely is totally forgotten material ever dragged forth from the unconscious and made conscious. But while this implies that most of the material dealt with during an analysis has not hitherto been entirely unknown by the subject, still Horney never rejects the unconscious. And neither does Fromm. Horney, in fact, regards the hypothesis of unconscious motivation as one of Freud's outstanding and most permanent contributions. Fromm everywhere implies the existence of an unconscious and makes particular use of it in one of his most interesting books, *The Forgotten Language,* where he develops at length the theory that the myth is to the race as the dream is to the individual. In the second place, Fromm and Horney, while they are both less deterministic than Freud, give far more weight to social conditioning than Sartre. Fromm especially, although he claims that human existence and freedom are inseparable, insists that if we could know the reasons why a person has become what he is, we could never pass any moral judgement. This conclusion is decidedly weak beside the existentialists' "totally responsible and wholly without excuse." Furthermore, the attitude toward the Self is not quite the same in Fromm and Horney as in the existentialists. Fromm and Horney urge that if the individual is to maintain good mental health and to achieve some adjustment higher than mere conformity, he must be free to develop his unique potentialities. But their view of these potentialities is closer to Aristotle than to Sartre. Although they never actually say that man has a dormant secret Self which is waiting to be revealed and given the chance to realize the form implanted in it like the oak in the acorn, one feels that this is their perhaps unacknowledged position. Fromm, in fact, uses the seed to illustrate his optimistic view that man is basically good and that evil results when his environmental situation prevents him from developing his powers and allows them, as it were, to rot. Such a view is obviously opposed to the existentialist view that man's Self never exists in any definite form but only as a Self-to-be-made by a free project launched in the direction of the future. With Fromm in particular there is also a hidden tendency to "objectivize," to assume that certain values are absolute even while he argues that all values are man-made and without eternal guarantee. The contrast between Sartre and Fromm could not be more strikingly illustrated than by their use of a familiar quotation from Dostoyevsky: "If God is dead, everything is allowed." We have seen that to the existentialist, this pronouncement indicates man's anguish and makes the burden of freedom almost intolerably heavy. But Fromm remarks comfortably, "If man is alive he knows what is allowed." In spite of the fact that Fromm and Horney are greatly concerned with man's present unhappiness, although they are, on the whole, future-oriented, they offer us at the very most an existentialism stripped of anguish.

While it seems to me that the existentialists may be profitably compared with Fromm and Horney in their general view of man and society, existential psychoanalysis in its technical aspect is most closely affiliated with phenomenological psychiatry. In part this close relation is due to common intellectual ancestry, for both these psychiatrists and Sartre have been profoundly influenced not only by Freud but by the ideas of Edmund Husserl, the founder of the school of phenomenology, particularly as interpreted and given an existentialist twist by Martin Heidegger. The phenomenological psychiatrists, however, owe a great deal also to the work of Karl Jaspers, whereas Sartre is not very sympathetic to Jaspers. Moreover Sartre has developed a concept of consciousness which orthodox phenomenologists would never accept. The question of influence, however, is a complicated one; Sartre has borrowed from individual phenomenologists, and the phenomenological psychiatrists, especially during the last decade, have been considerably influenced by Sartre. On the whole, this type of psychology has until very recently been prevalent chiefly in Europe, so much so that in 1954 Ulrich Sonnemann, formerly of the New School of Social Research, wrote a book with the express purpose of introducing this new theory to American psychiatrists. Unfortunately Sonnemann's work, *Existence and Therapy: An Introduction to Phenomenological Psychology and Existential Analysis,* is so abstract and so frequently almost unintelligible that it is not really informative. He does, however, give an admirable summing up of the existentialist (and phenomenologist) approach.

> We may say that it decidedly steers away from positivism, functionalism, instrumentalism, pragmatism, and operationalism, and toward a rediscovery of *spontaneous man in his world*. . . . Existentialism, to sum up, uncovers and questions exactly those constant and implicit assumptions of the functionalistic theories of man which to the functionalists themselves have become so completely self-evident that they are hardly aware of them, let alone of their aprioristic nature (p. ix).[9]

As Sonnemann indicates in his title, there are two different groups which share in common a peculiar emphasis on "existence." There are the phenomenological psychiatrists proper, of whom Eugene Minkowski, V. E. von Gebsattel, and Erwin Straus are probably the best known, and there are the existential analysts working in the tradition established by Ludwig Binswanger and continued by Medard Boss and Roland Kuhn.[10] The dividing line is not too clear. A man such as Franz Fischer might well be put on either side or both. In any case there is little point in listing names, and any attempt at examination of the theories of the individual psychiatrists would be inappropriate to our enterprise. What would be both pertinent and profitable, however, would be for us to consider briefly a book by the Dutch psychologist, J. H. Van Den Berg, *The Phenomenological Approach to Psychiatry.*[11] Van Den Berg, who is himself a follower of Binswanger, uses the term "phenomenological" to cover all these "psychiatrists of existence." What he has done is to point out what he believes to be the most crucial differences between their approach and traditional Freudian psychoanalysis, refraining from urging his own personal point of view and emphasizing only those positions which phenomenological psychiatrists hold in common. Although he is aware of Sartre's importance, he is by no means a follower of his and uses examples from Sartre chiefly to illustrate principles drawn from the clinical observations of phenomenologists.

Van Den Berg begins his book by introducing a hypothetical patient and describing his disturbed symptoms. The traditional psychoanalyst, he says, will treat this patient by making use of four fundamental concepts, each of which the phenomenologist will radically modify: *projection,* which involves the patient's attitude toward the world (and in part towards society); *conversion,* which is a manifestation of his relation to his own body; *transference,* which is a special example of his attitude toward other people and in particular toward the analyst; and *mythification,* which is his subjective remaking of his own experiences (implying a particular attitude toward time).

Following Van Den Berg's order of discussion, let us consider first *projection.* The patient has complained that the world looks different than it used to, that the houses all seem tumbledown and shut in on themselves, that the street and square are dangerously wide when he comes to cross them. The standard theory says that the patient has projected his own feelings into the environment. But Van Den Berg objects that this view simply proposes a mystery for an explanation. *How* could the patient put what is inside him into outside objects? The analyst, Van Den Berg argues, allows his interest in the patient to lead him to neglect the world, but it is a mistake to think that the patient and his world can be kept separate. None of us at any time lives in a world in which we see things only descriptively; rather we *always* surpass the object toward its signification. "Nothing gives us the right to regard our perception as being more true than that of the patient. It is also our perception that proves to us how and what we are" (p. 36). Therefore the analyst, according to Van Den Berg, should not waste time trying to verify for himself or for the patient that "the world is not like that." He should accept the idea that to the patient the world *is* like that, and he will begin to understand the patient when he gains an insight into the patient's world. The analyst should establish an "extrospective pathography" which describes "the pathological *physiognomy of the world* (Erwin Straus)."

All of this we have met already in the work of Sartre—though not specifically related to the problem of conducting an analysis. Sartre's basic definition of consciousness implies Van Den Berg's position. Consciousness is always consciousness *of* something, a never-ending active relationship between consciousness and the world, a world which has meaning only *for a consciousness*. Man experiences the external world as a complex network or hierarchy of instruments through which he may realize his potentialities. In his rational approach to reality he observes exclusively those relations between himself and the environment which he observes are sustained by all other people and which offer no inconsistency as he moves from one enterprise to another. But in his emotions man effects a magical organization of the world wherein he is content with a world which is responsive to his present impulses. Sartre's point (and Van Den Berg's) is not that the environment does not have any fixed physical structure, but that with the possible exception of artificial scientific investigation, one never sees everyday objects for what they are physically in themselves. One transcends them toward their subjectively established possibilities. Thus to a prisoner a gate may seem tremendous in size and strength, the central focus of the whole environment. To a visitor it may be only one architectural section among others of an imposing building. De Beauvoir's novels are particularly rich in passages illustrating these sudden subjective modifications of the environment. Take these examples chosen from *She Came to Stay*.

The first occurs in a scene where Francoise (like Lucien and Roquentin) is trying in vain to comprehend Being-in-itself, this time in the form of her jacket. The passage concludes,

> The jacket stayed there, indifferent, totally alien, and she was forever Françoise. Moreover, if she became the jacket, then she, Françoise, would no longer be anything more than it. Everything began spinning in her head, and she went downstairs and ran out into the garden.
>
> Later Francoise drank her cup of coffee with one gulp; it was almost cold; this was pointless; why was she thinking about all that? She looked at the murky sky. The one thing certain at this moment was that the present world was out of reach; she was not only exiled from Paris, she was exiled from the whole universe. The people seated on the café sidewalk, the people passing in the street put no weight on the ground; they were shadows; the houses were only a flat stage set with-

out depth. And Gerbert who was coming smiling toward her—he too was only a light and charming shadow (p. 123).

On another occasion Françoise is just entering a crowded room.

> She took in the scene at a glance: glamorous successful actresses, debutantes, respectable failures—it was a crowd of separate destinies come together to compose this confused swarming which made her a little dizzy. At certain moments it seemed to Françoise that these lives had interlocked expressly for her at that particular point in space and time at which she was standing; and at other instants it was no longer that at all. Everyone was scattered about, each one for himself (p. 147).

Next we may consider the problem of *conversion*. The patient claims that he suffers from ailments which medical examination cannot discern. The traditional theory explains this situation by saying that the patient "converts" his psychic illness into physical; he transfers the pains from his mind into his bodily organs. Here Van Den Berg argues that there is a hidden tendency to objectivize all the respective parts—pains and psyche as well as body—and that the theory quite openly presupposes a distinction between psyche and body as in the old soul-body dualism. But the idea that something nonspatial can be inside or outside anything, that man has a soul *and* a body, "is not comprehensible to anybody." Actually, says Van Den Berg, all that we know in so-called "conversion" cases is that psychiatrically disturbed patients frequently have physical complaints. In dealing with the problem we should realize that it is only on the reflective level that we *have* a body. I can hold up my hand and try to view it objectively as I would the hand of another. But this is not the way in which we ordinarily experience the body. On the pre-reflective level we *are* our bodies, so much so that in many "physical" acts—eating, caressing, sex—too much reflection on the physical processes may make it impossible to complete the act. As for psychic qualities such as shame or anger, what are these if not ways in which the body is lived? The physician in his examination of the body treats it as a thing severed from the psyche. He may be right in finding nothing wrong with the heart as a biological organ or with the muscles and reflexes of the legs. But the patient lives in a world where there is no such severance. His heart does beat rapidly with rebellion or fear. His legs do shake and give way beneath him. Traditional analysts, con-

cludes Van Den Berg, have understressed the interrelation of the body
and the world (the world as lived in by the subject, not the world which
can be summed up in the mathematical formulae of physicists and
chemists).

> The body, says von Gebsattel, *moulds itself* in close resem-
> blance to the plan of the world in which it finds its task sketched
> out, it assumes a shape, a *form:* a worker's form in response
> to the invitation issuing from a workshop, a warrior's form in
> response to the appeal of an arena, a lover's form in response
> to the erotic approach of the beloved. The pre-reflective body
> and the pre-reflective world are engaged in a continuous dia-
> logue. Both can only be understood from this dialogue (pp.
> 45-46).

Van Den Berg's view here is exceedingly close to that of Sartre, who
makes a comparable distinction between the Body-known-by-the-Other
and the Body-for-itself.* It is the first, of course, which is known by the
physician; it is also the body which I know if I deliberately look at my
arm or leg. In the latter case I am actually contemplating a psychic object in the same way that I can adopt a detached point of view apropos
of a hate or a fear at times when I am not actively living it. The Body-
for-itself is the body which I live, and it is wholly psychic. I *am* my
body. Without the body I could enter into no relation with the world
and its objects. With the body, which is, as it were, the master instrument by which I may realize the instrumental possibilities of the world,
I become the point of view which I adopt toward the world. I *am* my
relation to the world, and my body is everywhere ·in the world to which
I relate myself.

It is particularly interesting that both Van Den Berg and Sartre mention nausea as the physical manifestation of man's psychological (one
might almost say his metaphysical) orientation. Van Den Berg remarks
that the patient "often localizes his fear in the cardiac region; his general
dissatisfaction with life is identified with a bad taste in his mouth and
with a sensation of nausea in his throat" (p. 19). Sartre claims that "a
dull and inescapable nausea perpetually reveals my body to my consciousness." This nausea, this flat, insipid taste is always present as the

---

* Sartre adds also a third distinction, the Body-for-others. His discussion is
far more complex than I am indicating here, but I see no need to include more
of his analysis than is pertinent to the comparison with phenomenological psychiatry as summarized by Van Den Berg.

background of all my experiences; it is the indication to my consciousness of its contingency and its facticity.

> We must not take the term *nausea* as a metaphor derived from
> our physiological disgust. On the contrary, we must realize that
> it is on the foundation of this nausea that all concrete and
> empirical nauseas (nausea caused by spoiled meat, fresh blood,
> excrement, etc.) are produced and make us vomit.[12]

Van Den Berg proceeds next to the question of *transference*. The
standard theory assumes that the patient's feelings of hostility or dependency, which had originally been directed toward a dominating father
or mother or the like, are now *transferred* to the analyst, although he
has done nothing on his own to merit the excessive love or hate which
is suddenly bestowed upon him. Van Den Berg objects that the theory
treats emotions as if they were things which could be carried from one
place to another. But hate and love are inseparable from their objects;
they exist only as the hate or love of particular persons and things; they
cannot be "transferred." What we must look for in the patient is not
some half-forgotten episode in the past but a clue to his present orientation, so that we may see why he chooses to relate himself to *all* people
through hostility rather than friendliness, or to choose separation rather
than communication. As Van Den Berg develops his ideas on human
relations, he tries to show that our attitude toward others is inextricably
connected with our relation to the world and to our own bodies. In this
section he makes specific use of parts of Sartre's discussion of Being-
for-others, but paradoxically he is less close to Sartre in the conclusions
here than in those parts of the book where his parallel with Sartre is
apparently coincidental. This is probably because Van Den Berg's theory
of our relations with our fellow man is developed without any reference
to the subject-object conflict which Sartre finds so important. He does,
however, use Sartre's description of the caress—almost without change.
If I look at my hand, he says, paraphrasing Sartre, its appearance, the
arrangement of veins, etc. seems gratuitous, *de trop;* I find that no two
hands, not even my own, are exactly alike. The whole affair leaves me
somehow disturbed and dissatisfied. But if I caress a beloved body, then
suddenly my hand seems to me perfectly justified. "The caress cancels
the accidentality of my hand; it turns it into 'exactly that hand which it
should be fit for me to have' " (p. 55). Sartre employs this illustration
in connection with his study of desire. Van Den Berg uses it to illustrate the way in which another person enters in to modify my relations

with my own body, an application which I am sure Sartre would allow.

Again, Van Den Berg refers specifically to Sartre in retelling the famous keyhole example. He interprets it as demonstrating the way in which other people may modify my organization of the world. Van Den Berg speaks of the discovery at the keyhole as increasing the distance between the subject and his world. The events on the other side of the door have been very near; in fact, the watcher has "left his body outside the door and crept through the keyhole." But sudden discovery removes the inner room to a great distance where it will remain—unless the discoverer suddenly brings it close again by joining in with the game and taking his turn at keyhole spying. All of this is simply a repetition of Sartre's description of the Other's Look which effects "an internal hemorrhage of my world," making it "bleed in the direction of the stranger"; but the absence of all mention of the interplay of subject and object leaves Van Den Berg's argument less convincing and somehow more fanciful. Furthermore, he goes beyond Sartre—and to my mind beyond the facts—when he speaks of actually seeing with another's eyes, of entering into the country of which another is speaking, and other things which imply a break-through in that ultimate subjective isolation which Sartre and other existentialists never forget. On the other hand, Sartre would certainly agree that my way of "existing my body," my organization of my world, and my way of being-for-others cannot be separated even in analysis, but are one unified manifestation of my basic choice of Being.

Finally, Van Den Berg discusses the concept of *mythification.** As often happens, Van Den Berg's hypothetical patient gives a bad account of his youth. Yet the psychotherapist investigating finds that the past as the patient describes it does not jibe with the record of the past as confirmed by numerous other witnesses. Are we to conclude, as most psychoanalysts would, that the patient's neurosis has led him to effect a "mythification of his past"? He does not deliberately falsify, and Van Den Berg insists that the patient is in good faith. Yet our subject will resist evidence which would certainly be convincing to him if he were dealing with unemotional, factual memories. According to Van Den Berg the doctrine of "mythification" contains an error analogous to that which we saw apropos of the patient and "the world"; it assumes the existence of a past which is wholly neutral, a succession of absolute, non-signifying events against which the "mythification" can be measured.

---

* In speaking of the patient's "mythification of his past," Van Den Berg is following specifically the French psychiatrist Dupre.

But "this 'impartial' past never and nowhere occurs within the scope of human existence." The patient may or may not be accurate in describing the past as he has lived it, but even this is not of major importance. What is significant is how the past appears to the patient in the present. The task of the analyst is not to free the patient from the psychotraumata of the past but to liberate him from the meaning of these psychotraumata as they even now exist for him.

Van Den Berg's view of man's situation in respect to time is for all practical purposes identical with Sartre's, and both men are heavily indebted to Martin Heidegger. The position is essentially this: The past as lived is not a series of finished events; it depends upon the present, for we are continually remaking the past as we decide anew the meaning it will have in our present enterprises. But inasmuch as our present acts are determined by our projects of what is about to be, this means that the past comes to meet us from the future. Van Den Berg complains that psychoanalysts have given too little importance to the future, and he points out that it is frequently the patient's fear of the way his past will come to him out of the future which brings the patient to the analyst. Van Den Berg combines this emphasis on the future with the idea that the essence of man is choice. In words which might easily have come out of *Being and Nothingness* he writes,

> Man chooses the form in which he throws his past before him, he chooses the form in which he places himself in the future. He chooses a similar aspect of the future, that it becomes possible for him to live *on* (p. 75).

And again,

> The patient learns to choose differently. . . . The patient changes his past and in doing so gives a new aspect to the future, from which, as we know, this past continually comes to meet him (pp. 81-82).

The two most fundamental and most distinctive principles of existential psychoanalysis are the belief that man is free and the rejection of the unconscious. How does phenomenological psychiatry (at least as interpreted by Van Den Berg) stand on these? It would seem that in all of Van Den Berg's discussion of projection, conversion, transference, and mythification, the individual's freedom is necessarily implied. Man is presented as free to choose the meaning of his past, free to determine his own future. Unfortunately Van Den Berg never quite states his position in unmistakable terms. At one point he seems to make a reservation. Speaking of another hypothetical patient, one who must decide "how to place his broken leg in the future," he says, "He is—not quite—forced into a—not quite—*free* choice (Sartre)" (p. 77). Does this mean that Van Den Berg feels that Sartre's position is too extreme and must be modified? Or that he simply interprets Sartre's concept of facticity as being itself a factual limit of freedom which does not actually affect freedom as a psychological capacity? I suspect the latter, but one cannot be sure.

With regard to the unconscious there is no question as to Van Den Berg's position. Early in his book he suggests that the hypothesis of the unconscious is maintained because it makes it easier for the psychoanalyst to explain the processes of projection, conversion, etc., which would be difficult to accept without it. He asks, "For is not the unconscious defined as exactly that which eludes our attention? The unconscious is never experienced, so in an appeal to experience there is no sense at all" (p. 26). Toward the end of his discussion he points out that the approach which he has been presenting has been outlined with no recourse to *the unconscious*. There is no objection, he says, to our applying the adjective "unconscious" to those things which have escaped our attention (Sartre's levels of awareness or reflection), but we must not assume "an" unconscious "which would be supposed to exist as a second reality behind the phantoms of healthy and of neurotic life. There is but one reality: that of life as it is lived." The Freudian unconscious, Van Den Berg believes, is "the product of a premature cessation of the psychological analysis of human existence" (p. 83).*

---

* Since the problem of the unconscious is so vital to any psychoanalysis, I should like to refer the reader to Sonnemann's chapter on this subject. That his position is essentially that of Van Den Berg's can be seen from his opening paragraph. "The unconscious *per se* can be inferred from any experience of the emergence of our minds into a state of awareness, because the phenomenality of *emergence* as an event implies it: that state from which our minds emerge, relative to their subsequent states, is one of unconsciousness. It becomes evident that 'awareness' as we used it as well as 'unconsciousness' as we used it both require qualifications in the form of a genetive [genitive?], linking them with a content *of* which the subject is aware or of which he is unconscious; the habit of conceptual reification (*the* conscious, *the* unconscious), which is a convenience of thoughtlessness unless the reification stays aware of that requirement, became possible only at a moment in history when language, as was its specific fate during the nineteenth century, had sufficiently been flattened out—abstractified—to dim its phenomenal references so much that the tacit but constitutive 'of what' inherent in both concepts ('aware' and 'unconscious') could become relatively invisible" (p. 191).

Phenomenological psychiatry is certainly close to existential psycho-analysis, so close, in fact, that the comparison may very well result in our crediting Sartre with less originality than at first seemed due him. We must remember, however, that Van Den Berg is friendly enough to Sartre so that he has tended to stress parallels and even to modify his presentation under Sartre's influence. In any case, what should concern us here is primarily the question of whether there is any support for Sartre's psychology in the empirical work of practicing psychiatrists. If Van Den Berg's presentation of the phenomenological—and existential —approach is (as surely we must assume that it is) the result of com-paring the case histories and reports of the psychiatrists whom he men-tions, then we are justified, I believe, in saying that there is clinical evidence to support at least some of the claims of existential psychoanal-ysis. While it would be more satisfactory if Sartre had been in a position to offer his own empirical corroboration, at least we need not keep exis-tential psychoanalysis wholly isolated in a vacuum while it awaits the coming of its Freud.

# III. EXISTENTIALIST BIOGRAPHY

In the literature of humanistic existentialism, the psychology of freedom is everywhere implied. In many instances (e.g., Lucien, Daniel, Lulu, even Meursault and the Missionary) the fictional characters are presented almost as case histories illustrative of a new view of human personality. Yet since these beings are imaginary, they cannot of course serve as conclusive *evidence* for a psychological theory. So far as Camus is concerned, this does not matter. He makes no claim to be a systematic philosopher and is in fact opposed to the whole idea of explaining man wholly by rational principles. But the creator of existential psychoanalysis has quite understandably felt the need of demonstrating his method apropos of persons other than those whom he himself has invented. Thus we have two books of Sartre's which are literally case histories—his biographical studies. At the end of his presentation of existential psychoanalysis Sartre said that he hoped some day to show how the method could be used in biographies of Flaubert and Dostoyevsky. Instead he has given us Charles Baudelaire and Jean Genet. Under Sartre's treatment the inward struggles of the two men appear disturbingly similar in some respects. Still they are by no means the same, and it is only natural that Sartre would choose people whose lives seemed to him to illustrate principles which he had already been emphasizing in his work. Baudelaire and Genet form a particularly interesting pair in that Baudelaire is an example of a man who allowed his life to be determined by his first unhappy choice, whereas Genet, going through a somewhat comparable phase, made successive choices of Being until he finally realized his existential freedom.

Neither of these works is a biography in the usual sense. In *Baudelaire* Sartre assumes that the reader is already acquainted with the main events and influential persons in Baudelaire's life. In *Saint Genet, Martyr-Comedian* we learn of a few decisive events in Genet's career, but in all of the nearly six hundred pages there is nothing resembling a connected life history. Yet while both books make extensive use of the subjects' poems, novels, and essays, they are not interpretative literary studies. It is the writers and not their writing which primarily interest Sartre. At the same time, it is his intention to show that the man whose inward life is so carefully analyzed could—being what he was—have written only the literature which he did write; and to this extent it is the literature as well as the author which is interpreted.

On the first page of *Baudelaire* Sartre makes it clear that he has a thesis to prove. He begins,

> "He did not have the life which he deserved." Baudelaire's life seems to offer a magnificent illustration of this reassuring cliché. He certainly did not deserve that mother, that continual lack of money, that family council, that grasping mistress, nor that syphilis—and what could be more unjust than his premature end? Yet if we reflect on it, a doubt arises.

As doubt becomes conviction, Sartre attempts to show that Baudelaire had precisely the life which he chose to have. After more than two hundred pages of investigation he concludes, "The free choice which man makes of himself is absolutely identical with what is generally called his destiny." *Quod erat demonstrandum.* But the traditional biographies of Baudelaire offered to Sartre a more serious challenge than that implied in the vague assumption of an unjust Fate. To anyone steeped in Freudian psychology, Baudelaire appears to be an almost classic illustration of the Oedipus complex. His intensely emotional love of his mother and utter dependency upon her, his violent hatred of his stepfather, his ambivalent attitude of love and jealousy toward his own dead father—all these may be seen as causal factors to explain suspicions of Baudelaire's impotence, his need to protect his ideal loves from sex and to take refuge in debauchery, his sado-masochistic tendencies, his homosexual fantasies (if not actual experiences). All of these attitudes are expressed in only slightly disguised form in the poetry, which one may easily interpret as the sublimation of the incestuous desires, the immortal substitute for the child which Baudelaire did not beget by his mother. Sartre does not deny that Baudelaire secretly desired his mother, but he argues that the peculiar relation which Baudelaire insisted on maintaining with her, like every other of his relations and attitudes, can be best explained not as the result of an unresolved Oedipus complex but as the consequence of what Sartre calls a "theological complex which makes parents into deities."

The decisive incident of Baudelaire's life was the remarriage of his mother within two years after his father's death when Baudelaire was only seven. Baudelaire never recovered from the shock of it and took it as a personal affront. " 'When one has a son like me'—*like me* was understood—'one does not remarry' " (p. 19). In Sartre's view this crucial event meant more to Baudelaire than a sense of personal rejection accompanied by sexual frustration and jealousy. It coincided with and induced his first awareness of himself as a separate person. Until then he had seemed to himself little more than an emanation of his mother's divine personality; in her, existence was, so to speak, dissolved in the Absolute and *justified*. Now suddenly he was abandoned, and with a feeling that he had somehow fallen from grace, he realized that he existed alone and "for nothing." Self-discovery came unaccompanied by any sense of inner powers; it was no vision of self-fulfillment; it was pure exile and solitude. According to Sartre, Baudelaire chose to regard this first shock as an unjust affliction put upon a child too young to bear it, a blow which inevitably distorted the development of his life as surely as the twisting of a young tree. Thus it was both a grievance and an indication of a fatal flaw in his character. As Baudelaire created what was to be for him the meaning of his mother's remarriage, he thereby made that fundamental choice of Being which, Sartre claims, increased in complexity but never basically changed throughout his lifetime.

It was a choice which carried a discrepancy at its heart; the same psychic event produced in Baudelaire both hostility toward others and a fearful self-pity; upon the one he erected a freely created Self-for-others, out of the other he tried to form an absolute Being which he had to be—inescapably—for himself. Resentment at being thrust out of the incestuous Paradise made him react with rage and pride. He determined to make it seem that he himself was responsible for this otherness which had been so prematurely thrust upon him. He would convince the world and especially his mother that he willed to be this separate self, that his solitude was a mark of distinction. For the boy of seven the sense that he was "different" was not accompanied by anything positive to indicate his unique virtue. As Sartre says, the white blackbird who is rejected by the other blackbirds can comfort himself by looking at the whiteness of his wings. But "men are never white blackbirds." Looking into himself for a discernible guarantee of uniqueness, Baudelaire found for his contemplation only a pure self-consciousness. Like Narcissus he hung over his own image, watching himself and watching himself watch himself— but a Narcissus without love and forever frustrated. In first experiencing himself as a separate person, Baudelaire faced the fact that he was a free being. If he had been willing to accept himself as such—either when he was a child or later—his rage at his mother's remarriage would have been dissipated. But holding her responsible for the terror and dismay with which he "so prematurely" confronted his freedom, he chose to keep his resentment at all cost. In order to do this, he had in some way to deny his freedom, for he must convince himself and her that her act had branded a scar upon his very being. Thus the Being which he tried to grasp in himself—the Being that he *was*—was a Being marked with a deep and secret flaw. Naturally Baudelaire could not, any more than anyone else, ever pin down this Self and examine it. To do so he would have had to be simultaneously two different people. But this, Sartre maintains, is exactly what he tried to achieve. "Baudelaire is the man who chose to see himself as if he were another person; his life is simply the story of his failure" (p. 31). As we saw in the case of Daniel, self-punishment seems the clearest path to self-coincidence, and the theme of the self-tormentor is constant in *Flowers of Evil*. In the poem called "Heautontimoroumenos," Baudelaire writes,

> I am the wound and the knife!
> I am the blow and the cheek it strikes!
> I am the rack and the limbs it tears,
> Victim and executioner.

Unable to see his reflection in the moving water, Narcissus paints the image which he wants others to see, but never gives up hope of seeing this same image suddenly appear before him of its own accord in some new silent pool.

The result of Baudelaire's effort to find in himself an absolute Self was that he conceived of his life as a destiny. Because in his own mind this destiny was so closely allied with doom, he chose, Sartre says, "to live his life backwards." By the time he was twenty-five (he died at forty-six) Baudelaire had written most of his poems; his later creative work consisted largely in revising earlier poems, doing a few translations and a little critical writing, and launching never-to-be-completed projects which he had already outlined in his youth. The patterns of personal failure were firmly set: he had "established the definitive pattern for his relations with his parents, contracted the venereal disease with which he would slowly rot away, met the woman who would weigh like lead upon every hour of his life, and taken the one trip which was going to provide exotic images for his entire work" (p. 189). From this time on, Baudelaire did not change; he merely grew older and more depressed; his last years were a process of slow dissolution. His resignation to his own slow decay was reflected in his social attitudes. For him all the good things were in the past; present and future were corrupt and doomed to catastrophe. He was somewhat excited by the Revolution of 1848, but even there his chief hope was apparently that the revolutionists would set fire to the home of General Aupick, the stepfather he so hated.

The important problem for us, however, is not why Baudelaire failed to develop further as a poet or to write more poems. What is more significant is Sartre's attempt to explain the peculiar quality of the poems which Baudelaire did write. In his poetry as in his life, Sartre says, Baudelaire chose to celebrate evil for its own sake. The final title, *Flowers of Evil,* is exactly appropriate, and from their own point of view the judges who condemned the book were right in doing so. Sartre makes short shrift of Baudelaire's feeble public defenses—that his intention had been to describe vice in such a way that the reader would be horrified by it; or that the principle of art for art's sake gave the poet the right to imagine evil passions and to describe them without thereby either experiencing or condoning them. Instead, Sartre quotes as conclusive evidence a letter from Baudelaire to his publisher in which he says that no matter what lies he may continue to give the public, he has put into his book "all *my heart,* all my *tenderness,* all my *religion* (travestied), all my hate." The poems are flowers of evil in that their creator has deliberately set out to show all the seductive beauty of vice, to reveal a hidden loveliness where bourgeois morality tries to see only ugly depravity. But the rebellion is stopped midway. Baudelaire has not tried to say that what is generally considered evil is not really evil. On the contrary, he makes it clear that for him beauty and pleasure can exist only when they are supported by an accompanying awareness that they spring from evil. Their source is the recognition that evil is there and embraced. "The unique and supreme pleasure of love lies in the certainty that what one is doing is *evil.* Man and woman alike know from birth that evil is the source of all pleasure" (p. 86). To will evil for its own sake is an irrational attitude and one which demands a measure of bad faith; for it means that by recognizing certain things as good (hence desirable) and simultaneously choosing their opposite, one is deliberately willing what one does not want. If a person is to maintain this position, it will inevitably be because the holding of it enables him to fulfill certain contradictory inner demands. For Baudelaire, it enabled him to satisfy his hostility toward those who he thought had wronged him, and at the same time it allowed him to remain utterly dependent. In his poems he was fond of identifying himself with Satan—the perfect image, Sartre points out, of the sulky, rebellious child.

For the existentialist, the greatest creative act of a person's life is the creation of his own Good; that is, the invention of a system of values by which he gives his life form and meaning. According to Sartre, Baudelaire refused to make any attempt at arriving at standards which would be intellectually acceptable to himself; and by a Freudian-style sublimation he made his poems "the substitutes for the creation of the Good which he had forbidden himself to make." Preferring to be condemned by standards he could not or would not live by, rather than to develop a moral code which really satisfied him, Baudelaire inevitably suffered from a constant feeling of guilt. The feeling was certainly real and so intense that some critics have wondered if he were not after all guilty of some crime. But the most painstaking research has not uncovered the least suggestion of anything criminal. Others have tried to explain the guilty conscience as the result of his strict Catholic upbringing. While not denying that this influence is there, Sartre points out that any number of writers (Gide is an outstanding example) have made their rejection of childhood training a point of departure for working out a more acceptable ethical system. Baudelaire forced his mother into the position of being his judge, tried to do the same with some of his friends. He never questioned the validity of their judgements, though this did not mean that he ever made any real attempt to reform; he even commended the judges who condemned his book. In all of this, of course, he was flouting his disobedience and rebellion against those who stood as the champions of the Good. By simultaneously acknowledging the correctness of their code, he was achieving several psychological consolations. His revolt was paradoxically ennobled, for if he accepted the enemy's judgement, he had more at stake by going contrary to it. It also provided him with an escape from his own freedom and was consistent with his belief that his childhood "fall" had bestowed upon him an absolute and corrupted Being. Finally, his very guilt carried with it a secret hope of absolution. If without God everything is allowed, it follows as a corollary that with God some things are forbidden but anything may be pardoned. As a result of his "theological complex" (which is just another name for his first choice of Being), Baudelaire insisted on treating his parents as gods or idols; since all rules stemmed from them, he could hope that their love or compassion would forgive the erring child and receive him once more into the fold. He added another safeguard. Much of his suffering was really unnecessary. Financial troubles he certainly could have avoided (his patrimony was modest but adequate), he seems on the whole to have enjoyed the torments of his unhappy love affairs; even the venereal disease was hardly inevitable save as the predictable end of his deliberate debauchery. But by his afflictions Baudelaire could convince himself that he was already doing penance; more important, by viewing them as the result of the "flaw" which his judges had originally inflicted upon his character, he could see his torments as being in the deeper sense undeserved. Thus his suffering was a reproach to his mother and the General, and at the same time it undermined their authority by reminding both them and Baudelaire that they had themselves been guilty of injustice.

In so far as Baudelaire had any real belief in religion, Sartre claims that it was merely a projection of his parental relations. God was the stern Judge of the Old Testament, an image of General Aupick with the whip. (The comparison with Freud's concept of God as a projected superego is obvious.) Once again there was secret hope of absolution—if indeed Baudelaire actually believed in eternal punishment, which Sartre doubts. Although not denying that Baudelaire wavered between a dramatically asserted atheism and short-lasting conversions (both of them typical of his reactions in all moral questions where his parents' beliefs were concerned), Sartre doubts the truth, or at least the sincerity, of the death-bed repentance of which Catholic critics have made so much. Naturally it was helpful to Baudelaire to postulate an absolute Being as support for the absoluteness which he sought in his parents and in himself, and we find him engaged in a timid form of Pascal's wager.

> *Calculation in favor of God:* Nothing exists without a purpose. Therefore my existence has a purpose. What purpose? This I do not know. Therefore it is not I who have determined it.

> Therefore it is someone wiser than I am. Therefore I must
> pray to this someone to enlighten me. This is the wisest course
> (p. 68).

Here is the procedure which we have met before—assuming an externally established purpose in order to free oneself from the necessity of choosing one. At other times Baudelaire seems to have recognized that his God was only a psychic projection of himself. "Even if God did not exist," he said, "religion would still be sacred and divine. God is the only being who does not even need to exist in order to reign" (p. 67). The letter which seems to Sartre most clearly to cast doubt on the probability of Baudelaire's final conversion is one which Baudelaire wrote to his publisher three years before his death. In it he said,

> I shall explain patiently all the reasons for my disgust with
> the human race. When I am *absolutely alone,* I shall seek a
> religion . . . and at the moment of death I shall abjure this re-
> ligion to demonstrate my disgust with the universal stupidity.
> You see that I have not changed (p. 66).

The *Flowers of Evil* have a derived existence. Like Nothingness, which is utterly void of Being and yet which—like a shadow—cannot exist without it, Evil as such can be embraced only if one maintains a constant sidelong glance at the Good.

Furthermore, the Flowers are *artificial.* This is not merely to say that Baudelaire's poetry is a studied, carefully perfected art rather than spontaneous lyricism. In content as well as in form there is revealed a dislike of what is simple and natural. For Baudelaire, Sartre states, creativity is the very opposite of parturition; beauty, whether in art or in women, is never truth or nature unadorned. It is infecund, highly wrought, richly clothed, luxuriously useless. Sartre connects this artificiality with Baudelaire's perpetual pursuit of what he wanted to think was his inner Self. The man who spent his life convincing himself he *was* the carefully composed Self which he prepared for the eyes of others could not afford to relax and be natural. For him the idea of being himself by means of forgetting himself was dangerous in that it suggested the freedom from which he wished to escape. Especially in his love affairs and in the poetry inspired by them we can detect Baudelaire holding himself back. It is well known that Baudelaire's relations with women were of two distinct kinds. On the one hand, he found it necessary to bestow an exaggerated love and devotion upon women whom he idealized until they were worthy of him and who were at the same time inaccessible because of their already loving someone else. These he adored because of their very frigidity (to him), and his passion was hopeless because he willed it so. That he was impotent, at least with these women, is very probable. But throughout his life he frequented prostitutes, and his poems reveal that with them Baudelaire took a peculiar pleasure in ugliness, filth, and disease. Moreover, what most deeply satisfied him was to experience simultaneously the satisfactions of both kinds of relationships. When sporting with the prostitute, he kept before his eyes the image of the beloved ideal. He himself explained it—"A debauch with other women makes the mistress more dear. What she loses in sensual enjoyment she gains in adoration. The awareness that he needs forgiveness makes a man more eager to please" (p. 142). Sartre points out that Baudelaire himself could hardly have explained whether this habit of making the sexual act an experience *à trois* was for the purpose of increasing the pleasures he enjoyed with the harlots or whether his relations with them were simply to enable him to establish imaginary contact with the Angel. At any rate, two needs were satisfied. By thinking of her at the moment of sexual contact with another, Baudelaire caused the idealized Beloved to be besmirched and flouted in the same way that his mother and all other representatives of the Good were attacked by his misconduct. But perhaps more important, by imagining that the pure, chaste Judge was looking at him, Baudelaire seemed to be watching himself as he pursued his own pleasure. "She was like those mirrors which certain men of refinement use so that they may behold their pleasures reflected. She allowed him to see himself while he was making love" (p. 143).

It is in this connection that we can see most clearly the difference between Sartre's interpretation and the Freudian one. Almost any traditional analyst would see in Baudelaire's forbidden "good women" projected symbols of his mother. His desire for them and his sexual fiasco with them would be obvious repetitions of the original incestuous impulse and its repression. By this view, Baudelaire might enjoy more success with prostitutes who, because of their degraded position, would no longer be identified with the mother. Yet the presence of the mother-image in Baudelaire's mind would nevertheless allow for a more acceptable symbolic satisfaction of his desire for her. At the same time, the actual relations with prostitutes would be a violation of the child's "pure" love of his mother, and the whole business of sex would inevitably appear dirty and disgusting on the conscious level.

Anthony West in a review of a biography of Baudelaire points out that Baudelaire's fetishism accompanies and supports the hypothesis of an unresolved Oedipus complex.

> One of the great events in the sensuous life of a small child in the servanted, prosperous, middle-class house of the period of Baudelaire's childhood was the transformation of the familiar daytime mother into the elaborately made-up, scented, bare-shouldered, jewelled, and grandly dressed woman who came glittering into the nursery to say good night before vanishing to a dinner party downstairs, or, more excitingly, into a world of unknown pleasures in the lamp-studded darkness beyond the zone of the child's knowledge and experience. In Baudelaire's case, this recurrent excitement created a fixation on an ideal woman whom he could worship, fondle, and admire while she went through charades of dressing up but whom he could never possess.[1]

Whereas this Freudian interpretation explains Baudelaire's adult sexuality as deriving from and repeating the pattern of his infantile attachment to his mother, Sartre seeks to go back further and to show that Baudelaire's incestuous desire (both in childhood and in its all but acknowledged adult manifestation) and his relations with women other than his mother are all to be explained by a more fundamental choice of Being. Sartre argues that it was not Baudelaire's desire for his mother that made him seek out women who would exert a maternal authority upon him; it was rather that his need for authority led him to turn all women (including his mother) into judges. In the most fundamental sense Baudelaire's sexuality was not incestuous but onanist. In the same way that he needed an absolute set of standards to guarantee the nature of his revolt against them, so in his sexual life as elsewhere he required a background of artificiality and frigidity in order that he might at no moment lose sight of the Self he was so carefully creating (while at the same time convinced that it was bestowed upon him). It is in this way that Sartre explains the fetishism as being but one aspect of Baudelaire's peculiar, refined *volupté*. To be excited by women only when their beauty was elaborately clothed, bejewelled, and perfumed seemed to him—because it was more self-conscious—a more subtle and more highly developed sensuality than abandonment to naked female flesh. Similarly, sexual intercourse was vulgar and paltry beside the delicate delights of sensory contemplation. Sartre is probably right in suggesting that because Baudelaire refused to let himself go, he could never achieve the pleasure of complete sexual satisfaction in coitus and therefore made the nonsatisfied state of desire the most exquisite pleasure.

Preoccupation with the external stimulants to desire rather than with its fulfillment is reflected throughout Baudelaire's poems and stories. But in an early play, *The Drunkard (L'Ivrogne)*, there is a suggestion of something more serious. The play concerns a brutal husband who secretly hates his wife for her very goodness but who nevertheless insists on begging her to forgive him and to return to him. The scene takes place at a country crossroads. The husband is roused to violent desire by the visible signs of his wife's suffering and seeks to possess her on the spot. Maddened by her refusal, he sends her on to her death by giving her directions which will almost surely lead her to stumble into a well. Sartre suggests that even in this form the death is a symbol for the rape which Baudelaire really intended, the symbolic defilement of the beloved "good woman." Originally, however, Baudelaire had in mind something still stronger; the husband would kill the wife and *then* feel the sudden desire to violate her. Here, says Sartre, we see the real meaning of Baudelaire's *volupté*.

> Thus frigidity, which begins as a sterilization by coldness, finds at last its true climate, which is death. . . . Absence of life or destruction of life: these are the two extreme limits of the Baudelaire mind [*esprit*] (pp. 152-153).

The belief that one possesses and can contemplate a Self that is already fully finished comes perilously close to killing the Self that is alive.

Sartre claims that Baudelaire's attempt to find in himself the object-Self which he was for others resulted in a perpetual struggle against all that suggested giving in to natural impulse. This conflict was manifested in more than his moral life and sexuality. In his dress, in every taste and preference, in all the details of his daily living Baudelaire "wanted to be his own poem to himself." Take, for example, the famous dandyism. In part this was an expression of snobbism. Since the aristocracy of wealth or social position was closed to him, he sought visible signs of belonging to the eternal fellowship of immortal artists. But more than this, he was protecting himself from the Look of others by making them concentrate on the Self which he had designed for them. He would be observed and judged only on his own terms. Furthermore, it seemed in the mirror that he caught himself as he had composed himself. Thus the external dandy defended the real body from the gaze of strangers exactly as the Self which Baudelaire had invented for his own contem-

plation hid from him—at least in part—the freedom which he really was.
Sartre connects his dandyism with Baudelaire's habit of deliberately
circulating false scandals about himself. "A paederast, an informer, an
eater of children, and what have you. But while the gossips tore to pieces
the fictitious character, the real one remained sheltered" (p. 175). Some
biographers have taken the charge of homosexuality seriously, but have
never been able to prove that it was justified. Sartre, in view of the lack
of evidence, rejects it and feels that at most Baudelaire may have liked
to imagine that he was homosexual, and deliberately tried to give the
impression that he was so. But while the idea of being passive before
the desire of the male may have appealed to him, the type of object he
was making of himself demanded too much constant self-contemplation
for Baudelaire to risk letting another *treat* him as an object. "What the
myth of dandyism conceals is not homosexuality but exhibitionism" (p.
178).

While Sartre makes less use of the imagery of the poems than one
might wish, what he does say is illuminating and always consistent with
his basic interpretation. Take for example the image developed in *The
Giantess.*

> In Nature's spring when her creative powers
> Conceived strange progeny no man has seen,
> I should have loved to live voluptuous hours,
> A cat at the feet of some young giant queen!

Baudelaire's wish here, Sartre says, is one more manifestation of his
desire to be sustained in existence by the Other's Look.

> To draw to himself the Look of a giantess, through her eyes
> to see himself as a domestic animal, to lead the nonchalant,
> voluptuous, and perverse existence of a cat in an aristocratic
> society where giants, men-gods, decided for him and without
> him the meaning of the universe and the ultimate ends of his
> own life—such was his dearest wish. He wanted to enjoy the
> limited independence of a *bête de luxe,* idle and useless, whose
> games are protected by the seriousness of its masters (p. 64).

Sartre goes on to say that there is a strain of masochism in this revery,
and indeed Baudelaire's need to be consecrated as an object by his
Judges was in itself masochistic. Sartre admits that this dependency is
also comparable to that of the child. But where the Freudian would
attribute this infantile longing to childhood trauma and arrested sexual-

ity, Sartre claims that for Baudelaire infantile dependency symbolized the dream of being wholly enveloped by the Look which guaranteed protection against the terrors of individual freedom.

With regard to Baudelaire's more general use of images drawn from nature, Sartre develops along his own lines a view already suggested by an earlier critic. Georges Blin had said of Baudelaire that he "feared nature as a reservoir of splendor and fecundity and substituted for it the world of his imagination: a metallic universe, coldly sterile and luminous" (p. 124). Sartre says that Baudelaire's love for images which he derived from light, metals, and minerals is due to the fact that for him these things symbolized the cold, reflective intellect, which constituted the only life he valued. His own evil thoughts he seemed to see projected and objectified in "foul beasts," but his thought in general was exactly represented by steel, "the metal which is the most brilliant, the most polished, and the hardest to get a grip on." He loved the sea, says Sartre, because it is "a mobile mineral." Its brilliant, cold inaccessibility, its quick change of form combined with complete transparency offered an exquisitely precise symbol of the intelligence. "Thus by his hatred of life Baudelaire was led to choose from pure materialization his symbols of the immaterial" (p. 125). On the other hand, there are times when Baudelaire's attitude toward nature is vaguely mystic, as though everything in the world were permeated with a meaning pointing to some Beyond. And at such times Baudelaire seems to feel that the significant essence of an object hovers over it like an aura. "The words 'perfume,' 'thought,' and 'secret' are almost synonymous" (p. 205). Sartre explains these images as symbolic of Baudelaire's longing to grasp his own elusive existence as if it were a thing caught in the hollow of his hand. Far-off music, perfumes, subdued lights, the "secrets" of objects were like little given consciousnesses which he reached toward as toward his own incarnate thoughts. In addition, Sartre claims, Baudelaire disliked being pinned down to the brute reality of the natural. By making the world's meanings the important thing, he seemed to recreate the world, to make it over in his own image and so find himself within it. Sartre denies that there is in all this any genuine Platonism or even a serious acceptance of Swedenborgian mysticism, though admittedly Baudelaire borrowed from Swedenborg the idea of some mysterious "correspondence" between objects in the world and something higher. In so far as Baudelaire embraced any philosophical system, it was neither idealism nor mysticism which he chose; it was rather the work of Joseph de Maistre. But it was not a world of mystic meanings which Baudelaire sought in him. What satisfied in de Maistre's work was the assurance of a structured social and natural hierarchy and an absolute conservative politics. Baudelaire here glimpsed a Good so transcendent that even evil might be done in its name as "men with whips would make themselves its guardians." As with all who accept the doctrine of a natural caste system, Baudelaire saw himself among the elite. It is no wonder that he was also anti-Semitic.

Sartre's analysis is far more extended and detailed than I have been able to show here. At the end of it Sartre apologizes for the fact that his picture of Baudelaire must be made up of successive descriptions rather than offering the simultaneous revelation which a portrait would furnish. Then he makes a statement which is much more akin to romanticism, or at least to the more irrational branch of existentialism, than Sartre's work usually is. If we could but see Baudelaire for a moment, he says, these scattered observations would suddenly be unified as a total knowing acquaintance (*connaissance*). Sartre, like Heidegger, believes that we have a "pre-ontological" comprehension of a person so that we immediately sense what the person is, though it may take years for us to transform this vague awareness into explicit understanding. This view is, I think, an overoptimistic reliance on the validity of first impressions. If, however, we could suddenly see Baudelaire after reading Sartre's essay, then—assuming Sartre's interpretation is correct—we probably would feel that the "futile, arid, exasperated tension" which constituted the inner climate of Baudelaire's life was revealed in his dress, his mannerisms, "the dry cutting quality of his voice, the cold nervousness of his gestures"—the whole indicating a man who hated and distrusted the nature that was outside him and who held himself back at every moment in order that he might find only the "given" self which he had himself carefully created.

In evaluating this biographical study, we may consider it from two points of view. First, is it consistent with Sartre's requirements for such analysis as he has presented them in "Existential Psychoanalysis"? The answer here is clearly affirmative. Sartre has certainly presented a unified interpretation, viewing all of Baudelaire's life and achievements as a set of symbolic structures crystallized about the crucial event of childhood and the choice of Being which was Baudelaire's reaction to it. Every one of Baudelaire's attitudes, habits, acts, the themes and style of his poetry—all are taken as revealing. The study of imagery is done along the lines of the suggested "psychoanalysis of things." The biography utilizes all available evidence—Baudelaire's own statements, his creative writing, the testimony of his contemporaries—but treats no one source as especially privileged. Throughout the essay Sartre is careful never to take recourse to any unconscious, and he postulates the fact of Baudelaire's freedom both in making the original choice and in refusing to revoke it.

But if we forget the matter of Sartre's consistency and simply ask whether the biographical study is true, what then? Naturally no absolute answer is possible, and I suppose that ultimately we are thrown back on the question of which psychological position we decide is valid. If one believes that man is free and wholly conscious (though not always reflectively so), then the superiority of this study to the Freudian interpretation is obvious. If one does not, then the deterministic view possesses a certain neatness and finality. It seems to me that we really must accept one or the other. Any attempt to see Baudelaire as a man who in no way deserved or was responsible for any of his misfortunes is nonsense. The self-deception, the snobbism, the desires to give pain to those close to him, to rebel and yet to be assured of forgiveness are there and cannot be denied. Nor is it an adequate explanation to say that Baudelaire was a poor wanderer from the Faith who was tormented by his apostasy and who finally ended his life's search in a death-bed victory. The strongest argument in favor of Sartre's portrait is, I think, the fact that the Baudelaire who emerges is a total personality whose creative, social, and private lives are fundamentally consistent with one another in spite of superficial discrepancies.

Reviewers of the book (many of whom were willing to accept Sartre's interpretation of the *person* Baudelaire) have generally criticized it for not throwing light on Baudelaire the *poet*. To an extent the objection is justified. Sartre has at no time revealed any real love for poetry on his own part, and he has not tried to explain either Baudelaire's creative process or the beauty of the poems as they stand. On the other hand, he has certainly offered explanations for the themes, the style, and the images which we find in the poems. And he has sought to show why Baudelaire chose deliberately to limit the scope of his work and to leave much of it incomplete. The Sartrean interpretation is weakest exactly where the Freudian falls down. Why did Baudelaire choose poetry as the substitute for the libidinal-Oepidal satisfaction (Freud) or for the creation of his own value system (Sartre), and how was he able to create it so magnificently? Why was he not a famous lawyer or an unsuccessful poet? The Freudian theory offers no explanation. Sartre partially explains the choice of poetry in that it was a way by which

Baudelaire might remake the world of nature on a more satisfactory imaginative level. But since Sartre explicitly denies the existence of any such thing as "genius," we are left with the weak conclusion that either Baudelaire had simply a stronger-than-average need for imaginative creation or that his physiological "givens"—sense of rhythm, tonal sensitivity, etc.—were better developed. One thing Sartre does explain: that is, how Baudelaire's sense of "destiny" could both inspire in him the will to prove himself a great poet and yet limit his potentialities and bring about early destruction. For his initial choice of Being demanded precisely this—that he assert his distinctive, self-created uniqueness and yet prove to the world and himself that the injustice of others had branded upon him a flaw which made his failures and early decline inevitable.

In *The Roads to Freedom,* which Sartre was in the midst of writing when he did the *Baudelaire,* there is a character modeled after Baudelaire. This is Philippe, the young man whom Daniel desires to make his lover and fellow-collaborator.[2] It is easy to point out similarities between Baudelaire and Philippe. The backgrounds are similar; each has a stepfather who is a general; each loves his mother with an overintense emotion which is equalled in strength only by the jealous hatred of the man to whom she has given herself; both are self-tormentors; both feel that all the Good of the world is represented by their parents and that the only role left to themselves is defiance and a futile rebellion; both seek to escape their freedom in forms of bad faith. The interesting fact about this parallel, however, is that upon the ground of this similarity Sartre has woven an entirely different life history. Philippe is not a poet but a pacifist. His rebellion takes the form of flight when he is likely to be mobilized, a flight which is insincere; for when Philippe carelessly misses a train, he makes of the occasion a sign that he was not meant to go and returns to Paris. There he deliberately and foolishly attracts attention to himself by shouting in the street against the war, obviously because what he really wants is to be arrested, returned to the General, and punished. When war breaks out, he goes with the army but deserts when France collapses and he is in danger of being taken prisoner. When Daniel finds him, he is on the verge of committing suicide because he cannot bear the realization that he is a coward; but it soon becomes apparent that the suicide would never actually have come off. As we see him for the last time, Philippe appears ready to listen to Daniel's suggestion that it would be good to watch the Germans humiliate the General (cf. Baudelaire's wish that the Revolutionists of 1848 would set fire to General Aupick's house), and he seems to be drifting into a homosexual relation with Daniel, though his sulky narcissism and bore-dom make it unlikely that he will make any more real self-commitment in sensuality than he had made in politics.

One passage is particularly interesting. Philippe has just expressed to Daniel his hatred of the General.

> "I have an Oedipus complex," he went on. "The regular case-book type."
>
> "Is it your mother you're in love with?" Daniel asked with incredulity.
>
> Philippe made no reply. He had the self-important air of a victim of destiny.
>
> Daniel leaned forward. "Isn't it more likely you're in love with your stepfather?" he asked quietly.[3]

Daniel goes on to explain his theory, but Philippe rejects it with genuine derision. Here Sartre is undoubtedly having a bit of fun on his own. In his essay he had referred with an air of incredulity to the fact that some biographers have actually said that Baudelaire was in love with the General. Now he deliberately puts the suggestion in the mind of the perverted Daniel. But the passage—like the total picture of Philippe —is especially significant in that it illustrates another of Sartre's basic principles—that the abstract choice of Being becomes unique as well as concrete when it is lived by the chooser *in situation*. Philippe is not Baudelaire, for the world in which he lives is not Baudelaire's world. Where Baudelaire justified his conduct as the result of a metaphysical flaw and personal injustice, Philippe has ready at hand a reassuring psychological theory. Pacifism and collaboration are more obvious choices than poetry in France of the 1930's and '40's. Circumstances of Philippe's individual history make homosexuality more convenient than orgies with prostitutes. But in each case the choice itself was free, and so were the specific acts by which each man chose to manifest it.

In spite of Sartre's constant insistence that man is free, we might well wonder whether his *Baudelaire* does not after all illustrate Freud's con-cept of repetition compulsion. Granting that the initial choice was free, the fact remains that what Sartre shows us is a Baudelaire who deter-mined every one of his later acts in accordance with his early childhood reaction. Fortunately we have *Saint Genet, Martyr-Comedian* to demonstrate that even while the first crucial event remains central through a lifetime, the individual is free to modify his response. Sartre states explicitly that he is undertaking more than an interpretation of Genet's life and works. His purpose is

> To show the limitations of the psychoanalytical interpretation and of the Marxist explanation and to demonstrate that only freedom can account for a person in his totality, to let us see this freedom grappling with destiny, at first crushed by its fatalities, then turning back upon them in order that gradually it might direct them, to prove that genius is not a gift but the solution which is invented in desperate circumstances, to recover the choice which a writer has made of himself, of his life, and of the meaning of the universe—a choice which he reveals even in the formal characteristics of his style and composition, in the structure of his imagery, and in his own particular tastes—to retrace in detail the story of a liberation (p. 536).

To discuss fully Sartre's analysis of Genet's development is impossible, short of devoting a volume to this subject alone. The biography is, at least to me, the least satisfactory of Sartre's work from a literary point of view. There are some passages of a poetic beauty unlike anything in his other books, but they are not enough to redeem the unnecessary repetitions and the hundreds of pages of abstract and unclear philosophizing which are only slightly connected with Genet. Out of this morass we may profitably select for discussion Genet's original choice of Being, the various ways in which he tried to live this choice, his self-effected conversion and cure, and examples of Sartre's interpretation of the symbolic structures involved.

The crucial event of Genet's life was that moment at which the child was caught stealing, saw the finger of judgement pointed at him, and heard the words, "You are a thief." [4] The episode would not have been critical had Genet's situation been that of the average child. But as the illegitimate son of unidentified parents, he had first been made a State orphan and then given to peasants for adoption. Thus he could not take his position in the family for granted. It seemed to him that his very existence must be paid for by a burden of gratitude as heavy as the weight of original sin, and he felt that as a bastard he was an outcast, a stain upon the respectable community in which he lived. Sartre's interpretation of the decisive incident is basically this: "Society for reasons

of social utility took a child and made him a monster"; the child, feeling
that lawful existence was denied him, reacted by making of his life a
drama (the comedian *) and a sacred ritual of myth (the saint and
witness). It is Sartre's view that most of the suffering and crime in
society is caused by the fact that we have split good and evil into two
absolute categories. We judge acts and principles as absolute, we look
on the mores of society and the safeguards set up to preserve them as
sacred, and we tend to regard all those who do not fit within the fold as
*being* and *willing* Evil. Therefore the respectable people *(les justes)* and
the scum are divided by a cleavage comparable to the color line. *Les
justes* in particular dare not cross it even in their imagination, for to
sympathize and understand would be to acknowledge in themselves a
capacity for the evil which they have projected upon the unfortunates.

Genet's first reaction to the crucial event reminds one of Baudelaire's
original choice: he resolved to embrace and make himself responsible
for the alienation which had been thrust upon him, to *will* to *be* a thief.
In discussing this decision—as on many occasions in the book—Sartre
chooses passages from Genet's writing to show how a symbolic act reveals the significance of the original choice which governs it. In *Pompes
funèbres,* an elegiac novel commemorating a childhood friend who died
early, Genet speaks of the time when the boy accidentally put a maggot
into his mouth.

> He found himself caught between fainting from disgust and
> mastering the situation by willing it. He willed it. He forced his
> tongue and his palate to savor the hideous contact—deliber-
> ately, patiently. This will was his first attitude as a poet deter-
> mined by his pride. He was ten years old.[5]

Even though the boy in question is not Genet himself, Sartre is almost
certainly correct in saying that the attitude revealed is that of the child
Genet confronting the judgement which condemned him as a thief.

It is Sartre's claim (confirmed by Genet) that while Genet sometimes
stole out of need, the act of theft was primarily a symbolic ritual. In
part, it was a re-enactment of the original passion (the crucial event); in
part it was that he felt he had no lawful Being which belonged to him and
that he must steal his existence. In this sense theft was a creative act. He
stole in order to make himself a thief. A particularly illuminating episode

---

* It is important to note that in French the word *comédien* is not associated
exclusively with comedy but may also be used in the neutral sense of the English
"actor."

occurred when Genet as a young man was in a prison in Yugoslavia. His fellow prisoners started a game in which they tried to pick the pocket of a prisoner who was sleeping. By gestures they invited Genet to participate. He made the attempt and fainted before he could carry through. Genet himself refers to the moment as "supernatural." In a flash of illumination he saw that the prison cell was but a miniature image of the prison of the world where he was sent into exile far from the human sphere of his fellow prisoners. Sartre adds further explanation. Since the theft was to be a fictitious one performed beneath the gaze of others, and because the language barrier separated Genet from the other prisoners, the scene was a symbolic repetition of the original crisis when the child was caught stealing by adults with whom he could not communicate. In part, his reactions now are repetitions. By showing himself unable to perform the act, he chooses failure and rejection rather than successful integration in a society which condemned him to a humiliated position. But there is also something new. The original event was, in fact, the occasion of the death of the child Genet was and the man he might have been; the child Genet who lived on felt strongly the wish that he might wholly die. In the symbolic drama in the Yugoslav prison Genet can fulfill the wish which had almost destroyed him. In real life, of course, he had chosen, despite all, "to live the impossibility of living."

Sartre claims that Genet's later choice of himself as a passive homosexual was a natural consequence of his decision to *be* a thief. I cannot myself quite accept Sartre's idea that Genet became a homosexual because his discovery as a thief had come "as a surprise from behind" and seemed to him a violation. It is easy, however, to see both resolves as manifestations of that mixture of pride and resignation with which Genet determined to embrace the role of outcast which society thrust upon him. In his relations with "the toughs" *(les durs),* he sought both to lose himself and to find himself. On the one hand, his adored masters served as a kind of protection for him; their commands were absolute and fixed the day-to-day pattern of his life. To some extent submission seemed to give him a Being which others determined. But this form of self-evasion was only a minor aspect of his orientation. Its over-all significance is revealed in a pattern which is a variation on that which we have met in Daniel and again in Baudelaire. The "vertiginous word" of judgement had estranged Genet from himself as well as from society. In order to find himself, he must somehow feel that he *was* this object which others had condemned. As Sartre puts it, he was a Narcissus whose image had been stolen and who sought to find it again in the eyes of others. As the feminine partner he became a passive object; by watching another possess him, he seemed to possess himself. Pride and humiliation were curiously intermingled. Generally, the males of Genet's circle despised the homosexuals who took the female role, and Genet was careful to love where there was no hope of return. But there was more here than simple masochism. Sartre tries to show that for Genet the sexual act was a sacred ceremony which, while admittedly a travesty of the usual religious experience, nevertheless was heavy with mystic meaning. Instead of being raised to communion with the Good, Genet was transformed into "a contemptible female object," a mere instrument for another's use and pleasure. The moment symbolized not redemption but the original fall; even communion with his fellow men was lost and alienation intensified. Evil was there in a Presence just as real as that of Grace for the communicant believer. It was the instant at which Genet once again emerged triumphant from the conflict with his will, determined to keep himself in permanent opposition to the "good" society which had conferred upon him his Being as evil. The determination was all the more firm because it was forever accompanied by a secret longing to be accepted by this same society which had rejected him.

> Thus the sexual act which conferred upon Genet his destiny as a "prat boy" was a renewal of the crisis which had transformed him into a thief; in each case a child was pinned to the ground by the Look of strong, cruel men. But this time the crisis was provoked, consented to, and, just as in pschoanalytical therapy, it acquired a kathartic value (p. 109).

Humiliation because it was willed became a form of pride. There was also a concealed arrogance in Genet's attitude toward his lovers. On one level he worshipped their strength, their virile beauty, their criminal courage; they were gods of evil to whom he was willingly enslaved. Yet he was never really unaware that most of these qualities were projections of his own imagination. In his books there are several incidents where *le dur* is tested and found lacking. By a mechanism now familiar to us, the Genet-character who loves the fallen hero resolves to love the more because he is tempted to love less. But in real life such awareness was merely one aspect of Genet's proud resolve to recast all the events of his life in a drama which he himself was forever re-creating.

All this, of course, involves a choice of Evil for its own sake. Genet was not like the Marquis de Sade who, as Sartre reminds us, sometimes tried to dismiss his crimes as unimportant. ("My, what a fuss to make over spanking a prostitute!") The heroes of Genet's books gloat over their crimes, they commit murders which cannot possibly profit them and in situations where the idea of murder is particularly repugnant even to the murderer; their death on the scaffold is a moment of triumph. Genet himself never tried to reach these heights; his most serious crime—legally speaking—was housebreaking. But he was more than once guilty of an act which he and almost everyone else would agree to be one of the most contemptible—betrayal of a fellow thief for money. Sartre, whose ability to extend sympathetic understanding to all aspects of Genet's career is quite impressive, argues that Genet's motives here were not inspired by personal meanness or greed; and he offers as proof the fact that Genet insisted on being paid in the presence of those he had betrayed. Sartre's explanation is that Genet felt the need of proving to himself his absolute allegiance to Evil as such. If he merely substituted the class of criminals for the class of the respectable bourgeois and retained the old virtues of loyalty, devotion, etc., this would be to show himself content with the inferior position assigned to him. He would still be serving—in his own way—under the standard of the Good. Actually this choice was at no time really open to him, for Genet was never fully accepted by his underworld associates. He was too intelligent, too sensitive, too much preoccupied with his own inner drama. They looked upon him with suspicion long before he had given them cause; and Sartre claims that when he became actually a traitor, he was embracing the role thrust upon him, just as earlier he had made himself a thief because he had been made to think that such was his destiny. As a thief who was also a stool pigeon, Genet showed himself to be evil from the point of view of two different systems simultaneously. The act of betrayal was a crime committed by Evil against itself; furthermore, it was like a parasite sucking the forces of the Good; for in the strange bond established between police official and informer there was a remarkable paradox: the thief consented to serve the Good for the sake of Evil, but in the process he subtly compromised the representative of justice by making him an ally of Evil—albeit in the name of the Good.

Sartre argues that while Genet early lost his belief in God, he never lost his religiosity. Like the Christian saints, Genet felt that his life must be one of submission to a higher voice within him; he welcomed humiliation and suffering as signs that he was one of the Elect. But this god whom he served was nothing more than abstract, negative revolt. Constantly resisting any desire to be integrated in any existing community and unable to envision another society in which he might play a different role, Genet tried to be simply the Other to himself as well as to his associates. Naturally the goal was unattainable. It was only in fantasies and play-acting that Genet could convince himself that he both was and wanted to be the inevitably alien and rejected. The original resolve to accept his alienation as a destiny had been based on a proud determination to meet reality head-on. Gradually Genet came to see that he was living this destiny only by enveloping himself in rituals of myth and symbolism which had nothing to do with reality. It was at this point that he initiated the great reversal which ultimately freed him both from actual prison and from those tortures which he repeatedly inflicted upon himself. Frustrated and unhappy in his attempt to live reality as if it were myth, he began to create realities from his dreams. He turned to literature.

Genet first began to write as the result of an incident which, like so many others, emphasized his alienation and elicited from him a gesture of defiance. He had been put into a prison cell along with other prisoners who, like him, were still awaiting sentence. The rest were in ordinary clothes, but by a mistake Genet had been ordered to wear prison garb. Sitting like a bird of ill omen among them, he sensed their hostility and rejection. To pass the time away one of the men composed and proudly recited some sentimental doggerel addressed to his sister. Genet declared that he could do better, and wrote a serious poem called "The Death Sentence" *(Condamné à mort)*. The subject matter of the poem shocked his fellow prisoners; its style was totally beyond them. Genet was ridiculed and insulted, as he had no doubt anticipated. But he repolished the poem and began to write others. He put into them his own emotions, distorted and violent as they were. And gradually he began to think of his reader.

Slowly Genet moved from poetry to a poetic prose, from lyric introspection to the narration of fictionalized reminiscences. Then came *Our Lady of the Flowers (Notre-Dame des Fleurs)*.[6] In the writing of this novel, Sartre says, Genet underwent a conversion of which he himself was unaware, at least at the time; it was the death of the aesthete using words for his own amusement and pleasure; and it was the birth of the true writer recognizing that he had something to communicate and anxious that his reader should understand. Very early in the novel he says,

I shall speak to you about Divine, mixing masculine and feminine as my mood dictates, and if, in the course of the tale, I shall have to refer to a woman, I shall manage, I shall find an expedient, a good device, so that there may be no confusion (p. 27).

Again when he is describing the inner experience of the boy Culafroy alone at night—

When I write that the meaning of the setting was no longer the same, I don't mean that the setting ever was for Culafroy (later on, for Divine) other than what it would have been for anyone else, namely, wash drying on wire lines (p. 120).

At this point it is important for us to consider the novel itself. In the first place, it may serve us as a sort of test for the validity of Sartre's appraisal of Genet. Many of the reviewers of Sartre's book criticized him for making Genet not the subject of a biography but an excuse for the presentation of a special theory of existentialism. Moreover, we have noted that Sartre's Genet shares some things in common with Sartre's Baudelaire and with Daniel in *The Roads to Freedom*. But if we feel in looking at the novel that its author and the subject of Sartre's biography must be one man, then it does not really matter that Sartre may have added philosophy to biography or that he has found and created other people with certain reactions similar to Genet's.[7] Furthermore, *Our Lady of the Flowers* is in its own right germane to our discussion, for Genet's books are generally considered to be loosely associated with existentialist writing. I do not myself think that the work of Genet quite belongs with the literature of humanistic existentialism as I have defined it. Sartre points out that Genet's thinking is always essentialist. This judgement is perhaps more philosophical than literary, but in other respects Genet is quite unlike those existentialists whom we have been considering. He lacks the analytic rationalism of Sartre and de Beauvoir, the passionate concern of Camus. He specifically rejects the recognition of human solidarity which we have met in all these writers. While in a curious way he reveals to us the myths and case history of his own life, and while all his books are inestimably valuable as unique social documents, certainly his work is not the result of any conscious intent to improve society by holding a mirror up before it. Genet neither follows nor invents a philosophy or a social theory. He simply expresses himself.

Yet this is not to deny all connection between Genet and existentialism. The nature of this relation was accurately pointed out by Eleanor

Clark, writing for the *Partisan Review* almost three years before Sartre's book was published.[8] Genet, she says, "has actually created the bottomless moral world so successfully skirted and exploited by Sartre." In his familiarity with crimes which went beyond those of Caligula, he was "the living embodiment of what everybody else was talking about." This might sound as though Genet was nothing but a case study for the existentialists, but Clark goes on to point out that Genet's own work is written against a background of despair and intensity of experience such as one is accustomed to find in the moral preoccupations of existentialist literature.

Although Genet certainly has some things in common with the existentialists, I do not believe it correct to call him an existentialist—not, at least, unless the term is to be extended to what I consider an improper application, the work of the "Beat Generation." There, if we take pre-Zen Jack Kerouac, for example, we may find characteristics also present in Genet. In the works of both there is an aggressive, wholly negative individualism, a contempt for all middle-class, respectable values and all idealism, a tendency to hero worship which is not at all inconsistent with betrayal. In each case, the heroes' lives would be sordid by conventional standards but are filled with grandeur in their own eyes: intensity, whether joyous or painful, takes on a religious quality. Kerouac's Dean Moriarty too is called a saint. Yet both writers take it for granted that existence, as such, is painful and meaningless, though Genet's heroes escape via private myths of their own making, whereas Kerouac's characters are more inclined to try marijuana. Again the two are alike in the extravagance of their language, in lyrically poetic passages created out of the argot of their private worlds. Kerouac aims to write " 'without consciousness' in semi-trance . . . allowing subconscious to admit in own uninhibited interesting necessary and so 'modern' language what conscious art would censor." [9] Genet objects to anything suggesting automatism in writing and even within the novels stresses the self-conscious act of their creation. Yet most of his books were written rapidly within the aura of a single mood and give no less than Kerouac's the effect of immediate expression which seems spontaneously to create the form which is to contain it. Still, Kerouac beside Genet seems to be playing at evil, and the stakes are not so high. On every level Genet is more passionate, more fully committed; in form if not in style he is the more original. He has more to say, and what is most important of all, he listens to himself.

Genet has remarked that his books are not really novels because none of the characters ever makes a decision on his own.* In a sense this is true, for Genet deliberately and repeatedly breaks the dramatic convention by which fictional beings are treated as if actually existing in their own right. Yet certainly *Our Lady of the Flowers* is a novel, even though the creative process behind it is constantly drawn to our attention instead of being kept out of sight. It is a novel in the same way that paintings remain pictures even while the artist makes the pigment and brush strokes themselves centers of interest. Purely from the formal point of view, one may be reminded of *The Counterfeiters* by André Gide. But whereas Gide's book presents us with the notes for a novel which might have been written, Genet's shows us a novel in the very process of its writing. *Our Lady of the Flowers,* which Sartre has described as a book "soaked with tears and sperm," was written in 1942 while Genet was in prison. It is openly and admittedly a succession of onanistic fantasies woven into a story. Most of the characters who are gradually created for us are born from the pictures of handsome criminals which Genet has found in newspapers and pinned up on his cell wall. They are endowed with fuller life histories spun from Genet's imagination. Sometimes he tells us the actual episode on which a fictional incident is based, sometimes not. What emerges from all this is a novel within an autobiography, the autobiographer, of course, being the actual Jean Genet in his cell awaiting trial and sentence. The strange thing about this evil and beautiful book is that both stories (the autobiography and the novel) come equally alive—in spite of the fact that Genet is constantly reminding us that the fate of his characters depends upon their creator's whim.

There is a fairly complex plot, though it is not developed for us in chronological order. We know almost from the beginning that the hero, a homosexual called Divine, will die of tuberculosis, that Divine's greatest love, Darling *(Mignon),* will desert and forget Divine, that Our Lady of the Flowers, another lover, has committed a murder and will be arrested and guillotined. A series of controlled reminiscences shows us how all these events came about and relates some of the facts of Divine's childhood in the country. Here and there are interspersed passages

---

* At first thought this appears to be in sharp contradiction to Sartre's statement (quoted in Part One) that the characters must be set free from their creator and act in accordance with laws derived only from their own being-in-situation. Yet Genet's books admirably fulfill Sartre's requirement that the author be wholly inside or entirely out. Genet is definitely "in." If anyone is out, it is the characters, who are forever being reabsorbed in him as the sole hero.

called "Divinariana," which consist of bits of information about Divine's habits and preferences and quotations from Divine's more inspired conversation. In speaking of the adult Divine, Genet always uses the feminine pronoun, and he is amazingly skillful at portraying the complexities of this being who "felt as a woman but who thought as a man" and hence "found grammar an embarrassment." In speaking of Divine's childhood, however, Genet uses the masculine and Divine's real name, Louis Culafroy. Since Genet states specifically that Divine is Genet himself, the attitude which he takes toward this character is particularly interesting. At times the identification seems to be complete. More often Divine seems to be not so much Genet as the result of the half-sympathetic, half-satiric attitude which Genet adopted when contemplating himself. At one place he actually represents Divine and her lover as saying, "Jean, how glad I am to be living as Divine and to be living with Darling" (p. 62). Particularly important are the Culafroy passages, for there Jean-Divine is unmistakably contemplating the real child in the provinces whom Genet remembered as someone who had lived but who was forever separated from the man who took his place.

Despite these complicated levels of action and of reality, the novel *moves*. Naturally, in reading it one never gets outside Genet's own consciousness, and yet the technique is not really that of the "stream of consciousness" novel. It belongs rather with what may be called inner realism. While there is no concern to create a consistently naturalistic setting, nevertheless the real world is always present, whether it be the world of Genet's ill-smelling cell or the garrets in Pigalle. Against this background events are sharply focused and three-dimensional, so much so that one falls readily into Genet's trap and believes that the characters are flesh and blood even as their author declares them fantasy.

If we compare this portrait of Genet-Culafroy-Divine with Sartre's analysis of Genet, the similarities are completely reassuring. When the village Mother Superior asked the child Culafroy why he had stolen, his reply was, "Because the others thought I was a thief" (p. 169). Just before his transformation into Divine, Culafroy was forced by his first lover to grasp a snake in his bare hands. Giving in, the boy's revulsion turns into a sort of joyous tenderness. "Culafroy and Divine, with their delicate tastes, will always be forced to love what they loathe, and this constitutes something of their saintliness, for that is renunciation" (p. 116). Genet makes it clear that Culafroy felt that he was condemned by society and that he chose to transform this exile into grandeur by deliberately willing it and by wrapping it in the poetry of myth and ritual.

A man is great if he has a great destiny; but this greatness is of the order of visible, measurable greatness. It is magnificence seen from without. Though it may be wretched when seen from within, it is then poetic, if you are willing to agree that poetry is the breaking apart (or rather the meeting at the breaking-point) of the visible and the invisible. Culafroy had a wretched destiny, and it is because of this that his life was composed of those secret acts, each of which is in essence a poem, as the infinitesimal movement of the finger of a Balinese dancer is a sign that can set a world in motion because it issues from a world whose multifarious meaning is unavowable. Culafroy became Divine; he was thus a poem written only for himself, hermetic to whoever did not have the key to it (p. 241).

These passages and the book as a whole clearly justify Sartre's title, *Saint Genet*. Particularly the "Divinariana" are set up to show that in Divine is found "the essential form of the saint." But she is a saint without God—as Sartre says of Genet. It is chiefly on an episode in *Our Lady of the Flowers* that Sartre bases his claim that Genet, in what might be called a negative religious crisis, abandoned his belief in God. Culafroy sneaked into the village church and deliberately committed a sacrilege, profaning the Host. "And the miracle occurred. There was no miracle. God had been debunked. God was hollow" (p. 130).

What exactly was this saintliness? Sometimes Genet seems to equate it with suffering, especially a willed suffering. So that Divine may be a saint, he says, he will "strip her of all happiness," and Divine herself seeks rejection and misery, hopes that those she so passionately loves will remain indifferent to her. But more essential than martyrdom is detachment from the world. By never allowing anyone or anything but herself to determine the meaning or quality of her experiences, by investing every gesture and word with a host of imaginative significances, Divine subjected herself to the demands of the ideal. Yet she did not timidly withdraw from reality so much as she first embraced the world as it was, and then forced others to allow her to remake it in her own fashion. A particularly illuminating scene places Divine with Darling in a bar. As she sat there, she wore a crown of imitation pearls upon her head. Suddenly the string broke, and the pearls rolled over the floor.

> Condolences, to which malicious joy gives rich tonalities: "The Divine is uncrowned! She's the great fallen one! . . . The poor Exile!" . . . Then, Divine lets out a burst of strident

laughter. Everyone pricks up his ears: it's her signal. She tears her bridge out of her open mouth, puts it on her skull and, with her heart in her throat, but victorious, she cries out in a changed voice and with her lips drawn back into her mouth, "Dammit all, ladies, I'll be queen anyhow!" (pp. 150-151).

Then Divine did what required still more "grandeur of soul." She took the bridge from her head and fastened it back into place in her mouth. Sartre makes a great deal of this episode, which he finds to be not only a revelation of Genet's own habit of playing myth against reality, but an indication that at this stage of his life Genet was fully aware of the process. Divine, the fictitious woman wearing her faked jewels, ruled as a false queen over a society which, itself clothed in pretense, could not but take seriously the symbolism of the fallen diadem. Threatened in her position, Divine took the only way out. By daring suddenly to assert herself as she really was, as an aging faggot (she was only thirty but apparently quite decrepit), she used the false teeth as the symbol of her open acknowledgement of her humiliation. By the magnificence of her gesture, she made of the wretched denture a crown more compelling than the poor little pearls. The entire secret mechanism of Genet's life is here epitomized.

There are many things in the book which bear out the details of Sartre's interpretation of Genet, and all of them are related to the fundamental idea that Genet was a man who felt that his life was fatally determined by something outside himself and who reacted by constituting himself one of Evil's Elect. Sometimes the compulsion comes simply from things. Thus the pimp called "Our Lady" murdered a man chiefly because his tie was improperly tied and suggested to Our Lady the idea of using the great strength of his arms to pull the ends of the tie until they strangled the victim. Again Divine's mother thinks of murder because there happens to be a revolver at the bottom of a drawer. "It is not the first time that things have been the instigators of an act and must alone bear the fearful, though light, responsibility for a crime" (p. 20). More often there are suggestions of the attitude which Sartre develops into a full theory—that society has artificially divided and reified Good and Evil, and that the outcasts are the victims of this absolutism. When Our Lady has received the death sentence ("the apotheosis") and has been given over again to the guards, Genet writes:

He seemed to them invested with a sacred character, like the kind that expiatory victims, whether goat, ox or child, had in olden times and which kings and Jews still have today. The guards spoke to him and served him as if, knowing he was laden with the weight of the sins of the world, they had wanted to bring down upon themselves the benediction of the Redeemer (p. 249).

Sartre's claim that Genet made of his life a kind of Black Mass is borne out by Genet's consistent use of religious terminology, which, while deliberately perverted, is so intense and so pervasive as to suggest that it is blasphemy rather than simple disbelief. The mere names of the characters are suggestive. But there are dozens of stronger statements. "The Eternal passed by in the form of a pimp" (p. 15). "All eyes could read, graven in the aura of Our Lady of the Flowers, the following words: 'I am the Immaculate Conception'" (p. 228). And of Divine, Genet writes,

> As at other times, the days of big flush and gush, days of mystic debauch, she would say to herself, "Suppose I played at believing in God?" She would do it until she trembled.
>
> At the hour of Divine's death, she played so well at believing in God that she couldn't help having a bit of a transport.
>
> She saw God gulping down an egg. "To see," here, is a casual way of speaking (pp. 257-258).

Sartre explains this negative religiosity as simply one more manifestation of Genet's choice of evil for its own sake. Of course this choice had a social dimension as well as a philosophical one. Genet's decision to prolong indefinitely "the negative moment of freedom" meant that he held himself in permanent opposition to all established goods without setting up an alternative system of values in the name of which he might condemn these goods. Naturally he would be particularly vehement against the Church as the supposed repository and origin of all those standards by which society determined goods and evils. But I think there is more behind Genet's religious imagery than Sartre has suggested. Genet's blasphemy is not cynically detached; it is not even satiric. It is fervent and somehow compulsive. One could, of course, argue that the overvehement denial stemmed from an unacknowledged belief or at least a longing to believe. But I do not think there is any evidence to support the view that Genet was simply unwilling to listen to the secret demands of the heart. Admittedly Christian doctrine and ritual exerted a compelling attraction, but it was rather that mysterious fascination which is always exercised over us by the thing which most we hate. Or which we fear. To Genet, who had built his life upon the proud refusal to mitigate in any way the alienation to which society had condemned him, the need for the consolations of religion and the fear that he might be tempted to receive them as a substitute for real acceptance by society must have been equally overwhelming. Thus in a curious way his obsession with religion is the equivalent in reverse of that preoccupation with sin which we find so often in Fundamentalists. In the same way that Christian mystics will use sensuous imagery not only to describe their experiences, but by implied comparison to demonstrate the greater intensity of spiritual pleasures as contrasted with earthly ones, so Genet transfers the language of religion to his ecstasies of humiliation and to the morality of Evil.

There is still one other incident in *Our Lady of the Flowers* which is of particular interest in connection with Sartre's biography. This is the episode in which Divine's lover is offered the chance of turning stool pigeon for cash. Genet writes, "Darling accepted. He liked selling out on people, for this dehumanized him. Dehumanizing myself is my own most fundamental tendency" (p. 38). Sartre's more elaborate explanation of Genet's betrayals said that they sprang from his desire to serve Evil exclusively so that he feared to allow "good" values (loyalty, cooperation, etc.) even when they were in the interests of the cause to which he was devoted. Genet's own statement is simpler and, I think, more precise, but it amounts to the same thing. He was a man who held himself aloof from humankind and who hated even his own human condition. Yet it seems to me significant that it is Darling and not Divine who is the traitor. Genet is willing to endow his projected self with a wide variety of foolish and evil traits, even including responsibility for the death of a child,* but not betrayal. Does this mean, perhaps, that despite all, Genet could not quite separate himself from all human ties much as he might want to do so? Sartre claims that as a child Genet loved the adults who condemned him and that along with his defiance there is a longing for human affection and acceptance. In *Our Lady of the Flowers* there are several passages containing such a cry from the

---

* Divine does not murder the child directly but loosens a wire netting so that an accident is almost inevitable. That Genet considered such an act even worse than betrayal is indicated by the fact that Divine regards the crime as inexpiable and so decides that henceforth it does not matter what she does. It seems to me that the child involved is the young Genet-Culafroy, whose existence is cut off by Genet's decision to dehumanize himself. Such an explanation is consistent with the Sartrean interpretation which I have been following.

heart. Genet says of Divine, "For she really must be my age so that I can appease my need to talk about myself, simply. I feel such a need to complain and to try to win a reader's love!" (p. 159). Alone in his cell, Genet has a dream in which his victim pardons him, and he awakes with "the feeling of baptism." And on more than one occasion he considers suicide, "utterly weary of the land of the Chimeras—the only one worth inhabiting."

Sartre says that during these years Genet lived as if he were a victim of demonic possession and that Genet himself gradually broke the spell by his efforts in writing. "Ten years of literature equaled a psychoanalytic cure" (p. 501). This does not mean, of course, that he recognized the need for a cure or that he desired to change. When he first began to write, Genet was interested primarily in expressing himself to himself. Gradually the characters which he had created as mere projections of himself took on an objective reality of their own, and he began to feel the need to have others believe in them. But Sartre claims that Genet's desire to communicate to society was still the wish for an evil communication. Genet wanted to undermine society, Sartre says, by showing the beauty, the poetry, and the freedom of criminals' acts. In particular, he has attacked the comfortable doctrine that criminals are determined by poverty, bad example, and the like, that they are unfortunate victims who may be "cured" by rehabilitation programs. Genet's heroes are gloriously happy in their evil doing and look upon all attempts to "improve" them as merely laughable. If they recognize any determination by outside forces, it is only by such things as the too-tight tie which invites strangling, or the compulsive impulse to make the great gesture by confessing to a big crime when accused of a small one. Most important of all, Genet is so successful in enabling our imaginations to dwell for a time in this strange value world that the reader is compelled to recognize in himself a capacity for understanding (if not also of committing) acts which he considers to be entirely foreign to him. Furthermore, through his books Genet forces the society which has rejected him to accept him, but to accept him not as he might have been but as he is—as evil.

Sartre points out that Genet's works are profoundly disquieting. Whether we are to call them pornographic or not depends on our definition of the word, but certainly they are not like the usual pornographic novel. Genet shocks, but he does not snicker; he repulses and fascinates, but he never seeks mere titillation of the senses. This is due in part to his sincerity, but even more to the beauty of his writing, the emotional intensity, the rich imagery, the delicate prose rhythms, the imaginative power which forces our belief. And since beauty and pornography are rarely united, the reader is disarmed. Moreover, especially in *Our Lady of the Flowers,* we are never allowed to forget that to accept the book is to accept Genet. With the characters of other novels, one may judge them as persons independent of their author. But with Genet we are trapped. Just as we begin to feel that Divine and the others are after all fictional creations and may safely be allowed to win our sympathy and pardon, we are caught up short as Genet drags us back to his cell and reminds us that it is he who is determining what they shall do and be. We find ourselves his accomplices at the very moment at which he makes evil seem most real and most repugnant.

Yet at the end he too was caught in his own trap and impelled to change. "By infecting us with his evil, Genet freed himself of it" (p. 501). Sartre makes Genet's recovery synonymous with his self-realization as creative artist. In part this was due to the fact that the very act of writing for a public (no matter what the motive) is already an acknowledgement of human solidarity. Sartre had earlier indicated an abortive step toward a new life on Genet's part when he for the first time took up housebreaking instead of pocket-picking, shoplifting, and prostitution. In full-scale burglary Genet worked with an accomplice and with standard tools; he felt that he belonged to a profession. That the move was significant is indicated by his attempting for the first time to take the active role in homosexual relations (there is an echo of this in *Our Lady of the Flowers*). The attempt was a failure, however, even on the sexual level, and cooperation with his companion thief ended as usual in betrayal. But if one is to communicate in literature one cannot break the rules, and Genet wished from the start to be understood. Much as he loved language, and even single words for their own sake, he wanted them to be a means of enlightenment for the reader. "Therefore," says Sartre, "he reintroduced into himself order, truth, reciprocity, and the universal, all of which are, if I am not mistaken, qualities of the Good" (p. 504). Imposing order upon his writing, Genet sought order in his life and created it where it had not been. Toward his characters he could achieve what he had tried in vain to do with regard to himself; that is, he could assume toward them the point of view of the Other. Even the Jean Genet of *Our Lady of the Flowers* is no longer identical with his creator once Genet reads over what he has written. Yet in so far as he had intended these fictional beings as projections of himself, Genet could not look at them without at the same time seeing his own life in a new perspective. He could not, for instance, analyze Divine's way of playing myth against reality in the scattered-pearls incident without impairing his capacity to ensnare himself in his own dreams. The criticism and gentle ridicule which he directs against his heroes had a sharper edge when turned afterwards upon his living self. To understand is not only to pardon. To the extent that the self is fully comprehended it is subjected to new judgement. Sartre emphasizes especially the fact that Genet began to see himself differently in relation to time. He had been accustomed to look on present and future as destined, as merely the detailed working out of a repetitive pattern established by his past. This view permeates Genet's books; the characters do not *exist;* they live, each fulfilling the demands of his inner essence. But even as Genet objectified these "presents-made-past," the creative act demanded that he look at the future creatively. He had to see it as a reservoir of possibilities. In *Our Lady of the Flowers* he boasts that he alone shall decide the fate of Darling and Divine. Then what of the fate, the possibilities of Genet? His previous choices of Being—the Thief, the humiliated False-female, the Elect (for Evil) of God, the Saint, the Traitor—all had been variations on the decision to live as a fully determined (even if once and for all self-determined) Essence. The new choice was not only a choice to be a writer rather than to be a thief; it was a choice to *be* as one constantly in the act of creating his being (not a re-creation after an old pattern but a truly free pro-ject into an open future). This, at last, is the one kind of choice which existentialism recognizes as legitimate for man. It is legitimate because it is consistent with man's recognition that freedom to be rather than Being is what man really is.

In Genet's case the realization that he had freed himself from his past resulted finally in his freedom from prison. As French intellectuals began to read the books which were smuggled out of prison and privately printed, they set out to persuade the public and finally the authorities that Genet was a great author who deserved remission of sentence. When Genet accepted the offer of intercession suggested by Sartre, Cocteau, and others, he was doing more than seizing on a chance to escape. During the eight years between his pardon and the writings of Sartre's book, Genet had conclusively shown that the writer had replaced the thief. Sartre presents an interesting picture of the new Genet. His situation is deeply ironic. He has won respectability and freedom by books written with the express intent of undermining society. Upon one occasion he was introduced to one of the victims of his earlier activity, and the woman, graciously acknowledging the introduction, expressed the hope that Genet would continue with his work. To some extent, Genet's scorn of society for being thus duped has been a salutary tonic to the feeling of rejection and social inferiority which had haunted him since childhood. Yet in forcing society to accept him as he is, he has inevitably changed. Sartre makes no claim that Genet is wholly reformed in the usual sense. Genet has stated that he would not hesitate to steal if forced to it by need. Yet he has also said that he cannot steal for the gesture itself as he used to do. His occasional love affairs are more tests for friendship than serious passions or infatuations, and he seems to have a habit of using his influence to establish the young men in business and to help them arrange marriages, Genet becoming a kind of foster uncle to the new families! Thus tacitly he is admitting both that his earlier life was mistaken and that he recognizes the responsibility of helping those who might become as he himself had been. Inevitably he has experienced solitude and loneliness amidst all the lionization. *Les justes* admire him for his literary work, but always *in spite of* his crimes. Yet their acceptance, reserved as it is, has changed him. He is no longer at home among his former associates. His real friends are the artists and intellectuals, but their concerns are not his concerns; playing with ideas and art for their own sake does not interest him. But it is Genet and not Society who has chiefly won, and self-realization appears to have brought a measure of serenity and enrichment if not exultant joy. Sartre gives an odd twist to his final summing up: "Accepted, indulged and petted, Genet remains an exile in the midst of his triumph. So much the better! This new failure and the permanence of his exile safeguard his greatness" (p. 535).

I think that we may rightly call this biographical study a case history for the records of existential psychoanalysis even though there is no psychoanalyst—unless we are to assign the role to Genet himself. It is, of course an explanation and not a demonstration of therapy. There is nowhere a suggestion that anyone (certainly not Sartre himself) attempted to help Genet by psychological analysis or advice; on the contrary, Sartre emphasizes that Genet cured himself, and he uses this point as additional evidence that a human being is free to modify his personality structure, no matter how heavy the weight of hereditary and environmental pressures may be. One might raise the question as to whether or not Sartre can rightly say that Genet is cured. If one is to equate "cure" with a completely comfortable adjustment to society, with perfect conformism, then emphatically Genet is not cured. He has not returned to the Church; he has not married and raised a family; he has at no time publicly abjured his earlier life and expressed repentance. But no psychiatrist, I think, would ever make such demands. And if we did have such a person who still bore the name of Jean Genet, we certainly would not have Genet, the writer. Sartre's explanation of the means of Genet's recovery seems convincing enough to me. For an adult, writing books may, I suppose, be a more permanently valuable substitute for the play therapy which psychiatrists use in order to get children to act out their difficulties and so achieve a katharsis of them. Certainly Genet's writing increased his self-understanding, and literary creation was healthier and more satisfying than fantasy. Success in writing provided social acceptance and self-reassurance with which to heal the wounds inflicted by earlier rejection.

Sartre is more successful here than in his *Baudelaire* in showing why Genet turned to literature rather than to something else. With his constant sense that each act of his life must be clothed with symbolism and remade as a scene in a private drama, Genet was living creatively long before he ever set a word on paper. When he began to write, it was merely that for the first time he thought of himself as the author of the play rather than as an actor following a text. Thus for him literature was a means of escaping from the imaginary rather than of entering into it. Possibly we need no further explanation in terms of talent, genius, and the like. The best thing about Sartre's interpretation is the fact that the Genet who emerges is easily identified (as I have tried to show) with the Genet who comes to us from the pages of his own books. That Genet himself accepts his portrait is implied by the supporting evidence of conversations with him which Sartre quotes in his biography, and by the fact that Genet has allowed portions of Sartre's study to be published as introductions to Genet's works. Yet the strength of Sartre's method on one level seems to me to indicate a weakness on another. If we grant, as I think we must, that Genet was able through literature to accomplish a therapeutic self-analysis and subsequent readjustment, this seems to support Sartre's claims for the individual's capacity to break through the barriers of personality structure and to make a free choice of a new way of life. In addition, if Sartre's presentation of Genet is correct, this too helps to support the validity of existentialist principles inasmuch as Sartre has effected the analysis along the lines laid down in his "Existential Psychoanalysis." But since Baudelaire was never "cured" (perhaps fortunately for us), and since Genet achieved his own self-recovery, where in all this is there any suggestion that existential psychoanalysis can be other than an historical after-the-event explanation? Of course Sartre does not claim that his biography is anything other than this. At the same time his choice of the term "psychoanalysis" implies that he had intended to lay the groundwork for a therapy. It is somewhat disappointing that he has at no time suggested how one might use his approach to help the troubled solve their difficulties. Suppose that he had met Genet in his cell before Genet wrote that first poem. What would Sartre have said? But this is unfair. Once again we must remember that Sartre claims for his biographies only anticipations or suggestions of existential psychoanalysis. He hopes that it may sometime exist, but he has never himself claimed to be its Freud.

As though he felt the need to justify his lengthy study of an avowed enemy of present society, Sartre attaches to his biography a chapter telling us how we may profit by considering Genet's example. Calling Genet the Bukharin of bourgeois society, Sartre claims that from the point of view of the future we *(les justes)*, like Genet, will be made objects of judgement and condemned. Through our Manichaean splitting of Good and Evil and our projection of the latter upon the outcast groups, we ourselves are responsible for the Evil which we so strongly condemn. We should learn from Genet the consequences of our mistake and struggle to see that Evil is in reality the inextricable obverse side of the Good, the "negative moment of freedom," which can be overcome only when society achieves the synthesis of the two. All of which is very abstract and not profoundly illuminating. If it means anything, it means that only in a perfectly just society (a classless society) will there no longer be motivation for a totally negative revolt against all Good as it has been typified by Genet. More positively, Sartre has here added a social dimension to the psychological one, an analysis which shows man's situation influencing his condition without determining, hence destroying, his freedom. "The truth is that 'human reality' 'is-in-society' as it 'is-in-the-world' " (p. 541). Other people and the social structure are also a part of the facticity within which a freedom chooses itself.

As we read Sartre's analysis of Genet's life and attitudes, we might just as well be reading a discussion of young criminals in America or of twentieth-century delinquency in general. Genet's rejection of all the usual human values, his crimes which are without motive or for the sake of crime itself, his glorification of those who will destroy even themselves for the intensity of the experience or to make the grand gesture—all these are qualities which appear and reappear in the annals of police courts and the records of social workers. Genet and his like baffle because they seem to offer no point of contact by which we may measure them. One can understand a criminal who murders for a fortune or because of jealousy. But the boy who kills simply because his victim is there or because he draws on the murderer's sympathy—this goes beyond our comprehension. It seems that such criminals dare all for no purpose and in the name of no values. They suffer from loneliness and a sense of alienation; yet solitude is their ideal and conformity a threat to their very being. These contradictions Sartre has attempted to explain. To the extent that he succeeds, we may indeed profit from his Genet.

*Baudelaire* and *Saint Genet, Martyr-Comedian* are not quite the only examples of existentialist biographies. De Beauvoir also has written a long essay on a famous literary-criminal, "Must We Burn Sade?" *(Faut-il brûler Sade)*, which appeared at about the same time as Sartre's book on Genet. It is not necessary, I think, for us to consider this work in detail, for while it would not be fair to de Beauvoir to say that her biography of the Marquis de Sade shows no originality, yet her general approach parallels that of Sartre. She includes rather more than Sartre does in the way of specific information concerning the life history of her subject. But with de Beauvoir again one feels that it is the philosophical and general psychological implications which interest her much more than the man himself or his works. And once more it is the problem of evil with which she is chiefly preoccupied. The Marquis too is made out to be a man who did evil for its own sake, which is probably very true, and de Beauvoir, like Sartre, blames society.

> His thinking is clear—either do away with the poor or do away with poverty, but do not use half-measures and thus perpetuate injustice and oppression, and above all do not pretend to be redeeming these extortions by handing out a trivial dole to those you exploit.[10]

In the face of social hypocrisy which accepted inequality and suffering as inevitable, and before Nature whose injustice surpasses even that of men, the Marquis "chose cruelty rather than indifference."

It is reported that both Sartre and de Beauvoir have been writing their autobiographies. The first volume of de Beauvoir's appeared late in 1958 with the title *Memories of a Well-Bred Young Girl (Mémoires d'une jeune fille rangée)*. Its general structure is that of the conventional autobiography. There are memories of childhood, character sketches of the members of her family, relatives, and intimate friends, a somewhat reticent but extremely interesting account of her first acquaintance with Jean-Paul Sartre at the Sorbonne. Yet even here, especially in the first half of the book, the guiding motif is de Beauvoir's concern over society's habit of splitting and absolutizing Good and Evil. Early in the description of her childhood she writes, "The two major categories by which my universe was ordered were Good and Evil. I dwelt in the region of the Good where happiness and virtue reigned indissolubly united." [11] The progression of her narrative is determined in part at least by the various episodes which modify this initial optimism.

Existentialist biographies prove to be case histories of the kind which we have met already in existentialist fiction. All are consistent delineations of human character in accordance with a psychology based on a belief in human freedom. Theoretically we should find in these biographies greater variety than in the usual sort. Actually we find that the basic conflicts seem to be much the same. The subject of existentialist analysis must come to grips with the problem of whether or not to acknowledge his freedom and what to do about Good and Evil just as surely as Freud's patients must resolve or be determined by their Oedipus complexes and as the Christian martyr must wrestle with the Devil and win salvation by conversion. This is not to say that the existentialist approach is thereby proved to be distortion and falsehood. It may well be true. But as applied in biography, at least, it is the kind of truth which the skilled portrait painter may reveal on the faces of his subjects; it is not that of the X-ray plate.

# Possibilities

# POSSIBILITIES

---

Humanistic existentialism provides as its own support a psychology of freedom, and that is the real reason why we may rightly call its literature one of possibility. Freedom *is* possibility.[1] Abstractly, of course, possibility is neither positive nor negative, neither good nor bad. More than anything else it is a question. Like uncertainty, it simply means that something is not yet decided, that the future is open. If we consider closely any particular possibility, we find that logically it demands a background of impossibility. If we are able to say that a certain thing *may* happen, it is because we implicitly assert that totally prohibitive factors are not there. A thing is possible when those things which would utterly prevent it are impossible. It is possible rather than certain because there exists something opposed to it which is also possible. In the same way we have seen that freedom can exist only where there is a choice, and choice demands a limiting facticity. Man's factual condition, his mortal body, his position in time and place—these do not prevent freedom; they are the stuff of which it makes itself. The nonfreedom without which there can be no freedom is the fact that man cannot escape being free. The choice to be not-free is never open, and it is here that freedom finds its ultimate limit. There is a nearer limit too: no person can refute or remove the fact that existence is freedom for all others as well as for himself. Freedoms, as well as possibilities, may conflict with one another.

These "boundaries" serve not only to indicate the area within which freedom makes itself by its own succession of choices. A freedom is also qualitatively defined by the attitude which it takes toward its limits. An individual lives in good or bad faith according to whether he chooses to accept the inevitability of his own and others' freedom or spends his life erecting structures to hide either or both from himself and from the world. Within the framework of existentialism this either-or is itself a sufficient criterion by which to judge the positive and negative aspects of human possibility. But what if we stand apart and attempt to pass judgement upon the possibilities of humanistic existentialism? Does it offer any reasonable hope to man? Or are its enemies right in seeing in it only a confession of impotence and despair? Moreover, what of its literature? In proclaiming the freedom of man, has it lost its own freedom as literature? Before concluding our study of humanistic existentialism we must take one last, over-all, appraising look at the existentialist's Look and at the literature which presents it to our view.

## MAN-IN-THE-WORLD

Immediately there is a difficulty. From what point of view are we to make our appraisal? Obviously what we want is a point of view which is wholly objective, one so free from bias as to be entirely nonpersonal, hence acceptable to everybody. What is needed, in short, is that non-human objectivity which existentialism declares does not exist anywhere. If we could successfully establish such a point of view, we should thereby undermine existentialism at its foundations, and we should in this way achieve an absolute evaluation, albeit a destructive one. Failing this we could, of course, set up certain "natural" human needs and values and ask whether existentialism seems likely to satisfy them. This solution, unfortunately, is not so simple and obvious as it appears. It is precisely these values which the humanistic existentialists call into question and indeed the whole complex of thought and emotion which stands back of our way of defining a value. There is a sense in which we must have already chosen our values, our criteria by which to decide what demands are to be satisfied, before we are in a position to judge whether what existentialism has to offer is worthwhile or not. But if we do this knowingly, as it seems to me, we must admit that we are practicing existentialism in order to learn what it preaches.

Rather than seeking for some neutral ground on the basis of which I might, with a minimum of risk, list the debits and credits of humanistic existentialism—from my point of view, I propose that for our summary backward look we consider where we would place the philosophy of man which we have found in the work of Sartre, of de Beauvoir, and of Camus in relation to three fundamental questions: In what sense is their philosophy a humanism? Where do they stand with regard to the old idea that man is a creature of reason? Is there any place in their work for the ancient concepts of sin and salvation?

It is as a humanism that existentialism is most aggressive, both in its negative assertions and in its positive claims. All of our authors agree that man confronts a missing God and an indifferent universe. Of the three, de Beauvoir shows the least concern over God's nonexistence, yet what may be said to be consequences of the atheistic position are basic themes in her work: the individual's attempt to create a moral code he can live by and his effort to make his life meaningful in the absence of divine support or external guarantee. Sartre goes so far as to say that all of man's conduct—or at least all of his most basic desires and the bad faith which is for most men their natural environment—is the manifestation of man's wish to *be* God. Most persons, according to Sartre, would gladly forego their *human* being (i.e., being as for-itself) in order that the Self-cause (in-itself-for-itself) might live. But God does not exist, and man's sacrifice is abortive and in vain. Man cannot become his own self-contradictory ideal, nor is there any self-conscious Absolute existing independent of him as a pole for his derivative being. Just as he would have each man's being defined in terms of his consciousness, which is a nothingness, so Sartre's view of human nature and of the physical world hinges on the belief that God is missing there where man feels that He ought to be. Since there is no God, there is no human nature a priori. Each man exists first and by living defines his essence; mankind or human essence will have been what all men will have chosen to make it. Without God, the world of nonconscious reality—what Sartre calls the In-itself—has no significance whatsoever save as man writes a meaning upon it by making it the raw material of his projects. In so far as Sartre attempts any proof of the fact that God does not exist, he is concerned chiefly to show the illogicality and inconsistency of the concept of God as men have held it.[2] Camus, too, rejects any belief in a deity, not so much because such a faith would be irrational as because the traditional claim in God's righteous omnipotence is utterly at variance with the fact of human suffering. Camus' sense of man's forlornness derives less from the lack of a personal God and more from the absence of any response to man's questioning of the universe. Man desperately seeks a meaning in the world, a signifying relationship between himself and the rest of nature; what he finds is a nonrational, indifferent environment which renders the very question absurd.

Camus does not, however, go along with Sartre in saying that without God there can be no human nature. He feels that we must postulate some kind of human essence. It is needed to explain man's very sense of "the human." Without it there could be no solidarity among men; the Rebel would have no feeling that there are "limits" beyond which it "is not right" to go; no person would ever choose to give up his life to preserve an idea more precious than his own existence. Such conduct, Camus argues, is possible only because each man realizes his connection with something which includes and goes beyond him. The claim that essence thus precedes existence in human beings is the most important doctrinal difference between Camus and those who have called themselves existentialists. As I have pointed out earlier, the disagreement, while fundamental, is less consequential than one might expect. Camus never makes use of the notion of human nature in such a way as to try to establish specific human norms or to outline man's future. It does not provide for him an impersonal view upon the world of men and nature. It does not relieve the final isolation and loneliness of closed souls. Sisyphus finds happiness apart from the physical world, not in mystic communion with it; the Rebel joins hands with his fellow men in working for the good of all humanity, but neither he nor they have access to any reservoir of a priori thought. Sartre admits that all men share in common a facticity and an ontological status which he calls the "human condition." I cannot see that Camus' "human essence" is anything other than a name given to this common condition and our awareness of it. Camus is probably right in asserting that there are certain limits which no human project can transgress without undermining its initial premises and frustrating its own aim. Sartre and de Beauvoir say fundamentally the same thing when they claim that if metaphysical freedom is the reality and factual freedom the *sine qua non* for one individual, the same must be true for the rest of mankind. One cannot attack the rights of any man without thereby denying that Man has any rights at all.

This brings us to the more positive aspect of this humanism. To say that there is only man and not God, to place man in an alien universe utterly void of any human purpose—these are at most negative truths. It does not follow, however, that they make man unimportant. On the contrary, so long as man's nature is prescribed by God and his place in the scheme of things clearly mapped out, the gradual evolution of man's fate is rather uninteresting. The individual, of course, has a choice of joining up with the winning side or cutting off his nose with the losers. Nothing he does will contribute much to change the final outcome for mankind as a whole or to make humanity into one kind of thing rather than another. With an existential humanism, the question of man's destiny becomes for the first time all-important, for nothing is settled and everything matters. What men collectively, what man individually will make of themselves is left completely open. God has not defined the one, nor Freud the other. As a humanism, existentialism makes everybody responsible for everything—as Dostoyevsky said. Man's dignity stems not from his having been given a favored place in the universe but from the fact that while his existence is contingent, his life is his own creation.

We may ask next—how rational is this creative life of man? Or, more particularly, to what extent do these existentialists believe that a man in good faith can or should be guided by his reason? Practically nobody would hesitate to classify existentialism as an irrational philosophy. Inasmuch as the movement began as a protest against the attempt to imprison man within philosophical systems (especially, of course, the Hegelian system), and in so far as any existentialism lays great stress on the primacy of the individual and the importance of private emotions, we could not expect humanistic existentialism to adhere closely to the rationalist tradition. Nor does it. Its basic premises—the lack of any inscribed order in nature and of a definite place for man, a distrust of absolutist ethics, the denial of suprahuman purpose and meaning—these would disqualify it at the start. Yet while the work of Camus, de Beauvoir, and Sartre is in some ways as remote from Descartes as from Aquinas, it relies far less on the irrational than do other species of existentialism. These three have taken a position midway between the too trusting faith in reason held by the Enlightenment and that retreat into unreason in which the death of this faith has too often resulted. Recognizing that man's natural environment is uncertainty, and realizing that many times the stubborn demands of the heart cannot and should not be answered by dialectic, they have nevertheless sought by a relative, humanly restricted logic, a "logic of the absurd," to make assertions about man, to mark out limits, to distinguish between good and bad faith without ever laying claim to an impersonal, absolute knowledge.

Camus' way of balancing reason and emotion is not the same as that of the other two, though I believe that the difference lies more in mood and attitude than in philosophical theory. The contrast is nowhere more apparent than in their attitude toward the natural world. Sartre, once he has established that nonconscious reality points to no rational plan, that it is *de trop* like man himself, is no longer interested in it. Planets and mountains, sea breezes and sunsets—all are indifferently lumped together, distinguished only as that which is not man. The status of plants and animals Sartre has not, to my knowledge, ever defined. Presumably they too are part of the In-itself, which lacks all differentiation and significance until it is made the object of a consciousness. Sartre says that man lives by appropriating the world, by putting his mark upon it, by making of it a hierarchy of instruments for his projects. At no time have I observed him taking pleasure in the world for what it is in itself. It is significant that on the only occasion when Sartre speaks of loving one's familiar mountains, it is by way of illustrating the fact that one cannot feel the same about a terrain which has been conquered by an invader. De Beauvoir does little more. In her autobiography she tells how as a child she enjoyed making trips out of Paris into the country-side. Both in *The Mandarins* and in *She Came to Stay* the leading characters derive a measure of psychic comfort from camping out. One feels, however, that the experience is good for them chiefly as a kind of mental hygiene or release from tension. What seems to impress de Beauvoir most in this outdoor life is the sense of comradeship which develops when people live close to the earth—together. One does not find her contemplating the landscape alone.

Camus' attitude is altogether different. He does not, any more than the others, assign to the physical universe a reason for being. He makes no metaphysical distinctions between organic and nonorganic existents (save for the human, of course). The only rational result of man's attempt to make sense of the natural world is the concept of the absurd. Yet having once accepted the basic irrationality of things and man's consequent alienation from nature, Camus makes a partial return. He is a little like the existentialist lover, who after failing to become one with the beloved, learns to know the intense joy of recognizing and cherishing the other's separate being. The beauty of the world, the immediate sensuous enjoyment of what is simply there are for Camus absolute goods. The glory of the African sun and sea and mountains needs and allows no explanation. They provide no reason for living, but they make it possible for one to want to go on living. In attaching so much importance to this kind of direct experience, which is morally neutral and nonintellectual, Camus is closer to the German existentialists than he is to Sartre or de Beauvoir. In general his way of asserting the primacy of feeling over reason shows him to be more "existentialist" than they. The other two, even as they admit that the most important problems can finally be resolved only by a passionate choice, feel that they must furnish a rational justification for making the choice. Camus is willing to listen unashamedly to the cry of the heart even when reason is most convincing.

If there is nothing above man to give him purpose and meaning, if there is no absolute standard by which to judge men, is it logical to speak of human guilt? Have we simultaneously wiped out both original sin and the possibility of salvation? In the traditional Christian sense, we have. Man cannot be guilty before a missing God nor saved by his omni-absent divine Grace. Man's transgression, if there be such, can only be against himself or other men, and thence must come his forgiveness. The old words keep recurring in the writings of humanistic existentialism. The absurd, says Camus, is among other things "sin without God." Tarrou strives to become a "saint without God." In the work of de Beauvoir and of Sartre, the goal of sainthood appears mostly in perverted form as temptation (e.g., in the development of Goetz and Genet); yet these authors too cherish an ideal of moral purity.

In our examination of existentialist literature, we have met with the problem of evil in two different contexts. The first of these is the complex structure of good and bad faith. The fundamental principle is one of authenticity. The only way for a person to realize his true being is to recognize that his being is his individual freedom, that he is responsible for all his acts and determined by nothing. Here there is no question of being born in sin. Man renders himself unauthentic by pretending that his environment is a Serious World and submerging himself within it. This is wrong because it is false, and because it ultimately fails. No matter how hard one may try to glue down the wings of consciousness, it will soar free at the most inconvenient moments, leaving anguish in its wake. In this framework the traditional feelings of guilt and repentance become in themselves devices in bad faith as we have seen marvelously illustrated in the portrayal of Clamence and in the people of Argos. From this point of view, Freudian psychoanalysis, despite its humane intentions, serves to support the structures of bad faith—as we saw in the case of Lucien and Paula.

The second context is social. There are certain obvious possibilities for guilt, following as natural consequences of the position just presented: we must recognize the other's freedom; we must not seek to make of him an object nor try to force him to found our being by making an object of us. There is also a sense in which we are indeed, all of us, born in original sin. This is the obverse side of the statement that each one is totally responsible and wholly without excuse. We are guilty in two ways.

First, by my very existence, in everything I do, I make an assault upon the other's freedom. When I look at him, I bring into being his self-for-me. While he can never know exactly what this is, the very awareness of its existence is bound to influence his own idea of himself, hence his Self. Moreover, by my acts I help to frame the world within which he will make his choices. If in training a child I take all obstacles from his path and refrain from all dogmatic utterances in his presence, I thereby remove from him the opportunity of developing habits of endurance and resistance. If I hurt him for his own good, I am taking it upon myself to judge what is his good. Who is to say that this is "really" his good or even the good which he himself would ultimately have chosen? In so far as his own absolute freedom is his greatest good, I am the enemy. The fact that my acts—as objects in the world—may be distorted and made to serve ends which I had never intended does not relieve me from responsibility. If I take part today in a liberal revolution which becomes an oppression tomorrow, I have helped to create it, even though I may want to disown it. From this kind of guilt there is, of course, no deliverance. I must accept a "calculated culpability." To refuse my guilt would be to commit moral suicide, and that would be guilt of the worst sort. It would be as if the Christian should try to escape God's judgement by killing himself.

The second sort of guilt is less abstract and metaphysical. At least at the present state of civilization we are all born into a society based on the premise that the well-being and freedom of movement of a few must be sacrificed in order that the many may live and live better. I am not speaking here of the controversial issues of class consciousness, private ownership, and the like, though all three of the French writers would hold that such questions are pertinent. I am thinking rather of the existence of underprivileged peoples and of our own criminal groups. Reason says that there is no problem here. The situation is too bad, but it is inevitable, the "price we must pay." With some superficial help from us, the poverty-ridden nations will in the course of time solve their own problems; in any case it is obvious that we can do nothing drastic without impairing our own situation. As for the social outcasts, they have had their choice, they knew the rules of the game. Furthermore, what could we do? No community can function smoothly without removing those who refuse to cooperate and who actively impede the efforts of those who do.

The existentialists do not deny that these answers are true. But they remain dissatisfied. They accuse us of unfeeling complacency and self-righteousness. There is not one world of experience but as many total worlds as there are individuals. Are we justified in saying that some must be held back because others must not be endangered? Dare we claim that the inner aspect of a crime is the same as its exterior side? Meursault shot the Arab—indubitably. But was the murder for which he was condemned the same as the act which he committed? Whether it was or was not, how could the jury know? Society has a way of classifying not only the big acts but even the little ones as absolutely good or evil and rejecting as evil him who does not conform. If in resentment at the whole procedure an increasing number of persons show their hostility to Society by choosing Evil for its own sake, is it only the rebellious who are to blame? Up till now the existentialists, beyond advocating more social equality and the abandonment of capital punishment, have not offered any solution to this dilemma. Perhaps they cannot. Yet in their understanding portrayal of the downtrodden and in their sympathetic analysis of the motivations of the "infamous," they present perhaps their greatest challenge to the conscience—more accurately, the consciousness—of the modern world.

Existentialism (this existentialism) is a humanism. It is a theory of man for man. Perhaps the strangest thing about it is the fact that it takes infinite pains to show that what man most needs and wants is exactly what he cannot have. Many philosophers in the past have argued that man's deep-rooted craving for a God and for an intelligible world are clear indications that a rational deity must exist. This is still pretty much the position of the religious existentialists: since the universe does not make sense in human terms, there must be a suprarational Being to explain it. The humanists will have none of this. The belief that there exists exactly what man wants to believe exists is, on the face of it, suspicious.

One might well raise a question at this point. Admittedly nobody can *prove* that God does not exist or that there is not some as yet undiscovered rational order in life and nature. Since an idea about the totality of things must inevitably be what James calls an over-belief, is it necessary that all our over-beliefs be negative? Although no one of our three writers has posed the question in quite this way, I think we can find an answer consistent with their point of view. They might reply that the historical attempts to relate the supernatural to human affairs have not met the tests of reason and experience. If someone wants to postulate the existence of a deity or a meaning which is totally beyond human comprehension, let him do so. But he must admit that in this case, man is not affected one way or another. Perhaps at some time in the future there may live creatures who could find such existence significant. Meanwhile man is our concern.

## LITERATURE-IN-SITUATION

The literature of humanistic existentialism—like its heroes and like its psychology—exists *in situation*. In the first place, for the literature as for the individual, the traditions of the past are there as part of the matter out of which it must make itself. On the whole, its writers have chosen to assert themselves against the past. They have leapt over the intervening centuries to find their inspiration in the Greek concept of drama and in the universality of Greek myth; even here they have found in the myths a challenge to provide new interpretations of man and of the universe which are utterly at variance with the Greek view of things. Their criticism of the nineteenth- and early twentieth-century French novelists has been largely unfavorable; and yet the influence— whether positively or negatively by way of revolt—is unmistakably there. The twentieth-century writer in France does not and cannot write as though Stendhal, Flaubert, Zola, and Proust had never lived. In certain cases the debt to other novelists is a positive one and has been explicitly acknowledged. Of all previous writers, Dostoyevsky has had the most profound influence. Camus has stated that his thought owes more to Dostoyevsky and to *The Possessed* than to any other single author or book.* With Sartre and de Beauvoir the influence is somewhat less obvious. Yet I think it would not be an exaggeration to say that every one of their literary works, as well as those of Camus, is an examination of the consequences of Dostoyevsky's "If God is dead, everything is allowed."

---

* Early in 1959, Camus' dramatic version of *The Possessed* was produced in Paris, directed by Camus himself. Apparently the play has been quite successful. If I may judge from reviews, Camus has followed his usual practice of putting little of himself save his talent into his adaptations. I have not felt it necessary to discuss these in our study of his fiction.

Stylistically, on the other hand, it is American writers who seem to have made the most impression. Each one of the existentialists is eclectic in the sense that the variation in style from one book to another is considerable. There is, for example, as much difference between *The Stranger* and *The Fall,* or between *The Flies* and *Nekrassov* as there is between any two of the three writers with whom we have been chiefly concerned. Yet we may note, as almost every other critic has done, that *The Stranger,* with its matter-of-fact reporting, its short, concise, sometimes almost staccato sentences, is an obvious stylistic parallel to Hemingway. Sartre has remarked that he has been greatly influenced by Dos Passos and Faulkner. He adds,

> The technique of Simone de Beauvoir, also, was inspired by Faulkner. Without him she never would have conceived the idea, used in *The Blood of Others,* of cutting the chronological order of the story and substituting instead a more subtle order, half logical, half intuitive.[3]

The effect of Dos Passos is most obvious in Sartre's *The Reprieve.* Here a widely varied set of characters and events are connected only by simultaneity in time. We follow their separate careers in brief fragmentary narratives, sometimes shifting within a single sentence. In the same way that the U.S.A. may be said to be the hero of Dos Passos' trilogy, so the plot of *The Reprieve* is the story of the Munich conference; Sartre uses news bulletins to define the forward movement of time and to initiate the subsequent action much as Dos Passos does. On the other hand, the fact that Sartre has not employed this device either in the rest of this novel sequence or in any of his other books suggests that he found the method foreign to him and could not be content with a borrowed technique except for an isolated instance where it seemed peculiarly appropriate. The same might be said of Camus and de Beauvoir.

To me the problem of how humanistic existentialism came into being and what literary forebears may be claimed for it is not the important one. This literature takes its stand firmly in the present and looks toward the future. Although any attempt to "place" humanistic existentialism in the twentieth century will perforce be very superficial, I think we ought not to leave the authors whom we have discussed without giving some indication of their situation with respect to other writers of today.

To start with, we may ask whether, granting that the term "humanistic existentialist" is, in part at least, an arbitrary one, there is any reason to limit it to the work of Sartre, de Beauvoir, and Camus. Do these three stand apart, or are they simply three representatives of a tendency which is widely spread throughout today's literature? In one sense I believe we are justified in treating them as a unique group. I know of no other writer who combines *all* of the attitudes which we have found to be characteristic of humanistic existentialism: the concept of the absurdity of existence, the concern to justify man's resolve to live meaningfully in the face of an indifferent universe, the philosophical analysis of the basis for human solidarity, the ideas of authenticity and bad faith, the refusal to accept a society based on the assumption of absolute Good and Evil, a sympathy with those scapegoats who are sacrificed to social expediency, a feeling for the absolute value of the individual combined with the recognition that one cannot today live wholly innocently—all this based on an explicit or implied psychology which holds that every man is free but that we are all responsible for the situation within which a freedom must choose itself.

On the other hand, there are at least two French writers whose books express a point of view so close to that of our existentialists that one might well feel inclined to group them along with the trio. One of these is Vercors, whose novel, *You Shall Know Them,* presents clearly the existentialist concept of man's estrangement from nature. The other is André Malraux. He has been greatly admired by the existentialists. Since World War II he has turned from fiction to aesthetic criticism; but in the novels which he wrote during the late twenties and thirties, he was already anticipating many of the themes which we have met over and over in our discussion. Malraux' interest in exploring the meaning of the human, the metaphysical possibilities of man as a species, is indicated by the title of one of his books—*The Human Condition (La condition humaine).* In the truest sense his characters in choosing themselves choose for all mankind. Yet at the same time Malraux does not forget Man for men. In his novels human possibilities are revealed in the course of the very real and disillusioning struggles against oppression in Spain and in China. He is interested in re-evaluating both what might be called the metaphysical facts of man's situation and the specific possibilities which are offered to him in the twentieth century. Malraux, too, shows us men who struggle to be saints without God, who find solidarity in the midst of their ultimate isolation, who recognize the meaning of devotion and self-sacrifice in the face of the ultimate absurdity of things.

What makes it easy to link Vercors and Malraux with humanistic existentialists is that the literature which they write is one of situations and their view of man is sympathetic to that of the existentialists. If instead of looking for this particular combination, we should seek out writers who produce a literature of situations (in contrast to the literature of characters) without necessarily subscribing to the existentialist type of humanism or, on the other hand, writers who have merely made certain existentialist themes their main focus of interest, then the connections between humanistic existentialism and the rest of contemporary literature would be far too numerous to catalogue.

Sartre in defining the literature of situations seems sometimes to be setting it up as the ideal of what literature should be and at other times describing it as a recognizable existing trend, by no means limited to literature of which he would wholly approve. According to Sartre, the new approach is not interested in the careful portrayal of individual personalities. It moves away from realism toward myth in an effort to throw new light on the basic human situations, investigating the possibility of new choices apropos of the old metaphysical problems; at the same time it makes these choices concrete by reference to specific alternatives in today's societies. In finding examples to illustrate his theory, Sartre mentioned not only plays by Camus but also Anouihl's *Antigone.* The political content of the play was one with which Sartre was in agreement, but we could hardly say that Anouihl here was specifically existentialist, and he certainly has not shown himself to be so in his other works. Many of Sartre's fellow artists in France have been reinterpreting myths as a way of putting human situations into new perspective. Gide, for example, in his *Oedipus* and *Theseus,* finds in old tales new symbols for his own humanistic morality, and Gide's thought—save for its lack of political reference—is in many respects sympathetic with existentialism. Jean Giraudoux, whom Sartre has described as a charming, intelligent writer, fatally tempted by an anachronistic Aristotelianism,[4] has been rewriting myths and legends since the thirties. His more recent *Tiger at the Gates* is a particularly clear form of the drama of situations. We are back at Troy just before the beginning of hostilities. The familiar characters are neither the personalities of Homer nor new three-dimensional beings endowed with life by Giraudoux. They are universal types, personified human attitudes; the siege of Troy—when it comes about— will be every war. The message of the play seems to be the idea that if war is to come, nothing individuals may do to prevent it can be of any avail. It will come to pass because of the obscure workings of Fate or of historical necessity, because people in general want or expect it even if no single individual does. Another borderline example is Jean Cocteau. His *Orpheus,* for instance, uses the Greek myth for a point of departure and makes of it a new allegory of Love and Life and Death. But the surrealist technique blurs its resemblance to Sartre's literature of situations. Like certain forms of ritual, it seems to be its own sole reason for being. Rather than seeking to convey a message, *Orpheus* invites one to submerge in its play and flow of emotions; its symbolism is less intellectual than osmotic.

When Sartre described the theatre of situations in the mid-forties, he explicitly excluded American playwrights as being concerned only with theatre of characters. In the decade since then we have had both types playing side by side on Broadway. In fact I should say that our two most significant writers of serious drama epitomize the two trends. Tennessee Williams has consistently given us as pure a theatre of characters as one can find even in the works of such masters of it as O'Neill. When the social dimension is present, as in *The Glass Menagerie,* he is interested in it only as an environmental force molding and at the same time destroying a personality. The theatre of situations has been magnificently represented by Arthur Miller. In 1955, in a brief essay called "On Social Plays," Miller laid down a literary credo remarkably similar to Sartre's. He begins—like Sartre—with reference to the Greeks, who, I must say, are made to be all things to all people these days. Pointing to certain parallels between our age and Classical Greece, he argues for a concept of social drama which would be closer to the Greek ideal. He continues,

> The social drama, as I see it, is the main stream and the antisocial drama a bypass. I can no longer take with ultimate seriousness a drama of individual psychology written for its own sake, however full it may be of insight and precise observation. Time is moving; there is a world to make, a civilization to create that will move toward the only goal the humanistic, democratic mind can ever accept with honor. It is a world in which the human being can live as a naturally political, naturally private, naturally engaged person, a world in which once again a true tragic victory may be scored.

A bit later Miller extends the definition.

> The social drama in this generation must do more than analyze and arraign the social network of relationships. It must delve

into the nature of man as he exists to discover what his needs are, so that those needs may be amplified and exteriorized in terms of social concepts.[5]

I am not sure that Miller is altogether clear about the distinction he is making. Elsewhere in this same essay he says that any drama which helps to show us how to live is social drama, and he gives as examples Williams' *A Streetcar Named Desire* and most of the plays of O'Neill, thus—to my thinking—blurring the effect of everything which he has said. Moreover his tragedy, *A View from the Bridge,* appears to be straight application of Freudian psychology even if Miller himself believes that in it he has "somehow stumbled upon a hallowed tale," a myth which he cannot identify but which he feels exists somewhere outside his own creative imagination. Other of Miller's plays are clearly theatre of situations; while one would not say that they are precisely existentialist, they are not incompatible with the existentialist position. In *Death of a Salesman* the psychological analysis of Willy Loman is identical with Miller's interpretation and indictment of Society. Loman reflects Society; indeed he *is* his Society. His individual life is a microcosmic representation of the life around him. At the same time he is a product of Society, and Miller is remarkably skillful in showing the interplay of personal choice and social environment. One might say that the play is a study of Society's habit of trying to force people to become one with the social functions which they perform; it would be just as accurate to say that Loman represents the For-itself which tries to live as if it were only its Self-for-others. Or we could label Loman an example of Fromm's "market personality." In *The Crucible* the emphasis is political rather than more generally social. Here Miller comments on a twentieth-century problem by representing its parallel in an earlier historical crisis, the witch trials of New England. This is, of course, exactly what Anouilh did in *Antigone,* Sartre in *The Flies,* and (with some modification) what Camus did in *The Plague.* Sartre has adapted *The Crucible* in a film called "Witches of Salem." I have not had the opportunity of seeing this. If I may judge from a review of it, it seems that Sartre has followed the story closely, not making important changes as in his adaptation of Dumas' *Kean* but merely filling in with extra material to make the political content more emphatic if less historical.[6] This seems to indicate more than tacit approval of Miller's position.

Obviously the literature of situations is by no means restricted to humanistic existentialism. What distinguishes the latter is not only its concept of the function of literature and its literary method. Humanistic existentialism has as well its specific metaphysical and psychological assumptions and its own social commitments. What is unique is the total synthesis. If we were to search for parallels in details (even those details most typical of existentialism), we should be forced to examine practically the whole of modern literature. Possibly we could exclude the committed Catholic writers such as Evelyn Waugh and Graham Green, but they too have their off moments of near-existentialism. Even a random choice of more obvious examples is overwhelming, in geographical scope if nothing else. *Waiting for Godot,* by the Irish writer, Samuel Beckett, portrays the absurdity of existence, the futility of man's insistence on looking for something absolute to give meaning to his life. *I'm Not Stiller,* by the Swiss novelist Max Frisch, is vaguely theistic and obviously under the influence of Kierkegaard, but its analysis of the individual's relation to time is reminiscent of Sartre, Heidegger, and the existential analysts. The Italian Alberto Moravia, in his novel *The Time of Indifference,* depicts the predicament of a young man who cannot take seriously the roles offered to him and who suffers from being unable to engage himself passionately in anything—a younger, less philosophical Mathieu. In Greece Kay Cicellis' *No Name in the Street* is a superb treatment of the problem of the self-for-others. It concerns a closely knit group of young people who live so completely in and through the myths they have built up collectively that apart from the group they have no existence; when two of them try to split away and live as a couple, neither can any longer find the other—nor himself. In America John Barth's *The End of the Road* is of particular interest. It is a deliberate, careful satire of Sartre's thought, a *reductio ad absurdum* which is designed to show that if the theory is put into practice, it is utterly nihilistic. Although it seems to me a distorted application and not a convincing refutation, Barth's attack is thought-provoking, and it is more scoffing than downright hostile. The novel in several instances suggests that there may be after all a certain truth in some of Sartre's theories. In any case Barth offers no positive alternative.

For future critics who may try to describe the literary landscape of this mid-century, I suspect that the most interesting parallel and contrast with humanistic existentialism will be found in its relations to two other groups which have suddenly become important in the early fifties: the San Francisco "Beat Generation" and the British "Angry Young Men."

Naturally any such critical appraisal will have to wait for the future. To make generalizations about the still developing work of Camus, Sartre, and de Beauvoir is hazardous enough. The other schools are still newer, still more in process of change, and—especially in Great Britain—the individuals whom the public insists on grouping together show even more divergent points of view.

For both groups there is an obvious surface connection with existentialism. The Beatnik denizens of the West Coast bars have been popularly—and I think rightly—equated with the café existentialists in Paris. Jack Kerouac in *The Subterraneans* used "existentialism" as a kind of covering term for whatever his philosophical outlook was in those days. Just what he meant by it is hard to say. Extreme individualism, of course; a relentless intensity and craving to savor the most out of every present, passionate moment; revolt, too, against any kind of conformity. I feel that there is also at this earlier stage a genuine humanism in Kerouac, manifested sometimes as a sympathetic pity for the "forlornness" of humanity and again as an exultant acceptance of *all* the human condition. On the other hand, Kerouac has never given any indication that he is even aware of the intellectual side of existentialism, and one has the feeling that to him all preoccupation with moral questions is on a level with an old maid's fussing over her teacups. More recently, the association with existentialism has been pretty well forgotten in the feverish pursuit of Zen Buddhism. Theoretically, existentialism and Zen Buddhism are not so compatible that a transition could be made from one to the other without significant change in a man's way of life or in a novelist's approach to literature. Yet Kerouac seems to have accomplished it. Reviewers have been sufficiently free in condemning his use of Zen to justify moral irresponsibility in *The Dharma Bums*. The quality and sincerity of Kerouac's religious commitment are not for me to judge. Certainly he and those of his associates who have so eagerly reached out to lose the Self in the Not-Self and to find that in this world all things are illusion and the All is good, can no longer be related—even remotely—to existentialism. I question whether they are still humanists. Either-or is not both-and, no matter how high the mountain.

The Angry Young Men have been associated with existentialism chiefly through Colin Wilson, who actually has very little in common with the rest of them. In *The Outsider* it was apparent that for him "Outsider" and "Existentialist" were synonomous terms, and he applied them to a widely varied collection of persons ranging from Cardinal

Newman to George Bernard Shaw. The only requirement apparently was that the Outsider must be someone who felt himself to be out of step with society, who believed that the solution lay neither in better adjustment to the social nor in reform of society but rather in spiritual improvement, a process which isolated him even further but compensated with inner peace and mystic ecstasy. When reviewer after reviewer accused Wilson of using "existentialism" simply as a designation for any writer whom he admired, he defined his use of the word in a letter to *The Times Literary Supplement*. Existentialism, he says, cannot be summed up in the usual philosophical terms. It

> began with Kierkegaard's attempt to assert religious values against the materialistic trend of nineteenth-century thought. I feel, therefore, that a definition of existentialism which would cover all the different approaches to it—including M. Sartre's —would be: "An affirmation of man as spirit"—and therefore, as capable of salvation and damnation.[7]

The *Times* reviewer pointed out in answer to this letter that Kierkegaard was rebelling not against materialism but against Hegelian idealism, which is a quite different thing. Wilson's definition is much too inclusive. If all that is necessary is to conceive of man as spirit capable of salvation and damnation, then Dante and Aquinas are existentialists along with every other Christian writer. If the formula is interpreted so loosely as to make the words "spirit," "damnation," and "salvation" applicable in the work of nontheistic writers such as Sartre, then it is hard to see how anyone is *not* an existentialist.

Fortunately Wilson goes on to tell us. Those excluded would be materialists and Freudian determinists; in the strict sense it is true that they would be barred by humanistic existentialists also. On the other hand, Wilson says in *Religion and the Rebel* that "re-creation by self-analysis is the most fundamental meaning of existentialism,"[8] and this, while not the same as the concept of good faith, is at least tangential to it. In *The Declaration* he claims that the artist represents the highest consciousness of the age and must try to extend that consciousness to others.[9] This view is quite in harmony with the positions of Sartre and Camus, who would also agree that the artist "must become actively involved in the task of restoring a metaphysical consciousness to our age." Wilson's great difference from the French existentialists and, in my opinion, his weakness as writer and thinker lies in his never quite having made up his mind as to what man is or what is the meaning of the "religion" which the rebel is to embrace. At times Wilson seems to be wholly humanistic; he rejects the Church, he counsels men to look inward and to develop their own psychological potentialities. It is in this spirit that he considers Shaw the greatest existentialist of them all. At other times he seems to be more at home with visions and the saint's asceticism and wants us all to search for something higher than the everyday senses and consciousness. All of this is quite contrary to the doctrine of humanistic existentialism, which urges man to live by what he knows. Wilson says that his inspiration for *The Outsider* was William James' *Varieties of Religious Experience*.[10] The source is a good one, but I fear Wilson has muddied the waters of the spring rather than causing them to flow forth more abundantly.

There is one other specific connection between the British circle and Paris if we include Iris Murdoch. She has written a thoughtful study of Sartre, *Sartre, Romantic Rationalist,* in which she quite effectively demonstrates the interweaving in Sartre's work of certain seemingly opposed motifs of romanticism and rationalism. Her own novels are filled with psychological analyses obviously derived from Sartre's existentialism, but I cannot see that she has employed them in the interest of any new important idea. In fact she seems anachronistically to have adopted existentialist psychology for the purpose of creating a new-style literature of characters.

Speaking generally of both the Beats and the Angry, we may say at present that a tangential relation to existentialism has served them as a point of departure but that the connection is becoming much less apparent. Setting aside entirely those who have committed themselves to Zen Buddhism or other forms of Eastern mysticism, both English and American writers have remained "rebels without a cause," which is exactly what Wilson said the Outsider ought to be. Sometimes, as in the case of the pre-Dharma Kerouac, their revolt is at least roughly comparable to Jean Genet's. They strive to undermine society rather than to be better integrated in it or to modify it constructively—constructively from *any* point of view. Some of the Beatniks have found a way out in retreat to a primitivism and pansexualism somewhere between D. H. Lawrence and Henry Miller. In England the revolt is more closely associated with class distinction than it is in America. In John Braine's *Room at the Top* or in Kingsley Amis' *Lucky Jim,* resentment comes perilously close to being a small boy's envy of the rich kids whose fathers have better cars and who may look forward to going to more exclusive schools. Osborne's anger is deeper and more embracing. But when he seeks for a specific target, he can find nothing better than the Royal

Family, which is somehow anticlimactic. Most of these writers are distinctly uninterested in politics. (Doris Lessing may prove to be an exception.) Osborne's character Jimmy Porter, for instance, has found no noble causes and will certainly not try to invent any. Kerouac's heroes go through the world saying "Yes" to all of experience; Osborne's say "No," though their refusal is not resignation and still bears some trace of the passion of Sisyphus. But unless it takes a new turn in the future, the British movement seems to me, for all its clear sanity and dogged individualism, to come close to being a literature of despair. The American in its own boisterous and belligerent fashion at least looks for some way out and exults in the fight.

Even after so superficial a glance at the contemporary literary scene, if we look back again to the fiction of Jean-Paul Sartre, Simone de Beauvoir, and Albert Camus, it is evident that it is distinguished less by being a literature of situations than by the particular synthetic view which it takes of man's situation. To attempt here an encapsulated, purely aesthetic evaluation of their work would be difficult and for the purposes of this study not especially rewarding. This is partly because the three differ greatly from one another in style and in narrative technique, far more decisively than they do in their philosophy, though there too we have noted many instances of variation. Two generalizations I think we might safely make: All are stylistically eclectic and interested in experimenting with new forms. No one of them is ever willing to let form becloud the meaning. This does not mean that a clear statement of the message is attached to each work like the moral at the end of an Aesop fable. Like any worthwhile work of art, their books may legitimately allow several interpretations and may say to some readers more than was originally in the author's mind. At no time, however, does one feel that one is in a dream world where it is impossible to tell symbol from reality—as happens so often, for example, in the stories of Kafka—or that one simply does not know what is going on—as with the late writing of Joyce. Outside of these general statements there is little to be said apropos of literary method which would be significant and true for all three writers. Furthermore, tricks of style, choice of adjectives, ways of handling dialogue, plot foreshadowing, techniques for creating suspense, symbolic devices—such things are but the means selected by individual talents. They do not in any way stem from or determine the distinctive quality of the literature of possibility.

The specific plots are indeed determined by the literary and philosophical theory behind them, for it is by his choice of problem and by his way of resolving it that the author delineates the human situation for us. As we anticipated in Part One, there is wide variation in the type of plot chosen. We have found myth, near-allegory, thinly disguised autobiography, realistic tragedy, melodramatic comedy. In de Beauvoir's *All Men Are Mortal,* myth and what might have been a historical novel are wedded in a form which is almost but not quite science fiction. On the whole, myth or narratives set in distant space or time are employed when the author is concerned with philosophical concepts; more realistic, contemporary settings are for specific, immediate problems, for which man needs not only understanding but a solution. This is not always true. The German Occupation is present in ancient Argos for Sartre and in Oran for Camus, though we must add that both *The Flies* and *The Plague* are much more than political allegories. I do not think that any of the three authors is guilty of letting the idea get in the way of the plot in the sense that we feel the natural denouement has been distorted to make way for the doctrinal lesson. There are, however, a few examples where the plot *is* the development of an intellectual concept. This is emphatically the case with *Lucifer and the Lord*. It is partly so in *State of Siege* and *All Men Are Mortal*. It ought to have been the case in *She Came to Stay;* but in this novel de Beauvoir has so carefully and so skillfully developed the human complexities that it is only after finishing the book that one notes with amusement its step by step correspondence with Sartre's description of the subject-object conflict.

It is apropos of character portrayal that Sartre's literary theory is most radical, and it is in this respect that the existentialist work is most distinct from other literature. Two things are involved: the author's attitude toward the proper function of psychology in imaginative writing and the kind of psychology which he embraces. Camus and de Beauvoir are no more interested than Sartre in providing detailed psychological analyses of many-faceted, intricate personalities.[11] Among all these fictional heroes and heroines there is not a single instance—save for the sardonic portrait of Philippe-Baudelaire—of the Oedipus complex or of the struggle of the individual to free himself from the conditioning pressures of the family and environment or of any of the other familiar maladjustments which have filled the pages of the literature of characters. Meursault may have been condemned for not weeping at his mother's funeral; there is not the slightest suggestion that this was because he bore an unconscious hostility toward her or that he was repressing his affection because he had once wanted to sleep with her. His attitude toward his mother is the focal question at the trial, and we hear not one word about his childhood. Literature is no longer the handmaid and popularizer of psychology.

Yet if we are to be in any way convinced by these imaginary beings, their behavior must be consistent with some sort of psychological theory. In my interpretation of existentialist works, I have tried to show that the principles involved are those of a psychology based on freedom. For Sartre, obviously, our point of reference is existential psychoanalysis, and we have seen that the case histories of real persons "psychoanalyzed" by Sartre bear close resemblance to the fictional ones. Since de Beauvoir has explicitly stated her agreement with most of Sartre's psychology, it is proper for us to expect that her characters may be understood from the same approach. At the same time there is absolutely no reason why Camus should have written with existential psychoanalysis in mind or why his characters should be in any way at all explicable by Sartrean psychology. The fact is that we find no conflict of principles. Camus never argues against the existence of an unconscious, but neither does he at any time make it necessary for us to look for unconscious motivation. That he represents his fictional personages as free beings we have recognized again and again. It is possible to find in some of them obvious examples of the various structures of bad faith. Moreover, just as happens sometimes with Sartre's creations, Camus' heroes are often not three-dimensional personalities but embodiments of human attitudes. Thus Clamence is a portrait of the man who both enjoys and is destroyed by his self-conscious guilt. Caligula brings to life one type of reaction to the absurd. Other characters, even though they too may represent definite points of view, perhaps even specific intellectual ideas, seem to live for us as real people. Without our knowing very much of their everyday habits, they are nevertheless familiar to us. Rieux and Tarrou are like this—and d'Arrast. To be fair, I should say that so are Anne and Henri, and—distasteful as they may be—so are Daniel and Marcelle.

I believe that the possibilities for the literature of humanistic existentialism depend primarily on what Camus, Sartre, de Beauvoir, and those who may be influenced by them decide to make of this new concept of literary character and its accompanying psychology. In my opinion there is a danger involved in this tendency to abstract from human personality rather than to create synthetically. If one goes too far with it, one may very easily fall into an insipid variety of allegory. In addition, human traits and human situations, when stated abstractly, have a way of losing their uniqueness. In pleading for the free individual, existentialism can hardly afford to lapse into a vague universalism in its literature. I doubt that there is much likelihood that this will happen. If writers take the psychology of freedom seriously, they will not substitute new determinisms for the old Freudian ones.

So long as man is free to change, the literature which reflects him will find new possibilities. There is no danger that everything will have been said or all novelty exhausted. But literature too must be ready for the change. If a particular literature conforms too rigidly to established psychological, ethical, and philosophical principles, it can be transcended only as it is passed by and forgotten. The literature of possibility, which holds that there is no narrowly fixed, well-defined human nature, is ready to guide the process of its own development and eventual self-transcendence. Because it promises man an open future, its own future is open. When Fosca and that mouse finally reach the moon, there will be new tales to tell and new ways to tell them.

# AFTERWORD

THE CRITIC WHO CHOOSES TO STUDY the works of living authors runs the risk of seeing his book out of date – or at best incomplete – on the day of its publication. He may perhaps console himself with the thought that the further productions of those he has written about vindicate his original choice of them as significant – all the more so if they have shown themselves capable of going beyond anything which the critic had been able earlier to discover or anticipate.

For my own part, I find myself, three years after the completion of this book, not inclined to propose a revision. It does not seem to me that recent existentialist writing forces upon us a new appraisal of what went before. I see no necessity for remaking this particular part of my past and am content to let it rest in Being-in-itself, an object before the pitiless Look of the Other. Yet to say that new existentialist works do not demand a re-evaluation of what preceded them is not the same as maintaining that nothing important has appeared, that nothing has been added. Literature has not stood still nor been content with repeating itself, and I should like to cast a cursory appraising look on the output of these three years.

Albert Camus' death on January 4, 1960, in an automobile accident was surely one of the most gratuitous of tragic events in this absurd world. Columns in the press took on more of the quality of elegy than of straight reporting. For a remarkably long period critics seemed reluctant to assume the task of summing up the man's work, expressing almost unanimously the feeling that one could not properly close up the account for a writer who still had so much left to say.[1] This universal reluctance to abandon the hope of what would have been Camus' future was perhaps as great a tribute to him as the Nobel Prize which he received in 1957.

Simone de Beauvoir brought out in 1960 the second volume of her autobiography, *La Force de l'âge*. The book is amazing in its simultaneous sense of intimacy and breadth of scope. De Beauvoir relates in great detail her life between 1929 and the liberation of France in 1944. All is set forth from her personal point of view. Even the story of the Occupation, told in part by excerpts from her diary, is presented in terms of the private experiences of herself and Sartre and their friends. Yet her ability to grasp the universal in the particular, her consuming interest in the behavior of all around her, and her growing recognition that her own life was not and could not be separated from the cataclysmic events of a shrinking world, all combine to make the reader feel that he has lived through these years with France, not only with de Beauvoir.

The autobiography is a literary and cultural chronicle as well, a survey of the life of letters, theatre and cinema, and — though less completely — of art during this decade and a half. It describes de Beauvoir's and Sartre's struggles to win recognition for their own work. Most fascinating of all, perhaps, is de Beauvoir's discussion of the way in which her own books gradually assumed shape. In this study of the creative process there is far more than mere interest value for those already devoted to de Beauvoir's fiction. She conveys almost miraculously the sense of the inextricable yet discernible blend of external event and "intending" consciousness, the inspiring episode and the creative will to see in it something more than is objectively there, the later artistic transmutation into independent fictional being, the work as conceived, its tentative emergence, its final form.

*La Force de l'âge* confirms my belief that there is much of de Beauvoir herself in Anne (of *The Mandarins*) and in Françoise (of *She Came to Stay*). But it offers a wholesome corrective to any idea that these heroines are to be wholly identified with their author. In one particular respect I owe her an apology. Judging solely on the basis of her fiction and her philosophical essays, I had found nothing in de Beauvoir to indicate that she shared Camus' capacity for finding solace and psychic sustenance in the natural beauties of this world. Specifically I said of her, "One does not find her contemplating the landscape alone."

In her autobiography de Beauvoir reveals an almost frenetic

compulsion to walk over every inch of the terrain surrounding Marseilles, where she held her first teaching position. What distinguished her from the rest of the hike-loving Marseillaises was precisely the fact that she usually went by herself instead of with one of the organized groups. Throughout her life she has apparently covered on foot most of France and large sections of other parts of Europe. There was one mad midday jaunt through Arcadia in midsummer when Sartre, who on this occasion accompanied her, almost passed out.

Sartre's enthusiasm for out-of-doors contemplation was considerably less than de Beauvoir's. In their early meetings out in the country near Paris, she discovered that he "was allergic to chlorophyll. The verdancy of these pastures wearied him; he tolerated it only on condition of ignoring it."[2] On the whole, I think that de Beauvoir's passion for exploring every rock and hillock resembles that desire for possessing Being-in-itself which Sartre discusses in *Being and Nothingness* more than Camus' search for "an invincible summer" in the brilliance of Algeria's sea and sky. She confesses to a total lack of discrimination as she obsessively hunted down everything mentioned in her *Guide bleu,* no matter what it was. In Spain Sartre had to put his foot down when she wanted to interrupt their trip to go look at "a mountain of salt. 'Natural beauties, fine', he declared, 'but for natural curiosities, no!' " Yet I do not mean to imply that de Beauvoir was without true appreciation for the wonder of nature. We find from time to time descriptive passages of exultant delight reminiscent of Camus' lyrical essays.

> Amidst the bewildering stones where there was not the slightest sign of a path, I went on, watching for the arrows—blue, green, red, yellow—which guided me I knew not where. Sometimes I lost them, I searched for them, going around in circles, thrashing against the shrubs with their sharp aromas, scratching my skin on plants still new to me—the resinous rock roses, junipers, ilex, yellow and white asphodels. I followed over all the old tide-waiters' trails beside the sea. At the foot of the cliffs along these tortured coasts, the Mediterranean did not have that saccharine languor which often sickened me in other places. In the glory of the mornings it beat with violence against the promontories, in dazzling white, and I had the impression that if I plunged my hand into this sea, it would cut off my fingers.... From every lookout point, from every little valley I anticipated a revelation, and always the beauty of the landscape surpassed my memories and my expectation (pp. 95-96).

De Beauvoir revisited Provence, but this was no "Return to Tipasa." She recognized her reasons for having loved it all, but she realized that the terrain itself was not enough to explain her earlier mania. Unlike Camus, she finds the more lasting interest in the activity of her own consciousness.

> Often in life I took refuge in that strategem: to endow my activities with a necessity of which I was finally the dupe.
> It was in this way that at the age of eighteen I employed frenzy to save myself from boredom (p. 97).

During this period Sartre has brought out two works which must certainly be counted among the most significant of all his writing. These are his drama, *The Condemned of Altona (Les Séquestrés d'Altona)*[3] and *Critique of Dialectical Reason (Critique de la raison dialectique)*.[4]

To my mind, Sartre achieves an artistic perfection in *The Condemned of Altona* which he had never quite attained earlier. The play is richer, more self-contained, more complete. It reaches beyond itself only in the way that all great art does, demanding that we ourselves develop its further implications in our own subsequent reflections. The philosophical and political themes may be further developed in Sartre's essays, but our understanding of the play never depends on anything outside itself. The characters are fairly complex; they come alive as themselves, but they never become personalities interesting only for themselves. Sartre seems here better than anywhere else to have given flesh and blood to his theatre of situations without at any time returning to the old theatre of characters.

In some ways the new drama points back to two earlier works. Sartre has called it a *"No Exit* with five characters."[5] The shifting relationships move less mathematically than in *No Exit,* but there is a similar use of the disintegrating Third, the same sense that each person by the demands which he makes upon the others, keeps both them and himself prisoners. This Hell is of the characters' own making, and it is laid at Altona in Germany. We have left myth for history. Sartre is nevertheless depicting one situation in terms of another, and in this respect he is doing once more what he attempted in *The Flies.* In the story of Franz, the reluctant Nazi in bad faith and with uneasy conscience, Sartre holds up to France the troubling reflection of her own role in Algeria.

As early as 1958 Sartre had remarked in *France Observateur* that a fruitful subject for a play would be "The disintegration which might come about inside a family, due to the silence maintained by one recalled from duty in Algeria." In *The Condemned of Altona* Sartre is indeed treating "the silence of those who come back," but he lays the scene in Germany. Asked whether he thought that the particular circumstances of the Algerian war would in any way change the essential meaning of a play concerned with "Germany's bad conscience," Sartre answered:

> "Absolutely nothing would be changed. It is a question of a man's relations with others. And also, of course, of a man with himself."[6]

I suspect that the drama has profited by the transposition. Sartre has avoided the pitfalls of the obvious propaganda piece, and he has gained the advantage of dealing with a problem already rounded off, as it were, by history.

In this era of the anti-play, Sartre's dramatic technique remains rather conventional. The only interruption to realistic chronological development is a series of insets presenting scenes from the past. In these Sartre carries one step farther a device employed in *No Exit*. In the earlier play each of the protagonists describes actions which he or she sees taking place on earth, a last glimpse of what he had left behind. In *The Condemned of Altona* the scenes are played before our eyes. Again just one person "sees" them. Only this time he takes part himself as he recalls or is supposedly relating the events to other people. The material is carefully restricted to what he wants the others to hear though it is never falsified. The complication and denouement of the plot are determined almost equally by acts in the present and by the characters' reaction to what is revealed from the past.

Following the main outline of the story as it took place rather than as it is unfolded in the play, we find the following: In Nazi Germany Herr von Gerlach, a wealthy shipbuilder, learns that his son Franz is sheltering an escaped Jewish rabbi. The father informs Goebbels personally. S.S. guards come after the prisoner and kill him as Franz watches helplessly. Franz is pardoned on condition that he enlist in the army. As an officer, Franz throughout the war considers himself an anti-Nazi but nevertheless does everything necessary in order to win. Nothing but victory, he believes, can justify the means employed. When Germany loses, Franz feels that only the greater atrocities on the part of the Allies can excuse the war guilt of the Germans. A fair beginning has been made by the bombing of Hiroshima, and Franz anticipates with mingled horror and longing the inhuman punishment and degradation of a ruined Germany. A crisis is precipitated when his sister Leni provokes an anti-Semitic American officer by calling him a Jew. The man attempts to rape her; Franz kills him. Again the father uses his influence and gets permission for Franz to leave the country unharmed. Franz refuses to go and shuts himself up in an upstairs room, leaving his father to arrange a pretended flight to Argentina. Franz tells himself that he has retreated because he cannot bear to watch his country's agony. Much later he confesses that the real reason was his unwillingness to be a witness to her resurrection. If what awaited defeated Germany was prosperity, then he had betrayed his ideals for nothing. For thirteen years Franz sees nobody but Leni, whose incestuous love he halfheartedly returns. Leni, Sartre's representative of the proudest and most cynical of the bourgeoisie, feels humiliated at the idea of giving herself to anyone but a Gerlach. She is annoyed by Franz' need to defend himself, not, apparently, disturbed by the acts which had made him feel guilty.

Most of the time Franz spends nourishing a delirium. He imagines he is witness for the defense for the twentieth century before a tribunal of Crabs in the thirtieth century. The Crabs are constantly watching him, trying to catch him off his guard. Franz makes speech after speech into a tape recorder, trying to find an adequate defense. Meanwhile Leni sustains his delusion that Germany remains in ruins; she gives him horrifying descriptions of suffering orphans, famine, oppression, concealing entirely the fact that the von Gerlach firm is but one of many enjoying new heights of prosperity.

It is at this point in the story that the play opens. The father, knowing he is about to die of cancer, tries to compel Leni and Franz' brother Werner to swear that they will never leave the house at Altona during their lifetime. Joanna rebels, refusing to let her husband's life be sacrificed to Franz' madness. The father makes a secret bargain with her—if she can manage to see Franz and persuade him to grant his father an interview, he will release Werner from his oath.

Joanna has not one but several interviews with Franz and finds even in his madness a truth and power which she had never felt in her husband. Knowing that knowledge of Germany's real situation would cure the delirium but kill Franz, she falls voluntarily into the habits of Leni. It is Leni who destroys their relation. Madly jealous, she tells Franz the truth about the world outside, and she informs Joanna that Franz, who had claimed to be tormented by the fact that he had refused to go to the limit to insure his country's victory, had voluntarily tortured Russian partisans. Joanna rejects him. Franz scorns Leni and descends to meet his father. The two men are reconciled only in a suicide pact. Leni realizes that they have set out to drive her car over a nearby cliff. She ascends the stairs to take her turn as "the sequestered" in Franz' room. Joanna and Werner leave the stage with faces void of all expression. Only the tape recorder is left, playing back Franz' "best speech for the defense," in reality a violent condemnation of our century.

Of all the characters Joanna most resembles those of earlier existentialist literature — especially the studies of bad faith. Although supposedly her decision to see Franz is motivated by her desire to protect her husband's independence, it becomes apparent that she had never loved Werner. Leni, remarking brutally that "some marriages are funerals," accuses her of having married only because she knew she had failed as a cinema actress (reminding us of Paula in *The Mandarins*). Franz sees in her a person who refused everything (her decision to give up her career) so as to conceal the fact that she had been rejected (reminiscent of Genet). Joanna herself confesses that she tried to watch herself, to find herself in the image on the screen but could never see what the public saw. What puts her under the spell of Franz is primarily his promise to declare that she is beautiful and to bear witness to the fact before all eternity. In all of this we see that attempt to catch a crystallized self, that pursuit of the in-itself-for-itself which permeates almost all of Sartrean literature.

Sartre's treatment of Franz is especially significant if we consider him in relation to Sartre's views as expressed in "Existential Psychoanalysis." Franz is a person who has consented to, or even willed himself into a delirium. Faced with the alternatives of killing himself or living with the knowledge of his guilt, Franz refuses to recognize the dilemma and creates a third path: he chooses madness, which allows him to construct a make-believe world where he is no longer the accused but the witness for the defense.

Sartre makes it very clear that Franz is both author and prisoner of his delirium. His feeling that he must defend himself and his century before the Future is certainly genuine. The tribunal of Crabs is real enough for him to be seriously upset when he thinks he may have betrayed to them thoughts which he does not want the Crabs to know. He is sufficiently convinced of the reality of a ruined Germany so that when the delusion is destroyed, he does indeed die as Joanna had foreseen. Yet there are many indications that Franz has to work at this self-deception. At one point he himself suggests to Joanna that Germany is swimming in prosperity, then quickly covers his ears, "Useless! Useless! I will not believe you." There is more resignation than shock in his final acceptance of actuality when Leni forces it upon him. Early in the play Franz admits that he values his madness above everything else. His father and Leni never do fully believe in it. In the last interview with Joanna, Franz moves back and forth between lucidity and senseless ramblings. Joanna realizes that at this moment he seeks his imaginary world partly as a refuge from her. Sartre writes into the stage directions, "As he speaks, she regains control of herself and hardens; she understands that Franz is trying only to protect his delirium" (p. 161). It would be a mistake to think that Sartre intended his portrait of Franz to be taken as a typical picture of any delirium or thoroughgoing psychosis. Yet in this borderline case he suggests the curious intermingling of freedom and a willed loss of freedom which perhaps accompanies and renders possible all psychotic rejections of a more objective reality in favor of the arbitrarily constructed world of the mentally ill.

In conveying the particular style of Franz' madness, Sartre uses material objects as psychological symbols. For example, Franz' room is covered with oyster shells, which he has the habit of picking up and rubbing against one another in moments of distress. The reflection of his desire to retreat into the dark shelter of the shell is obvious. The choice of crabs for his judges is interesting on another level and as related to Sartre himself rather than to his fictional creation. One might suspect that Sartre had chosen crabs as the only inhabitants in the thirtieth century either under the influence of H. G. Well's *The Time Machine* or by the same sort of evolutionary fantasy as that which led Wells to choose a giant marine creature as the last form of life on our dying planet. That there is a little more behind it than this, one might surmise upon recalling that in *Nausea* Roquentin's tormented imagination insisted on seeing the configurations of his hand

and fingers turn into the shape and movements of a crab. De Beauvoir in her autobiography supplies pertinent and illuminating information.

During the years 1934 and 1935 Sartre suffered from semi-hallucinatory images. They began when he allowed a physician friend to give him mescaline as a scientific experiment. Unlike the other subjects, who experienced fantastic delights, Sartre seemed to see monstrous images fastened upon the objects in the room, and in particular, swarming crabs. For some time afterward he continued to be troubled by these distorted pseudo-perceptions: a black spot dancing in space, houses with grimacing faces, covered with eyes and open jaws, and forms of marine life trotting along behind him. They never became full-fledged hallucinations. Sartre was always aware that the visions were not really there but inside his own consciousness. He did not believe in their objective existence, but he was haunted by the fear that some day he might believe. De Beauvoir describes his extreme depression.

> Abruptly he said to me, "I know what it is. I'm in the first stages of a chronic hallucinatory psychosis." As they defined it in those days, this illness was one which within ten years would end up fatally in insanity.[7] I protested furiously, and not, for once, out of wishful thinking but from common sense. Sartre's case in no way resembled the beginnings of a hallucinatory psychosis. Neither the black spot nor his obsession with the houses with jaws indicated the birth of an incurable psychosis. Moreover I knew with what facility Sartre's imagination ran to catastrophe. "Your only madness is to believe yourself mad," I said. "You will see," he answered me somberly (pp. 217-218).

For some months the visions persisted, pursuing Sartre even on his vacation in Italy, where for one long night in Venice a lobster followed after him. But the Venetian lobster was the last of them. They did not return.

Later Sartre and de Beauvoir together concluded that the experience expressed a profound unrest and basic anxiety in Sartre. De Beauvoir explains it by saying that at the age of thirty he "was not resigned to passing from 'the age of reason' to 'the age of man'." Although he liked teaching and enjoyed his students, Sartre felt oppressed by the hollow pretensions of the bourgeois world in which he felt himself a prisoner. Furthermore "he was committing himself to a path already marked out in advance. His only adventure would be the books which he would write." And these were not going well. His first novel had been rejected. What was ultimately to be *Nausea* still required a great deal of work. The publisher Alcan had accepted only the first, less original half of Sartre's study of the imagination.

> We both had absolute confidence in his future; but the future was not always enough to illuminate the present. Sartre had put so much ardor into being young that at the moment when his youth was leaving him, there would have had to be over- whelming joys to console him for its loss (p. 219).

I have referred to this episode in Sartre's life not just because I find it interesting in itself nor because it furnishes a chance clue to the otherwise insignificant choice of crabs for Franz' judges rather than owls, snakes, or hoptoads. I think that it furnishes us a valuable aid both for our interpretation of Franz and for our understanding of Sartre's view of the relation of the free consciousness to abnormal mental states. At a time when the life he wanted to lead seemed ir- remediably bogged down in concessions to the Serious World, Sartre's consciousness projected the situation by means of the disagreeable, oppressive and almost irresistible images. He could not prevent him- self from letting them come to his attention, but he was able to deny them acceptance as anything other than the imaginations which they were. Evidently Sartre recognized that had his hopes been weaker, his reasons for rejecting the present situation more compelling, he might well have given in to the temptation of the fantastic, yielding to its pressure rather than struggling against it. Franz has gone but a step further. By struggling to deny external reality rather than facing it, by presenting himself as a witness before the Crabs instead of the accused before mankind, he can bear his guilt by restructuring it. Yet he has not retreated so far into the imaginary that he is not dimly aware that it is his act of will which determines which world he will live in. At those moments when he renews his original choice, he is not mad but in bad faith.

Even in his delirium Franz is partly right. He believes that he will be judged by the future, and the anxiety with which he rejects each of his attempts to find just the right defense testifies to his realization that his guilt cannot be erased. To this extent he is not the mad Franz von Gerlach but in very truth the century he claims to defend. Sartre said in an interview,

> The whole play is constructed from the viewpoint of a future which is simultaneously false and true. The recluse's madness lies in his considering himself—in an effort to avoid feeling guilty—the witness of a century which is in the process of disappearing and in addressing himself to a superior tribunal. All he says is absurd, to be sure, and not a true commentary on this century, but I wanted the spectator to feel himself to some degree in the presence of this tribunal. . . . Or, quite simply, in the presence of centuries to come.[8]

Franz' own sense of guilt and Joanna's rejection of him both underscore Sartre's belief that no appeal to political expediency can justify the torture of individuals either in Nazi Germany or French Algeria. The final scene with the father makes the point still more forcefully. Herr von Gerlach feels that he has instilled his own destructive passions in his son. He pities Franz and loves him, but he states flatly that he cannot accept him. Like the Father in Kafka's *The Judgement,* he sentences his son to death, and the son accepts the verdict as just. But Franz insists that his father face death along with him. The father's consent signifies more than simply his realization that the only thing in life which still held him had been the desire to see Franz once more. It is also the acknowledgement of his own guilt.

When the Nazis wanted to buy some of his land to be used for a concentration camp, von Gerlach let them have it: "If I had refused my property, they would simply have bought it somewhere else . . . and I would have made enemies inside the Government." Like Franz, the father insisted that he loathed the Nazi leaders but that he had to obey them. Franz asks in reply,

> Whom did they obey? We hated Hitler, others loved him. Where's the difference? You furnished them warships, and I furnished them corpses. Tell me, what more could we have done if we had idolized him? (p. 44).

The father can only respond with another question. "Then is everybody guilty?" Sartre's answer is yes. As Franz puts it, you can destroy a people either by condemning them as a whole or by forcing them to repudiate their chosen leaders. "The second way is the worst." The Germans are responsible for the actions of the leaders they support. Repudiation of them in 1946 is a guilty evasion. But so is the act of those French who would merely disassociate themselves from the oppression and torture of Algerians by French officials.

In the play there are several suggestions of the existence in Franz of a hidden love of cruelty and evil. In self-disgust he realized that it was the prisoners themselves who filled him with horror as he saw them in the concentration camp—their dirt, vermin, sores—their fear. He confesses to Joanna that he doesn't really care about the orphans concerning whose fate he was constantly inquiring. Most important of all is his memory of the scene where he watched the S.S. guards kill the rabbi.

> I hated Hitler. Before, and after. But that day he possessed me. Where there are two leaders, either they must kill each other, or one must become the other's wife. I was Hitler's wife. The rabbi was bleeding and I discovered at the heart of my powerlessness some strange assent (p. 206).

From then on, Franz, resolving never to be again without power, pursued it to the limit by giving orders to kill or torture others.

It is possible, I suppose, to conclude that Sartre here is claiming that there exists in man a fundamental animal cruelty or basic evil.[9] I myself do not think it is quite accurate to go so far. In the first place, Franz' momentary approving assent was inseparable from the sense of his own impotence, a reaction closer to masochism than to sadism. Even if we grant the existence of bestial possibilities in every man, I do not see that they are any more fundamental than their opposites. The guilt which would not let Franz accept rehabilitation in the post-war world was ultimately stronger than the rationalizing which he invented to excuse his torture of the partisans. Neither the "butcher of Smolensk" nor his martyred victims represent the essentially human. Each existent must choose for himself between them. It is surely in this spirit that we are to understand the lines in Franz' "best speech for the defense."

The century would have been a good one if man had not been

marked down by his cruel, immemorial enemy, by the flesh-eating species which had vowed his destruction, by the hairless, malignant beast—by man....The beast was hiding, we surprised his look suddenly in the depths of our neighbors' eyes. Then we struck—legitimate self-defense. I surprised the beast, I struck, a man fell. In his dying eyes I saw the beast still alive, myself....From whom, from what do I find this dull rancid taste in my mouth? From man? From the beast? From myself. It is the taste of the century (p. 222).

There are two respects in which *The Condemned of Altona* is closer to Sartre's later *Critique of Dialectical Reason* than to *Being and Nothingness*. Unlike Orestes in *The Flies*, Franz is not concerned with metaphysical despair. He is not mankind suddenly aware of a missing God. Insofar as he is more than himself, he is man in the mid-twentieth-century, confronting the specific political problems of his time. His discovery is not that he is an exile from Nature but that he has been one of the actors in a history which did not follow the course he had designed for it, which turned back upon him and accused him of having played the wrong role.

This last point—that the action of history transforms our roles and directs our efforts toward an end we would not have chosen—is brought out still more strongly in the case of Herr von Gerlach, owner of "the greatest business enterprise in Europe." Having devoted his life to building it up, vainly hoping that Franz might carry on the dynasty, he realizes he has become a mere figurehead, "a hat on a flagpole." The firm no longer needs either him or his son. It has grown too big for any owner. At the moment it runs itself; it recruits and trains its own managers. Soon the State will step in, perceiving that private investment is no longer enough.

The idea that other people may change the meaning of my acts by bringing about consequences which I had never desired is not new to existentialism. But when Sartre developed the idea earlier, he generally spoke in terms of the actions of specific people. The process which von Gerlach refers to resembles much more the dialectical movement of History as interpreted by Marx. In the *Critique* Sartre comes much closer than heretofore to the idea of an inevitability in history. He never speaks of this inevitability as if it were the result either of some superhuman mind or of the mechanistic functioning of absolute economic laws to which men's lives are subject. In fact the tendency to construct an autonomous historical process without men as its conscious agents is the very thing which Sartre thinks has corrupted Marxism from within and retarded its progress to the point of retrogression. Nevertheless it is possible to say—at least when looking backward into history—that given man's existence in a world characterized by scarcity, and given a certain stage in the development of men's self-realization as a group or class, and given a certain stage of industrialization, one kind of a solution was possible for a particular society and another was not. A single individual might choose to work with the current or against it, but he could no more alter the overall, eventual outcome than a man could, by throwing himself upon the railroad tracks, prevent the Denver Zephyr from finally reaching Chicago.

In all of this Sartre emphasizes a new concept of his, the *praticoinerte*. This includes the material environment. It encompasses also objective human structures—the formal rules of a language, public opinion as expressed or manufactured by press or radio, any "workedover" matter which serves to modify my actions by the mere fact of its being there. In *No Exit* Sartre declared that "Hell is Others." In the *Critique* he says that Hell is the *pratico-inerte*. This is because it "steals my action from me." Sartre goes into considerable detail to show that even raw matter, once men have allowed it to enter into the human sphere, takes on a weight of its own so that it is entirely correct to speak of its "provoking" or "allowing" or "prohibiting" events.[10] Thus with von Gerlach's shipbuilding firm. Human desires and human actions began it; human needs sustained it. Yet the factories themselves, the network of commercial relations which had been established set up objective requirements which had to be met if the firm was to continue to exist. The movement of social forces— again put in motion by thousands of individual projects and maintained by their constant renewal and development—even though they might assume a form no longer recognized by the initiators—rendered the existence of von Gerlach less necessary than his creation, made him the servant of his product. This unanticipated and unwanted end, which comes about naturally and logically as the result of human activity in the *pratico-inerte,* Sartre calls a "counter-finality."

*Critique of Dialectical Reason* is a very important book. It is admittedly somewhat shocking to existentialists, and some may possibly decide that if existentialism is to realize its best potentialities, it must take another path than the one which Sartre has chosen to follow. Sartre declares flatly that the only philosophy today is Marxism. Existentialism is one of many subordinate ideologies. Yet is an important one, particularly because existentialism and it alone is able to reinsert into our interpretation of history, human action and the individual project, without which Marxism seems destined to become an abstract theory without relation to living men and women. As for freedom, Sartre has never gone back on his original statement that men are psychologically free. Yet in the *Critique* this freedom seems to count for little with him. It is practical freedom which matters, the freedom to live "beyond the mere production of life." If it is ever achieved by mankind, then Marxism itself will have been surpassed because it is no longer needed. A philosophy of freedom will take its place. Meanwhile Sartre devotes his existentialist thought to revitalizing Marxist social and political theory. He analyzes man's situation in a world of scarcity, the gradual emergence of the we-group, intent on making a common history in the interests of common ends, and the gradual decline of the we-group into institutions and the reified relations of the *pratico-inerte*. But I do not think it appropriate for me to try to discuss the *Critique*, both because it is much too great an undertaking for what is essentially a postscript and because — with the exception which I have indicated — it is not as yet significantly reflected in Sartre's purely literary work.

# REFERENCE NOTES

In references to French sources I have added the title and author of English translations where I have known that they exist. Page references, however, are to the French edition and the translation of quotations is my own unless I have explicitly stated otherwise.

## REFERENCES FOR "INTENTIONS"

1. I shall be discussing these areas of disagreement in appropriate chapters. For Camus' most explicit refusal to be called an existentialist, see "Non, je ne suis pas existentialiste," *Les Nouvelles Litteraires,* November 15, 1945.
2. Henri Peyre evidently shares my belief that one may profitably read Camus in the light of existentialism. His summing up of the problem is formulated in two brief statements with which I am in full agreement. "Albert Camus refused repeatedly to be labeled an existentialist. But for all practical purposes he is one, at least in his philosophy of the absurd, in his constructive and moral pessimism, in his portrayal of the alienated man in *L'Étranger (The Stranger),* and in his plays." Some pages later, "We have already noted that Camus never belonged to the existentialist 'sect' and did not subscribe to the (undefined) creed of the group. But, in fact, he matured in the same ideological climate, hailed the same masters (Nietzsche, Kafka, Kierkegaard, and Husserl), shared the same general assumptions: the death of God, unconcern for essence and stress upon existence, the absurd, humanism in the sense that the man freed from belief in God must love and serve men all the better, and so forth." *The Contemporary French Novel* (New York: Oxford University Press, 1955), pp. 218-19 and footnote on p. 243.

## REFERENCES FOR PART ONE

1. *L'Homme révolté* (Paris: Gallimard, 1951), pp. 338-39. Eng. trans. by Anthony Bower, *The Rebel* (London: Hamish Hamilton, 1953). Unless other-

wise indicated, all page numbers refer to the French edition and the translation is my own.

2. "Forgers of Myths, The Young Playwrights of France," *Theatre Arts*, XXX, No. 6 (June, 1946).
3. Jean-Paul Sartre, *L'Existentialisme est un humanisme* (Paris: Nagel, 1946), pp. 59-60. Eng. trans. by Bernard Frechtman, *Existentialism* (New York: Philosophical Library, 1947).
4. *L'Homme révolté*, p. 327.
5. "Forgers of Myth," p. 325.
6. *Op. cit.*, p. 330.
7. *Le Mythe de Sisyphe* (Paris: Gallimard, 1942), p. 159. Eng. trans. by Justin O'Brien, *The Myth of Sisyphus and Other Essays* (New York: Knopf, 1955).
8. "Qu'est-ce que la littérature?," *Situations II* (Paris: Gallimard, 1948), p. 316. Eng. trans. by Bernard Frechtman, *What Is Literature?* (New York: Philosophical Library, 1949).
9. *Op. cit.*, pp. 262-63.
10. "We Write for Our Own Time," *Virginia Quarterly Review*, XXIII, No. 2 (Spring 1947), p. 243.
11. "The Artist and His Time," included in the American edition of *The Myth of Sisyphus and Other Essays*, p. 212. O'Brien's translation.
12. *L'Homme révolté*, p. 339.
13. *Speech of Acceptance upon the Award of the Nobel Prize for Literature—December 10, 1957*, trans. by Justin O'Brien (New York: Knopf, 1958), pp. ix-x.
14. "The Artist and His Time," p. 210.
15. *Le Mythe de Sisyphe*, p. 138 and p. 156.
16. Camus made this statement in an interview with Jean Bloch-Michel. A fairly long quotation from the record of the interview is included by Albert Maquet, *Albert Camus: The Invincible Summer*, trans. by Herma Briffault (New York: George Braziller, 1958), pp. 196-97.
17. Included in *L'Exil et le Royaume* (Paris: Gallimard, 1957). Eng. trans. by Justin O'Brien (New York: Knopf, 1958).
18. It is an interesting fact that Sartre, whether knowingly or not I cannot say, has given the Erinyes what was probably their original form. As Jane Harrison demonstrates in her *Prolegomena to the Study of Greek Religion*, the Erinyes almost certainly developed from the Keres, tiny winged creatures who seem in the beginning to have functioned almost like bacteria, causing putrefaction, disease, etc.
19. For fuller discussion of this point see my article, "Myth and Human Experience," *Classical Journal*, LI, No. 3 (December 1955), pp. 121-27.
20. *Théatre* (Paris: Gallimard, 1947), p. 80.
21. "Explication de L'Etranger," *Situations I* (Paris: Gallimard, 1947).
22. "Forgers of Myths," p. 326.
23. *Théatre*, p. 165.
24. *Saint Genet, comédien et martyr* (Paris: Gallimard, 1952), p. 12.
25. "M. François Mauriac et la liberté," *Situations I*, p. 44.
26. *La Peste* (Paris: Gallimard, 1947), p. 329. Eng. trans. by Stuart Gilbert, *The Plague* (New York: Knopf, 1954).
27. "Qu'est-ce que la littérature?," p. 75.
28. *Op. cit.*, pp. 304-5.
29. *L'Homme révolté*, p. 335.
30. *Op. cit.*, p. 319.
31. *Op. cit.*, pp. 326-27.

32. *Op. cit.*, p. 324.
33. *Op. cit.*, p. 341.
34. *Op. cit.*, pp. 331-36.

## REFERENCES FOR PART TWO

### I. THE DEFINITION

1. The clearest presentation of this position may be found in Simone de Beauvoir's discussion of Sartre's view. Cf. *Pour une morale de l'ambiguïté* (Paris: Gallimard, 1947), p. 17. There is an English translation by Bernard Frechtman: *The Ethics of Ambiguity* (New York: Philosophical Library, 1948).
2. *The Outsider* (Boston: Houghton Mifflin, 1956), p. 26 *et passim*.
3. Vercors, *You Shall Know Them*, trans. by Rita Barisse (Boston: Little, Brown, and Company, 1953). Vercors' real name is Jean Bruller.
4. Eugene O'Neill, *Long Day's Journey into Night* (New Haven: Yale University Press, 1956).

### II. BAD FAITH AND THE SERIOUS WORLD

#### 1. THE MEANING OF BAD FAITH

1. Sartre uses the work of art as an illustration of existentialist ethics in *L'Existentialisme est un humanisme*, pp. 75-77. See Note 4 in Pt. I.
2. *Op. cit.*, pp. 29-31.
3. *L'Être et le Néant* (Paris: Gallimard, 1943). Eng. trans. by Hazel E. Barnes, *Being and Nothingness* (New York: Philosophical Library, 1956). Page references are to the English translation.
4. A. J. Ayer, "Jean-Paul Sartre," *Horizon* (July, 1945).
5. *L'Invitée* (Paris: Gallimard, 1943), pp. 61-62. Eng. trans. by anonymous translator, *She Came to Stay* (New York: World Publishing Company, 1954).

#### 2. A STUDY OF BAD FAITH

1. *L'Enfance d'un chef* is contained in a collection of Sartre's stories, *Le Mur* (Paris: Gallimard, 1939). Eng. trans. by Lloyd Alexander, *The Wall and Other Stories* (New York: New Directions, 1948).
2. For full discussion of Sartre's theory of emotions, see his *Esquisse d'une théorie des emotions* (Paris: Hermann, 1948). (Originally published in 1939, *Actualités scientifiques et industrielles* 838) Eng. trans. by Bernard Frechtman, *The Emotions: Outline of a Theory* (New York: Philosophical Library, 1948).
3. I have discussed this subject and used the same example in an article, "Jean-Paul Sartre and the Haunted Self," *The Western Humanities Review*, X, No. 2 (Spring 1956), pp. 119-28.

#### 3. MANIFESTATIONS OF BAD FAITH
#### BAD FAITH IN PREJUDICE

1. *Réflexions sur la question juive* (Paris: Morihien, 1946). Eng. trans. by George J. Becker, *Anti-Semite and Jew* (New York: Schocken Books, 1948).

A portion of the book was published separately as Number One in the Partisan Review Series, by an anonymous translator, as *Portrait of the Anti-Semite* (New York: Partisan Review, 1946). Page references are to the Partisan Review publication.

2. *Nekrassov* (Paris: Gallimard, 1956), p. 79. Eng. trans. by Sylvia and George Leeson, *Nekrassov* (London: Hamish Hamilton, 1956).
3. Cf. *The Emotions,* especially Ch. 3.
4. Not contained in the Partisan Review publication.

## BAD FAITH IN POLITICAL ATTITUDES

1. Simone de Beauvoir, *Pour une morale de l'ambiguïté,* pp. 142-43 and section entitled "L'ambiguïté" in Ch. III, *passim.*
2. "Qu'est-ce qu'un collaborateur?" *La République Francaise.* In two parts: I "Aspect social de la collaboration," Vol. II, No. 8 (August 1945), pp. 5-6, and II "Aspect psychologique du collaborationisme," Vol. II, No. 9 (September 1945), pp. 14-17.
3. *L'Etat de Siège* (Paris: Gallimard, 1948), p. 233.
4. *Le Sang des autres* (first published in Paris by Gallimard, 1945, but page references are to the de luxe edition published in Lausanne by Marguerat, 1946). Eng. trans. by Roger Senhouse and Yvonne Moyse (New York: Knopf, 1948).
5. "Qu'est-ce qu'un collaborateur?" p. 16.

## BAD FAITH IN RELIGION

1. I regret that I have been unable to discover the author of these lines. I take the liberty of quoting them anonymously on the theory that all limericks are public property.
2. *Le Diable et le bon Dieu* (Paris: Gallimard, 1951), p. 177. Eng. trans. by Kitty Black, *Lucifer and the Lord* (London: Hamish Hamilton, 1952).
3. *Les Chemins de la liberté* (Paris: Gallimard. *L'Âge de raison,* 1945; *Le Sursis,* 1945; *La Mort dans l'âme,* 1949). Eng. trans. by Eric Sutton, *The Age of Reason and The Reprieve* (New York: Knopf, 1947). Eng. trans. by Gerard Hopkins, *Troubled Sleep* (New York: Knopf, 1950). Page references are to the American editions.
4. *The Reprieve,* pp. 406-7.
5. *The Age of Reason,* pp. 394-95.
6. *L'Homme révolté,* p. 55.
7. *L'Exil et le royaume.*

## BAD FAITH IN HUMAN RELATIONS

1. *Must We Burn Sade?* trans. by Annette Michelson, contained in *The Marquis de Sade* (New York: Grove Press, 1953).
2. Simone de Beauvoir, *Le Deuxième Sexe* (Paris: Gallimard, 1949). Eng. trans. by H. M. Parshley, *The Second Sex* (New York: Knopf, 1953). Page references are to Parshley's translation.
3. Albert Camus, *La Chute* (Paris: Gallimard, 1956). Eng. trans. by Justin O'Brien, *The Fall* (New York: Knopf, 1957).

4. Philip Thody, *Albert Camus. A Study of His Work* (London: Hamish Hamilton, 1957), pp. 76-81.
5. Camus' statement is from an interview which is quoted in part by Albert Maquet, *Albert Camus: The Invincible Summer*, pp. 197-98.
6. Justin O'Brien's statement is quoted by Maurice Dolbier in an article, "From the French and the Incoming Mail," *Herald Tribune Book Review*, March 3, 1957, p. 2.

## 4. CONCLUSION

1. Eugene O'Neill, *The Iceman Cometh* (New York: Random House, Modern Library Paperback, 1946). Originally copyrighted by Eugene O'Neill in 1940.

## III. RECOGNITION AND ENGAGEMENT

### 1. TO LEAP OR NOT TO LEAP

1. Albert Camus, *Le Malentendu. Caligula* (Paris: Gallimard, 1944). Eng. trans. by Stuart Gilbert (London: Hamish Hamilton, 1946).
2. Albert Camus, *L'Étranger* (New York: Pantheon Books, 1946), p. 114. (Originally published in Paris by Gallimard, 1942). Eng. trans. by Stuart Gilbert, *The Stranger* (New York: Vintage, 1954).
3. William James, *Essays on Faith and Morals* (New York: Longmans, Green, 1947), pp. 1-31.
4. *Letters of William James,* edited by his son, Henry James (Boston, Atlantic Monthly Press, 1920), Vol. I, pp. 199-200. Permission to reprint granted by Paul R. Reynolds & Son, 599 Fifth Avenue, New York, N. Y.
5. Albert Camus, *Lettres à un ami allemand* (Lausanne: Marguerat, 1946), pp. 72-73.

### 2. THE ABSURD MAN

1. This and the explanation by Camus which follows may be found in the "Avant-Propos" which Camus wrote for a special edition of *L'Étranger,* by Albert Camus, edited by Germaine Brée and Carlos Lynes, Jr., copyright © 1955, Appleton-Century-Crofts, Inc. The translation which I have quoted is from "Preface to 'The Stranger,'" *The Nation*, CLXXXV, No. 16 (November 16, 1957), pp. 355-56.
2. Albert Camus, "Noces à Tipasa," contained in a collection of Camus' essays, *Noces* (Paris: Gallimard, 1950), p. 13.
3. Albert Camus, "Retour à Tipasa," contained in *L'Été* (Paris: Gallimard, 1954), pp. 157-58. This passage is the source for the title and central theme of Albert Maquet's book, *Albert Camus: The Invincible Summer*.
4. For a particularly forceful presentation of this view, see Thomas Hanna, *The Thought and Art of Albert Camus* (Chicago: Henry Regnery, 1958), especially Chs. III and IV.
5. *L'Été*, p. 32.
6. *Noces*, p. 63.
7. *L'Été*, p. 123.
8. *La Femme adultère* is contained in *L'Exil et le royaume*.

9. D. H. Lawrence, "Sun," contained in *The Woman Who Rode Away and Other Stories* (New York: Knopf, 1930), p. 43.
10. Jean-Paul Sartre, *La Nausée* (Paris: Gallimard, 1938). Eng. trans. by Lloyd Alexander, *Nausea* (London: Purnell and Sons, 1949).
11. Albert Camus, "L'Énigme," *L'Été*, pp. 134-35.
12. Albert Camus, "La Comédie," *Le Mythe de Sisyphe*, pp. 107-15.
13. Both Sartre's and Dumas' plays are contained in *Kean* (Paris: Gallimard, 1954). Eng. trans. of Sartre's play by Kitty Black, *Kean or Disorder and Genius* (London: Hamish Hamilton, 1954).
14. Albert Camus, *Le Mythe de Sisyphe*, p. 87.
15. Simone de Beauvoir, *Tous les hommes sont mortels* (Paris: Gallimard, 1946).

## 3. ENGAGED FREEDOM

1. *L'Homme révolté*, p. 21.
2. Sartre discusses the "We-subject" and the "Us-object" in *Being and Nothingness*, pp. 413-30.
3. This short essay has been quoted in its entirety by Marjorie Grene in her discussion of Sartre's concept of "The New Revolutionary." *Dreadful Freedom. A Critique of Existentialism* (Chicago: University of Chicago Press, 1948), p. 98. Her discussion of Sartre's early social theory and its relation to World War II is excellent. The translation of the essay which she quotes is by Ramon Guthrie and originally appeared in *The Republic of Silence*, compiled and edited by A. J. Liebling (Harcourt, Brace and Co., 1947), pp. 498-500. I have substituted the word "freedom" where Guthrie uses "liberty," since I have throughout this book been using "freedom" for the French *liberté*.
4. Grene, *op. cit.*, pp. 99-100.
5. Jean-Paul Sartre, *L'Existentialisme est un humanisme*, pp. 90-94. Sartre's reference to "L'humanisme existentialiste" seems to me to justify my use of the term "humanistic existentialism," though the designation is, of course, my own and not that of any of the writers I have been discussing.
6. *Ibid.*, p. 74.
7. *Being and Nothingness*, pp. 541-42.
8. *Ibid.*, pp. 554-55.
9. Simone de Beauvoir, *Pour une morale de l'ambiguïté*, p. 218.
10. Simone de Beauvoir, *Pyrrhus et Cinéas* (Paris: Gallimard, 1944), p. 112.
11. *Ibid.*, p. 116.
12. *Ibid.*, pp. 16-17.
13. *Ibid.*, p. 69.
14. *Ibid.*, pp. 70-74.
15. *Pour une morale de l'ambiguïté*, pp. 119-24.
16. Simone de Beauvoir, *Les Mandarins* (Paris: Gallimard, 1954). Eng. trans. by Leonard M. Friedman, *The Mandarins* (New York: World Publishing Company, 1956).
17. Edna St. Vincent Millay, "Passer Mortuus Est," *Second April* (New York: Harper and Brothers, 1921). This quotation appears through the courtesy of Norma Millay Ellis.
18. Tarrou's account may be found in pp. 269-79 of *La Peste*.
19. My source for this statement is Philip Thody, *Albert Camus: A Study of His Work*, p. 38.
20. Robert Champigny, "Existentialism and the Modern French Novel," *Thought: Fordham University Quarterly*, XXXI, No. 122 (Autumn 1956), p. 381, note.

21. For a discussion of this phase of Camus' career, see Germaine Brée, *Camus* (New Brunswick: Rutgers University Press, 1959), pp. 26-30.
22. Thomas Hanna discusses Camus' recent political articles and interviews in Chapter VII, "The Political Philosophy of Revolt," of his book, *The Thought and Art of Albert Camus.*
23. *L'Exil et le royaume.*
24. *Ibid.*
25. Albert Camus, *Les Justes* (Paris: Gallimard, 1950). *Les Justes* is generally considered as one of Camus' original plays rather than among his adaptations. Germaine Brée, however, points out that Camus follows rather closely an earlier work by the Russian Boris Savinkov. This he apparently knew in a French translation, *Souvenirs d'un terroriste* by Bernard Taft. Cf. Brée, *Camus,* pp. 154-56.
26. *L'Homme révolté,* pp. 206-16.
27. Fyodor Dostoyevsky, *The Idiot,* trans. by Constance Garnett (New York: Modern Library, 1935), p. 406.
28. Jean-Paul Sartre, "Máterialisme et révolution," *Les Temps modernes,* I, Nos. 9 and 10 (June-July 1946). There is a translation in English in Jean-Paul Sartre, *Literary and Philosophical Essays,* trans. by Annette Michelson (New York: Criterion Books, 1955).
29. Jean-Paul Sartre, "After Budapest," *Evergreen Review,* I, No. 1, pp. 5-23. This article is a translation of an interview published in the Paris *Express,* November 9, 1956.
30. For discussion of this speech see Francis Jeanson, *Sartre par lui-même* (Paris: Editions du Seuil, 1957), pp. 158 ff.
31. Contained in *Le Mur.*
32. *Troubled Sleep,* pp. 255-56.
33. Jean-Paul Sartre, *Les Mains sales* (Paris: Gallimard, 1948). Eng. trans. by Lionel Abel in *Three Plays.*
34. Jean-Paul Sartre, *L'Engrenage* (Paris: Nagel, 1948). Eng. trans. by Mervin Savill, *In the Mesh* (London: Andrew Dakers, 1954). In quotations I have used Savill's translation.
35. My translation of some remarks of Sartre's taken down in shorthand and quoted by Francis Jeanson, *Sartre par lui-même,* pp. 48-49.
36. Henri Alleg, *The Question* (New York: Braziller, 1958).
37. Simone de Beauvoir, *Les Bouches inutiles* (Paris: Gallimard, 1945).

## REFERENCES FOR PART THREE

### I. EXISTENTIAL PSYCHOANALYSIS

1. Sartre's discussion of existential psychoanalysis is contained in Part Four, Chapter Two of *Being and Nothingness.*
2. *Ibid.,* p. 561.
3. For an evaluation of Freud in these terms, see Karen Horney, *New Ways in Psychoanalysis* (New York: Norton, 1939), p. 45.
4. Jean-Paul Sartre, "Présentation," *Les Temps modernes,* Vol. I, No. 4 (January 1946), p. 17.
5. *Being and Nothingness,* pp. 567-68.
6. *Ibid.,* p. 54.
7. *The Second Sex,* pp. 51-52. I have slightly altered Parshley's translation.
8. *Being and Nothingness,* p. 54.

## II. HUMANISTIC EXISTENTIALISM AND CONTEMPORARY PSYCHOLOGY

1. Erich Fromm, *Man for Himself. An Inquiry into the Psychology of Ethics* (New York: Rinehart, 1947).
2. Erich Fromm, *Escape from Freedom* (New York: Rinehart, 1941), p. 27. Jean-Paul Sartre, *Baudelaire* (Paris: Gallimard, 1947), p. 19. Eng. trans. by Martin Turnell, *Baudelaire* (Norfolk: New Directions, 1950).
3. The work of Harry Stack Sullivan, especially his dynamic view of the Self, would also be interesting to examine from the point of view of existentialism. But Sullivan is less well known to the nonspecialists and seems to me in any case not so significantly parallel to Sartre as are Fromm and Horney.
4. Erich Fromm, *The Sane Society* (New York: Rinehart, 1955).
5. Erich Fromm, *Man for Himself.*
6. Erich Fromm, *Psychoanalysis and Religion* (New Haven: Yale University Press, 1950), p. 114.
7. *The American Journal of Psychoanalysis*, XIV, No. 2 (1954), pp. 123-27.
8. Karen Horney, *New Ways in Psychoanalysis* (New York: Norton, 1939), p. 156. This book contains Horney's own comparison of her theory with that of Freud.
   Ultich Sonnemann, *Existence and Therapy. An Introduction to Phenomenological Psychology and Existential Analysis* (New York: Grune and Stratton, 1954).
10. In 1958 considerable excitement was evoked in this country by the appearance of *Existence: A New Dimension in Psychiatry and Psychology,* edited by Rollo May, Ernest Angel, and Henri F. Ellenberger (New York: Basic Books, 1958). This includes introductory essays by May and Ellenberger and translations of selected works by the phenomenologists (Minkowski, Straus, von Gebsattel) and by the existential analysts (Binswanger and Kuhn). Rollo May is inclined to attach little importance to Sartre's contribution to psychology and says of "Existential Psychoanalysis" that it "has very little to do with psychoanalysis or, for that matter, existential therapy" (p. 15, note). There are, however, several passages in the book where the authors make specific use of Sartre's work.
11. J. H. Van Den Berg, *The Phenomenological Approach to Psychiatry. An Introduction to Recent Phenomenological Psychopathology* (Springfield, Illinois: Thomas, 1955). I am indebted to Dr. Harold Kelman, editor of the *American Journal of Psychoanalysis* for introducing me to Van Den Berg's book. In several articles published in the *Journal* Dr. Kelman seems to be moving in a direction sympathetic to existential psychology. See especially his series, "Life History as Therapy," published in the *Journal,* XV, No. 2 (1955); XVI, Nos. 1 and 2 (1956).
12. *Being and Nothingness,* pp. 338-39.

## III. EXISTENTIALIST BIOGRAPHY

1. Anthony West, "A Fallen Angel," a review of *Baudelaire* by Enid Starkie, *The New Yorker,* April 12, 1958, p. 142.
2. The obvious parallel between Philippe and Baudelaire has been pointed out by at least two other critics: Iris Murdoch, *Sartre, Romantic Rationalist*

(New Haven: Yale University Press, 1953), p. 20; Francis Jeanson, *Sartre par lui-même*, p. 116.

3. *Troubled Sleep*, p. 168.

4. At a later point Sartre remarks that whether this episode was real or imaginary does not greatly matter. He has been criticized for taking so lightly the question of whether the event which he makes so fundamental to his discussion ever occurred. But of course he means that it doesn't matter whether there was one particular time at which Genet was caught stealing, when a finger was actually pointed and the specific words uttered. Genet often refers to such an event. He writes of "the melodious child" which died in him and attributes the cause of death to "un mot vertigineux." The essentials of the story are certainly true: that Genet stole as most small children do and that suddenly or gradually persons in his environment made him feel that in his case the theft was evidence of an irreparably corrupt nature. For critical discussion of Sartre's interpretation of Genet's childhood, see a review of the biography: Maurice Nadeau, in "Mercuriale," *Mercure de France,* CCCXVI, No. 1070 (October 1952), pp. 300-6.

5. Quoted in *Saint Genet, Comédien et Martyr,* p. 61.

6. *Notre-Dame des Fleurs* is contained in Jean Genet, *Oeuvres complètes* (Paris: Gallimard, 1951). In selecting quotations I have preferred to use the English translation by Bernard Frechtman, who has achieved a mastery of underworld argot which I can never hope to equal. *Our Lady of the Flowers* (Paris: The Olympia Press, no date).

7. This is the conclusion of Maurice Nadeau in the review referred to above.

8. Eleanor Clark, "The World of Jean Genet," *Partisan Review,* XVI, No. 4 (April 1949), pp. 442-48.

9. Jack Kerouac, "Essentials of Spontaneous Prose," *Evergreen Review,* II, No. 5 (Summer 1958), p. 73.

10. *Must We Burn Sade?* trans. by Annette Michelson, contained in *The Marquis de Sade* (New York: Grove Press, 1953), p. 68.

11. Simone de Beauvoir, *Mémoires d'une jeune fille rangée,* (Paris: Gallimard, 1958), p. 18. There is an English translation by James Kirkup, *Memoirs of a Dutiful Daughter* (New York: World Publishing Company, 1959).

## REFERENCES FOR "POSSIBILITIES"

1. That freedom equals possibility is a central theme in the philosophy of the Italian existentialist, Nicola Abbagnano. It is discussed most fully in his book, *Possibilità e Libertà* (Turin: Taylor, 1955). Professor Abbagnano feels that the French existentialists have given entirely too much emphasis to the idea that man is *condemned* to be free. He himself prefers to stress the positive side of freedom as possibility.

2. I have discussed Sartre's attempt to refute the idea of God, in my introduction to *Being and Nothingness.*

3. Jean-Paul Sartre, "American Novelists in French Eyes," *Atlantic Monthly,* Vol. 178 (August 1946), pp. 114-18.

4. Jean-Paul Sartre, "M. Jean Giraudoux et la philosophie d'Aristote," *Situations I.*

5. Arthur Miller, "On Social Plays," contained in *A View from the Bridge* (New York: Viking Press, 1955), pp. 7-8 and p. 12.

6. The source of my information concerning "Witches of Salem" is John McCarten's column, "The Current Cinema," in *The New Yorker,* December 13, 1958.

7. *The Times Literary Supplement,* Friday, November 1, 1957, p. 657.

8. Colin Wilson, *Religion and the Rebel* (London: Gallancz, 1957), p. 131.

9. Colin Wilson, "Beyond the Outsider," *The Declaration,* ed. by Tom Maschler (New York: Dutton, 1958), p. 35.

10. Colin Wilson, *Religion and the Rebel,* p. 315.

11. Germaine Brée, who is an ardent admirer of Camus and who objects strongly to grouping him with the existentialists, remarks repeatedly in her study of his work that he is not interested in the Freudian-style analysis of character and that he is much more concerned with basic human attitudes and situations.

## REFERENCES FOR "AFTERWORD"

1. I have recorded my own reactions to the world's reception of the news of Camus' death in "Measure of Magnificence," *Prairie Schooner,* XXXIV, No. 2 (Summer 1960), pp. 115-19. Camus left pages of an unfinished novel, but I have seen no indication as yet that these were nearly enough complete for publication.

2. Simone de Beauvoir, *La Force de l'âge* (Paris: Gallimard, 1960), p.17.

3. Jean-Paul Sartre, *Les Séquéstres d'Altona* (Paris: Gallimard, 1960). Eng. trans. by Sylvia and George Leeson (New York: Knopf, 1961).

4. Jean-Paul Sartre, *Critique de la raison dialectique* (Paris: Gallimard, 1960). Only one volume of the planned two volumes has appeared so far.

5. Sartre described the play in this way in an interview reported in *France Observateur,* September 10, 1959. At this time the play was still in rehearsal.

6. *Ibid.*

7. This episode in Sartre's life probably provided the inspiration for his short-story, "The Room."

8. Sartre made this statement in an interview with the editors of *L'Express.* Sections from the interview have been printed under the title, "The Theater," trans. by Richard Seaver. *Evergreen Review,* IV, No. 11 (January-February 1960), pp. 143-52.

9. Philip Thody is inclined to take this view and calls *The Condemned of Altona* "the most pessimistic play that Sartre has ever written." *Jean-Paul Sartre: A Literary and Political Study* (London: Hamish Hamilton, 1960), p. 132.

10. I have already expressed these ideas apropos of Sartre's *Critique* in a review of the book, "Jean-Paul Sartre and the Outside World," *Chicago Review,* XV, No. 1 (Summer 1961), pp. 107-112.

# INDEX

# A NOTE ABOUT THE AUTHOR

HAZEL E. BARNES, Professor of Classics at the University of Colorado, holds an A.B. from Wilson College and a Ph.D. from Yale, and has done post-doctoral work at Columbia University and the University of Hawaii. Before joining the faculty at Colorado, Miss Barnes held teaching posts at the Woman's College of the University of North Carolina; Pierce College, an American college for Greek students near Athens; the University of Toledo; and Ohio State University. She has contributed articles and reviews to numerous scholarly and literary publications, is the translator of Sartre's *Being and Nothingness* (1956), and is co-author, with Donald Sutherland, of HIPPOLYTUS IN DRAMA AND MYTH (1960), published by the University of Nebraska Press (BB 103).